REDISCOVERING STANISLAVSKY

Konstantin Stanislavsky (1863–1938) was one of the most innovative and influential directors of modern theatre and his System and related practices continue to be studied and used by actors, directors and students. Maria Shevtsova sheds new light on the extraordinary life of Stanislavsky, uncovering and translating Russian archival sources, rehearsal transcripts, scores and plans. This comprehensive study rediscovers little-known areas of Stanislavsky's new type of theatre and its immersion in the visual arts, dance and opera. It demonstrates the fundamental importance of his Russian Orthodoxy to the worldview that underpinned his integrated System and his goals for the six laboratory research studios that he established or mentored. Stanislavsky's massive achievements are explored in the intricate and historically intertwined political, cultural and theatre contexts of tsarist Russia, the 1917 Revolution, the unstable 1920s, and Stalin's 1930s. *Rediscovering Stanislavksy* provides a completely fresh perspective on his work and legacy.

MARIA SHEVTSOVA is Professor of Drama and Theatre Arts at Goldsmiths, University of London. She is known internationally for her books and other publications, which have been translated into numerous languages, and her participation in theatre festivals as well as scholarly events abroad, and her multimedia broadcasts. She is the co-editor of *New Theatre Quarterly*.

REDISCOVERING STANISLAVSKY

MARIA SHEVTSOVA

Goldsmiths, University of London

CAMBRIDGE
UNIVERSITY PRESS

University Printing House, Cambridge CB2 8BS, United Kingdom

One Liberty Plaza, 20th Floor, New York, NY 10006, USA

477 Williamstown Road, Port Melbourne, VIC 3207, Australia

314-321, 3rd Floor, Plot 3, Splendor Forum, Jasola District Centre, New Delhi - 110025, India

103 Penang Road, #05-06/07, Visioncrest Commercial, Singapore 238467

Cambridge University Press is part of the University of Cambridge.

It furthers the University's mission by disseminating knowledge in the pursuit of education, learning and research at the highest international levels of excellence.

www.cambridge.org
Information on this title: www.cambridge.org/9781107607033
DOI: 10.1017/9781139151092

© Maria Shevtsova 2020

This publication is in copyright. Subject to statutory exception and to the provisions of relevant collective licensing agreements, no reproduction of any part may take place without the written permission of Cambridge University Press.

First published 2020
First paperback edition 2022

A catalogue record for this publication is available from the British Library

Library of Congress Cataloging in Publication data
NAMES: Shevtsova, Maria, author.
TITLE: Rediscovering Stanislavsky / Maria Shevtsova.
DESCRIPTION: Cambridge, United Kingdom ; New York, NY : Cambridge University Press, 2020. | Includes bibliographical references and index.
IDENTIFIERS: LCCN 2019019435 | ISBN 9781107023390 (hardback)
SUBJECTS: LCSH: Stanislavsky, Konstantin, 1863-1938–History and criticism.
CLASSIFICATION: LCC PN2728.S78 S49 2020 | DDC 792.0233092–dc23
LC record available at https://lccn.loc.gov/20190194354

ISBN 978-1-107-02339-0 Hardback
ISBN 978-1-107-60703-3 Paperback

Cambridge University Press has no responsibility for the persistence or accuracy of URLs for external or third-party internet websites referred to in this publication, and does not guarantee that any content on such websites is, or will remain, accurate or appropriate.

For Sasha, always

Contents

Preface		*page*	ix
Acknowledgements			xiii
Note on the Text			xv
1	Context I		1
	The Road to the Moscow Art Theatre		1
	Ensemble Theatre		7
	Utopian Communities		21
	Silver Age Metaphysics		37
2	Context II		43
	Stanislavsky and Politics		43
	Theatre in Revolution, and Meyerhold		57
	The Art Theatre in the Stalin Years, 1926–1938		67
3	Actor		87
	'The Life of the Human Spirit' and Russian Orthodoxy		87
	'*Ya yesm*': 'I Am' and the Subconscious		101
	Several Problems of Translation		104
	Yoga; the Superconscious; Inspiration and Orthodoxy		109
	The Theatre of Emotional Experiencing		121
	Ethics and Discipline		124
4	Studio		129
	A Chart of the Studios		129
	Sulerzhitsky and the First Studio		132
	The Second Studio		149
	The Third Studio		156
	The Fourth Studio		158
	The Bolshoy Opera Studio		161
	The Opera-Dramatic Studio		169

viii *Contents*

5 Director 180
    The Society of Art and Literature 180
    Two Directors 184
    Production Scores and Musicality: Chekhov and Gorky 190
    'Reality' and *The Lower Depths* 201
    Rehearsal Notes: *Cain* and *The Marriage of Figaro* 205
    Director-Pedagogue: *Othello, Romeo and Juliet, Hamlet* 218
    What Is a Director? 226

Epilogue: Legacy 235
    Which Stanislavsky? 235
    Perspectives: France, Britain, Germany 241
    Now: The 'Human Being' 255

Bibliography 270
Index 279

Preface

On hearing that my new book was about Stanislavsky, a friend remarked in the quiet inflections of Russian irony that of course we knew everything about Stanislavsky. I smiled, understanding perfectly what he was telling me and replied that, yes, we did not know enough about the Stanislavsky whom we knew so well and so we needed to rediscover him – or discover him for the first time, if such was the case.

I had understood as well my scholar friend's implicit reference to my lifelong study of contemporary theatre and related theoretical and interdisciplinary principles, and his curiosity as to why I was now concentrating on Stanislavsky whom history had already placed. My study as a whole was pivoted on the work of European directors and especially of those whose theatre companies and productions I had faithfully followed – some for four decades and more. Having taken this approach during my student days, I pursued their ongoing work despite the considerable difficulties posed to research by the constraints of time, space, organization, travel and cost. In other words, I practised what I preached, reminding my many students over the years that continual research on a living director was research on a living archive as well as the creation of an archive for the future. In the case of a historical figure like Stanislavsky, museum archives as well as archives of other kinds were fortunately available, providing a glimpse of what our own eyes, ears, remaining senses and intelligence might have perceived in the past.

After the brief discussion with my friend, I found myself thinking on more than one occasion that there was something to be said for having contemporary theatre as a reference point for Stanislavsky, all the more so because I had direct contact with my material. I have been privileged to observe the rehearsals of some of 'my' directors at varying degrees of proximity and to engage in various, often sequential, conversations with them. As my research on Stanislavsky progressed, it became quite clear that observing in the flesh directors as different as Giorgio Strehler and Robert

Wilson were from each other and from Stanislavsky – each working in very different socioeconomic and cultural circumstances – gave me lenses through which to see Stanislavsky anew, not solely artistically as an ensemble actor, stage director and lighting designer (bound to be a discovery for some readers) but as a managing director of the Moscow Art Theatre, publicist, fundraiser from private and public sources and more besides. What, then, could be said of such practitioners in the Russian context as close to him as Lev Dodin and Anatoly Vasilyev, each in his respective way in a direct line from Stanislavsky? Looking backwards from them to Stanislavsky also gave me invaluable insights into his manifold achievements and just how colossal a figure he really was in his time and still for ours. What Dodin and Vasilyev can show about Stanislavsky as well as themselves and the transmutations of the theatre as a range of specific practices comes through my last pages titled 'Legacy', as occurs with the other internationally renowned theatre practitioners who appear in that panorama.

The vistas of Stanislavsky's future into the twenty-first century are far from exhaustive in these closing pages, as I point out. But a comprehensive study of Stanislavsky such as the one offered in this book must situate him first and foremost in the multiple contexts of his 'split' life: those that define it before the 1917 October Revolution and the rapidly changing, identifiable shifts of the years that follow this Revolution and segue into Stalin's no less volatile 1930s.

The first half of his life involved him in activities almost entirely neglected by Stanislavsky scholarship, although they nurtured his aspirations for the theatre. These were the extraordinary cross-arts explorations – painting, sculpture, ceramics, architecture – generated in the rural Abramtsevo commune founded by the railway magnate and family friend Savva Mamontov not far from Stanislavsky's family estate. And it was near enough to Moscow to facilitate interconnection with Mamontov's Private Opera Theatre, making both of them significant precursors of Sergey Diaghilev's World of Art and the Ballets Russes. The way major visual artists, composers and opera singers, most notably Fyodor Chaliapin, shared and combined their talents and skills inspired Stanislavsky to realize the collaborative, harmoniously integrated stage productions that became the signature of the Art Theatre. His opera productions, when he eventually turned to them in the 1920s and 1930s, followed suit.

The second half of Stanislavsky's life was fraught with difficulties on every front that also engulfed the Art Theatre as he harnessed moral imperatives and political subterfuges to protect his life's work.

Preface xi

Stanislavsky's correspondence with Stalin is but one of many channels through which he navigated to avert numerous dangers, frequently unsuccessfully, and not always in accord with Vladimir Nemirovich-Danchenko with whom he had co-founded the MAT. Among the company's opponents in the field of the theatre were the Proletkult, the Blue Blouse groups, Agitprop and TRAM whose main features are detailed in my book to throw into relief both the MAT's rejection of politics and Meyerhold's embrace of them together with his vital contribution to the revolutionary theatre. Meyerhold's and Stanislavsky's lifelong friendship has, in my view, been underestimated and misrepresented, even during this turbulent period when political engagement, just as much as political misalignment, was the target of terror and death.

Much has been written in English about Stanislavsky's System and here is to be found another perspective – that of the worldview which underpins the System's practical purpose and is rooted in Russian Orthodoxy. Stanislavsky's religious outlook shapes the worldview that envelops his search for the organic actor-creator for whose benefit he elaborated the System until his dying day. Many of Stanislavsky's early influences, which included Old Believer Orthodoxy and the 'heretical' beliefs of Lev Tolstoy, not to mention Isadora Duncan's unaffected, natural dancer, find their niches across my book.

Much less is known about Leopold Sulerzhitsky's fundamental contribution to the First Studio (1912) and its working particularities, but I have consulted as many disparate sources as possible – in the paucity of available information – in order to draw his working biography and give some substance to his name. Sulerzhitsky has been invariably linked to Mikhaïl Chekhov, Yevgeny Vakhtangov and Nikolay Demidov (when the latter is remembered at all), but, once mentioned, is invariably passed over. He taught First Studio actresses Serafima Birman – also a director – Lidiya Deykun and Sofya Giatsintova (when women are remembered in the Art Theatre Pantheon), but his link to them has had a similar fate.

One of my most daunting tasks was to chart the time, duration, character and achievements of the six studios that were affiliated with the MAT or were directly Stanislavsky's responsibility. Such was the case of his first opera studio and its various avatars as well as the second, the Opera-Dramatic Studio (1935), in which Maria Knebel, who had been a member of the Second Studio, learned and taught. It is my firm conviction, arrived at only after assiduous research, that the two opera studios cannot be separated from the other four – nor, indeed, from the unofficial 'first', the Povarskaya Studio, run by Meyerhold at Stanislavsky's request and funded from his purse; and this inclusive coverage *within* a comprehensive study of Stanislavsky is, to my knowledge, the first of its kind in any language. Only when these studio-laboratories and their intensive work are set side by side does it finally become clear just how central they were to Stanislavsky's artistic endeavours. Their importance as models – even when unacknowledged models – for laboratory and workshop theatre research throughout the twentieth century and still today in the twenty-first cannot, in my view, be overestimated.

All things considered, Anglophone research, by contrast with Russian research, knows little about Stanislavsky's work as a director, with the exception of his early productions, most notably of Chekhov and Gorky plays. Yet his directing, including the team directing of not uncommonly three directors of one work, where Stanislavsky was often an overseer, covered a relatively wide span in which he was no less an innovator than he was in the domain of acting. Mine was an exciting journey through Russian archival sources, transcripts of his rehearsals and scores and plans of his early and 1920s productions, as well as rehearsal-lessons from his Opera-Dramatic Studio and details of several of his opera productions. The latter is the least examined and yet one of the most fruitful areas not only of his directing work but of his work as a whole, shedding a great deal of light both on the actor and the newly developed actor-singer who helped him to expand his sights. I would hope that my readers travel with me on this journey, together with the other journeys of my book, with a similar joy of discovery.

Acknowledgements

My greatest thanks must first go to the Leverhulme Trust whose award of a Research Fellowship allowed me to undertake the research necessary for this book; and, second, to the entire staff of the Moscow Art Theatre Museum and especially to Marfa Bubnova and Maria Polkanova, respectively director and vice-director of the Museum and custodians of its K. S. Stanislavsky archives. I am extremely grateful to both for granting me permission to reproduce for my front cover Aleksandr Golovin's design for Scene 5 ('The Balcony') for *A Mad Day or The Marriage of Figaro* (1927), so suggestive, in a painterly way, of the vibrant physical movement Stanislavsky sought for this production.

My requests from the archives were brought with the deft hands of Yelena Sekirova and Yevgeny Konyukhin, while items concerning Leopold Sulerzhitsky came from Yekaterina Shingareva; sincere thanks, too, to Valentina Kuzina, Tatyana Asaylova and, particularly, curator Galina Sukhova, who shared my passions for the painters and sculptors cited in my book, and to Nina Demyanova at the door. The librarians of the MAT Museum, Maria Smoktunovskaya and Lyudmila Medoshina, were always helpful. I am infinitely grateful to Zinaïda Udaltsova, scholar and editor par excellence, who, working near my desk, became curious and struck up a conversation with me that turned into several more to my benefit. All warmly welcomed me, and Maria Polkanova and her team sustained me unforgettably in other ways. Anna Ovchinnikova, in charge of the Stanislavsky House-Museum, also received me with open arms, generously giving her time to answer my questions. I owe great thanks to Yelena Mitrofanova, vice-director of research at the Abramtsevo State Museum, for her tour of the magic world within this rural estate; and to Svetlana Trifonova for her kind invitation to the holy seat of Sergiyev Posad.

For their kind courtesy and efficiency, I thank the librarians at the STD (Union of Theatre Professionals) Library in Moscow and those of the renowned and beautiful St Petersburg State Theatre Library founded in xiv *Acknowledgements*

1756 by Empress Elizabeth Petrovna, who appears in this book. Opposite, founded also by Elizabeth in the same year, is the Aleksandrinsky Theatre. I owe to its artistic director and theatre director Valery Fokin, as to Aleksandr Chepurov, the Aleksandrinsky's head of research and Chair Professor of Russian Theatre at the Russian State Institute of Scenic Arts (RGISI), a great debt of long standing for their hospitality, knowledge and support.

In Riga I am indebted to another generous friend and theatre scholar, Guna Zeltina, for facilitating access to the National Library of Latvia, the library of the National Theatre, whose librarian Rita Malnice I deeply thank, and the Riga Russian Theatre, which was opened in 1883. Both of these theatres are, of course, closely associated with Mikhaïl Chekhov, who is one of my main protagonists, and the second had previously hosted other MAT artists, as noted in my pages. The Russian Theatre was named after Chekhov in 2006.

I owe most of what I know about the theatre to the work of all the living directors whose names I cited as I wrote, even if I did not quote them directly, and others too, who do not appear here at all. And, knowing how busy and hard-working theatre directors are, I cannot thank enough the remarkable directors from whose enriching conversations and more formal interviews over the years I draw in these pages: Eugenio Barba, Yury Butusov, Lev Dodin, Declan Donnellan, Valery Galendeyev, Oskaras Korsunovas, Katie Mitchell, Luk Perceval, Peter Sellars, Anatoly Vasilyev.

My gratitude extends to Stephen Barber, Laurence Senelick and Rose Whyman for their firm support of my project; to Dassia Posner and Andrei Malaev-Babel; to Stéphane Poliakov in France; in Russia to Vadim Shcherbakov; in Poland to Dariusz Kosinski and Tomasz Kubikowski – wonderful scholars all. Many more have helped in numerous, different ways, among them: Rida Buranova, Philippa Burt, Wendy Cobcroft (a lifetime's worth of debt), Dina Dodina, Roman Dolzhansky, Jaroslaw Fret, Rogelio Armando Nevares Guajardo, Olga Galakhova, Dorothy Gray, Nika Kosenkova, Yekaterina Kupreyeva, Magdelena Madra, Natasha Pavlutskaya, Elvira Pirkova, Yevgenia Rozanova and, never last, Aleksandra Shevtsova.

Note on the Text

I have primarily used the Russian eight-volume collected works of Stanislavsky published in 1954–61 (*Sobraniye sochineny v vosmi tomakh*) because its explanatory notes are more complete than those of the nine-volume edition of 1980–99 (*Sobraniye sochineny v devyati tomakh*). However, I have cross-checked both, necessarily citing material only available in the second edition. My references appear as *SS* 8 or *SS* 9, as the case may be, followed by the volume number and then the page(s) cited, thus: *SS* 8, 3, 309 or *SS* 9, 5, 126–7.

To help my readers, my references to and also to my translations of *Moya zhizn v iskusstvye* (*My Life in Art*) and *Rabota aktyora nad soboy* (*An Actor's Work on Himself* [*aktyor* grammatically a masculine noun]) are followed by the corresponding references in English translation, when they exist in English (many do not). Citations from several other books in Russian are given their corresponding source in English, albeit not always. Where Stanislavsky's letters are concerned, I cite Laurence Senelick's edition in English for the same reason of reader access to them, while I myself always worked from the two Russian editions and register any discrepancy in our translations.

My friendly transliteration from the Cyrillic alphabet is intended for readers with no Russian. Thus I delete soft and hard signs and write the terminals й and ий as y and the letter ы as y as well; я as ya; ю as yu. However, I have kept the familiar English spelling of names – Scriabin, for instance, instead of Skryabin, or Chaliapin instead of Shalyapin, and so Meyerhold, Tchaikovsky, and other well-established spellings.

I use the word System in upper case to distinguish Stanislavsky's from any other kind of system and, as well, to distinguish it from the comically inflected but disparaging usage of the word in quotation marks of his critics in the early years of the MAT. Stanislavsky wrote 'system' in quotation marks when citing the latter but, most important of all, also when he wished to stress the temporary and provisional nature of the term.

xvi   *Note on the Text*

Stanislavsky did not believe that an actor's work could be confined to, or be defined by, sets of exercises and rules. Hence his 'system' in quotation marks drew attention to the inadequacy of the term for the continually developing creative process that is an actor's work. Otherwise, he simply wrote it without quotation marks and in lower case, in accordance with usage in the Russian language.

CHAPTER I

Context I

The Road to the Moscow Art Theatre

Born in 1863 in Moscow as Konstantin Alekseyev to a wealthy manufacturer of gold and silver thread, he took the name 'Stanislavsky' after a ballerina whom he had admired as a boy. He experimented with this name when he joined his father's factory at the age of eighteen, adopting it permanently in 1885 as he increasingly played in amateur theatres other than the Alekseyev Circle in which, since childhood, he had developed his imagination with his siblings and family friends. Custom obliged him, as others of comparable or superior social standing, to take a pseudonym for the stage, largely because many Russian actors had been serfs. They included the renowned Mikhaïl Shchepkin and Glikeria Fedotova, whose truthful characterization was to inspire Stanislavsky, Shchepkin by reputation (he died the year Stanislavsky was born) and Fedotova through personal contact. In addition, he was aware of the significance of his father's upward social mobility, which separated Stanislavsky by four generations from his peasant ancestry. Vladimir Nemirovich-Danchenko, co-founder with him of the Moscow Art Theatre (MAT) in 1897, would ungraciously evoke Stanislavsky's origins when referring to him, throughout their forty-year collaboration, as 'our merchant' and to his allegedly deficient literary culture.

The immediate prompt, however, for Konstantin Alekseyev's capitulation to social pressure was his parents catching him red-handed performing in a risqué French vaudeville. His was an indulgent father who had responded to the family's enthusiasm for making theatre by building a theatre in their Moscow home as well as at Lyubimovka, their country estate. Sergey Alekseyev had also nurtured his children's love for going to the theatre – ballet, opera, plays, the circus – whether Russian or presented by touring companies from abroad. Nevertheless, he was a paterfamilias in the patriarchal mould of tsarist Russia, and he was now going to exercise his authority. He firmly pointed out to his son that material of finer quality, co-actors less inclined to drink, swearing and blasphemy, and improved working conditions would better serve his artistic dreams. This was all very well from a sternly moral point of view, but Stanislavsky learned much from the fun, vivacity, timing and speed of lightweight and saucy material, invariably from France.

Stanislavsky was to remember his father's lesson when, on the demise of the Alekseyev Circle in 1888, he formed the Society of Art and Literature, replacing operettas, melodramas and lover-in-closet farces with reputable plays (Ostrovsky, Tolstoy, Shakespeare) and contemporary ones from the foreign repertoire (Gerhart Hauptmann). He exchanged, as well, the doubtful venues of his freelance activities for clean, ventilated spaces, while his day job helping to run the family factory paid for them. Societies, like the modest, often domestic Circles on which the Alekseyev Circle had been patented were common enough urban occurrences, also in Russia's far-flung regions. Together with the serf theatres of noble estates before them (serfdom was abolished in 1861, soon leading to the end of serf theatres), they offered small-scale alternatives to the monopoly of the five Imperial Theatres in existence until the 1917 October Revolution, three in St Petersburg and two in Moscow. In the latter city, the Bolshoy was reserved for opera and ballet and, in the adjoining square, the Maly for drama.

The Maly Theatre became a state theatre in 1824 and was enlisted under the 1756 charter of Empress Elizabeth I, the daughter and eventual successor of Peter the Great who had 'westernized' Russia while introducing monarchic absolutism to the country. Her edict had declared theatre to be a state institution tasked with providing high artistic quality, although the subsidies for Russian theatre were significantly below those for the French and Italian theatres resident in Russia at that time: Russian theatre, in the eyes of the Europeanized court, was simply inferior.[1] The Maly, hailed as the 'Second Moscow University' (the University was founded in 1755 with the support of Elizabeth I), proved to be a cultural hub for Russian talent, and it was here that Shchepkin and Fedotova garnered their fame.[2] Stanislavsky was to say in his 1926 *My Life in Art*

---

[1] Robert Leach and Victor Borovsky (eds.), *A History of Russian Theatre*, Cambridge University Press, 1999, 54.
[2] Ibid., 223.

that 'the Maly Theatre, more than any school ... was the key factor in directing the spiritual and intellectual sides of our life'.[3]

The monopoly of the Imperial Theatres was abolished in 1882, thereby opening the way for private theatres, and so, eventually, for the MAT. As models of cultural influence, the Imperial Theatres guided Stanislavsky's ambitions for the amateur Society of Art and Literature, which had opera and drama sections, the former headed by Fyodor Komissarzhevsky, a lauded opera tenor who had taught Stanislavsky singing; his son, a successful theatre director in St Petersburg, would emigrate to England in 1919 and, known as Theodore Komisarjevsky, would attempt to consolidate his career there. The importance of Stanislavsky's singing training cannot be stressed enough, for, apart from its technical benefits for acting such as placing the voice and encouraging clear diction, it enabled him to phrase the tones, intonations, tempi, breathing and rhythmic patterns, and cadences of speech not only for the musicality of his and fellow actors' performances, but also to improve the overall arc of the productions he directed for the Society. These gains would be of great use to his work in the future. So too would his skills in drawing and watercolours for the visual composition of his productions.

The Society venture was attractive to the intelligentsia, that distinctively nineteenth-century Russian conglomerate of individuals whose education and culture, according to Geoffrey Hosking, 'plucked [them] out of one social category without necessarily placing them in another'.[4] However, it must be noted, the same education and culture were indispensable for their aspirations to some kind of social status and esteem. Set outside Russia's strict social hierarchy, they thus belonged to the *raznochintsy*, the people of disparate ranks thrown back on their own resources to forge a place for themselves; Anton Chekhov, who was one generation removed from serfdom, was representative of this mixed intelligentsia. It was from them, and especially from the liberal professions among them – doctors, lawyers, writers, teachers – that, in its early years, the MAT would generally draw its audiences. In the meantime, during the ten or so years it took to build up the Society's credentials, Stanislavsky honed his acting and directing

---

[3] *Moya zhizn v iskusstvye*, SS 8, 1. All translations from this book are mine. Note my 'spiritual and intellectual sides of our life', which accurately translates Stanislavsky's words and corrects Jean Benedetti's 'mental and intellectual development', since 'mental' does not have the same meaning as 'spiritual'. Moreover, 'mental' weakens Stanislavsky's point that the Maly profoundly affected people's moral constitution and their emotional capacities to deal with life. See *My Life in Art*, trans. and ed. Jean Benedetti, London and New York: Routledge, 2008, 29.

[4] *Russia: People and Empire, 1552–1917*, London: Fontana Press, 1998, 263.

4 Context I

skills to equal the best that the Maly had offered in its heyday. So impressive had Stanislavsky's achievements become that the well-established playwright, critic and acting teacher Nemirovich-Danchenko sought him out to start a 'new theatre' intended to shake up the professional Russian theatre which, in his as well as Stanislavsky's view, was mired in 'simple, workable technical tricks'.[5] Further, in Stanislavsky's words: 'the theatrical profession was, on the one side, in the hands of barmen and those of bureaucrats on the other. How could the theatre flourish in such conditions?'[6] His answer, throughout his lifetime, was that it could not.

Stanislavsky's summary in *My Life in Art* of their eighteen-hour meeting contains his impassioned account of the 'inhuman conditions' in which actors, 'these servants of beauty ... spend three-quarters of their lives'[7]: filthy, airless and unheated quarters, more like stables than dressing-rooms with planks for wardrobes and cracked, unlockable doors; ice-cold wind blowing from the street onto the stage where rehearsals took place; damp prompters' boxes causing tuberculosis, and many more vividly observed details based on Stanislavsky's own experiences. The fervour of his account suggests that priority would be given to 'surroundings that would be fit for educated human beings', for only then could 'proper, decent behaviour from actors' be expected and become an integral part of company ethics.[8] Ethical behaviour was a point on which he and Nemirovich-Danchenko were to insist to the end of their days. Both men also agreed that beauty was not the prerogative of a select few and, for this very reason, the MAT would be open and accessible (*obshchedostupnoye*) to all.

Their views, in this, were liberal, although even liberal attitudes had been touched by the populism of the *narodniki* ('advocates of the people' – *narod* means 'people' or 'folk') who, in preceding decades, had 'gone out' to teach the illiterate peasantry but who, by the turn of the twentieth century, had become socialist revolutionaries, ready to bring down tsarist autocracy. The fact that the censors had definite ideas as to what was suitable for the people, urban as well as rural, meant that any lingering hopes Stanislavsky and Nemirovich-Danchenko may have had about showcasing their envisaged theatre as something of a *people's* art theatre had to be dropped, along with the adjective *obshchedostupnoye*, which they had originally attached to the word 'art' in their chosen name. For the censors, as for the remaining tsarist bureaucracy, the very notion of 'open accessibility' was potentially seditious. Yet, later, nothing in the reigning

[5] *My Life in Art*, 159. [6] Ibid. [7] Ibid., 162. [8] Ibid., 161.

system of control could prevent Stanislavsky from giving a lecture in the fateful year of 1905 about the 'high artistic mission' of the theatre, which 'more than any of the other arts' could 'withstand the oppression of censorship and of religious and police restrictions'.[9]

The issue of how the MAT could be socially inclusive did not really become a pressing one until the revolution of February 1905, when the persistent struggles between the authorities and the champions of social reform, among them factory women demonstrating against their working conditions in St Petersburg, came to a head on 'Bloody Sunday' in that capital city. This critical landmark in increasingly deteriorating relations – a peaceful mass petition to the tsar had turned into a massacre – was followed by a series of strikes. Strikes in Moscow encouraged several members of the MAT, which on Stanislavsky's insistence had always counted the stage technicians and all support staff, not least the doormen and cleaners, to vote to close down the theatre for six days in solidarity with the city's workers.[10] Further strikes in November cut electricity supplies, which closed down all theatres for a considerably longer period.

Fear stalked the streets. The political turbulence aggravated the artistic crisis within the MAT – by no means the last crisis in its history – which foregrounded its uncertainty as to whom, and for whom, the theatre was performing in an unstable country, riddled with injustices. The MAT had already wound down artistically in 1904, at around the time of Chekhov's death. Chekhov had become the house playwright, and his loss was all the more keenly felt because the company had enjoyed close ties with him, while Olga Knipper, one of its founding members, was his widow. The issue of social inclusivity was not to become urgent, however, until the MAT was forced by circumstances way beyond its control to encounter the completely new audiences thrown up by the October Revolution.

A decree signed in December 1919 by Lenin and Anatoly Lunacharsky, a literary and theatre critic who had recently been appointed Commissar of Enlightenment, nationalized all theatres which, the MAT not excepted, gave out free tickets to factory workers, other proletarian groups, and soldiers on leave from the battlefronts of the Civil War (1918–21) in order to 'educate' and 'enlighten' – in the current thinking – an emerging

---

[9] Quoted in I. Vinogradskaya, *Zhizn i tvorchestvo K. S. Stanislavskogo. Letopis* (*Life and Work of K. S. Stanislavsky. Chronicle*), Vol. 1, Moscow: Moscow Art Theatre Press, 2003, 488. All translations throughout this book from Vinogradskaya's compilation are mine.

[10] Ibid., 520.

6 Context I

participant public;[11] and this public was beginning to be engaged not only with the theatre, but also in every area of civic life, having been deprived of civil liberties and responsibilities by centuries of repressive monarchies. Nationalization meant renaming the MAT an 'academic theatre', hence changing its acronym to MKhAT (Moscow Art Academic Theatre – MAAT). Lunacharsky's rather pompous label was part of his strategy to protect the Art Theatre from left-wing accusations that it was 'bourgeois' and thus noxious as well as obsolete. Stanislavsky, although well aware of Lunacharsky's benevolent ploy, soon discovered that a title he had found galling to begin with had made no substantial difference. By 1925, he was able to vent his frustration, writing to his son Igor that the most 'insulting' term going was '"academic theatre"', amid many abuses and obstructions fomented by the Art Theatre's antagonists.[12]

Lunacharsky was an unconditional Bolshevik who believed, within the frames of reference of the Communist Party, that the proletariat had become active in history instead of remaining its faceless victim. But he was also an old-style humanist who valued the cultural legacy of the privileged classes, which, being a means for enriching lives, necessarily had to be shared with this recently empowered proletariat. The October Revolution had finally made it possible to open the doors to the dramatic, musical and performance treasures of the Art Theatre, the Maly and the Bolshoy. Lenin, while prepared to tolerate the Art Theatre, had serious doubts about the validity of the 'bourgeois' Bolshoy, which he thought should be razed to the ground. Lunacharsky countered by arguing vigorously that, with the overthrow of the old regime, all the institutions protected by his policy had passed to the 'masses', their rightful heirs. The Bolshoy building survived, while its repertoires were slowly acclimatized to the changing society.

Theatres, whether seen as keepers of tradition or companions of revolution, were expected to supplement the ideological tutoring of the population carried out variously, not least by straight-out propaganda. Russia and the territories of the former Russian Empire became the USSR in 1922. Just how the Art Theatre could artistically serve ('these servants of beauty') an altogether different people, the newly evolving Soviet people, without being enslaved by the Soviet state, art and beauty intact, ineluctably

---

[11] Lunacharsky headed the *Narodny Komissariat po Prosveshcheniyu* (the People's Commissariat of Enlightenment), usually known by its acronym Narkompros. *Prosveshcheniya* is frequently translated as 'education', since the Russian word encompasses this idea.

[12] Laurence Senelick (selected, trans. and ed.), *Stanislavsky – A Life in Letters*, Routledge: London and New York, 2014, 464, letter of 3 June.

preoccupied Stanislavsky. He dealt with the problem and its practicalities, including the negotiations required to survive Stalin's multiple versions of the 'oppression' he had spoken against in 1905, as intelligently and shrewdly as he could until his death in 1938.

Stanislavsky's is a story of riches to rags. The prosperous Alekseyev factories, which had traded internationally and had enjoyed international prestige, were confiscated after the October Revolution, leaving the entire Alekseyev family destitute. Stanislavsky took responsibility for his extended family both economically and in terms of its moral well-being. But, above all else, his is also a story of attainable ideals and indomitable spirit. Regardless of personal upheaval, serious illness, fear, political interference, cumulative state domination, pervading social turmoil and the volatility of theatre practice across the board, Stanislavsky unfailingly kept in sight the 'high' mission of his life in art.

Ensemble Theatre

Among the numerous innovations bequeathed by Stanislavsky and the MAT to the world is his radical idea of ensemble theatre. This was not, for Stanislavsky, merely a case of getting a group of people together to form a company along the lines of a 'corporate' team. Nor was it an ad hoc arrangement to stage this or that piece of work – what today is called project-based theatre. Still less was it a vehicle for the star system fostered in the later nineteenth century by the hierarchical structures of the Imperial Theatres in Russia and the actor-managers and entertainment-commercial theatres of Europe and the United States. Ensemble theatre was a matter of like-minded people with a 'common goal', who *wanted* to be together and were fully dedicated to making theatre permanently together according to this goal;[13] they also shared the same expectations and values, which Stanislavsky often spoke of as common 'foundations' and 'ideas'.

The 'many creativities' of the writer, actor, director, designer, musician and other collaborators were to be merged harmoniously in a piece of work whose various 'creative elements' – word, music, light and so on – would come together in a unified and structured 'whole' (Stanislavsky's *tselost*).[14] Such a collective input of individual talents required a balance between individual interests and those that took hold integrally in the work being

---

[13] The quotation is from *My Life in Art*, 74.
[14] *SS* 8, 5, 428, and *SS* 8, 6, 75, 280; *SS* 8, 6, 367, especially, for 'creative elements'.

8 Context I

made. It is helpful to seize Stanislavsky's meaning by thinking of the work being made as a transcendent entity to which everyone involved had to 'submit'.[15] Stanislavsky's 'submit' is telling, since it suggests that he was well aware of the push-and-pull and drive for prominence and brilliance of powerful 'creativities'. His envisaged harmonized 'whole' was in sharp contrast with the piecemeal results of competing competencies, as well as rivalries between actors predominant in the nineteenth century.

The framework he conceived for ensemble activity enabled Stanislavsky to reconsider the role of the stage designer who, by past practice, had become accustomed to arranging the scenic 'picture' (Stanislavsky's word) independently of the actors' and the director's wants and needs.[16] When he found in Viktor Simov a like-minded scenographic partner rather than an artist merely hired temporarily for the job – and Simov was to design in close consultation with Stanislavsky and the MAT for most of his life – Stanislavsky gave the very role of designer its full range and significance, probably for the first time in theatre history. The role was one of constructing space rather than illustrating it and, in addition, of providing not decorative backgrounds for situations but a visual insight into, and an interpretation or even synthesis of, the core aspects of a production. This role, a liberating one in so far as the designer was not a subordinate but an equal partner in the process of making a production, was to be a shaping force of twentieth-century theatre, extending to the present in the twenty-first century. Here, indeed, in the designer's place at the *centre* of theatre work along with all other collaborators can be seen a long-lasting consequence of Stanislavsky's advocacy of ensemble practice. The piece of work fashioned collectively, that 'transcendent entity', as described above, was neither a 'thing' nor a 'product', but an *embodiment* of the collective effort invested in its making.

Despite his eighteen-hour deliberations with Nemirovich-Danchenko in 1897, Stanislavsky did not draw up a fully detailed blueprint for ensemble theatre. He was not a theorist as such. It took him a lifetime to contour his thoughts and to test and revise them in different ways in different periods, as much through his stage practice – rehearsals included – as his teaching. His observations regarding ensemble theatre are scattered

---

[15] *Moya zhizn*, 86. Benedetti in *My Life*, 74, erroneously translates the Russian verb for 'to submit' (*podchinyatsya*, thus Stanislavsky's 'submit to a common goal') with the English verb 'to work' (Benedetti's 'work towards a common goal'). However, as is clear from my text above, Stanislavsky's reference to submission is vital for his idea that collaborators need to respect the goal and the artistic 'whole' (*tseloye*) above their personal interests.

[16] *SS* 8, 5, 428.

Ensemble Theatre

over a wide range of sources, going from his private notebooks, diaries and letters, quotations and commentaries among students and friends, public speeches on designated occasions, and of course *My Life in Art* and *An Actor's Work on Himself, Part One* (1938) and *Part Two* (1948), as well as *An Actor's Work on a Role* (1957), which Stanislavsky had planned as a sequel (never completed) to the preceding book. The main points from across these sources have been extracted for these pages and are treated in clusters of ideas rather than in chronological sequence. Clarity of exposition must rely on some interpretation, and this includes my analogy with music below, which is appropriate for Stanislavsky's practical knowledge of singing and his musically endowed approach to the theatre, but is not to be found in precisely these words in Stanislavsky's writings.

The MAT was to be a platform for actors of a *new* type. Such actors were to agree with the principles of artistic and personal unity on which the MAT was based. Consequently, they were to be prepared to reject the star system that had indulged egos excessively, fostering the individualism, narcissism and exhibitionism of actors whom Stanislavsky identified, according to his well-known aphorism, as loving themselves in the theatre instead of loving the theatre in themselves.[17] If the ensemble blueprint took years to be fleshed out, this feature of ego-abnegation for love of the theatre was defined right from the start. Yet let there be no misunderstanding. The 'individualism' denied by the MAT cannot be confused with 'individuality', which Stanislavsky prized and encouraged in actors without fail.[18] Time and again he referred to the necessity of nurturing individuality both for the sake of the actors' own abilities and for the highest potential of the ensemble which, in his view, could not be

[17] The exact aphorism is 'love the art in yourself, not yourself in art' in *An Actor's Work: A Student's Diary*, trans. and ed. Jean Benedetti, Routledge: London and New York, 2008, 558.

[18] The theme of the actor's individuality runs right through Stanislavsky's classes, as recorded in shorthand and transcribed and compiled by Konkordiya Antarova in *Besedy K. S. Stanislavskogo v Studiya Bolshogo teatra v 1918–1922* (*K. S. Stanislavsky's Conversations in the Bolshoy Studio Theatre 1918–1922*), general ed. and introduction by L. Ya. Gurevich, Moscow and Leningrad: All-Russian Theatre Association, 1939, especially 54 and also on the teacher's obligation to bring out the student's individuality so that it flourishes thereafter in his/her professional work. See 80–2 for the 'best human strengths' (Stanislavsky) 'in concert' (my gloss). A wayward version of Antarova's book in English is titled *Stanislavsky: On the Art of the Stage*, trans. David Magarshack, London: Faber and Faber, 1950. This being unreliable, I refer only to Antarova's transcription in the chapters that follow.

For Stanislavsky's view of the actor, in which many of the points cited are summarized, see his 1928 'Iskusstvo aktyora i rezhissyora' ('The Art of the Actor and the Director') in *SS* 8, 6, 232–42, commissioned by the *Encyclopaedia Britannica* and published as 'Direction and Acting' in Vol. 22, 1929–32, 35–8.

realized without the development of individualities in concert, as equals among peers.

An ensemble was absolutely necessary for the 'collective creativity' and 'collective creation' – recurrent phrases in Stanislavsky's vocabulary – that defined the 'new theatre' he and Nemirovich-Danchenko had founded.[19] The actors of this kind of theatre could be nothing but united by a common purpose, and they were to be deeply connected to each other by how they acted: acutely listening to and hearing each other and co-ordinating each nuance of sound, glance, gesture and action so that the overarching movement developing from moment to moment was like the music played by an orchestra. It did not matter whether the music was on a grand symphonic scale or intimate like a chamber orchestra. The point was that the playing – acting – was inseparably together, constructing the line, texture and density of the piece so that nothing was outside it, going it alone, so to speak. This finely tuned and tuned-in ensemble playing was indispensable for any group identified as 'ensemble theatre'. How Stani-slavsky attempted to realize such playing, and how it led his productions at the MAT and activated his laboratory-studios are discussed in subsequent chapters of this book.

As Stanislavsky saw it, ensemble playing worked best when it worked consistently, and this was reason enough to believe that ensemble theatre should be a *permanent* group and endure over the long term. He spared no effort to have the Art Theatre survive, which it did for decades, irrespective of outside political and other pressures, its own vicissitudes, shortcomings and failures, and the disappointments experienced, as well as caused by, its various members – founding members, too, not excluding Stanislavsky and Nemirovich-Danchenko, and younger recruits. Stanislavsky well knew that duration allowed actors to grow and change as everyday human beings as well as artists, since their body, spirit and successive emotional inner states, in short, everything that they were becoming in the flow of life, were integral to the very process of acting. The ensemble both facilitated and protected this motility, while channelling its energy so that nothing went randomly into the ether, away from the work undertaken.

The ensemble was equipped to capture and focus energy because actors were not obliged to waste it by getting to know each other, as do strangers

---

[19] To be found, for example, in *SS* 8, 3, 254. Benedetti in *An Actor's Work* omits this section, which refers specifically to collective and united creativity. For other strong references, see *SS* 8, 3, 416, *SS* 8, 5, 428–9 (reflections of 1908) and *SS* 8, 6, 369 (1938); the dates in parenthesis suggest Stanislavsky's consistency of thought on 'collective creativity' from the pre-Soviet to the Soviet period. See also Senelick, *Stanislavsky*, 593, letter of circa 29 September 1935 to his sister Zinaïda.

Ensemble Theatre

in entertainment and/or project-based theatre when they come together for the first time and then disband after their work is done. Working within the same group of people was immersive and continuous, and both immersion and continuity inspired and sustained individual and collective confidence, while safeguarding the members of the group against fragmentation, dislocation and isolation. In this, an ensemble was akin to a family and, in its devotion, it was comparable to a church. In a notebook of 1908, Stanislavsky reflected on the vital need for a 'theatre-church' in a period of religious decline, and observed how practitioners 'demanded new art or new buildings, wanted a theatre without actors, or dreamt of turning spectators into theatre participants', whereas 'no one has tried to purify himself and pray in the theatre. What a mistake!'[20] In the same entry, he likened actors to 'priests', thereby suggesting the sacredness of their purpose.

Ensemble theatre, for Stanislavsky, was also a permanent *repertory* company bound to the principles of energy, growth, change, immersion and continuity here noted. Productions in stock made them available for actors to improve them over time, as the MAT's founding actors, in fact, did for the first decade or so of the company's existence. Thereafter, they were less willing to renew and reconstruct what they felt they had already mastered, unlike Stanislavsky, who ceaselessly revised his roles. But, then, they were less committed to researching acting than he was, and a number of them mistrusted the younger actors' enthusiasm for his new findings, which they soon critically dubbed his 'system'. Stanislavsky noted ruefully their complaints, during the mid- and later 1900s, that he had 'turned rehearsals into an experimental laboratory and that actors were not guinea-pigs'.[21] Regardless of their disparagement of his efforts to find a common basis for acting ('system') – fundamental, in his view, for pulling actors in the same direction so that, instead of pursuing individual paths, they all performed the same production – Stanislavsky remained firm in his belief that a repertory ensemble provided actors of differing abilities with prime opportunities for learning from each other.

Intrepid (or obstinate), Stanislavsky expressed his wish in a letter of 1929 to the 'MAAT collective' that younger members take advantage of what their seniors could still teach them.[22] He said this as if to counter the attitudes of a post-revolutionary period, when the younger generations were vigorously questioning the authority of the older ones, especially

---

[20] *SS* 8, 5, 420, my translation.   [21] *My Life*, 257.
[22] *Stanislavsky – A Life*, 525, letter of 31 December 1929.

when the imprecation 'bourgeois' came to hand as they sought to fit in with the current political regime. He said it, moreover, despite his own misgivings, ever since the company first toured the United States in 1923, about whether the established company actors were capable of learning anything new. He had written at the time to Nemirovich-Danchenko, who was keeping the rest of the Art Theatre open and performing in Moscow, that the older actors 'don't want to [work] in a new way, and the old way is impossible'.[23]

There is still another important aspect to be considered. An ensemble company such as the MAT was in a strong position to build up lasting relations with audiences who would come to know its distinctive approach to performance as an *ongoing* group. There was never any doubt in Stanislavsky's mind that spectators were far from passive onlookers, or merely empty receptacles to be filled from the stage. He saw them as active and participatory because they communicated their feelings back to the stage in a myriad of subtle as well as quite ostentatious ways (their soundless relay of intense concentration, for instance, or, by contrast, their audible shuffling). They thus influenced performances in the moment and indicated to actors where they might consider modifying them in the future. A spectator in the process of connecting and interacting with the players became, in Stanislavsky's words, a 'co-creator', 'one of the collective creators' of a performance.[24] His view that spectators were interactive was totally modern (for Stanislavsky they were interactive by their very nature) and the issue of co-creative spectatorship and how it functions is still a concern of the early twenty-first-century performing arts, evident in such cases as 'participatory', 'promenade', 'immersive' and 'one-on-one' theatre.

The MAT was to enjoy the benefits accrued from its ensemble practice when it first performed abroad in 1906. After discussions with the company, Stanislavsky and Nemirovich-Danchenko engineered this three-month European tour to kick-start it out of its artistic impasse. In Berlin, Dresden and Leipzig, and then elsewhere along its journey, which included Prague, Vienna and more cities in Germany before going to Warsaw, the MAT saw again what it had first discovered in the hamlet of Pushkino, near Lyubimovka. These were the weeks of concentrated preparation in idyllic seclusion of *The Seagull*, planned for the MAT's inaugural season in 1898. The discovery was this: learning as one body, with all parts interconnected, as happened between the instrumentalists of an orchestra, was a potent catalyst for productive work; meanwhile, the experience of

---

[23] Ibid., 416, letter of 14 February 1923.   [24] *SS* 8, 6, 87, notes of 1918–19.

Ensemble Theatre 13

synergized learning was stored up in the collective body memory, allowing actors to source and renew it afterwards. The productions taken on tour – the Chekhov stalwarts *Uncle Vanya* (1899) and *The Three Sisters* (1901) among them – relied heavily on this principle of reinvigoration to give performances that were fresh and full of life. The foreign critics invariably noted the latter qualities, stressing the extraordinary ensemble work of the actors (who, in their view, surpassed similar attempts in Germany) and its musicality, harmony and emotional depth, together with the co-ordination of the scenic whole.[25] There was praise, as well, for the directing.

Reviewers had caught what Stanislavsky saw not as being set features of ensemble theatre but its 'processes', his term suggesting the *organic* rather than fixed nature of creativity, in which Stanislavsky profoundly believed – intuitively believed, one could say – but had not yet tried to formulate in words: verbalization was to come in the ensuing years. Put differently, processes are about something coming into being, something that gradually takes shape and form to which a name, if it is necessary, is assigned only after the event for the purposes of differentiation. In Stanislavsky's view, as will be clear in the chapters to follow, acting, directing, devising from etudes and imaginative flashes, intuitions and insights are part and parcel of organic creativity made flesh.

The MAT did not always live up to Stanislavsky's expectations of what an ensemble theatre could or should be, and Stanislavsky and Nemirovich-Danchenko's disagreements with each other, dating from before the tour, many to do with Stanislavsky's burgeoning System of acting, destabilized the situation. Many more difficulties, stemming from the Art Theatre's Chekhov years, were bound up with what proved to be two irreconcilable directorial positions: Nemirovich-Danchenko's, which was primarily literary, stressing the priority of the author and the author's text, and Stanislavsky's, which was theatrical and so *of* the theatre, stressing the right of the theatre to shorten, reorganize and otherwise modify the author's text – while retaining its kernel ideas – when this was beneficial for scenic work; in Stanislavsky's case, then, the necessities of performance took priority over the words on the page as such – that is, words did not dominate but were components of an integrated performed whole.[26] The October Revolution subsequently played a major part in the rocky

---

[25] *Zhizn i tvorchestvo*, Vol. 2, 6–29 for varied commentaries.

[26] Olga Radishcheva's remarkable study of the difficult relations between Stanislavsky and Nemirovich-Danchenko throughout their forty-year collaboration details the rift that occurred between them over the role of the director in staging plays and the kind of direction that was desirable. Their disagreement began relatively innocuously with *The Seagull* in 1898, tapered away

14   Context I

course that the Art Theatre was to take as it found itself face to face with immense economic hardship. Quite predictably, in sequential post-revolutionary circumstances on a cataclysmic scale, the company was obliged to undertake another tour, this time to the United States, with performances in Berlin, Prague, Zagreb and Paris en route, in that order. Paris saw [a] 'colossal success, general acclaim, fantastic press', as Stanislavsky jubilantly reported.[27]

There was never any doubt that this tour was for anything but foreign currency – Stanislavsky wrote of the actors 'actually starving';[28] and the government, while shilly-shallying over whether to give the troupe permission to travel, for fear that it might never return, recognized that political mileage would be had from a display of renowned 'Soviet' art. On the side of the United States, there were also commercial as well as culturally and politically invested interests. Stanislavsky was to write afterwards that the main initiators of the tour years before it actually took place had been the company's impresario Morris Gest and the journalist Oliver Sayler who had spent time visiting various theatres in Moscow and was an Art Theatre enthusiast;[29] and, according to Stanislavsky, Sayler 'played an important role in our journey' writing numerous newspaper articles on the Art Theatre and broadcasting radio lectures across the United States before its arrival to spread the word and prepare potential audiences. Sayler's book *The Russian Theatre under the Revolution* (1920), republished in 1922 as *The Russian Theatre* (most likely in order to take the incendiary edge off his title) was to have similarly preparatory and publicity value. Intensive preparations involved printing cheap playtexts in English of the productions that spectators would hear in Russian. These were sold out within a few hours. Stanislavsky refers also to the advertising and organizing help of Nikita Baliyev (Chapter 2), a former Art Theatre shareholder and actor who now ran a theatre in New York.

Contrary to original intentions, the tour lasted for two years, from September 1922 to early summer 1924, mainly because its first performances in 1923 in the United States (New York, Chicago, Philadelphia,

---

with *Uncle Vanya* in 1899, but came to a head during their co-direction of Gorky's *The Lower Depths* in 1902 and again, when co-directing *The Cherry Orchard* in 1904. See *Stanislavsky i Nemirovich-Danchenko. Istoriya teatralnykh otnosheny. 1897–1908 (Stanislavsky and Nemirovich-Danchenko: A History of Theatre Relations. 1897–1908)*, Moscow: Artist. Director. Theatre, 1997, especially 100–1, 124–5 and 155ff.

[27] *Stanislavsky – A Life*, 403, telegram of 5 December 1922 to Nemirovich-Danchenko.

[28] Ibid., 398, letter of 26 May 1922 to composer, pianist and conductor Sergey Rachmaninov, who had left Russia in 1917, settling in the United States.

[29] *SS* 8, 6, 408, endnote 72.

Boston) had incurred prohibitive expenses, leaving the company in debt to their impresario, who had arranged a contract greatly to his own advantage. The (now) MAAT was forced to return to perform in Europe and then go back again to the United States in the hope of recouping its losses. Meanwhile, their impoverishment amid North American riches had triggered off in the actors what Stanislavsky saw as money-grubbing and the 'putrid, decomposing rot' caused by its single-minded pursuit;[30] not that he condoned his own pursuit of 'damned dollars' to pay for his tubercular son Igor's cure in Switzerland.[31]

Further, besides Igor, he had thirty and more relatives in Moscow to feed. Stanislavsky's personal situation was little better. He was embarrassed to appear in the United States in his threadbare trousers and worn-out shoes beside his splendidly dressed hosts at occasions in his honour; and he felt ill at ease at lavish banquets, having lost the habits of wealth in the economic straits of Soviet life. The Art Theatre's circumstances were anything but capitalist luxury, which their political enemies in the Soviet press accused them of enjoying; and, while Stanislavsky maintained the dignity of the poor, he was bound up in moral contradictions regarding his own actions – like scrambling for 'damned dollars' while, contradictorily, defending moral fortitude – from which he suffered shame.

Other than the obligation to bear such humiliations, Stanislavsky began to face his gnawing disillusionment with the company. In 1923, he gave in to despair. 'One must get accustomed to the idea', he wrote to Nemirovich-Danchenko, 'that the Art Theatre is no more' for 'no one and nothing has a *thought, idea,* big *goal*'.[32] He, Nemirovich-Danchenko, had already understood this several years before, and now it was undeniable. Yet why did the 'Americans so extol' the company? Stanislavsky's almost eureka reply to his own question was: 'the ensemble!'[33] His principles for harmoniously integrated stage work had been so deeply implanted that they had withstood the negative influences weakening the troupe on other fronts, mainly of their daily life, seemingly without so much as a sign of resistance against them from the actors.

However, Stanislavsky also saw the broader, more positive, picture. He foregrounded 'America's might', the size of the country's towns and the endless queues for tickets at the box office, concluding that, by comparison

---

[30] *Stanislavsky – A Life,* 444, letter of 6 April 1924 to his family.
[31] Ibid., 437, letter of 12 February 1924 to Nemirovich-Danchenko.
[32] Ibid., 415, letter after 14 February 1923, following the date indication in *SS* 9, 9, 78; Senelick's translation modified by MS, substituting his 'outstanding' with 'big'.
[33] Ibid.

with Europe's smaller-scale wealth, 'one can only do business in America'.[34] Such thoughts led him to avow that the MAAT needed American dollars to keep the company and the studios going in Moscow and that, in fact, only the MAAT of the old guard – '*the first group alone*' – could be a 'dollar-making machine'.[35] (He had ruled out the studios as cash benefits.) Stanislavsky was clearly thinking like the tried and tested entrepreneur that he was in his father's factory. He believed, above all, in the sanctity of art, but was not impractical regarding finance and how it supported art.

He praised the American public, who had seen the best talents from Europe, and praised, almost without reserve, the country's great actors: 'We do not have an actor like Warfield, who plays Shylock' and 'Barrymore as Hamlet, although not ideal, is very charming'.[36] His admiration knew no bounds for the lavish resources available to Belasco's *Merchant of Venice* and, across the board, the quality of lighting and lighting technology ('which we can't begin to imagine') and the impressive number of competent stage hands together with a foreman 'we would not ever have dared to dream of'. Compared with America's incomparable advantages, the only thing the Art Theatre could really offer was its unique ensemble work – and this was considerable, if not priceless, as the Americans had realized. He referred as well to a letter by the investor Otto Khan who said that the MAT had 'brought America not the cut-and-dried clauses of a commercial treaty, but the living Russian soul for which America had felt a bond'.[37] In such a context, Stanislavsky found it all the more reprehensible that the company was frittering away the '*idea*' and its 'big *goal*', which galvanized an ensemble.

In 1924, a complete year later, Stanislavsky returned to his theme of how the company's impressive ensemble playing risked being undermined by a visibly compromised ensemble unity. The Americans were 'perplexed and excited' by the presence of not just one striking 'individuality' (Stanislavsky was surely thinking of America's love of stars) but of 'six excellent actors in a single production'.[38] But he was dismayed by the actors' lack of discipline, bad behaviour, carping attitudes and heavy drinking – in short, by the lack of ethics, which had sustained the MAT at its beginnings and without which, he stressed, there could be no talk of 'a group, a troupe'.[39] He worried about the repertoire – 'the oldest stuff we've got' (at the heart of which were the Chekhov productions) – and

[34] Ibid., 417.   [35] Ibid., 418.
[36] Ibid., and also for following citation; *SS* 9, 9, 80–1 from which MS translates.
[37] Ibid., 419; *SS* 9, 9, 84.   [38] Ibid., 438–9, letter of 12 February 1924.   [39] Ibid., 438.

Ensemble Theatre 17

about the actors routinely falling back on 'earlier acting techniques, which have turned into the bad cliché of the Art Theatre'.[40]

Reality had invaded the ideal of 'ensemble' and, Stanislavsky feared, the fierce conditions of Soviet Russia, together with pressure on the MAAT from its opponents to perform socially topical and politically acceptable material would hinder its restoration. Nevertheless, he was certain, having witnessed the impact of the Art Theatre's very *practice* of ensemble theatre in Europe as well as in the United States, that this was, indeed, its unique and defining characteristic. Ensemble practice had also become its brand image as much at home as abroad. 'People', he wrote to Nemirovich-Danchenko, as they discussed the MAAT's opening season on its return to Moscow, 'are expecting an ensemble', and, while he had lost faith in the old guard's ability to maintain the ensemble they had once created so powerfully together, he doubted that the 'newly introduced youngsters' in Moscow would 'achieve one'.[41] The season would open with Gogol's *The Government Inspector* (part of the 'oldest stuff'), and 'people', Stanislavsky was aware, were expecting the 'elders' (*stariki*) to play it. However, 'the acting of the old-timers in *Government Inspector* is so-so'.[42] Stanislavsky had not spared his own acting in the United States from his criticism. It, too, had suffered from a damaged ensemble.

There were, nevertheless, happier notes in his reflections of 1924. He thought of the pleasurable discoveries in this hitherto unknown continent, which he and his colleagues had first approached with some misgivings, anticipating skyscrapers that blocked out the sun and similarly prefabricated stereotypes. On 17 May 1924, the day their ship left New York, Stanislavsky wrote a letter in his and the Art Theatre's name titled 'To the American People', to be published in the American press.[43] He explained that he was not used to speaking with spectators through newspapers – the ease of public dialogue through this medium was 'strange' to him, while 'in America a newspaper addressed the whole country'. He thanked the American people for their generous hospitality and open receptivity, likening them to the Russian people, and thanked them, too, for how they had treated their fifty-four-week tours in a foreign tongue with so much attention and respect. Stanislavsky's tribute, if rather stiffly written, was sincere, as were two articles on the tour published in journals in the

---

[40] Ibid., 409, letter of 10 January 1923 to Maria Lilina, his wife, a founding actress of the MAT; and 442, letter of 12 March 1924 to Nemirovich-Danchenko.
[41] Ibid., 457, letter of 10 July 1924.   [42] Ibid.
[43] *SS* 9, 9, 151–2, published in this edition for the first time; *Stanislavsky – A Life*, 446–7.

18 Context I

Soviet Union in May 1923 and August 1924.[44] In both of these he was keen to dispel any doubts about his appreciation of theatre and theatre audiences in the United States (which suggests that he had been misreported).

However concerned he may have been to set the record straight from every angle, suspicions about the MAAT's loyalties to the Soviet Union had grown during the company's time abroad and, on its return, vociferous Communist groups increasingly threatened its security, along with that of the remaining 'academic theatres', the Bolshoy in the forefront of their condemnation. Additionally, Stanislavsky's personal relations with Nemirovich-Danchenko continued to degenerate in tandem with Stanislavsky's deteriorating health, on the one hand, and, on the other, with internal politicking among company members. The generation of actors undergoing 'Sovietization' was more aggressive than the *stariki* about getting on in the world, but the demands of external politics on them all depleted their energies and lowered morale. These factors were so invasive that Stanislavsky, after his heart attack while performing Vershinin in *The Three Sisters* in 1928, followed by an obligatory two-year treatment abroad, began to take some distance from the MAAT, which was fast becoming an institution co-opted by the state, to find alternative ways of realizing his wishes for it.

Nevertheless, Stanislavsky held fast to his vision throughout these continual, frequently insurmountable difficulties in order to help himself and the colleagues in sympathy with him to keep aspiring to it. He had the highest hopes regarding the younger ones from the six laboratory-studios that he had set up from 1912 to 1935 (the last being the Opera-Dramatic Studio in his home), with the intention of exploring, teaching and developing his System. The Opera-Dramatic Studio gave him special opportunities for enriching the System through the crossover of dramatic and music theatre in which various techniques thought to be exclusive to the one – voice production for the tempo-rhythm of singing, for example – proved to be transformative for the other. The studios were a means, as well, of keeping the ensemble flame burning and, at the same time – the case particularly of the first three studios – of replenishing the Art Theatre with new blood. Only through steadfast aspiration, he was convinced, could the goal of ensemble theatre come closer, and his own dogged faith, or even what some of the founding members of the Art Theatre saw as

---

[44] 'Stanislavsky ob Amerike' ('Stanislavsky about America') in *SS* 9, 6, 491–5, and 'Khudozhestvenny Teatr za granitsey' ('The Art Theatre Abroad'), 495–501. My translation.

Ensemble Theatre

mere stubbornness, caprice or eccentricity, was an example in itself of the compelling power of such aspiration.

Striving for ensemble theatre did not – and does not – inevitably have to lead to the inwardly explored 'psychological theatre' associated with Stanislavsky. On the contrary, history has shown that the idea and the ideal of ensemble theatre can give rise to a whole range of theatre aesthetics. Vsevolod Meyerhold, who had participated in the Pushkino experience and had played Konstantin Treplev in *The Seagull*, also worked within the principles of ensemble theatre after he left the MAT in 1902. Yet he produced not only one genre and style different from that of the MAT, but a series of them, the most prominent and daring being Constructivist theatre, which he based on the biomechanics that he elaborated with his actors. Yevgeny Vakhtangov, the student whom Stanislavsky had loved the most, forged another genre, 'fantastic realism' (also known as 'magic realism') out of his company's ensemble work.[45] Mikhaïl Chekhov, Anton's nephew, whom Stanislavsky considered a 'genius' actor, sought ensemble coherence in which powerful artistic individualities like his own could breathe freely within theatricalized, stylized, modes of performance.

The varieties cited are Russian grown, coming out of Stanislavsky's school, regardless of their divergence from the 'psychological realism' characteristic of the MAT. Others, elsewhere – for example, Bertolt Brecht's 'epic theatre', Tadeusz Kantor's 'theatre of death', Ariane Mnouchkine's 'theatricality' (*théâtralité*) and Elizabeth LeCompte's techno-improvisatory The Wooster Group – are salient types of theatre outside Russia generated from ensemble-theatre practice, and which, most probably, could only have been generated from it; and there are many more, both inside Russia and beyond, down to the present day, encompassing Jerzy Grotowski's 'holy theatre' and the groups derived from, or inspired by, Grotowski.[46] The Théâtre du Soleil, Mnouchkine's non-realistic, indeed, vehemently anti-realist theatre, is a highly visible example of an enduring ensemble: it originated in 1964, in a decade when Mnouchkine strongly advocated Stanislavsky's model (it was in tune with the spirit and politics of co-operatives favoured by the counter-culture of the 1960s), and this ensemble is still active according to its collectivist ideals as the 2010s draw to a close.

---

[45] See Christopher Innes and Maria Shevtsova, *The Cambridge Introduction to Theatre Directing*, Cambridge University Press, 2013, 77–93.
[46] Ibid., 229–52.

20   Context I

Looked at retrospectively from the twenty-first century, ensemble theatre proves to have been a radically innovative idea-and-practice because, whatever else it had sparked off, it spawned, not necessarily directly from Stanislavsky (his indirect impact was, in any case, enormous), numbers of different aesthetic approaches while maintaining its singular operative principles, which have sustained them all. Its diversity within longevity bears witness to the magnetism of ensemble theatre.

These very principles set the Moscow Art Theatre apart right from the start, for, while functional ensemble companies were in existence, led by such significant managers and directors as André Antoine in Paris and Otto Brahm and Max Reinhardt in Berlin, they were 'ensembles' in so far as they were a cohort of people carrying out the same task – performing– without being seamlessly unified by their style of acting and artistic convictions; and without holding beliefs and everything else that makes up a common 'worldview' to cement their relations. Reinhardt's Deutsches Theater (he succeeded Brahm in 1905) came the closest to this encompassing idea of ensemble – an achievement knitted together with related achievements (seeking to make productions integrated wholes, co-operation with dramaturgs) on which Stanislavsky congratulated Reinhardt in 1930 for his theatre's twenty-fifth anniversary.[47]

But that was Stanislavsky looking back at a colleague's success in which he saw reflections of his and the MAT's contribution by their very own example. In the nineteenth century, however, there had been no such precedent to rely upon. Even the Saxe-Meiningen Court Theatre, which Stanislavsky first saw in Moscow in 1890, having missed its first 1885 tour, derived its apparent unity not from the synergized, symbiotically attuned acting that Stanislavsky was to pursue with the MAT, but, rather, from the co-ordination of costumes with the historical subject and setting of plays, and with the visual and sound effects to illustrate them; cohesion, where actors and acting were concerned, was to be found only in the immaculately organized crowd scenes.

Aleksandr Ostrovsky, Russia's most important playwright of this period, noted in 1885, after his initial excitement over the Meiningen's crowd scenes in *Julius Caesar*, that 'the impression I got was no more powerful than the impression I would have got from the march of a well-drilled regiment or the dancing of a well-trained *corps-de-ballet*'.[48] This technically articulated unison had been achieved, moreover, on the orders of the

---

[47] *SS* 9, 9, 426, letter of 24 May 1930.
[48] David Magarshack, *Stanislavsky: A Life*, London: Faber and Faber, 1968, 40–1.

director Ludwig Chronegk: command was his method. To add insult to injury, 'the leading actors are bad and the leading actresses are worse', and they too 'always played at the word of command'.[49]

Five years later, Stanislavsky seemed little disturbed by the Meiningen's lack of actor connectivity and oneness, noting, instead, his gratitude for having witnessed incomparable 'directorial devices' – offstage crowd noise in *Julius Caesar*, mechanized gliding gondolas in *The Merchant of Venice* – that 'revealed the essence of the productions'.[50] Pictorial detail of this kind was intrinsic to the fundamentally photographic 'naturalism' of the last decades of the nineteenth century, above all at Antoine's Théâtre Libre (1887–95), and Stanislavsky was not free of its influences at the Society of Art and Literature. His debt to the Meiningen variation on it showed then, and subsequently, in the verisimilitude of dress and furniture in his stage environments – with a big difference, however, that makes all the difference in that Stanislavsky, in a highly innovative move, constructed these environments to help actors act in the 'new' MAT way. In other words, his details of setting at the MAT were less about telling and illustrating a story and passing a social message through it, as was largely the case of European naturalism, than a *support* for the actors' imagination and creativity during a performance.

Additionally, as Stanislavsky openly acknowledged, he modelled himself, when a young director, on Chronegk's despotic methods.[51] Nevertheless, the impact of the Meiningen 'was something less than a theatrical Road to Damascus', as Jean Benedetti accurately observes.[52] And it was less than an epiphany precisely because Stanislavsky was already broaching the problem of how to stage convincingly without complete recourse to command or, for that matter, to the heavily ostentatious eye-and-ear-catching external effects that quashed the actors' inner impulses, preventing them from becoming fully, viscerally, engaged in their acting. The Art Theatre was where he would do his utmost to develop his precocious insights.

Utopian Communities

Stanislavsky's vision of ensemble theatre emerged from within a thickly intermeshed socio-political and cultural context that sheds considerable light on the MAT project. Of uppermost importance, although sorely

---

[49] Ibid., 41.   [50] *Zhizn i tvorchestvo*, Vol. 1, 23–4.   [51] *My Life*, 115.
[52] Jean Benedetti, *Stanislavski: His Life and Art*, London: Methuen Drama, 1999, 41.

neglected by studies of Stanislavsky and the Art Theatre, both in Russia and abroad, is the fact that the last third of the nineteenth century and the first two decades of the twentieth were highly conducive to belief in togetherness and to its actual implementation for multiple reasons to be sketched shortly. The established word for this coming together was *sobornost*, that is, people's willingness and aptitude to form a congregation and steadfastly *be* one. *Sobornost* was most likely Stanislavsky's starting point for his image of an ensemble and its 'collective creation', a phrase he modulated according to visible social changes but without losing its primal connection to the spirit of togetherness. *Sobornost* resonates with Russian history and has powerful cultural connotations, including those to do with the nineteenth-century Slavophil doctrine of pan-Slavic unity.

By the same token, this word has deep roots in Russian Orthodoxy and its fundamental idea that human beings must live in a believing community, for, without this community, they are doomed to such manifestations of spiritual poverty as egoism and greed. Stanislavsky had been brought up in a regularly church-going family and in the creed and rituals of Russian Orthodoxy, and, although as a late nineteenth-century, Russian-style liberal he disagreed with the ultra-conservative outlook of the Orthodox Church, he observed Orthodox customs. It should not come as a surprise, then, to discover that a priest (*svyashchennik*) was called in to hold a service at Pushkino, blessing the actors and their shared enterprise before work began. Lack of space in Moscow had forced Stanislavsky to find an alternative in the country, and lack of money meant that the actors had to do the daily household chores themselves. Stanislavsky, who really did not know how to boil the proverbial egg, set the example by being the first to take up domestic duties. What he *did* know, however, was that the actors had been gathered to live and work together for a common cause, with shared responsibilities for each and all, and this was enough to be a community.

Stanislavsky was no stranger to communities. Savva Mamontov, the railway magnate who was his cousin by marriage and in whose house in Moscow only several streets away the Alekseyev children had spent countless hours making costumes and stage props, had bought the estate of Abramtsevo near Moscow in 1870 with the express purpose of establishing a colony of artists on the property. Abramtsevo artists would soon become key painters, designers, sculptors and ceramicists of Russian art history. There was Ilya Repin, a leader of the Wanderers (*peredvizhniki*), the painters who initiated mobile exhibitions to make art accessible to the people by bringing it to them – a practical instance of the social perspective

Utopian Communities

of 'accessibility' that Stanislavsky was to take up for the MAT; and there were the brothers Viktor and Apollinary Vasnetsov, Valentin Serov, Mikhaïl Vrubel, and Yelena Polenova and her brother Vasily whose portraits and landscapes reflected his faith in beauty while paintings on religious subjects, several on the life of Christ, reflected his Orthodoxy.[53]

The collective aim of the Abramtsevo artists was to combine the arts with the crafts, Vrubel notably moving with ease from his imposing mystical *Demon* paintings to stained glass mosaics and ornamental glazed ware (majolica). Their sculpture, woodwork and pottery workshops, complete with apprentices on three-year courses and guests eager to learn, produced brightly coloured pieces for use in the artists' homes, as in Mamontov's Abramtsevo and Moscow residences. Polenova ran art classes for local peasant children, in keeping with the intelligentsia benevolence of the Abramtsevo nest.

The young Stanislavsky had occasion to visit Abramtsevo with his family during the summers spent at Lyubimovka and to absorb the excitement of the colony's activities. In 1878, Stanislavsky, then fifteen, saw the first 'living pictures' performed at Abramtsevo (after the *tableaux vivants* in which Mamontov and Abramtsevo artists had participated in Paris). On their return home to Lyubimovka nearby, he had his family perform versions of this new form of theatre, later relished by the Symbolists.[54] The Alekseyev family was part of the wider group involved with the Abramtsevo Circle, yet Stanislavsky's links with this world of visual sensuality were woven in other ways as well. Isaac Levitan, the landscape painter who was a pupil of Polenov and an intimate friend of Chekhov, called frequently at Abramtsevo in the 1880s, when he exhibited with the Wanderers. His subtle, so-called mood canvases had their counterpart in Chekhov's countryside stories and, of course, in his plays; Dr Astrov's passionate speeches in *Uncle Vanya* about the natural environment and the need to protect it reflect both Chekhov's and Levitan's ecological views. Simov, a painter, who was to become Stanislavsky's designer, was part of the Abramtsevo Circle and a great admirer of the Wanderer group. The Wanderers' feel for an unassuming, everyday kind of rural Russia permeated his designs for the MAT, especially for its Chekhov productions.

---

[53] Polenov's travels to Rome and then to the Middle East, including Jerusalem, were palpable in his religious paintings, as documented in Tatiana Mojenok-Ninin, *Vassili Polenov: Chevalier de la beauté*, Rouen: Editions points de vue, Association Vassili Polenov, 2013, 127–49.

[54] Eleonora Paston, *Abramtsevo: Iskusstvo i zhizn* (*Abramtsevo: Art and Life*), Moscow: Iskusstvo, 2003, 326.

24   Context I

Abramtsevo studios were architecturally harmonious in carved wood, according to what their artists imagined to be an authentic folk style; they painted the icons and frescos of the small church constructed on the estate, features of its exterior suggesting the decorations on village houses. Indeed, they concentrated on free reconstructions of an elemental 'old Russia' and its folklore, primarily legends and fairy tales. Polenova wrote stories modelled on folk tales. Repin soon began painting actual rather than imaginary scenes of archaic Russian life, recording a heritage that was to disappear faster than he or any of his companions realized. Romantics in their gaze backward, they also looked ahead to putting firmly into place a veritably national, quintessentially Russian visual culture comparable in stature to the established visual cultures of western European countries.

Stanislavsky's education in the visual composition fundamental to his directing seriously began here, while Repin's example of painting the cruel realities of degraded humanity was to show in Stanislavsky's visual detail for his production of *The Lower Depths* by Maksim Gorky in 1902. The influential theatre critic and MAT commentator Nikolay Efros described Stanislavsky's fastidious approach to detail of costume and setting as 'ethnographic' and 'archaeological'.[55] According to Efros, these were habits of socio-historical veracity translated into pictorial idioms that Stanislavsky had acquired from directing at the Society of Art and Literature before French and German 'naturalism' became popular in Russia. Indeed, Efros' astute assessment alters the gaze to notice how deeply these habits infiltrated such early MAT chronicle-like productions as *Tsar Fyodor Ioannovich* (1898) and *The Death of Ivan the Terrible* (1899), both by Aleksey Tolstoy (allegedly a distant relative of Lev Tolstoy, but not so). Here as elsewhere – and beyond Gorky – Stanislavsky's idioms were certainly more 'ethnographic' and Abramtsevo-inspired than 'naturalistic' in the footsteps of western Europe.

The Abramtsevo artists echoed, with vestiges of *narodnik* zeal, the folk-nationalistic sentiments that had begun to surface among an earlier generation, most distinctly in Modest Mussorgsky's songs, operas and instrumental music; and such contemporary composers of note as Nikolay Rimsky-Korsakov were rapidly taking up Mussorgsky's baton. Mamontov, when he launched his Private Opera Theatre in Moscow in 1885, produced operas on Russian tales and themes alongside his impressive Italian

---

[55] *Moskovsky Khudozhestvenny Teatr. 1898–1923 (The Moscow Art Theatre 1898–1923)*, Moscow and St Petersburg: State Publishing House, 1924, 148.

repertoire, sometimes helping to stage them as well as the operas he had composed himself.

The ambitions of the Private Opera Theatre were prodigious for a small organization. The bass-baritone Fyodor Chaliapin, soon to become the most sought-after singer on the world stage, sang twenty different roles in his three seasons with the Private Opera Theatre, including fourteen new creations; and not only did Mamontov firmly encourage him to sing the title role of Mussorgsky's opera *Boris Godunov*, the acme of his exceptional artistry, but he also taught Chaliapin to understand how the new, pro-active designers and others working together at the Private Opera Theatre in 'an atmosphere of trust and friendship' had combined 'all the arts – music, poetry, painting, sculpture and architecture', and dramatic characterization harmoniously.[56] This type of creativity of threading, weaving and texturing is precisely what Stanislavsky had learned under Mamontov's tutelage-by-example at the Private Opera Theatre, and its image stood before him in 1918 as he remembered Mamontov's 'authority regarding art' and his credo that it was 'necessary to accustom the eye of the people (*narod*) to beauty in stations, churches and in the streets'.[57] The musical education he received in this exceptional context came to his aid when he experimented with grand opera in the 1920s and 1930s (Chapter 4). In matters of art, Chaliapin would become one of his most important points of reference for the rest of his life.

'Beauty', understood as multifaceted sensory stimulation, was the kernel of the Private Opera Theatre. The resounding success of Mamontov's first season was Rimsky-Korsakov's *The Snow Maiden*, based on Ostrovsky's play. Viktor Vasnetsov's bold folk-style, ethnographic design in vibrant colours had contributed to the sensation caused by the work, and more was whipped up by the following seasons, Rimsky-Korsakov's operas of magic and mystery usually at the top of their lists. Stanislavsky would direct Ostrovsky's play at the MAT in 1900 with visual flair and a beguiling fairy-story atmosphere – Simov's 'old Russia' costumes echoed Mamontov motifs – but it failed to stir audiences. He was fascinated by opera's capacity for enfolding multiple artistic elements into drama, and responded enthusiastically to Mamontov's occasional requests for help with various productions, also singing in *King Saul* composed by Mamontov in 1890.[58]

---

[56] Both phrases are Chaliapin's, cited in Victor Borovsky, *Chaliapin*, London: Hamish Hamilton, 1988, 115 and 123.
[57] *SS* 8, 6, 96–7 and 100.   [58] *Zhizn i tvorchestvo*, Vol. 1, 115.

Beside the Vasnetsov brothers, Vrubel, with whom Stanislavsky came into contact more than once and not only through Mamontov, drew designs and made sets for the Private Opera Theatre, as did Serov but also, on occasion, Simov. Vrubel performed as well, when Mamontov was short of performers. Levitan painted scenery, but avoided playing on the stage. By now Konstantin Korovin, the impressionist painter who had travelled to France and Italy with Mamontov in 1888, had become part of the Abramtsevo community, sketching *en plein air* the subjects of his canvases; Stanislavsky asked him to provide the sets for his 1891 *Foma* after Fyodor Dostoyevsky's *The Village of Stepanchikovo* for the Society of Art and Literature. In 1895, he asked Vrubel to design the costumes for his production of *Othello* (1896), notably those for Desdemona to be performed by his wife, Maria Lilina.[59]

Stanislavsky's great debt to the Private Opera Theatre and the Abramtsevo community generally for a visual culture that buoyed up his entire professional life largely remains uncharted territory. Yet his account in *My Life in Art* of how, according to his 'director's and actor's habit', he squeezes his body into the frame of a Vrubel painting (undoubtedly one of Vrubel's *Demon* paintings) to 'become physically accustomed to it, not from without but from within' is a visual tour de force in itself, let alone a strong clue to Stanislavsky's affinities.[60] Stanislavsky's is an extraordinarily exact analysis of Vrubel's idiosyncratic lines: sloped shoulders, lengthened arms and fingers, a turned-out waistline – all constituting the 'inner substance of the painting'. While gliding from detail to detail, Stanislavsky articulates precisely what distinguishes Vrubel's painting: its 'forms', which meld with 'inner substance' in a non-representational, abstract way, and so much so that they are 'too abstract, non-material' to submit to Stanislavsky's attempts, both as an actor and a director, to give them corporeal shape. And, as Stanislavsky visualizes how he would be acting Vrubel's painting, he merges painting and acting so that the one contemplates and illuminates the other. Visualization from within an action to externalize it concordantly in form became a cornerstone of his System.[61]

The activities interlacing Abramtsevo and the Private Opera Theatre stimulated the kind of multidimensional cross-arts development delineated in the previous paragraphs, and Mamontov went further afield to finance *The World of Art* headed up by Sergey Diaghilev in St Petersburg in 1899. Diaghilev used the journal to publicize the eponymous group of artists he

---

[59] Ibid., 170.　　[60] *Moya zhizn v iskusstvye*, 278–9; *My Life in Art*, 243–4.
[61] Preliminary principles of such visualization are in *SS* 8, 2, 69–95; *An Actor's Work*, 60–85.

was gathering around him, organizing international exhibitions to show off their talents. Vrubel and Serov were involved in this group, rubbing shoulders with Aleksandr Benois, Aleksandr Golovin (he had joined the Abramtsevo Circle in 1898) and Leon Bakst, who would become renowned designers of the Ballets Russes, managed by Diaghilev in Paris between 1909 and 1929. Benois would briefly design and direct for the MAT, most notably Pushkin's *Mozart and Salieri* in 1915, while Golovin, an exceptional painter of colour and light, designed elegant sets and costumes, which he together with Stanislavsky lit exquisitely, for Beaumarchais' *The Marriage of Figaro*, part-directed by Stanislavsky in 1927. Stanislavsky's collaborations with these two major artists showed that he was more than capable of renewing contact, as the years passed, with old family connections to the advantage of the Art Theatre.

Mamontov's financial partner for *The World of Art* was Princess Tenisheva, whose artistic community at Talashkino, her estate near Smolensk, shared Abramtsevo's perceptions and ambitions. These two pioneering phalanxes of Russian art, combined with Mamontov's no less pioneering Private Opera Theatre, were most certainly forerunners of the Ballets Russes, whose musical, visual and dance brilliance intended to outshine anything that they had done. The Ballets Russes also magnified 'Russianness' to an unprecedented degree, shocking Paris audiences with the 'primitive' (which they equated with 'Russian') *The Rite of Spring* in 1913, and titillating them and other international audiences afterwards with a brand of Orientalism like no other, born of the Russian Empire that extended to Central Asia and the Far East.

The MAT's inaugural production *Tsar Fydor Ioannovich* in 1898 had already evoked a similarly 'exotic' world through its opulent, ethnographically inspired sixteenth-century costumes and architectural sets, calling up the 'authentically Russian' promoted by Abramtsevo, Talashkino and the Private Opera Theatre. There was, after all, a similarly national impulse in Stanislavsky and Nemirovich-Danchenko's desire, when founding the MAT, to transform *Russian* theatre rather than theatre 'in general', the phrase Stanislavsky would use when coaching actors to avoid conjuring up diffused images of characters and aim, instead, for specific characterization. Furthermore, both men considered that identifying the MAT with Russia was a prerequisite for its immortality, first in Russian culture, and then beyond national frontiers. They were keenly aware of the immense significance of their 'common idea' – in actual fact, the MAT's innovations *did* make world history – and this guiding light kept them together both through their cordial friendship and strained relations (even when they no longer spoke with each other but communicated only by letter), as it bound them through the frequently overwhelming political pressures and stresses of the future.

Stanislavsky was acquainted with Diaghilev and, like most cultivated Russians who travelled in Europe extensively, he knew of Diaghilev's successes abroad, not least with Russian opera. Stanislavsky was all the more likely to keep his eyes and ears open because of his love of music and ballet since childhood and his training in singing. His musical passions had found a channel other than theatre performance in the mid-1880s, when he served on the Directorial Board of the Russian Music Society and Conservatoire alongside Pyotr Tchaikovsky. Stanislavsky greatly appreciated the acclaimed composer's ballets and operas, directing scenes from Tchaikovsky's *Cherevichki* and *The Queen of Spades* in 1897, these being his first experiences of opera directing. Diaghilev, who moved within much the same cultural circles as Stanislavsky, saw and praised his 1903 performance of Brutus in *Julius Caesar*, directed by Nemirovich-Danchenko (although Stanislavsky loathed the role, the production and his performance in it).[62]

In short, the whole network of interlocking entities and values, interests, agreements, expectations, aspirations and perspectives identified in these pages were part and parcel of Stanislavsky's social class and 'habitus' – Pierre Bourdieu's pithy term for the dynamics of socially generated cultural appreciation, understanding, adaptation, appropriation and behaviour, which are mediated by institutions as much as by relatives, friends, friends of friends and acquaintances whose shared values, interests and so on form a cohesive social group.[63] Habitus, of whatever kind it may be, gives a social group definition ('structures' the group, in Bourdieu's language) within the 'umbrella' structure of society. The personal richness Stanislavsky's habitus offered him involved direct knowledge of artistic currents, which nurtured his creativity while broadening his culture without diverting him from his chosen path.

---

[62] *Zhizn i tvorchestvo*, Vol. 2, 421. See also Senelick's commentary on Stanislavsky's performance of Brutus, *Stanislavsky – A Life*, 164–5.

[63] Bourdieu elaborates his concept of habitus from book to book, but perhaps the most comprehensive account is in *Le Sens pratique*, Paris: Le Seuil, 1980, 87–98. Bourdieu stresses that, apart from involving thoughts, perceptions, aspirations and behaviours, among other aspects itemized in my text, 'habitus' generates practices or what could be called value-embedded actions and how they are carried out. Although Bourdieu never wrote about the theatre, 'habitus' is extremely useful for studying this field and precisely because the theatre is practice. See Maria Shevtsova, *Sociology of Theatre and Performance*, Verona: QuiEdit, 2009, especially 83–102.

Utopian Communities

The ferment of these years and their lasting impact cannot be underestimated, but nor can the philanthropy that sustained it. Mamontov's patronage was on a grand scale, as was that of Savva Morozov, the tycoon benefactor and major shareholder of the MAT. Morozov not only kept the MAT from financial ruin, but he also housed the company in a building reconstructed in 1903 by Fyodor Shekhtel, the foremost architect of the Modern Style (the Russian version of Art Nouveau) that graced the dawn of the twentieth century.[64] The sculptress Anna Golubkina, whose rare gifts Auguste Rodin had recognized when he taught her in Paris, carved the façade above one of the building's doorways which, in the Modern Style, appeared to be rolling forwards between sea and air.

Not only was Shekhtel's architecture a striking example of this most recent of Europe's modernist trends, but the new theatre also boasted a revolving stage – a great innovation of the time – as well as state-of-the-art lighting technology, which Stanislavsky enthusiastically used to great advantage, becoming an adept light designer himself. The Art Theatre was equipped to leave the old world behind. Further, with its new writing, acting, directing, visual culture and ensemble organization, it was ready to face the twentieth century and, more still, to help shape it irrevocably. Shekhtel gave his services gratis, in keeping with the open and generous ethos of the group of merchant-patrons in focus here who belonged to a broader group comprising builders of roads, schools, hospitals, medical clinics, churches and other necessities of the 'civilization' that they wished to spread across a Russia in need of modernization. These benefactors' perception of Russia as 'backward' was part of their habitus and thus of their transformative actions to bring Russia forward, level with Europe.

Stanislavsky's father's philanthropic deeds were on a smaller scale. Yet, whether donation was munificent or modest, Stanislavsky must surely have imbibed the philanthropic good will surrounding him. He constructed a 300-seat theatre for the workers of the Alekseyev factory, opening it in 1904, one year after Shekhtel's completion of the MAT premises that Stanislavsky finally thought worthy of 'educated human beings'. Scholarly research has forgotten the factory theatre, but it would seem, even from the minimal information available about it in the MAT Museum archives, that the workers were not solely audiences for productions brought in according to 'art' standards, but that they staged and performed

---

[64] Stanislavsky's eulogy on Morozov is unusually effusive for so private a man, which indicates his profound recognition of Morozov's humane generosity and his affectionate gratitude to him. *Moya zhizn*, 244–7; *My Life*, 213–15.

30 Context I

productions themselves – with such enthusiasm that they stopped going frequently to the church across the road, to the consternation of its priests.[65] The factory, left completely in his charge after his father died in 1893, had put Stanislavsky squarely in the merchant class, as identified by the census at that time, listing 'industrialists' in this same category. The terminology shifted to 'capitalists' with the growing politicization of all sectors of society, and its negative connotations weighed in after 1917. Until then, come what may, and regardless of his inherited status, Stanislavsky lived his parallel life at the Art Theatre.

Still, merchants were not a uniform class, and Stanislavsky's intimate friends, Mamontov and Morozov, together with Pavel Tretyakov, who was part of the Alekseyev clan by marriage, adding to its intermesh of influential people, were especially prominent figures within a wider compass of public benefactors. A rapid profile of Tretyakov shows him to be a textile merchant and a judicious collector of contemporary Russian paintings, who left his wonderful canvases to the museum in Moscow that bears his name to this day. His collection showcased Abramtsevo artists and the Wanderers, including Levitan who stayed in Polenov's house when he visited the colony, evoking its surroundings in some of his landscapes. Then there was his 'rival' Sergey Shchukin, also a textile merchant, who was a great collector of contemporary western European art, notably French paintings and especially paintings by Matisse and Picasso, and whose art gallery in Moscow founded the first museum of modern art in the world. Shchukin intended to bequeath his collection to the people of Moscow. In the event, it was nationalized in 1918. Not to be forgotten is Aleksey Bakhrushin, a leather industrialist in the entourage of patrons constructing a country and its heritage, who, during his lifetime, bequeathed his home and vast theatre collection, which he started in 1896, to the city of Moscow.

These men, who were such a powerful presence in Stanislavsky's universe, were united within their social class by their commitment to arts patronage, but three of them, Morozov, Tretyakov and Shchukin, were distinguished within it by the fact that they were Old Believers. The Old Believers were a breakaway Orthodox group and political dissenters who had built their communities on strong egalitarian lines in Northern Russia, the Urals and Siberia. They had protested against reforms within the Orthodox Church in the seventeenth century and had adhered, without wavering, to their schismatic position ever since. Like nineteenth-century

---

[65] *Zhizn i tvorchestvo*, Vol. 1, 455.

Utopian Communities

anarchists, they defied authority, having been inured against it by Peter the Great's persecution of them and by continual attempts thereafter to crush them. Their values of industriousness, reliability, sobriety, education and high ethical standards were 'values characteristic of Orthodox monasticism', crowned by their 'view of all actions as a holy task or a religious feat'.[66]

By the beginning of the twentieth century, the Old Believers had produced mighty industrialists and a 'number of enlightened patrons of the arts and charities, creators of innovative industrial technology, and collectors. ... And they acted as patrons of scholarly research'.[67] Mamontov's patronage of the journal *The World of Art* is to be seen in this context for, although not an Old Believer, he thought and behaved like one in his conviction that art was blessed and a blessing, and served the common good. His support for research, which turned out to be groundbreaking due to the calibre of its contributors, outweighed Diaghilev's commercial uses of the journal for advertising his art exhibitions inside and outside Russia. But, after all, Diaghilev was a scintillating impresario, and he had no claims to higher motives.

The values of work, integrity, ethical behaviour and so forth, on which Stanislavsky founded the MAT, corresponded to Old Believer values, although his, too, was not an Old Believer family.[68] The title he was to choose for his lifelong commitment, *An Actor's* Work *on Himself* (my emphasis), reflects this complicity, and his book makes it clear that, for Stanislavsky, work, art and acting were tightly intertwined. Stanislavsky's 'work' was not a matter of utilitarianism or expediency, or, for that matter, of excessively intensive productivity, as was to be pursued in the Soviet era. It responded to Stanislavsky's calling, to a moral-spiritual aspiration encompassed by the Old Believer notion of 'holy task'. The theatre, which he equates with art, is his holy task; acting is his holy task, and acting, as he conceives it, cannot be achieved without morally grounded and selfless work.

Acting/working of this deeply giving kind is capable of penetrating the 'life of the human spirit', the phrase Stanislavsky repeats too frequently in

---

[66] Dmitry S. Likhachev, 'Religion: Russian Orthodoxy' in *The Cambridge Companion to Modern Russian Culture*, ed. Nicholas Rzhevsky, Cambridge University Press, 1998, 47–8.

[67] Ibid., 48.

[68] Golubkina, by contrast, was from such a family. Educated at home more systematically than Stanislavsky and, like him, given the freedom to be strong-willed and independent – these were acknowledged Old Believer traits – she participated in the construction of the MAT with complete conviction in its social and artistic goals.

his writings to be discarded as something he did not altogether intend to say. 'Spirit', whatever else it means for him, refers to the non-material but nevertheless indelible component of human beings, like air or microbes; and 'spirit', in the religious terms familiar to him from his upbringing and social milieu, is the connection of human beings to God. Stanislavsky's allusions to the theatre as a 'church' presuppose that the theatre has a sacred dimension, lifting it up along the vertical going towards divinity.

All of this is to indicate that the habitus of Stanislavsky's formative years left an indelible mark on how he viewed and practised the theatre, and continued to view and practise it in the official atheism of the Soviet Union. Mamontov, in particular, must have been a mentor to Stanislavsky. His letter of 1899 to the younger man reminds him of his 'holy task of art' (*svyatoye delo iskusstva*) in words that Stanislavsky could easily have spoken himself and does, in fact, use.[69] In another letter of 1903, Mamontov repeats his encouragement in quasi-biblical language by referring to Stanislavsky's 'work in art' as a 'high, sacred sermon'.[70] Such details suggest that more attention surely needs to be paid than has been the case to aspects of the Orthodox faith underlying Stanislavsky's understanding of the theatre. Integral to that faith is a belief in beauty as a conduit to God, and as a manifestation of God. It has been argued that 'beauty determined the nature of Orthodoxy in Russia' being ever-present in its 'emphasis on ceremony, church singing . . . pleasing architectural forms . . . and church ornament and decoration'.[71]

There is no reason to doubt that faith in beauty had guided Mamontov's and Morozov's patronage of the arts. A similar faith is behind Stanislavsky's hopes for his and Nemirovich-Danchenko's 'new theatre'. In other words, Stanislavsky's allusion in *My Life in Art* to actors as 'servants of beauty' is fully serious, with no frills, let alone ironic inflections, attached; and his call on discipline and dedication to prevent acting from becoming banal and be beautiful is, in such a framework, nothing but an expression of humility. *My Life in Art* shows that Stanislavsky's is neither a pretentious nor elitist notion of art/theatre. It is a religious one that he transforms and adapts to secular conditions, for art (theatre) comes from humble devotion sustained by hard work; it is labour and creation; it is the space of congregation; it is the space of communion (*sobornost*) – Stanislavsky's word for this interactive coming together is *obshcheniye*; and, while it is not the same as religion, it has the dignity and sanctity of religious affect. Art, although ostensibly secular, has a calling akin to a

---

[69] *Zhizn i tvorchestvo*, Vol. 1, 260.   [70] Ibid., 412.   [71] 'Religion: Russia Orthodoxy', 40–1.

Utopian Communities

spiritual one. Beauty, which art incarnates, has spiritual power and, in so far as it improves people, making them better human beings and also making them feel better as human beings, it has healing power as well. The notion that art is a force for healing is deeply embedded in Orthodoxy – more so in Old Believer Orthodoxy – and Stanislavsky inherited it effortlessly from within his habitus, without ever needing to underline its validity for him.

Stanislavsky's idea of art (theatre) as a binding force has some connection with Lev Tolstoy's *What Is Art?* (1897), as might have been expected, given the particular character of the networks of people being discussed here and the overlapping variations on their collective habitus. Other points in common with Tolstoy to do with 'feeling' and 'experiencing' will be focused upon in Chapter 3. Of immediate relevance is Tolstoy's thesis that art is communion, by which it is linked to religion, for religion unites people. Liturgy, for Tolstoy – and, when referring to it, he means Orthodox liturgy – is far more than the ceremony of faith: it is the religious expression of human communion. Art worthy of its name must aspire to this kind of *sobornost* or being together, Tolstoy's first touchstone for art. His second is folk song because, in his view, the latter conveys feeling in a simple, unaffected way, enveloping listeners and holding them together as one. Folk dance, he argues, has the same unifying capacity. Stanislavsky, although receptive to Tolstoy's general line of thought, never proposed liturgy, or, for that matter, folk/peasant performances, as models for the theatre.

Tolstoy's position was radical in the extreme, as unthinkable for Stanislavsky as his draconian criteria for what was acceptable in art. And Tolstoy was ruthlessly uncompromising. From Shakespeare's plays to Wagner's operas, with novels, poetry and concert music in between – Tolstoy tossed them all out for this reason or that, but mostly because they failed his tests of simplicity and transparency which, to his mind, were the portals of communion and divine grace. He had little time for the plays of Chekhov, for whom he had deep personal affection, although he greatly appreciated Chekhov's short stories; and he shrugged off Stanislavsky's 1902 staging of his own play *The Power of Darkness*, although he had agreed in 1895 to Stanislavsky's textual readjustment for an eventual production, in deference to Stanislavsky's experience of the theatre.[72] Sofya, Tolstoy's wife, thought it presumptuous of this upstart to importune her celebrated husband in this way.

---

[72] *Zhizn i tvorchestvo*, Vol. 1, 164.

Tolstoy's dismissal of art as it actually was mirrored his demolition of the Orthodox Church and tsarist absolutism, both of which, he insisted, had perverted their missions. The Church had lost sight of the teachings of Christ, as written in the Gospels. The tsar had failed his people. Tolstoy's Christianity – anarchist in its total repudiation of all institutional authority – turned its wrath against the private property, oppression, injustice, inequality and hatred that had caused social divisions and had denied the peasants all rights, their foremost right being the land which they still worked for their masters: Aleksandr II had failed to grant them land when he freed them from serfdom by decree in 1861.

Tolstoy was a formidable figure, attracting countless 'Tolstoyans' to his side. His indefatigable writings and activities, all denouncing the iniquities of Russian society, made him a moral beacon for the entire nation. On his death in 1910, Stanislavsky wrote: 'How fortunate we have been to have lived in the time of Tolstoy, and how terrifying to remain on earth without him. It is as terrifying as losing your conscience and ideals'.[73] Among Tolstoy's numerous actions as the nation's moral conscience was his success in arranging the passage for 5,747 persecuted Dukhobors ('spirit wrestlers') to western Canada (1898–99), where their descendants are still to be found.[74]

The Dukhobors had been pacifists for generations and refused to serve in the tsar's army, thereby incurring the wrath of the tsarist authorities. They lived by the religious and ethical precepts of their community alone, and Tolstoy idealized them, seeing in them the image of Christ, the suffering human being. Their non-resistance (also called 'passive resistance') to autocracy exemplified his own doctrine of non-resistance and non-violence, which he taught to his innumerable international visitors and disciples, including Mahatma Gandhi with whom he corresponded and who deployed it to great effect in India's struggle for independence against the British. Tolstoy raised funds in Russia for the Dukhobors' journey, approaching Stanislavsky, among many respected members of the intelligentsia, wealthy merchants and enlightened aristocrats, for

---

[73] SS 8, 8, 208–9, letter of 10 November 1910 to Nemirovich-Danchenko; Stanislavsky – A Life, 290, offers a different translation.

[74] Leopold Antonovich Sulerzhitsky, Povesti i rasskazy. Stati i zametki. Perepiska. Vospominaniya o L. A. Sulerzhitskom (Accounts and Stories, Articles and Notes, Correspondence, Memories of L. A. Sulerzhitsky), ed. Yelena Polyakova, Moscow: Iskusstvo, 1970, 168–256; L. A. Sulerzhitsky, To America with the Doukhobors, trans. Michael Kalmakoff and introduction by Mark Mealing, Regina: Canadian Plains Research Centre, University of Regina, 1982, 17. See also Aylmer Maude, A Peculiar People: The Doukhobors, New York: Funk and Wagnalls Company, 1904, especially 1–44.

contributions to his cause.[75] With the help of his followers in England, he gathered large donations from the English Quakers.

It is here that Tolstoy's story intersects that of the Art Theatre, and it does so through Leopold Sulerzhitsky. The transportation of the Dukhobors was a phenomenal feat, but it would have been quite impossible without Sulerzhitsky, a staunch Tolstoyan who had offered to accompany the Dukhobors to Canada. On his return to Russia in 1900, Sulerzhitsky came to know Chekhov and Gorky in Yalta and then Stanislavsky in Moscow, whose rehearsals of *The Snow Maiden* he had managed to attend. He became directly involved in theatre activities, and Stanislavsky, who had read his account of the Dukhobors' journey, invited him in 1906 to be his assistant, paying his salary out of his own pocket. The Art Theatre management had declined to do so for financial reasons. Nemirovich-Danchenko was outraged that Stanislavsky had chosen a mere 'amateur' to help him.

Sulerzhitsky quickly became Stanislavsky's closest friend. Stanislavsky asked him to direct the First Studio, formed in 1912, where Sulerzhitsky emphasized using the body, not least because, from the perspective of Orthodoxy (but not of Tolstoy), it was a conduit to and from the human spirit, as he taught the System that Stanislavsky was then elaborating. In all his dealings with the Studio, Sulerzhitsky highlighted the Tolstoyan principles of integrity and communal co-operation; these, in any case, had been among the founding principles of the MAT, and Stanislavsky was keen to encourage them in the First Studio – indeed in all the studios he was to establish. The profound connection between the two men was bound up, as well, in their agreement that the mind, body and soul were integrated rather than separate entities, or even antagonistic ones, and that their integration was precisely what the actor had to work on in a holistic manner.

Sulerzhitsky hoped to build on these principles away from the burdens of everyday life, and so, in the summers of 1913 to 1915, he took First Studio actors to the rural Kanev on the Dnepr river in Ukraine and Yevpatoria in Crimea, both being regions of the Russian Empire. Here, in the light of Tolstoy, they learned from local peasants how to till the soil. In the light of the Dukhobors, they learned to live communally. Stanislavsky had bought them a plot of land in Yevpatoria for these purposes and visited the commune, which included his daughter Kira and Vakhtangov. Sulerzhitsky's death at the age of forty-four in 1916 from

[75] *Zhizn i tvorchestvo*, Vol. 1, 234.

the nephritis he had contracted while arranging the affairs of the Dukhobors in Canada put an end to the adventure. Tolstoy preached love and brotherhood, but Sulerzhitsky paid for them with his blood. Stanislavsky was devastated by his passing, and was never to find so close a friend again.

The romanticism of Yevpatoria, a place the communitarians could call their own, must have been intoxicating, and Stanislavsky could not have failed to recognize its advance on Pushkino. Pushkino, home of *The Seagull* rehearsals, was a short-term sanctuary, as was, for a few summer months in 1905, Meyerhold's experimental laboratory-studio, which moved thereafter to Povarskaya Street in Moscow for an equally short time. Stanislavsky had supported the laboratory personally and financially until his factory's financial losses because of revolutionary unrest throughout 1905, the great costs of studio refurbishment and studio salaries in Moscow, and Nemirovich-Danchenko's opposition on the grounds that it 'was absolutely of no use to the MAT' forced Stanislavsky reluctantly to close it down.[76] Yevpatoria, on the other hand, was not a fleeting occurrence, but one sustained over three years whose duration provided a more viable test of its potential. In addition, the moral and social benefits derived from the experience were intended to help the First Studio's research on the actor who, more than a trained-up player, was to be an enlightened human being.

Utopian communities were most definitely in the air, but they were not only in the air, for there was no denying their concrete existence. Tolstoy, alone, inspired communities to be set up hither and yon, one settling at Telyatinki, more or less on his doorstep at Yasnaya Polyana, to the horror of his long-suffering wife whom he continually accused of giving him a 'hard time'. She writes scathingly in her diary about this latest encroachment upon her life: 'There have been a number of Tolstoyan communities,

---

[76] Plans, itemized expenses and projects of this 'theatre-studio' of 'young forces and new forms' show how seriously Stanislavsky took the venture, as did all who participated in it. See K. S. Nos. 14548–14580, 3818 and 13233 in the archives of the Moscow Art Theatre Museum. Stanislavsky lost 75,000 roubles on the studio, a huge sum of money for this period. For details regarding Meyerhold, see Oleg Feldman (documents compiled and ed.), *Meyerhkolda nasledie* (*Meyerhold's Legacy*), Vol. 3, Moscow: Novoye Izdatelstvo, 2010, 34–40. See 40 for Nemirovich-Danchenko's hostility towards the studio enterprise.

Feldman's meticulous research indicates that economic factors were of the utmost importance in Stanislavsky's decision, and thereby debunks the myth that he was envious of Meyerhold's experiments and curtailed them for this reason. Stanislavsky also compensated all the collaborators of the studio to the tune of six months' salary each. Among them was the composer Ilya Sats, who became the head of the Art Theatre's Music Section in 1906 and wrote the music for the MAT's 1907 *Drama of Life* and *The Blue Bird* in 1908.

Silver Age Metaphysics

but they all collapsed because people had such a "hard time" living together'.[77] Just how 'hard' people found it to live together was to become apparent also in Sulerzhitsky's 'Tolstoyan' Kanev and Yevpatoria communities (Chapter 3).

Silver Age Metaphysics

Sofya Tolstoy's exasperation came from years of frustration with her husband's dissensions, but there was no getting away from practices that had become culturally ingrained. Russia, as Orlando Figes asserts, had been a 'breeding ground' for several centuries for 'Christian anarchists and utopians', and countless other sects burgeoned, year on year, on her soil.[78] According to Figes, in the 1900s, 'the theosophists, the anthroposophists, the Symbolists, Rasputinites and mystics of all types started to see in these sects an answer to their yearnings for a new and more "essential" kind of Russian faith'.[79]

However, even when 'Russian faith' as such was not the issue, the 'isms' of the cusp of the 1900s, starting with Symbolism, blossomed in the Russian Silver Age. The dates of this Age are conventionally given as the early 1890s (when not 1900) to the early 1920s (when not to 1917), and some of its major precursors, as well as pioneers, have already appeared in the preceding pages of this book.[80] The MAT, it must be remembered, was itself part and parcel of the Silver Age, contributing enormously to its manifold brilliance. Other pioneers, who were either directly related to the MAT or are now taken as contextual markers for it, show no less significantly the fertile terrain that nourished Stanislavsky's work.

Thus, in accordance with the Silver Age, Symbolism was welcomed with open arms at the MAT in the plays of Maurice Maeterlinck, first staged there in 1904. Anthroposophy, a significant feature of Silver Age esotericism, made its entrance under the banner of Rudolf Steiner but in the figure of Mikhaïl Chekhov to whom Stanislavsky had first spoken about Steiner before 1917.[81] Chekhov appears not to have read Steiner in

---

[77] *The Diaries of Sofia Tolstoy*, trans. Cathy Porter, Surrey: Alma Books, 2009, 132.

[78] Orlando Figes, *Natasha's Dance: A Cultural History of Russia*, London: Allen Lane, 2002, 308.

[79] Ibid., 345.

[80] John E. Bowlt's title gives his preferred dates. Thus, *Moscow and St Petersburg, 1900–1920: Art, Life and Culture of the Russian Silver Age*, New York: The Vendome Press, 2008.

[81] Michael Chekhov, *The Path of the Actor*, ed. Andrei Kirillov and Bella Merlin, London and New York: Routledge, 2005, 13. For Chekhov's observations on Steiner's influence on his approach to theatre practice see 160, 187–8 and Kirillov's Note 39, 210.

38 Context I

Russian translation until 1918, but he took to Steiner's esoteric elaboration of Christianity, passing it through the yoga he had practised during his studies with Stanislavsky and Sulerzhitsky in the First Studio. It was here that Chekhov forged the warm friendship with Vakhtangov that gave rise to a highly productive artistic collaboration, especially regarding the work of actors. The more Chekhov studied Steiner, the more he moved away from Stanislavsky's anything but other-worldly System, despite its spiritual base, and, eventually, from Vakhtangov's more secular and politically activated than religious or metaphysical imagination.

Yoga had come to the First Studio with Nikolay Demidov, who taught it to all Studio actors. He was Stanislavsky's son Igor's gymnastics tutor and, besides knowing the theatre practically from his manger-director father during childhood, he had studied 'traditional' medicine, psychiatry and Tibetan medicine. Demidov became a family friend, discussing the System with Stanislavsky, assisting him with teaching actors and with editing several drafts of *An Actor's Work on Himself,* for which Stanislavsky gratefully thanks him in his preface, as well as for his 'precious instructions, materials, examples'.[82] Also a friend of Sulerzhitsky, Demidov was well aware of the experimentations under way in the First Studio – he, together with Igor, joined the Yevpatoria community in 1915 – and, while he had doubts about the feasibility of the System, he had few about the creative intentions of the Studio.

Vakhtangov died of cancer in 1922, aged thirty-nine, leaving Stanislavsky heartbroken, once again. He had lost a kindred spirit, not as close as Sulerzhitsky, but, even more painfully, he had lost 'the hope of Russian art'.[83] Chekhov, who took charge in 1923 of the First Studio, as it was evolving into the independent Second Moscow Art Theatre (MAAT2), was by then under attack from the hard-line left factions of the 1920s for his anthroposophical beliefs. Essentially, Chekhov's anthroposophy was a convenient pretext for their political ambitions at a time when the arts were intermingled with politics and, as well, were used transactionally for political reasons. Within a few years he understood that, notwithstanding the political conflicts in society at large, political splintering and divisions of allegiance and intention within the MAAT2 set him at odds with its majority inclination to 'fit in with the Soviet system', as the Art Theatre

---

[82] *SS* 8, 2, 8. Benedetti omits this preface in *An Actor's Work*. For further details see *Nikolai Demidov: Becoming an Actor-Creator,* ed. Andrei Malaev-Babel and Margarita Laskina, trans. Andrei Malaev-Babel with Alexander Rojavin and Sarah Lillbridge, London and New York: Routledge, 2016, 1–7.

[83] *Zhizn i tvorchestvo,* Vol. 3, 196, from an inscription of 18 April 1922 on Stanislavsky's photograph to Vakhtangov, now mortally ill.

Silver Age Metaphysics 39

scholar and editor Zinaïda Udaltsova puts it.[84] Seeing that he was no longer able to build up his own kind of theatre, he left Russia in 1928, going to Berlin, Paris, Riga, Dartington Hall in England and Connecticut in the United States before settling in Hollywood, where he died in 1955.

Chekhov was a dazzling 'individuality' in the Pleiad that had risen from the MAT. He stunned colleagues and audiences alike with his compelling performances of the insane king in August Strindberg's *Erik XIV*, directed by Vakhtangov in 1921. For some time now, he had been in search of an acting style that projected what was other than obvious reality, or was on the edge of it, and this resonated with a strand of anthroposophy concerned with finding how to make visible the invisible spiritual world. Take, for instance, Chekhov's idea that the actor did not need to seek a character from within: the character, lured by the imagination, would come from without, like a visitation, to the actor.[85] His theory of the 'psychological gesture', by which the actor physicalizes a character's mysterious, hidden impulses, can be understood in terms of the 'ineffable' that was central to anthroposophy, together with its interest in the expressivity of the body. A good number of Chekhov's ideas on acting came together in his stellar creation of the role of Hamlet in 1924 at the MAAT2, directed by Valentin Smyshlyayev, Vladimir Tatarinov and Aleksandr Cheban, with Chekhov, effectively, as the fourth director. Smyshlyayev, issuing like Chekhov from the First Studio, is foregrounded in the following chapter.

The invisible was a hallmark of Symbolist drama which, in Russia, was generally written by poets – thus Andrey Bely, Aleksandr Blok and Valery Bryusov, to cite only the most well known of them.[86] Bely was an anthroposophist who encouraged Chekhov to take a studious approach to the subject. He was, at the same time, a theorist of Symbolism, who urged the 'transformation of theatre into a shrine', a goal that, at first glance, looked deceptively like Stanislavsky's until closer inspection proved

---

[84] Personal conversation 13 April 2017. Udaltsova, a great admirer of Mikhaïl Chekhov, queries his hints as well as the claims of his acquaintances abroad that imminent arrest because of his anthroposophical views forced him to emigrate. For Chekhov's account, see *Literaturnoye naslediye* (*Literary Legacy*), ed. Maria Knebel et al., Vol. 1, Moscow: Iskusstvo, 1995 (with supplementary material added to the 1986 first edition), 181–2, 246–7 and 249.

[85] Michael Chekhov, *To the Actor*, London and New York: Routledge, 2002, 21–34 and 63–76 for the 'psychological gesture'.

[86] In any case, separation of writers by literary genres was never a Russian practice. Virtually all the great Russian writers from Pushkin, Gogol, Tolstoy and, of course, Chekhov to the Symbolists here noted and well beyond them wrote in multiple forms – poetry, plays, novels, essays, treatises and so on.

it was quite different.[87] Stanislavsky thought of the theatre as comparable to a place for prayer and so for the cleansing necessary for the 'life of the human spirit'. Bely's 'shrine' was to the chimera of wherever vertiginous fantasy took a creator: the 'shrine' was for crystallized poetic experience. And so it happened that, in 1921, years after Bely's theoretical pronouncements, he and Chekhov turned his delirious novel *Petersburg* into a weird and wonderful theatre piece. Chekhov played the role of the ghostly, grotesque Ableyukhov, a civil servant, who was Bely's emblem of the 'unreal' city built by Peter the Great on water, shrouded in mist. None of Chekhov's performance extravagances could have been too extravagant for this phantasmagorical work.

Years earlier, in 1906, Meyerhold had taken a similarly visionary direction when he staged Blok's *The Fairground Booth* in St Petersburg. Overnight, Meyerhold's production became a rallying point for Symbolists of all stripes, even though Meyerhold, like Blok, had cast a satirical eye on the play's mystics. Stanislavsky, whom Blok liked and admired, valiantly attempted to grasp Blok's plays, to Blok's good-natured amusement at his efforts. But Stanislavsky was not cut out for the vagaries of Symbolism, as his lame 1904 short-play Maeterlinck productions, *The Blind*, *Interiors* and *The Intruder*, had shown.

The Fairground Booth in Meyerhold's hands was groundbreaking for its mixture of genres, going from balletic *commedia dell'arte* to clowning, and for its championship of the *cabotinage* (ham acting) that Stanislavsky had banished from the MAT. Each and every aspect of Meyerhold's multi-layered production supported the stylized acting favoured by Symbolist theatre. Vera Komissarzhevskaya, daughter of Fyodor, Stanislavsky's singing teacher, was probably the Symbolist actress par excellence, with her highly expressive, highly theatrical manner that appeared to be evoking something in existence beyond her actual performance.

Komissarzhevskaya had hired Meyerhold to direct in her theatre in St Petersburg to promote Symbolism, the antithesis, from her point of view as much as Meyerhold's, of the MAT's psychological-realistic work. The Symbolist poets-novelists-critics had a field day smashing what they took to be the MAT's claims to lifelike art. Most vocal among them was Bryusov, who had been on Stanislavsky's payroll when he collaborated with Meyerhold in the 1905 laboratory financed by Stanislavsky and who

---

[87] Quoted in Konstantin Rudnitsky, *Meyerhold, the Director*, trans. George Petrov, Ann Arbor: Ardis, 1981, 85.

Silver Age Metaphysics

argued that art was artifice and so anything but 'like life'.[88] Bruysov's *The Fiery Angel* (1908), which teamed with demons and witches, and demonstrated his knowledge of the occult, corroborated his assertion. Then, on top of the home-grown Symbolists, there were the imported ones like Strindberg, favoured by Vakhtangov, and Maeterlinck, preferred by the MAT.

The visual and musical arts abounded in allusions to the invisible universe. Demons flew across Vrubel's dark, overwrought canvases, while newer artists, turning their back on the nineteenth century, burst into the twentieth with arms outstretched. Vasily Kandinsky, by contrast with Vrubel, sought to materialize in luminous compositions the intangible correspondences between spiritual experiences and colours; Marc Chagall, to materialize the mystical flights of the soul. Kasimir Malevich painted his intimations of spaces aeons away, so far beyond the ken of ground-bound mortals that they could only be intuited through the most abstract of forms; and so his black-square pictures, just like his white-square counterparts, appeared to dissolve into nothingness. The first of Malevich's black squares had made its appearance in the Futurist opera *Victory Over the Sun* (1913) whose *zaum* (language beyond rational understanding) by Aleksey Kruchenykh, with a prologue by *zaum* poet Velimir Khlebnikov, was meant, with glints of humour, to blow the mind away. The music by Mikhaïl Matyushin was to do much the same, albeit in the dissonant, anti-lyrical idiom of Russian Futurism, which, preoccupied by abstractions rather than the immediately knowable of daily experience, was more cerebral than sentient and sensual.

Nerve-end sensation was the Symbolists' aperture to the 'beyond'. It took the composer Aleksandr Scriabin, who was heavily influenced by theosophy, to soar into the heavens with his notes of many colours and there find ecstasy. His 1908 symphonic *Poem of Ecstasy* was nothing if not the apotheosis of his quest for absolute spiritual freedom, already announced to the fanfare of trumpets, the instruments of angels, in *The Divine Poem* written four years earlier. It has been said that Tolstoy was profoundly moved by Scriabin's music and, if the anecdote is not true, then its invention expresses true insight into Tolstoy's own quest.

And what of Stanislavsky in this maelstrom of utopian journeys, some, with Malevich and Scriabin in the lead, travelling into the farthest reaches

---

[88] 'Realism i uslovnost na stsene' ('Realism and Convention on the Stage'), essay of 1908 reprinted in *Teatr. Kniga o novom teatre* (*Theatre, A Book about the New Theatre*), Moscow: GITIS, 2008, 202–14.

of the cosmos, hoping to touch infinity? Stanislavsky responded to Scriabin's inimitable sounds with a sense of recognition and, in the coming years, had his compositions played at the convivial Monday meetings held at the MAT.[89] He may have soared in spirit with Scriabin, but his feet stayed on the ground. Stanislavsky's limitless capacity for inventiveness, for unexpected, astonishingly imaginative turns was legion among those who took part in, or witnessed, his rehearsals.[90] However, for all his flights of the imagination and intimations of the divine and the cosmic 'beyond', he was closer to the earth, intent on establishing on it the natural, fully organic creative actor within a creative community: actor and community were mutually inclusive and, together, they gave the theatre both its concreteness *and* its sacred dimension.

[89] See, for scattered references to Scriabin, *Khudozhestvenny Teatr. Tvorcheskiye ponedelniki i drugiye dokumenty 1916–1919* (*The Art Theatre: Creative Mondays and Other Documents, 1916–1919*), compiled and commented Z. P. Udaltsova, Moscow Art Theatre Press, 2006.

[90] See, for example, Vsevolod Meyerhold's letter of 28 June 1898 (during rehearsals of *The Seagull*) to his first wife Olga in Jean Benedetti (selected, ed. and trans.), *The Moscow Art Theatre Letters*, London: Methuen Drama, 1991, 28; Maria Knebel, *Vsya zhizn* (*My Whole Life*), Moscow: All-Russian Theatre Society, 1967, 213–56; Aleksandr Gladkov, *Teatr. Vospominaniya i razmyshleniya* (*The Theatre: Recollections and Considerations*), Moscow: Iskusstvo, 1980, 236–51; V. O. Toporkov, *Stanislavsky na repetitsii: Vospominaniya*, Moscow: AST-Press SKD. 200, especially 75–155 on *Dead Souls* (1932) and in English as *Stanislavsky in Rehearsal: The Final Years*, trans. Christine Edwards, New York and London: Routledge, A Theatre Arts Book, 1998, 76–152; Boris Zon, 'Vstrechi s K. S. Stanislavskim' ('Meetings with K. S. Stanislavsky') in *Teatralnoye naslediye. K. S. Stanislavsky. Materialy. Pisma. Issledovaniya* (*Theatre Legacy. K. S. Stanislavsky. Materials. Letters. Research*), ed. I. E. Grabarya et al., Moscow: Academy of Sciences of the USSR, 1955, 444–91.

CHAPTER 2

Context II

Stanislavsky and Politics

The utopian states of being cherished by Silver Age artists took shape, in counterpoint, as revolutionaries articulated their materialist visions of a just and equal society, steered by the modern proletariat. Several Silver Age artists noted in the preceding chapter – Malevich, Blok, Bely, Bryusov – and others besides, saw no contradiction between their quests for transforming aesthetics and those of revolutionary politics to change the world. The first owed their strengths to metaphysics, while the second were grounded in the 'scientific materialism' popularized by Marx and adapted by Lenin and the Bolsheviks to Russian circumstances. The revolutionaries distinguished 'scientific materialism' from 'utopianism', which they generally dismissed as idealistic thinking, even though utopian sparks had also to ignite their imagination so that they could envisage a new world.

The actual reality of making such a world was the foremost challenge after the monumental overturn by the October Revolution of millions of lives, hewing a context that would redefine them all. The changes implemented in the coming two decades were massive, transforming social structures, social classes, emotions, moralities, psychologies and behaviours, and, in Stanislavsky's case, his entire class and clan habitus. Stanislavsky's world was split into two: the world of the nineteenth century, which had nurtured him, and the world of the twentieth blazoned after 1917 in which he would live fewer years – twenty-one, to be exact – but which required a colossal readjustment of the outlook, attitudes and expectations that he had incarnated, as every habitus is absorbed in the flesh.

The 'new' was a term that had become like a mantra for the Silver Age, and the 'new' engendered by the post-revolutionary context was multiple, volatile and generally unpredictable; and it was ubiquitous. A full account of these 'new' phenomena is not possible in the restricted space of this

44 Context II

book. Nor is it possible to do more than simply identify the political events after 1905 that led up to the complete turn-about of the tsarist universe, sealing conclusively with the October Revolution and the rise of Stalin the fate of the country and so of the MAT. A few bold strokes will have to suffice to place and perceive Stanislavsky and the Art Theatre as clearly as such briefest of outlines can allow.

The causes of the demise of tsarist Russia are exceedingly complex, but the events happening in its last phases, all of which reoriented the direction of Stanislavsky's life, can be broken down reductively, as follows. The mass social protests of 1905, during which year Russia's war with Japan ended in abject defeat, had forced Tsar Nicholas II to concede to the establishment in 1906 of the Duma, Russia's first parliament. In the same year, the Constitutional Democratic Party (Kadet) was formed. The liberals, Stanislavsky and Nemirovich-Danchenko discreetly among them, welcomed these steps towards democracy with relief. Democracy was not guaranteed, however, as a second and then a third Duma followed in the ensuing struggle between parliamentary forces and royalists until a revolution in February 1917 precipitated Nicholas' abdication. The Provisional Government, ushered in almost immediately, gasped and expired. The diplomatic wranglings, military humiliations and heavy loss of life during the First World War had also taken a heavy toll on this transient government's battle for authority.

The second, decisive insurrection in October 1917 in Petrograd (the Germanic-sounding 'St Petersburg' was renamed due to the war against Germany) swept the Bolsheviks to victory. Valentin Smyshlyayev, who had joined the MAT in 1913 and then its First Studio two years later, was in turn incredulous and aghast at the 'political blindness' of his peers amid the 1917 crises and their breezy talk of the freedom of art, while they ignored the fight for freedom at their very door: the tsar had abdicated, they said, and a government had been assembled, so what more could the people want, and why had they let themselves go to wrack and ruin?[1]

Smyshlyayev, the son of 'professional revolutionaries', was a card-carrying Bolshevik, the only one among the Art Theatre artists, and his political know-how was useful in calming the 'hysterics' (Smyshlyayev) of his good friend Chekhov whose neighbourhood came under heavy fire

---

[1] Smyshlyayev's diaries in Maria Polkanova (compiled and ed.), *I vnov o Khudozhetsvennom. MXAT v vospominaniyakh i zapisyakh 1901–1920 (More about the Art Theatre. The MKHAT in Memoirs and Notes, 1901–1920)*, Moscow: Avantitul, 2004, 40–139, and especially 70 (for the citation), 100–4, and 107 for the Studio's anti-Bolshevik sentiments.

Stanislavsky and Politics 45

from Moscow insurgents, who had taken to arms in solidarity with Petrograd.[2] His political credentials were of great value in 1919, when, on 30 August, Stanislavsky and actor Ivan Moskvin were arrested and imprisoned by the Secret Police (*Cheka*) on the mistaken charge of collusion with the White Army. The Civil War raged across Russia's far-spread territories, and the offensive taken by the Whites against the Red Army in Moscow had precipitated the arrest of alleged counter-revolutionaries. Smyshlyayev's horror at his teacher's plight was spurred on by his love for this 'wonderful, fascinating old man! ... What imagination, boldness, talent!';[3] and he spared no effort in running between political offices and inept officials until he secured Stanislavsky's and Moskvin's release.

Smyshlyayev's distraught reflections on that day of shock focused on Stanislavsky 'who is a coward' so 'God knows what he is going through', the fear that had paralyzed the Art Theatre as a result of his arrest, and Stanislavsky's undoubted innocence: 'After all, in politics – he is a child'.[4] Smyshlyayev agonized over Lunacharsky's absence from Moscow: had he been there, Stanislavsky would have been released immediately. He could not have guessed Lunacharsky's fury over this breach of his protection of the Art Theatre on his return to Moscow; or his outrage at the mass arrests of intellectuals and public cultural figures who had been members of, or had been sympathetic to, the Kadet, which Dominic Lieven maintains had the support of the 'majority of educated Russians'.[5] Lunacharsky openly expressed his anger to Lenin, as did the people's writer Gorky.[6] Both strongly felt that the new, fragile government could not afford to alienate educated groups who, with encouragement, would most likely become reconciled with it. Gorky, twice imprisoned for his connections with revolutionaries, who became core Bolsheviks, was a celebrated publicist, essayist and novelist and an authoritative figure in Russia. The MAT had performed two of his plays in 1902, *The Lower Depths* with resounding success. A third, *Children of the Sun*, was performed in 1905.

Smyshlyayev's loyalty to Stanislavsky and to the goals of the First Studio did not prevent his involvement with the Proletkult (short for 'Proletarian Culture') which, already hostile to 'bourgeois' culture, fairly quickly also

---

[2] Ibid., Polkanova's Introduction,15; also 104 for Smyshlyayev's diary entry of 1 November 1917. All translations here and following are mine, unless otherwise stated.

[3] Ibid., 100, 23 October 1917.   [4] Ibid., 125–6, 30 August 1919.

[5] *Towards the Flame: Empire, War and the End of Tsarist Russia*, Allen Lane Great Britain, 2015, 167.

[6] Katerina Clark and Evgeny Dobrenko with Andrei Artizov and Oleg Naumov, *Soviet Culture and Power: A History in Documents*, trans. Marian Schwartz, New Haven and London: Yale University Press, 2007, 7.

became the enemy of the pugnacious and flamboyant, equally anti-bourgeois, avant-garde Left. This rift occurred, even though Meyerhold, who was aligned with that Left, had some jurisdiction over early Proletkult activities when Lunacharsky appointed him in 1920 to head the Theatre Section (TEO) of the Commissariat of Enlightenment. In the saddle of this organization, whose project was to politicize the 'masses', Meyerhold took up the slogan of 'Theatrical October' as he proceeded to demonstrate that the theatre could serve the revolution in a thousand ways, from street theatre, pageants and mass festivals to performances in factories and, indeed, in old-regime venues, as well.

Meyerhold had already joined the Bolshevik Party and, in 1920, he set up the RSFR1 Theatre as his platform for adventurous theatrical experimentation with a revolutionary message. His theatre differed in tone and method from the crudely utilitarian theatre of the Proletkult, and it marked him out as a man ready for the Left Front in Art (LEF), a loose association he was to establish with the playwright Vladimir Mayakovsky in 1922. The Art Theatre's disdain for Meyerhold's swagger was equal only to his contempt for its failure to ride with history. He was soon to write an article in 1921 about Stanislavsky's 'isolation' – this 'genius of pure theatricality', who had forsaken his true nature and succumbed to the 'art foisted upon him by the literary-bourgeois management of the Art Theatre'.[7] Meyerhold's insult to the 'management' was principally meant for Nemirovich-Danchenko, but an insult to Stanislavsky was also lodged in his craftily formulated attack.

The Proletkult, which enjoyed its greatest freedom between 1918 and 1922, was founded by Aleksandr Bogdanov who, like Lunacharsky, was from the intelligentsia. Bogdanov's enthusiasm for a culture made by and for the proletariat *without* reference to 'bourgeois' antecedents – on this he disagreed with Lunacharsky – resulted in the appearance of hundreds of Proletkult groups in large conurbations as well as smaller towns. The Proletkult network saw to raising literacy and numeracy levels, and its adherents taught the rudiments of playwriting, stagecraft, musical composition and painting to aspirant proletarian artists. The terminology 'proletarian' was problematic since the Civil War had decimated the working class. Huge numbers of working men had died in battle; factories

---

[7] Vsevolod Meyerhold and Valery Bebutov, 'Odinochestvo Stanislavskogo', ('Stanislavsky's Isolation') in V. E. Meyerhold, *Stati. Pisma. Rechi. Besedy* (*Articles, Letters, Speeches, Conversations*), Vol. 2, Moscow: Iskusstvo, 1968, 30–4. An extract from this essay is cited in Laurence Senelick and Sergei Ostrovsky (eds.), *The Soviet Theatre: A Documentary History*, New Haven and London: Yale University Press, 2014, 108.

had fallen into disuse and, at the end of the Civil War, when the cities could offer neither work nor bread, hungry worker-soldiers of peasant origin returned to the countryside to eke out a living. As Sheila Fitzpatrick points out, the Bolsheviks defined the proletariat as an *industrial* proletariat and its heavily depleted ranks had been filled out by menial-job seekers, journeymen, white-collar workers and students, putting its identity into question for most of the 1920s.[8] Nevertheless, these heterogeneous groups claimed the proletarian status privileged by the proletarian state.

Proletkultists were inevitably caught up in the fluidity of class definition. Some, like the playwrights Pavel Bessalko and Valerian Pletnev, were plebeian: the first was the author of *The Bricklayer* which, a 'favourite in Proletkult organizations ... was also used as a model for theatrical improvisations in the Red Army'; the second emphasized themes on 'the workers' struggle'.[9] Others, however, like the theatre director and film-maker Sergey Eisenstein, were from the intelligentsia, but concurred with the popular revolt against pre-revolutionary classics in favour of subjects and forms adequate to the revolutionary era. In 1921 Eisenstein, together with Smyshlyayev, directed *The Mexican* after Jack London and a 'miniature' production of *The Avenger* by Pletnev after Paul Claudel (albeit hardly a proletarian writer) for the Proletkult's Central Studio in Moscow.[10]

Eisenstein went on to direct three more plays between 1923 and 1924 for the First Workers' Theatre under the aegis of the Moscow Proletkult. The last of them was *Gas Masks* by the LEF writer Sergey Tretyakov, which he staged in the Moscow gas works without sets or other accoutrements of 'bourgeois' theatre – costumes, make-up, footlights.[11] In 1925, Eisenstein's first film, *Strike*, the seed of his prolific film innovations, which guaranteed his world fame, was completed with financial aid from the First Workers' Theatre, backed by Pletnev who, by then, was at the helm of the Moscow Proletkult.

Eisenstein's was a prodigious talent. He had been a student of Meyerhold to whom he revealed his great discovery, montage, which became his main cinematic technique. Meyerhold took it up for the theatre and

---

[8] *The Cultural Front: Power and Culture in Revolutionary Russia*, Ithaca and London: Cornell University Press, 1992, 16–19.

[9] Lynn Mally, *Culture of the Future: The Proletkult in Revolutionary Russia*, Berkeley and Oxford: University of California Press, 1990, 141–2.

[10] *Ivnov*, 19.

[11] Jay Leyda, *A History of the Russian and Soviet Film*, Princeton: Princeton University Press, 1983, 181.

reciprocated with the gift of biomechanics for actor training, whose great influence was palpable in *Strike*, as in Eisenstein's subsequent films. Biomechanics dates from about 1921, when Meyerhold started devising methods for the execution and control of precise movements and gestures after Frederick Winslow Taylor's studies of efficient labour in factories in the United States.[12] Meyerhold's was a response to the perceived needs of a society in transit between revolution and socialism, and Taylorism had become identified in the Soviet Union with current Soviet scientific research on the relationship between movement and the human brain.

Meyerhold's emphasis on the execution rather than the meaning of action was prescient, for the ideological tide had begun to turn away from the rhetoric of being proletarian to the *function* of the proletariat, gathering pace in the second half of the 1920s. The proletariat, irrespective of who actually constituted it, had to function productively in Soviet industry to bolster up an alarmingly deficient economy. As the pressures of economics accelerated, so the attractions of cultural education and exploration waned. Both the Proletkult, on the side of education, and the avant-garde Left, whose wild fantasies in its earliest phase Lenin had described as 'hooliganism', were to be the losers in the tidal wave. So, too, by a most cruel twist, was Meyerhold, who had proclaimed the coming of a machine age mastered by physically and intellectually advanced human beings whose superior virtues he had demonstrated with biomechanics.

Eisenstein left the Moscow Proletkult after *Strike* to concentrate on making films. In the meantime, Smyshlyayev had been part of the Proletkult leadership from 1919 to 1922, heading up its main theatre workshops, copied from the Stanislavskian studio prototype.[13] (Indeed, studios of that ilk mushroomed everywhere for any and every art-education activity, unwittingly testifying to Stanislavsky's unexpected but widespread influence in this domain.) And it was in these co-operative ventures that he acquainted aspiring actors with Stanislavsky's work. His reputedly extensive and fruitful use of Stanislavsky's System emboldened him to write a treatise on the subject, together with an account of the processes of directing. Smyshlyayev published his book *Teoriya obrabotki stsenicheskogo zrelishcha* (literally, *Theory of the Development of a Stage Show*) in 1921,

---

[12] 'Aktyor budushchego i biomekhanika', 1922 ('The Actor of the Future and Biomechanics') in *Stati*, Vol. 2, 486–9; as 'Biomechanics' in *Meyerhold on Theatre*, trans. and ed. Edward Braun London: Methuen, 1969, 197–200.

[13] For details regarding Smyshlyayev's Proletkult productions and contribution to Proletkult theatre in general, see D. Zolotinsky, *Zori teatralnogo oktyabrya* (*The Dawn of Theatrical October*), Leningrad: Iskusstvo, 1976, 288–367.

Stanislavsky and Politics

rewarded for his labours by attention and applause, except from Stanislavsky, the man whose approval mattered to him the most.

Stanislavsky, who appears never to have known that Smyshlyayev had intervened to save him and Moskvin from incarceration, was appalled by Smyshlyayev's 'self-satisfied' plagiarism of his System, which he had by no means finished or even legitimated by a published explanation of his own.[14] Worse, Smyshlyayev had regurgitated his flawed vocabulary and idiosyncratic expressions. Worse still, Smyshlyayev had proved to be a 'bad and backward disciple' by his superficial, muddled exposition and misrepresentation of his [Stanislavsky's] working principles, and his claims to have discovered the 'well-worn' but now 'fashionable' practices of 'collective creativity' and 'collectively devised plays through rehearsals'. Here Stanislavsky must have been thinking, clearly indignantly, about his own, tried and tested practice of collective creativity, etudes and devising on the go, which his disciple had so blatantly co-opted; and he gives no sign of knowing that, irrespective of Smyshlyayev's pilfering, his System, even in its developing stages, had by then 'begun to permeate widely the practices of various theatres, studios and theatre schools'.[15]

The year 1921 was overwhelming for Stanislavsky. Apart from professional anxieties – Vakhtangov, too, like Meyerhold, was urging him to drop the Art Theatre – there were personal traumas. Stanislavsky's brother Georgy was arrested in Crimea in 1921, and Stanislavsky had pleaded in vain with the high-ranking All-Union Central Executive Committee (VTsIK) for his release.[16] Georgy's whereabouts were unknown and buried, too, in the silence of the authorities. In the event, he and his three sons were shot.[17] Additionally, Stanislavsky, who had already been reduced to poverty, had had to fight against eviction from his family apartment of twenty years. Since 1918, this apartment had also served him as an Opera

---

[14] *SS* 8, 6, 1959, 114–15, undated diary entry of 1921. See also Senelick, *Stanislavsky – A Life in Letters*, 393–4. It must be noted that the vocabulary and general configuration of ideas in Smyshlyayev's book, although crude, indicate that he had mined Stanislavsky's teachings as far as Stanislavsky had developed them by the end of the 1910s. However, nowhere does Smyshlyayev acknowledge that his source was Stanislavsky, which also goaded Stanislavsky into condemning him for plagiarism. See *Teoriya obrobotki stsenicheskogo zrelishcha*, Izhevsk: Proletkult Publication, 1921 at the MAT Museum, No. 10714/43/ 5394.

[15] *I vnov*, 23.

[16] *Sobraniye sochineny*, Vol. 9, Moscow: Iskusstvo, 1999, 31–2, letter of 22 February 1921 on his brother and 28–31, letter of 14 January 1921 on his eviction. See also *Stanislavsky – A Life*, 387–8, and 384–6, respectively.

[17] G. Brodskaya, *Alekseyev-Stanislavsky, Chekhov i drugiye. Vishnyovosadnaya epopeya (Alekseyev-Stanislavsky, Chekhov and Others. A Cherry Orchard Epic)*, Moscow: Agraph, 2000, 386.

Studio, where he carried out laboratory research on acting with singers under the auspices of the Bolshoy Theatre. He had also shared it with strangers when the government introduced communal living as part of its policy against private property and, as well, to regulate a housing crisis. His stern, factual letter to the Council of People's Commissars to let him stay was greeted with prevarications, and the apartment, demanded by the garage on the ground floor, was expropriated, leaving Stanislavsky homeless. With Lunacharsky's help, the matter went up the hierarchy to Lenin, on whose orders a replacement apartment big enough to house his Opera Studio was to be found.

Stanislavsky's courageous and business-like letters in such politically charged circumstances – moreover, his brother's arrest endangered Stanislavsky, together with his extensive family – have nothing of that 'child' in politics conjured up by Smyshlyaev. On the contrary, they prove, as do the very facts of his arrest and eviction, and his brother's arrest and disappearance, not only how politics invaded his life, but also how adult were his dealings with its consequences. The letters referred to in the preceding paragraph were not common knowledge during Stanislavsky's lifetime, nor were they published in the first Soviet edition of his letters in the 1950s. They saw the light of day only after the dissolution of the Soviet Union in December 1991 in the post-Soviet edition of them in 1995. Yet the evidence spells out and extends information that could have been gleaned previously – from Stanislavsky's correspondence during the American tours, for instance, most of which was published in the 1950s. Nevertheless, despite evidence that is now undeniable, the myth of Stanislavsky's political naivety and political incompetence lives on into what will soon be the third decade of the twenty-first century, its longevity perversely seeming to validate it.

There are three main reasons for this strange indulgence. The first is the excision of these vital letters in the 1950s' publication, an omission entirely bound up with a regime that was still protecting itself and determined to control the country after the Second World War. A regime bent on retaining power and saving face in multiple areas, where it would be brought to shame, is not likely to seek out its crimes, errors and cover-ups and willingly avow them. The second reason is expediency. After the tumultuous 1920s had finally caved in to the totalitarian 1930s, it suited the Soviet regime politically, during the 1930s (and for decades afterwards), to put Stanislavsky on a pedestal because – irony of ironies – of his devotion to art. Why? Because when art is sequestered in its domain, doing what it is 'meant' to be doing, it is separated from the imbroglios of

Stanislavsky and Politics

politics; consequently, it is prevented from exposing and contesting the rule of the state, or from fomenting rebellion against it.

Paradoxically, the Russian totalitarian state, much like all totalitarian states, also needed the reverse: to put politics into art because art was a channel for reaching hearts and minds. Infiltration was done most efficiently with didactic art, but art could be stealthy and infiltrate minds imperceptibly, thus aiding politics by not 'doing' politics. Whether and how Stanislavsky fell in with the political players who enforced the rules is not the point here: Fitzpatrick, for instance, claims that he was 'an accomplished flatterer of the powerful'.[18] The point – and this is the third reason for the longevity of the Stanislavsky myth discussed here – is that, until the collapse of the Soviet Union, the myth of Stanislavsky the political 'child', upon which other myths like his alleged administrative incompetence have been encrusted, served not only the political sphere, both at home and abroad, but also the interest groups in other spheres, notably culture and education. Interest groups within such cultural and educational institutions as theatres, drama schools and universities profited from the myth-making that not only pictured Stanislavsky playing the victim, the 'holy fool' or the befuddled handmaiden of power unaware that he was a handmaiden, but that also drew extremely entangled circumstances in the crude strokes of political cartoons. Groups of this kind were not – and are not, today – exclusive to Russia.

Consider, too, that a man who has undergone acute personal suffering at the hands of politics is not in the least likely to be politically naive. Stanislavsky screened his suffering from peering eyes and also, on occasion, from himself, but this did not mean that he was incapable of fathoming and admitting its causes. His letters during the Art Theatre's tours in the United States clearly show that he was more than capable of accurately assessing the political motives behind certain social gatherings, advertisements and press releases; and he was alert to the political interpretations that could or would be made of them in Soviet Russia.[19] He understood perfectly well how Soviet newspapers misconstrued interviews and feature

---

[18] *The Commissariat of Enlightenment: Soviet Organization of Education and the Arts under Lunacharsky, October 1917–1921*, Cambridge University Press, 1970, 140.

[19] See especially the letters in *Stanislavsky – A Life*: 401–3, letter between 10 and 17 October 1922 to Nemirovich-Danchenko from Berlin en route to New York; 403–10, letter of 10 January 1923 to Lilina; 415–20, letter of 14 February 1923 to Nemirovich-Danchenko; 423–4, letter sometime in April 1923 to Lilina; 426–7, letter of 21 May 1923 to his family; 433–6, letter of 28 December 1923 to Nemirovich-Danchenko; 441, postscript to letter of 12 February 1924 to Nemirovich-Danchenko.

52 Context II

articles by American writers; conversely, how they were manipulated by anti-Soviet sentiment in the United States. He dealt adroitly with gifts, invitations and requests to be photographed that could compromise him, without offending his hosts and well-wishers.

The importance of such details need not be exaggerated, but whether they are noticed at all and how much weight they are given, other than to discredit the watchful Soviet bureaucrats and spies who dogged Stanislavsky's footsteps has, once again, to do with vested interests; and among the latter appeared the proto–Cold War interests that made Stanislavsky a venerated model (when not a mummified one), on one side of the war, and, on the other, little more than the pawn of an 'evil empire', made to march to the tune of whichever ideology was going – the 'masses', Soviet behavioural psychology, 'socialist realism' – while immunized against danger by the 'privileges' bestowed on the MAAT. Such 'privileges' were, in actual fact, basic survival. More still, the weight attributed to this or that aspect of Stanislavsky's working biography has to do with perception and how preconceived ideas skew perception. Pre-packed perception is thus the fourth main reason for the myth about Stanislavsky's political naivety and why it has endured: well-inculcated and even only lightly acquired 'received ideas' have reproduced it in a chain reaction (together with other myths sticking to him, like his lack of business sense and managerial know-how).

Correction of outlived myths posing as 'truths' is necessary for helping to straighten the picture, not least by pausing in front of its unobtrusive details. Stanislavsky's eviction from his home involves the Opera Studio. This is obvious in the canvas. However, in its shadows hovers Zinaïda Sokolova, Stanislavsky's older sister on whom the eye must rest. Sokolova, his assistant at the Bolshoy Opera Studio, relied entirely on him financially. The cause was nothing less than political – the revolution's confiscation of the family fortune – and that event alone might have jolted Stanislavsky into picking up political acumen of some kind. Sokolova's misfortunes were many. 'Bandits' (of unknown identity) had killed her doctor husband in a village where the couple had opened theatre and crafts workshops for local peasants, and a school for the blind.[20] The crafts workshops may have been inspired by Abramtsevo, or possibly specifically by Polenova's art classes in the village near the Abramtsevo estate.

Sokolova had melded the Abramtsevo spirit and Alekseyev philanthropy with *narodniki* deeds only to be forced back to Moscow, dependent on her

---

[20] *Alekseyev-Stanislavsky*, 388.

brother to keep her from starvation. It is little wonder that Stanislavsky heavily petitioned the authorities for enough space to hold his Opera Studio in the apartment to be allocated to him in a *kommunalka* (a conglomeration of small communal apartments, more often single rooms, with shared facilities – kitchen, toilet, bathroom – for all occupants). Stanislavsky was comparatively privileged to have more family space than the residents on the floor below, and a toilet adjacent to the room dedicated to Studio purposes, which was for the family and Studio participants. A bathroom with a bathtub for his personal use was added in later years, when illness made such a luxury a necessity.[21]

Stanislavsky's passion for research aside – he was developing his System together with actor-singers – the Studio had to continue, for it provided Zinaïda with a meagre income and a modicum of dignity. In addition, he had to keep alive his brother Vladimir, on whose musical knowledge and sense of rhythm in acting he could rely to instruct the Bolshoy actor-singers. His siblings lived in small rooms on the floor above. Stanislavsky's insistence to the government that it meet his family needs required some political competence to frame his case and help to tip the balance in his favour.[22]

Stanislavsky and the Art Theatre continued to work against adversity. The daunting conditions of 1919 – food, fuel and housing shortages, infestation, political unpredictability, moral collapse, and anxiety – caused a group of actors to escape on a summer tour to Ukraine. Stanislavsky opposed the move for he could ill afford their absence at a time when it was imperative that the theatre build up amicable relations with the government. Most unfortunately, the celebrities Olga Knipper-Chekhova and Vasily Kachalov were part of the departing group (known subsequently as the 'Kachalov group'), and the departure of such important actors was bound to elicit mistrust.

The Civil War made the journey riskier than any of them had realized, and the White Army cut off their return to Moscow, forcing them to flee abroad. Their travels took them back and forth to Prague, where a splinter group decided to stay permanently, taking the name of the Moscow Art Theatre of Prague.[23] The rest of the troupe returned to Russia at the end of

---

[21] Information provided by Maria Polkanova, Deputy Director of the Moscow Art Theatre Museum and Anna Ovchinnikova, Head of the K. S. Stanislavsky House-Museum on Leontovsky Lane.

[22] It was gratifying to discover, as research consolidated my hypotheses, a similar point of view in Rima Krechetova, *Stanislavsky*, Moscow: The Young Guard, 2013.

[23] See Laurence Senelick, 'The Accidental Evolution of the Moscow Art Theatre Group of Prague', *New Theatre Quarterly*, 30, No. 118 (2014), 154–67.

54 Context II

the Civil War, having been cajoled by Nemirovich-Danchenko's promise of a tour to the United States. Three years had passed. The company that had stayed behind in Moscow was divided in its attitudes towards the prodigals. Stanislavsky greeted them coolly, but they were necessary for the American tour, permission for which Lunacharsky had negotiated with the Politburo, the uppermost layer of the Communist Party.

Documents only recently in open access in Russia shed light on a delicate situation. Lunacharsky had deviously masterminded a loophole in the dictate to 'prohibit travel', which had been announced full blast by 'the new authorities trying to halt uncontrolled emigration': the Art Theatre was to be allowed to travel to the United States on the condition that the First Studio, then performing in western Europe, come back.[24] The documents in question give a glimpse of the dangers to which the MAAT had been exposed, including the potential charges of treason against the Kachalov group for its long absence, and against the Prague Group for its defection. The leadership's suspicion of the Art Theatre percolated downwards. Thus the rank and file among Proletkultists and avant-gardists could be nothing but wary of it, even though Smyshlyayev's political trustworthiness may have subliminally eased their misgivings. What is certain is that Smyshlyayev's enthusiastic teaching had made the Art Theatre seem less foreign to his proletarian students, thereby putting a brake on knee-jerk rejection of it and what, prejudicially, it was presumed to represent. His teaching also prepared workers to be spectators at this theatre.

The seeming paradox of Smyshlyayev's Proletkultist endeavours – here he was, a revolutionary, supporting 'bourgeois' art – was no more paradoxical than any other paradox in these years of embryonic and disappearing entities, uncertainties, ambiguous attitudes, and tenuous, confused or divided loyalties. The Proletkult was a telling case in that the success of its goals for an independent, non-bourgeois culture depended on the 'gifted artists and teachers' who were largely not proletarian, even in the accepted loose sense of the word at the time, but who 'came with the express purpose of serving the working class and the revolution'.[25] The Symbolists Bely and Bryusov taught Proletkultists literature, and Malevich and the Constructivist artist Lyubov Popova taught them to paint. The Constructivist designer, painter, installation artist and photographer Aleksandr

---

[24] *Soviet Culture and Power*, 9. See also the remaining documents, 11–22.
[25] *Culture of the Future*, 112.

Rodchenko, friend of Meyerhold and Mayakovsky, ran courses on designing book covers and political posters for Proletkult festivals.

Popova, from a wealthy textile family, was an exceptionally gifted designer as well as painter, and she broke with all previous conceptions of scenic design in her composite block structure for Meyerhold's *The Magnanimous Cuckold* in 1922. Her assembly of juxtaposed flat surfaces, wheels, pulleys, ladders and stairs was neither decorative for the sake of pure pleasure nor illustrative of something else, whether of an interior or a landscape. Still less was it an immersive environment for character acting, which had become the hallmark of Art Theatre design thanks to Simov's reversal of nineteenth-century pictorial – fundamentally two-dimensional and decorative – design norms. It gave actors, who were now Meyerhold-trained biomechanical actors, opportunities to run, jump, climb and swing, but, more radically still, it determined their movements, symbiotically binding the actor, the movement, the space created through movement, and the design. Popova's design-object was useful and was to be *used*, and its functional purpose in an unexpected shape coincided exactly with the ideas Rodchenko was teaching at the Proletkult about function defining the form of design. Rodchenko went on to design *The Bedbug* by Mayakovsky for Meyerhold in 1929, showing through yet another artistic genre into which he crossed with ease that he was among the most creative, if not also notorious, avant-gardists of the age. Popova's revolution in the theatre was stopped short by her untimely death in 1924 of scarlet fever, one of the many diseases rampant in these problematical years.

The Proletkult movement reached its peak in the early 1920s, tapering down till the end of the decade, when Rodchenko made his theatre debut. Its decline was principally due to the Communist Party's strategic decrease of funds for its activities in order to weaken it politically. At the height of its powers, the Proletkult boasted half a million members, its strength in numbers and popularity giving it the appearance of an alternative party. Perhaps, as has been suggested, it was turning into a 'people's party' in competition with the 'official' Communist Party.[26] It is unlikely that the Proletkult would have challenged the power elites, but its position on culture was definitely a political irritant. Lenin vehemently opposed the idea that a proletarian culture had a separate, self-made identity that set it apart; this was not possible because proletarian culture and communism were one and the same thing.[27]

---

[26] Ibid., 221.   [27] *The Cultural Front*, 22.

In conjunction with his doctrine, Lenin insisted that nothing other than a canonical, classical bourgeois culture – 'bourgeois' not altogether a sneer in Lenin's vocabulary on this point (although his residual doubts remained about the Bolshoy Theatre) – would equip the proletariat for the modern communist world. The proletariat had been deprived of a heritage that it was imperative to appropriate, as property had been appropriated. It must be remembered that, in the Russian context, and particularly in the immediate post-revolutionary context in which Lenin was thinking, 'culture' was inseparable from enlightenment-education. For this very reason, when Lenin set the New Economic Policy in motion in 1921 to save the country from economic disaster – NEP allowed limited private enterprise as part of *his* experiment – knowledge was put on a pedestal as *the* value of values. The NEP period coined the words 'bourgeois specialist', and bourgeois-specialist knowledge and know-how, in whichever field they were used – the sciences, business, technology, practical application (electricity, plumbing), or the arts – had to be learned and reapplied to the altered conditions of post-revolutionary society.

All this goes a long way to explaining why the government not only tolerated the Art Theatre, but also actively promoted it after 1924 as the bastion of culture for present and future proletarian generations – providing that it heeded Communist Party demands for adjustments and revisions of its productions. Add to this the fact that, unlike all the revolutionary theatres – Meyerhold's theatre, the TEO, the Proletkult theatres, the Blue Blouse (to be met shortly), and more still – the Art Theatre was, to all intents and purposes, politically *disengaged*, and its absence from the scene of political struggle meant that, theoretically at least, it could never become actively contentious nor, consequently, pose a threat to the powers in command. Stanislavsky was Tolstoyan enough to understand the advantages of standing on the moral high ground and avoiding the partisan politics that weaken that moral high ground. An urgent priority of the 1920s was the job of consolidating the Soviet state. Where Meyerhold agreed with the policy, in his own way, Stanislavsky withdrew into the Tolstoyan non-resistance typical of his behaviour in the face of tsarist politics and, once again, now, when the communist epoch's unavoidable realities faced him. His heart attack in 1928, followed by recuperation for two years in Germany and France, kept him out of circulation for a while and, basically, out of trouble.

The 1920s unfolded, and the economy, stimulated by NEP, saw the rise of predatory newly rich 'Nepmen' who were satirized by the 1917 anti-capitalists, notably by Mayakovsky in his plays as well as verse and propaganda cartoons, illustrations and posters. But the time of topical satire, as of the grass-roots effervescence typical of Proletkult festivals, was fading fast. Growing numbers of strong-armed 'agitational propaganda' groups (Agitprop) began to eclipse the Proletkult as they brashly set about re-educating the 'masses' to fortify the Communist state. Stalin, who succeeded Lenin on his death in 1924, eradicated NEP in 1928, supplanting it in that same year with his First Five Year Plan whose objective was a fully controlled state economy, all efforts concentrated on industrialization and the collectivization of agriculture. By then, the Proletkult and the avant-garde Left were closing down, and the MAAT was staffed with Party clerks whose job it was to keep an eye on this seat of 'bourgeois' culture secured for a population that was worn out by successive policies from which it was still waiting to reap promised rewards.

Theatre in Revolution, and Meyerhold

Meyerhold swiftly threw in his lot with the October Revolution, directing, in 1918, his first version of Mayakovsky's *Mystery-Bouffe* (the second in 1921), with abstract sets and costumes by Malevich. According to the renowned scholar Konstantin Rudnitsky: '*Mystery-Bouffe* was the first fully and thoroughly political play in the history of Russian theatre' in so far as it was 'without love, without psychology, without plot in the previous traditional sense. Its actual subject was contemporary political life'.[28] Meyerhold was a highly accomplished artist who, in the preceding decade, had spurned psychological introspection and realism in the theatre for a theatrical theatre (*uslovny teatr*) whose modes, in his hands, were stylization, physicality and the techniques of the 'grotesque', that is, exaggeration, extravagance and startling juxtaposition of opposing elements. Meyerhold's 'grotesque' was the lynchpin of his 'theatricality' (*teatralnost*), honed to show that theatre was always *theatre*. As his theatre became increasingly politicized, he revamped his earlier variations on the *commedia dell'arte*, fairground farces, circus and music hall, which were core to his pre-revolutionary notions of popular theatre, by drawing upon the current entertainment-cum-propaganda vernaculars of activist theatre intended for the 'masses'.

The theatricality of *Mystery-Bouffe* was witty, and celebratory as well as programmatic. It was trumped, however, by Nikolay Evreinov's theatricality, which he had cultivated attentively in St Petersburg to prove that

---

[28] *Meyerhold, the Director*, trans. George Petrov, Ann Arbor: Ardis, 1981, 253.

58 Context II

theatricality was the *sine qua non* both of the theatre and daily life. His 1920 mass spectacle *The Storming of the Winter Palace*, mounted on the site of the October Revolution to commemorate its anniversary, was one of the most ambitious 'staged' (that is, not spontaneous) celebrations of the twentieth century, and also one of the most extraordinary instances of street-and-square popular theatre to be seen in Europe. It would outdo the participatory theatres of the twenty-first century by the mega-numbers of its performer-participants and its vast scale and intensity.

Evreinov led a team of ten to reconstruct, step by step, the events at the Winter Palace that had brought down tsarism. More than ten thousand performer-participants took part. Professional actors playing the main protagonists were mixed with ordinary people who played the people, while some played themselves as they were then. Soldiers, authentic fighters of only three years before, were banded together with reinforcements to heighten the drama. Sailors of the now famous Battleship Aurora, moored nearby and from which the canon shots that had set off the October Revolution were fired, were back in post.[29] So convincing was this reconstruction that people who came upon the scene by chance at first believed that another revolution was taking place before their very eyes.

Evreinov appeared to be on the left of the political spectrum, but nothing in his writings proves that ideology had motivated him to mount this supersize interactive spectacle. Lack of evidence opens the event to conjecture. Thus it is possible to assume that he produced it for the sheer pleasure of the spectacle itself, and for the satisfaction of seeing how the boundaries between theatre and life could disappear. This hypothesis would fit in with his theories about the 'theatricalization of life' whose axioms 'life as theatre' and 'the theatre in life' dovetailed with his hero Oscar Wilde's notion that life imitated art rather than the reverse.[30] Evreinov eventually concluded that there could be no place for him in a Russia hell-bent on using art for social and political ends rather than letting it be for 'art's sake' (also Wilde's credo), and he emigrated to Paris in 1926.

Given Evreinov's appetite for 'theatricalization', *The Storming of the Winter Palace* might have been his attempt at a gigantic open-air cabaret. He had had plenty of experience directing cabarets at The Crooked Mirror, which was modelled on Moscow's famous cabaret The Bat, managed by Nikita Baliyev, (Chapter 1), who had founded it in 1908.

---

[29] Spencer Golub, *Evreinov: The Theatre of Paradox and Transformation*, Ann Arbor: UMI Research Press, 1984, 53–77.
[30] *Teatralizatsiya zhizni*, Moscow: Vremya, 1922.

The Bat closed its doors in 1922 after Baliyev's emigration to Paris in 1920 and then to the United States, where Stanislavsky met up with him once more when the MAAT was playing in New York. By that time, Baliyev had set up a show based on his most successful numbers at The Bat with performers from the Russian diaspora, which ran to sold-out houses. Then again, since Evreinov appears not to have been deeply politically invested in *The Storming of the Winter Palace*, the 'mass action', as he called it, may have been his fanciful take on a *kapustnik*, albeit not in a comical way. A *kapustnik*, or 'cabbage party', is a practice originating with Shchepkin who, during Lent, when theatre performances were forbidden, met with fellow actors, literally to 'play the fool' informally among themselves. The MAT turned this fun into a more structured series of spoofs that the actors performed for their own entertainment after the hard work of public performance. In 1910, the company introduced a twist on the *kapustnik* by making it public, selling tickets for the event, as for any other perform-ance. The *kapustnik* as a generally private, theatre-family tradition is upheld in the Russian theatre to this day.

A *kapustnik* would typically burlesque some aspect of what had been performed, or laugh at people's foibles, which everyone knew about, or at mishaps during rehearsals. Stanislavsky had participated in similarly playful revelries at the Society of Art and Literature, and probably at Mamontov's Private Opera Theatre, and he enjoyed them with Art Theatre groups at The Bat, where his quirks of character were the butt-end of jokes. *Kapustnik* parties generated camaraderie and a sense of bonding and community vital to ensemble theatre. Evreinov's outdoors event created a similar sense of belonging, this time among thousands: a shared experience en masse that at once inspired feelings of solidarity and celebrated it. Looked at from the twenty-first century, Evreinov's event, although recognizably a political festival, might be seen additionally as an example of performativity in a mass dimension, and a mass acting out of desired identity associated with the revolution.

'Theatricality' had plenty of room for the play-acting and *cabotinage* that Stanislavsky spoke about pejoratively, but which Meyerhold relished, exploiting them more than ever before in his post-revolutionary produc-tions. Mayakovsky had updated *Mystery-Bouffe* in 1921 to include topical references (emphasis on engineering, 'saboteurs' of communism, the up-and-coming breed of Nepmen), and his satire lent itself admirably to play-acting and clever tricks. Its roughly hewn theatricality was quite different from the elegantly contoured festive theatricality of Vakhtangov's *Princess Turandot*, staged in the same year as a joyful antidote to the hardships of

60 Context II

life in a society under renovation. Here, actors slipped in and out of role for audiences to see, and addressed them directly while they sang, danced and performed athletic numbers, all of it to say that this was indeed the 'return of theatre to the theatre'.[31] Vakhtangov, as Rudnitsky notes, harked back, with this phrase, to Meyerhold's 'pre-revolutionary formulation'.[32]

Meyerhold thought that the life-affirming theatricality of *Princess Turandot*, the crowning achievement of Vakhtangov's tragically short career, was out of date in a society that called for a tougher approach. What he failed to acknowledge was that the production's message of hope spoke to a society that, burdened almost beyond endurance, had not yet lost all hope. Its optimism, by contrast, had not escaped Stanislavsky, and it was plain to see at the performance that he had enjoyed and admired it thoroughly. His few reservations did not concern the joy of making theatre, patent in *Princess Turandot*, but Vakhtangov's 'fantastic realism' which, by attempting to merge inwardly felt empathy with extroversion, risked privileging what was spectacularly on show. Stanislavsky feared that theatricality's incessantly giddying displays might send it toppling; if it crashed, it would reveal that it was nothing but a bag of tricks, after all. Behind his ascetic attitude lies Stanislavsky's old opposition to theatrical hyperbole and, in more recent years, to revolutionary hyperbole.

Audiences thought differently from both Meyerhold and Stanislavsky, since *Princess Turandot* captivated city workers newly exposed to the arts, as well as adept intelligentsia theatregoers. There were working men in the new audiences who delighted in Vakhtangov's theatricality whose edges, they recognized, were softer than Meyerhold's. But the Art Theatre appeared to be out of the equation altogether. A makeshift survey by the theatre critic Mikhaïl Zagorsky, which appeared in *LEF*, the journal of the eponymous association founded by Meyerhold, reported that four railway employees, who had attended *Mystery-Bouffe* in 1921 and an unspecified '"bourgeois" performance of the Art Theatre the same day', allegedly found the difference between the two 'colossal'; at the Art Theatre they had felt nothing but 'terrible boredom and utter disappointment'.[33]

The Art Theatre had already had to stomach undisguised audience dissatisfaction. Audiences, whether working-class or surviving intelligentsia, had voted with their feet by staying away from *Cain* at the Art Theatre the year before, forcing Stanislavsky to close down Byron's Mystery in

---

[31] Cited by Rudnitsky in *Meyerhold*, 285.   [32] Ibid.
[33] Quoted in Robert Leach, *Vsevolod Meyerhold*, Cambridge University Press, 1989, 34.

Theatre in Revolution, and Meyerhold   61

three acts (which he had shortened) after only eight performances. Stanislavsky had intended to make the production, in which a brother killed a brother while Lucifer struggled against God, a parable on the Civil War. The production may not have been ready to be shown to the public, as Stanislavsky was to claim in *My Life in Art*, but his recourse to the Bible was bewildering in times when God was proclaimed to be dead, *pace* Dostoyevsky's polemic against Nietzsche in *The Devils* to prove the necessity of God's existence.

Stanislavsky's choice of *Cain* would have had personal resonance, linking him to his Orthodox faith, as to his idea of the theatre as a church. However, his biblical subject was confusing, and his scenic attempts to modernize liturgical vocalizations and ritualistic groupings and movements were just as confusing, if not absolutely alien, to the spectators of 1920. Their response to *Cain* could not have been any different, given the surge of the louder, faster, and generally more raucous visual and sonic 'languages' filling the theatres, let alone the streets and political rallies and meetings. *Cain*'s purchase on what was 'contemporary', as Stanislavsky saw it, was feeble by comparison, and feeble, too, when compared with *Mystery-Bouffe*, which had also reworked a biblical narrative – not the story of fratricide, but of Noah's ark and the resurrection of the world. Crucially, and unlike *Cain*, Mayakovsky's makeover was a parody – except when it came to the victorious proletariat. Mayakovsky's regenerative flood was, of course, the October Revolution.

The Magnanimous Cuckold, following *Mystery-Bouffe*, surpassed the latter's physical acting for it was 'coloured', in Rudnitsky's words, 'by the agility of sportsmen'.[34] A cluster of productions succeeded this 'first and possibly only show in which the principles of stage Constructivism were applied thoroughly'.[35] If Meyerhold had not co-ordinated his other stage elements around design as completely as Rudnitsky may have wished, they were, nevertheless, led by design; and design, instead of illustrating or representing something, determined the spatial arrangement for the actors' work. The actors in these productions continued to construct space on the go and to treat space as a workstation – in effect, as a construction site. What continued as the actors worked on this site was the rigour and exactitude of movement pre-empted by biomechanics.

The systemic, ordered approach of Constructivism meant that busy activities spun out of simple subjects, which were often of little literary value, were prevented from descending into chaos, even when their overall

---

[34] *Meyerhold*, 293.   [35] Ibid., 290.

effect might have struck spectators as chaotic. Thus Meyerhold directed a cohesive group of works that spectators and critics in thrall to him invariably found exciting. These were: *Earth Rampant* (1923), a feverish production on the Civil War by Tretyakov whose design-construction was by Popova; *Lake Lyul* (1923), a melodrama involving capitalists and revolutionaries; *D. E.* (1924, *Dayesh Evropu – Give Us Europe*), featuring capitalists, workers, soldiers, tap-dancing, a live jazz band and, most exciting of all, Meyerhold riding 'out of the audience on a motorcycle with a side-car' which was 'raised to the stage by a trapdoor elevator';[36] *The Teacher Bubus* (1924), which drew the critics' attention 'more to Meyerhold's employment of biomechanics than to the intrinsic qualities of the play'; *The Mandate* (1925), a comedy by Nikolay Erdman on contemporary social climbers; and Ostrovsky's *The Forest* (1924), the only production of an established play of this group, which, like most of its other productions, was divided into episodes. Episodic fragmentation and montage from fragments were typical of stage Constructivism. Nemirovich-Danchenko found *The Forest* 'very boring';[37] but, then, he disliked Meyerhold, and had an axe to grind, starting with the Povarskaya studio for experimentation that Stanislavsky had entrusted to Meyerhold in 1905 against his wishes.

Meyerhold's devices chilled and thrilled to the hammer and bang of cars, cranes, field telephones, machine-gun fire and spontaneously sung army songs or *The Internationale*, as well as political interjections from the audience. The atmosphere was that of mass rallies, the whole simulated for the feel of 'theatre' rather than reproduced as 'history', as ostensibly had been the case of *The Storming of the Winter Palace*. Trucks and armoured cars rode on to the stage in *Earth Rampant*, attended by a jubilant Lev Trotsky, Stalin's arch-rival for the leadership, whom Stalin was to oust in 1926 and exile in 1929.[38] Blackouts and blazing searchlights threw episodes into relief; slogans and images were projected on screens, flaunting the new art of the cinema, with a nod to Meyerhold's friend Eisenstein. The actors caricatured local and foreign villains, using their trademark biomechanical as well as acrobatic and circus skills.

In 1926, Meyerhold directed a canonical play, once again, *The Government Inspector*, breaking it down into episodes and adding pieces of other writings by Nikolay Gogol in order to immerse spectators in a 'total'

---

[36] Account in *The Soviet Theatre*, 162; second quotation, 164; third, 159.
[37] Ibid., 159, letter of 3 February 1924 to his secretary Olga Bokshanskaya.
[38] Ibid., 157 (Trotsky's presence reported by Yury Annenkov, artist and designer).

Theatre in Revolution, and Meyerhold

Gogolian universe. The production was not about 'contemporary political life' (Rudnitsky's words, as quoted above) nor brazenly political, but it was contemporary and political in the sense that its brilliant comedy on self-important officials, self-seekers, imposters and toadies could be taken as an exposure of comparable figures who vied with each other to run Soviet Russia in the present.

These productions of the first half of the 1920s displeased the upper echelons of the Communist Party, who judged them to be out of touch and tendentious in the wrong way. They waved revolutionary banners, when the revolution was over, harped on the Civil War, when that was over, too, and ironized on petty capitalists, when the leaders allowed small-scale capitalism temporarily, and then, when this opportunistic capitalism was officially under review. Lunacharsky's words in 1921, when he sacked Meyerhold within a year of appointing him to the TEO, summed up what would be the leadership's official point of view three and more years later: Meyerhold's 'Futurist artistic forms' (the reference was to *Mystery-Bouffe*) were 'incompatible' with 'the real requirements of post-Revolutionary social life'; 'Futurist' posters, rallies and propaganda 'were necessary for Revolution' but not when 'the Revolution had grown stronger, been victorious and had moved on to construction'.[39] Meyerhold's productions of his Constructivist phase, especially after *The Magnanimous Cuckold*, were poster-and-rally strident, and there could be no doubt that they were 'leftist' rather than in the 'correct' Party position, which was to the right of 'leftist' on the political spectrum.

The sticking point, in Meyerhold's case, was always his politics, while his 'artistic forms' were merely a pretext for the criticism levelled against him. His continually revolutionary attitude seemed undesirably too close to Trotsky's left-side notion of 'permanent revolution'. Trotsky, unlike Lenin, Stalin and Stalin's allies, insisted that continual revolutionary action was necessary, since 'construction', using Lunacharsky's term, was still some way off. Furthermore, Stalin propagated the dogma of 'socialism in one country', that is, socialism, first of all, in and for the Soviet Union conceived as 'one country', whereas Trotsky held to the theory that socialism had to be fought for internationally, that is, in all countries simultaneously. At a time when political allegiances were a matter of life and death, it sufficed for Meyerhold to *appear* to be close to Trotsky in the eyes of Stalin's winning faction in 1926 to make life enormously difficult for him and, ultimately, to condemn him. Tragically, that is exactly what

---

[39] *Meyerhold*, 280–1.

befell Meyerhold during Stalin's reign of terror from 1936 to 1939, which included real as well as alleged Trotskyist sympathizers – also within the leadership's upper ranks – in its extensive witch-hunt.

Yury Annenkov's account (note 38) of how Trotsky had joined in the commotion of *Earth Rampant* and had interrupted the performance with a speech from the stage, shows that 'incriminating' evidence against Meyerhold was there for the asking, if and when required. The fact, too, that Trotsky, in his *Literature and Revolution* (1924), gave Meyerhold's theatre his stamp of approval, contrasting its relevance for the present and the future with the 'bourgeois' irrelevance of the Art Theatre, did not do Meyerhold any favours, either at the time or subsequently. And, since perilous misalliances are at issue here, it is important to remember that Meyerhold had a long-standing friendship and collaboration with Mayakovksy to whose early works the Communist Party, in the words of Lunacharsky, was 'cold and even hostile' and particularly to 'those in which he appears as the trumpeter of Communism'.[40]

Hostility against Meyerhold did not abate. Mayakovsky's last work with him was *The Bathhouse* in 1930, a satire on the idiocies of bureaucracy for which both the playwright and the director came under malicious attack. The critic Vladimir Yermilov, who was influential in the right quarters, barked: '*The Bathhouse is unintelligible for mass audiences*' (italics in the original).[41] In the same year, Mayakovsky, disillusioned with communism, alarmed at the centralization of the state, vilified for his last play, and unlucky in love, shot himself.

No one could have foreseen Mayakovsky's bitter end so soon, slightly more than a decade after the October Revolution and after he and Meyerhold had become an inspiration to many, including factory workers. Among them were comrades who, in 1923, set up the Blue Blouse workers' theatre troupes, thus called because their factory uniforms were also their clothes for performing.[42] Their topical, poster and journalistic 'living-newspaper' performances were the successors of Mayakovsky's political cartoons and humorous reports on current affairs in pictures and captions – his famous ROSTA windows – as of Meyerhold's gymnastic theatre escapades. By a type of beneficial contagion, Blue Blouse groups were at their best during Meyerhold's concentrated Constructivist period of 1922–25; and their exploitation of theatrical devices intertwined with political militancy became a nuisance for policy makers, as had

---

[40] Ibid., 281.   [41] *The Soviet Theatre*, 332.
[42] See Frantisec Deak, 'Blue Blouse: 1923–28', *The Drama Revue*, 17 (1972), 35–46.

Theatre in Revolution, and Meyerhold 65

Meyerhold's theatre. In 1927, when word came from on high to merge Blue Blouse with TRAM (Theatre of Worker Youth), there were some five thousand Blue Blouse groups and more than one hundred thousand members of the organization. The power of numbers was eloquent, as in the case of the Proletkult and, like the Proletkult, the Blue Blouse organization had to be curbed to ensure one-party and one-ideology control. The fact that Blue Blouse performances had become stale and repetitive by 1927 was inconsequential.

Stanislavsky, abroad from September 1922 until August 1924, missed these and many other critically important political, social, cultural and specifically theatre developments as they were happening, defining the context and the parameters in which, and by which, he and the Art Theatre would be measured on their return. The pressure and even trepidation of re-entry into this unknown world would have to have been dealt with, and the rapidity, acceleration and expansion of change in tentacular fashion meant that the Art Theatre travellers had to get their bearings and orient themselves quickly, above all in the field of the theatre. How Stanislavsky and the Art Theatre took up a position in that field's state of play was vital for their future. They had already taken a position in the past to honour their achievements in the theatre of emotional experiencing (*perezhivaniye*), but the latter was simply not in keeping with the ambient theatricality, in whichever way it was politicized.

Stanislavsky, moreover, still had a great deal of research to do on the theatre of *perezhivaniye*, and he was convinced of its justification and so of its resilience against pressures and trends. However, although Stanislavsky's teachings had spread to various institutions in Moscow, as in the provinces, there were fewer allies for the MAAT than ever before among the proactive theatre professionals, excluding the Hebrew-speaking Habima with which Stanislavsky had always had close relations, teaching and directing the company on occasion. He had also arranged for Vakhtangov to train many of its actors. But this alliance was impermanent. In 1926, Habima went on tour to New York, where some of the troupe remained while the rest emigrated to Palestine.

Otherwise, the tendency among the directors and companies whom Stanislavsky had known before his departure was theatricality, modified according to taste. Those of greater note were Sergey Radlov, a former student of Meyerhold, who was less inclined to mass-spectacular theatre than his teacher; Aleksandr Granovsky, head of the State Jewish Theatre (whose 'circus' *Mystery-Bouffe* Stanislavsky saw and discussed with the company in 1921); and Aleksandr Taïrov, progenitor of 'synthetic' theatre,

66   Context II

where actors were supposed to dance and sing as well as they could act (criticized by both Stanislavsky and Meyerhold for different reasons), and whose Kamerny Theatre had survived politics, regardless of its openly championed aestheticism of forms and stylization for visual impact. As for the politically didactic theatricality of the 'masses' that had multiplied during his absence – Stanislavsky's aversion not to amateur actors as such, but to theatre for agitational purposes of any kind at all would have prevented him from even considering that agit-theatre could be included in the theatre field, let alone exist within sight of the Art Theatre.

There was only one, Meyerhold, in whom Stanislavsky could seriously be interested, irrespective, on the positive side of their relations, of their agreeably shared MAT experience and continuing friendship, and, on the negative side, of the sarcastic shots that Meyerhold could not resist firing in public, not so much at him as at the Art Theatre as a bourgeois institution. Given that Stanislavsky was tied as by an umbilical cord to his progeny, a shot against it was widely perceived as a shot against him – from which was derived the unhelpful myth that the two men were perpetually against each other. Stanislavsky lived with the bullets and their friendship survived. When still in New York, he was keen to discover what Meyerhold's 'new art' consisted of, having gleaned from hearsay that his exploits were far from insignificant when his 'gimmicks' were removed.[43] Stanislavsky's interest was sharpened by his awareness of the Art Theatre's inadequacies and where, in actual fact, it really *was* obsolete. After his return to Moscow, having had a chance to survey the situation, Stanislavsky wrote in 1926 to his son in Switzerland of the 'new plans, contexts and possibilities' for the Art Theatre:

> All sorts of colours and lines and forms of the scenic-painting designer are over-familiar and obsolete . . . The most correct path of all is Meyerhold's. He is proceeding from general scenic and directorial possibilities and principles. And he determines them boldly and simply (it is impossible to say the same thing regarding the acting aspect, which is weak in him).[44]

Stanislavsky's musings on the generally 'enormous dimension' of the Art Theatre's proscenium stage had him fully approve Meyerhold's abolishment of 'curtains, draperies, borders, and so on'.[45] Stanislavsky had seen and greatly appreciated *The Mandate* in 1925, commenting enthusiastically but also with humility that, in its closing act, 'Meyerhold has achieved

---

[43] *Stanislavsky – A Life*, 442, letter of 12 March 1924 to Nemirovich-Danchenko. See also I. Vinogradskaya, *Zhizn i tvorchestvo*, Vol. 3, 325.
[44] Ibid., 470, letter of 14 February 1926.   [45] Ibid.

what I am dreaming of.[46] Six months after his letter to his son, he finally saw *The Magnanimous Cuckold* in repertoire, but found 'nothing new' in it.[47]

Stanislavsky's disappointment in this work did not deter him from accepting Meyerhold's invitation to an exhibition of designs for his productions, going from *The Dawn* by Emile Verhaeren in 1920 to *The Mandate* in 1925, and his intense excitement apparently knew no bounds as he admired what *was* entirely new.[48] It was indisputably there in the boldly experimental, three-dimensional forms and radical spatial arrangements of these designs. Stanislavsky pored over models and photographs, going from the geometrical figures and planes of *The Dawn* to the sculptures of *The Mandate*, which were large wooden screens that moved on wheels to shape abstract 'settings'. Stanislavsky's awakening to the visual arts at Abramtsevo and Mamontov's Private Opera Theatre had not failed him: here was the 'new' of Meyerhold's theatre to be prized and reckoned with.

The Art Theatre in the Stalin Years, 1926–1938

Stanislavsky's priority on his return from the United States, in agreement with Nemirovich-Danchenko, was to overhaul the MAAT entirely: restructure it administratively and thus also set up a parliamentary-style management; blend the Second Studio into the Art Theatre so as to fill out its numbers (many had actually remained in the United States), rejuvenate it and give the juniors the time and scope to draw on the experience of the seniors (the First and Third Studios had become independent theatres, so were out of the project); come up with a new repertoire and, above all, with new playwrights for it. A new repertoire was urgent if the MAAT was to find its place in the radically changed historical conditions.

Playwrights other than potboiler propagandists were few, and the most opportune plan of action, while waiting for a windfall, was to tour the old *Tsar Fyodor Ioannovich*, *Uncle Vanya* and *The Lower Depths* with the amalgamated company. A two-month tour in 1925 included Tbilisi, Baku and Odessa, where Stanislavsky performed his famous role of Astrov and the not so acclaimed Satin; the seniors took heart, and the juniors gained confidence. Their triumphs on the road and, in Moscow, with Ostrovsky's *The Ardent Heart*, another so-called old-fashioned piece, but which the public received well, was followed by the breakthrough on which they had

---

[46] *Zhizn i tvorchestvo*, Vol. 3, 403. [47] Ibid., 478. [48] Ibid.

68   Context II

pinned their hopes: a contemporary play that they could take seriously. This was Mikhaïl Bulgakov's *The Days of the Turbins*, adapted by the author from his 1925 serialized novel *The White Guard*, set in the Civil War. The actors formerly of the Second Studio took charge of the project, with Ilya Sudakov as the production's director; Stanislavsky rehearsed and supervised selected scenes. Stanislavsky spoke of his renewed hope in this 'second Pushkino' as he contemplated the unity of the older and younger members, which made the Art Theatre a harmonious 'family' once more.[49]

Collaboration with Bulgakov took the play through seven redactions, to Bulgakov's perpetual annoyance, but Stanislavsky had grave misgivings as to whether the Glavrepertkom (Main Repertoire Committee), which the government censor had established during the Art Theatre's absence, would accept it in its first version. There was nothing 'naive' about Stanislavsky's fears, for, after a run before this committee, *The Days of the Turbins* was, indeed, rejected and sent back for revision to make it seem less like an apologia for the White Army, as for the Whites, generally.

From here on, the saga of *The Days of the Turbins* escalated. The production's fate hung in the balance for months until it was finally passed by the censor at a preview shortly before the opening of the 1926 season, only to be savagely lambasted by left-wing theatre critics, who are to be distinguished from the creative avant-garde LEF group comprising Meyerhold, Mayakovsky, Eisenstein and company. The latter, in any case, along with Taïrov from another camp altogether, poured out bile of their own onto the production. The officially tolerated critics on the left regurgitated clichés: *The Days of the Turbins* was pro-White, was 'written from the old standpoint of the Russian intelligentsia', was counter-revolutionary, lacked the peasant and proletarian characters obligatory for contemporary writing, and similar imprecations, which caused Lunacharsky to fulminate against these 'yapping little monsieurs' and their customary 'MAAT-baiting'.[50] He argued, logically, that the production had been passed by representatives of

---

[49] Ibid., 462.

[50] Anatoly Smeliansky, *Is Comrade Bulgakov Dead? Mikhaïl Bulgakov at the Moscow Art Theatre*, trans. Arch Tait, London: Methuen Drama, 1993, 92 and 111–12, respectively. See also 70–114 for Smeliansky's brilliant account of the insults and debates of the entire sequence. Note that Smeliansky in his Russian original quotes Lunacharsky's '*moskakh layushchykh*', that is, 'barking pugs' (or 'pug dogs' – not '*monsieurs*', as translated, which, in any case, would have to be '*messieurs*'). See Smeliansky, *Mikhaïl Bulgakov v Khudozhestvennom Teatre*, Moscow: Iskusstvo, 1986, 142. Lunacharsky's witty reference is to Ivan Krylov's widely known fable *The Elephant and the Pug*, in which a pug, barely as high as the elephant's foot, barks noisily but senselessly at this huge animal 'to let it be known that it [the pug] is strong'.

The Art Theatre in the Stalin Years, 1926–1938

the government together with the supreme censorship bureau in the land, so there was no sense in protesting.

Lunacharsky insisted on the value of this 'first political play on our horizon to raise serious socio-political matters', knowing better than to activate further spite by referring to the production's acting of the highest quality, which had gripped audiences.[51] Lunacharsky's defence of the MAAT was lost, and the inflated critics, aided and abetted by equally inflated political playwrights, savaged him, in turn, for his pains. *The Days of the Turbins* was removed from the repertoire at the end of the 1926–27 season, causing Stanislavsky to appeal to the chairman of VIsIK (Executive Committee of Soviets) to intercede and save the actors, whose energies had been sapped by the ceaseless ferocity. The production was reprieved for the year of 1928. Then, in early 1929, it was categorically banned.

V. N. Bill-Belotserkovsky, one of the protrusive playwrights of the moment 'yapping' at the MAAT, but who had real clout in the RAPP (Russian Association of Proletarian Writers), had written to Stalin a month or so before the final interdiction, urging him to ban *The Days of the Turbins* for its right-wing views. Stalin's reply on 1 February 1929 reveals exactly where the thinking was to go and how the terms for proscription would be set in the near future. He explained that '"right-wing" and "left-wing" refer to people who deviate in one direction or another from the pure party line', but did not apply to literature and theatre.[52] 'Most correct' for these spheres were the concepts of 'a class nature, or even the concepts of "Soviet" and "anti-Soviet"'. *The Days of the Turbins* was 'not all that bad', since, irrespective of Bulgakov, it was 'a demonstration of the crushing force of Bolshevism'.

Stalin's stupefying subversion of Bulgakov's composition can only be matched by his dismissal of *Flight*: '*Flight* in its present form [that is, without some recognition of the Bolsheviks' actions as 'the will of the workers and peasants'] is an anti-Soviet phenomenon'. Far more was involved in these pronouncements than directions for the theatre. Stalin's redefinition of the parameters of the debate was to have fatal consequences from the later 1920s and throughout the 1930s, dispatching millions of citizens for 'anti-Soviet' sentiments or activities as 'enemies of the people' to the state forced-labour concentration camps, the infamous gulags, when they were not directly sent to instant death.

Stalin let the matter lie for the time being, allowing Bill-Belotserkovsky and his allies their victory. However, he was to tergiversate and revoke the

---

[51] Ibid., 108.   [52] *Soviet Culture and Power*, 56–7 for all the citations from Stalin's reply.

ban on *The Days of the Turbins* in 1932, after his prescriptions on the 'correct' concepts of 'Soviet' and 'anti-Soviet' had taken effect. His judgement was lapidary: the play and the production revealed the retrograde mentality of the Whites and thereby explained why the Reds had defeated them. Furthermore, he liked the production enough to see it fifteen times – more than any of its belligerent critics would have done! In the meanwhile, two or so years before Stalin's dialogue with Bill-Belotserkovsky was to unfold, the MAAT had started to prepare *The Armoured Train 14–69* by Vsevolod Ivanov, who had been in the Red Army during the Civil War and whose play recounted the strenuous fight of peasants and workers in the Far East against the Whites. There were two directors, Sudakov and Nina Litovtseva, while Stanislavsky contributed mainly to the crowd scenes. The production was to be the MAAT's offering for the tenth anniversary of the October Revolution, but, when performed, it too inflamed the left critics, who damned it as 'an attack by the kulaks [wealthy peasants] and the intelligentsia'.[53]

Stanislavsky, when appealing to Stalin for *The Days of the Turbins*, was thus also obliged to plead for the 'half-banned' *The Armoured Train 14–69*, as he put it to Lilina, adding ruefully, 'It's a pity the whole thing wasn't'.[54] Such was his damning assessment of the play. However, he knew that, if theatre politics were ubiquitous, the invasion of politics into the theatre was inescapable. The ban on *The Days of the Turbins* was a foregone conclusion, but to expose the Art Theatre to the accusation that it was incapable of honouring 1917 was tantamount to signing the company's death warrant. With this calamitous prospect before him, he merely shrugged off the more or less concurrent ban on *Uncle Vanya* (presumably for its politically damaging 'pessimism'), telling Lilina: 'They suggest instead of *Uncle Vanya* staging *The Cherry Orchard* (Oh!!!).'[55] She would have understood his groan in parentheses, since Stanislavsky had long been fed up with the sentimentalist and related ready-made ideas about Chekhov, which he scornfully called 'Chekhoviana', and believed, in any case, that *The Cherry Orchard*'s central tale of gentlefolk and the loss of their estate was not for the times.

By the same token, he knew which traps would be laid to catch out the incautious. In correspondence earlier in 1927 with Golovin, the scenographer of *The Marriage of Figaro*, he observed that the Communist officials who were monitoring the MAAT ('they', as noted to Lilina) had

---

[53] Cited in *Is Comrade Bulgakov Dead?*, 113. [54] *SS* 9, 9, 284, letter of 19 August 1927.
[55] Ibid.

The Art Theatre in the Stalin Years, 1926–1938   71

demanded a 'revolutionary' production, an order that was 'dangerous' because the term 'revolutionary' had come automatically to mean agitprop methods.[56] On 21 February of the same year, he had courageously addressed a Narkompros meeting from this very angle, insisting on the distinction between art and 'naked tendentiousness' and denouncing the latter as harmful for the Soviet theatre, especially for its growth and quality in the longer term.[57] He battled on in the name of that artistic integrity published in 1926 for all to see in *My Life in Art*; and, for all his efforts to stage something within his purview that would be acceptable to the authorities, here was *The Armoured Train 14–69* stirring up conflict when it was as 'revolutionary' in content (if not in method) as the MAAT could get.

The production, after Stanislavsky had gone to great lengths to have it reinstated – the MAAT simply could not be seen to have failed the October Revolution – finally succeeded in persuading at least a few of the left critics of its political merits.[58] It was, to boot, a public success. *Untilovsk* by Leonid Leonov[59] (1928), the next production to fit Lunacharsky's category of 'socio-political matters' was not successful, although it was the only text in Lunacharsky's bracket that genuinely interested Stanislavsky. He saw in Leonov a new playwright with whose help the MAAT could build a new repertoire. He believed that Leonov had talent and that *Untilovsk* was a truly contemporary attempt to understand the human degradation to be found in backward Russian villages; and the play showed, without resorting to political slogans, the 'revolution through the human heart' and the 'rebirth of the human heart'.[60] These Stanislavskian motifs on the 'life of the human spirit' were echoed in Simov's scenography, which recalled the desperation of that 'primitive' Russia captured in several paintings by Repin and the Wanderers. None of it passed muster, least of all the text, which the admired Proletkult activist and RAPP chief Platon Kerzhentsev dismissed outright for its drawing of 'human putrefaction'.[61] *Untilovsk*, directed by Vasily Sakhnovsky, who had begun his directing career with Komissarzhevsky junior and had joined the MAT in 1925, was banned after twenty performances.

---

[56] Ibid., 268, letter of 4 February 1927.
[57] *Zhizn i tvorchestvo*, Vol. 3, 519–21, and 521 for the quotation from his notes.   [58] Ibid., 581–3.
[59] Not to be confused with Leonid Leonidov the Art Theatre actor cited in this book.
[60] *Zhizn i tvorchestvo*, Vol. 4, 15.
[61] O. A. Radishcheva and E. A. Shingaryova (eds.), *Moskovsky Khudozhestvenny Teatr v russkoy teatralnoy kritike 1919–1930* (*The Moscow Art Theatre in Russian Theatre Criticism, 1919–1930*), Moscow: Artist. Director. Theatre, 2009, 247.

72   Context II

The next blow for the Art Theatre was *Flight*, which, caught in Stalin's cavils with Bill-Belotserkovsky, had its wings clipped, and was banned in 1929. The ban on this, Bulgakov's second play for the MAAT, now on Whites fleeing via Crimea to Constantinople and Paris, was predictable, one might have thought, and several Art Theatre elders certainly thought so. However, the ex–Second Studio actors, flushed with their triumph in *The Days of the Turbins*, had failed to anticipate the inevitable fall. *The Days of the Turbins* was *the* production that had made their name as artists; it had been for them what *The Seagull* had been to their seniors, and it had provoked a major, prolonged debate on the role of theatre in society, all of which wrote them and Bulgakov into history. It thus did not dawn on them that *Flight* might be a leap too far for safety.

The four 'socio-political' plays (Lunacharsky's adjective) cited earlier played a role in the Art Theatre's struggles to find its place in Soviet Russia. *The Days of the Turbins* was eventually to bring the Art Theatre glory, but *The Armoured Train 14–69*, which had had a relatively easier time, was never to become a ticket to immortality. Still, regardless of its minor status, this production requires attention for its central role of another kind. It can be seen from two perspectives: as the MAAT's reconciliation with the October Revolution and Soviet power, or as unadulterated opportunism for the sake of the theatre's survival. Stanislavsky's attitude, both private (to Lilina) and public (to the Executive Committee of Soviets) indubitably smacked of the latter. Even so, he knew what he was doing. He could not have been clearer about the urgency of the MAAT's current situation than in this letter to Kachalov on the day after the production's premiere:

> Yesterday at the premiere, in the presence of Rykov [key member of the Politburo], the government, the critics, and friends of our theatre, at the moment of the first showing of our eight-months' work, at a time when the theatre is trying with its last remaining strength to win back its former position and right to exist in a new Russia, in front of the new severe audience – *you were drunk*.
>
> A greater insult, offence and pain I have never experienced.[62]

Is this a brutal and censorious Stanislavsky? Yes, but the stakes were inordinately high, as high as the MAAT's very '*right* to exist' (my emphasis).

The intermesh between Stanislavsky's creative efforts and reigning politics had now become extremely tight, as they could never have been

---

[62] *SS* 9, 9, 299, letter of 9 November 1927.

The Art Theatre in the Stalin Years, 1926–1938

in the Art Theatre's youthful period, or on the curve of the 1905 revolution, or even on that of the October Revolution; and it would tighten so much from 1927 onwards that an account such as this one is compelled to observe that whatever concerned the MAAT from the point of view of artistic endeavour axiomatically called upon the contextual political factors from which nigh everything was inseparable. And so it was that the company in the Soviet context – in actual fact, *contexts*, given the fluctuating changes – the least inclined to take up a political position ended up, despite itself, in the political fray; furthermore, not just in the fray, but also in a pivotal position within it, as the following pages show.

Stanislavsky's *cri de cœur* to Kachalov was acute in an acute situation, but the MAAT's tribulations kept increasing during the 'cultural revolution' of 1928 to 1931. Stalin's first Five-Year Plan had begun in 1928 and 'cultural revolution' was, in large part, the result of the leadership's need for technicians, managers and administrators for the implementation of the Plan. 'Cultural revolution' was also a consequence of the pressures exerted on the leadership by the Communist rank and file to purge the old Communist intelligentsia (Lunacharsky was a perfect example), together with the 'bourgeois specialists' primed during NEP. According to the newly empowered and upwardly mobile workers, both of these groups had unfairly gained the upper hand. It was high time, they insisted, that the new *proletarian* intelligentsia reaped the rewards of its labour and replaced them. In point of fact, Fitzpatrick argues, the 'substantive proletarian aspect of the cultural revolution was the promotion of workers to responsible jobs and their recruitment to higher education'.[63]

It must be added that, at this moment in time, acquiring a tertiary education, especially one with practical ends, like technical subjects and engineering, was considered to be far more important than acquiring an artistic-literary culture. Furthermore, while education and career progression were steps towards necessary social justice, they were highlighted in such ways as to incite feelings of social revenge by which any privileged individual or institution, thus the MAAT, was debunked and debased, and risked liquidation. The period of renewed 'class war' had begun.

It was in this state of affairs that the MAAT suffered another round of attacks, now from the Komsomol (Communist Youth) theatre groups, the most belligerent of which was TRAM (Theatre of Worker Youth). According to Katerina Clark, TRAM, which originated in Leningrad

---

[63] Sheila Fitzpatrick (ed.), *Cultural Revolution in Russia, 1928–1931*, Bloomington and London: Indiana University Press, 1978, 32.

(formerly Petrograd), 'proved one of the few truly viable ones in the sense that it was able to turn agitational dramas about factory life into pithy, rollicking and enormously popular productions (no mean feat)'.[64] On its 1928 tour to Moscow, TRAM impressed Lunacharsky and fellow cultural bureaucrats on whose patronage it depended.

However, the tide was swiftly turning. Within a year, Lunacharsky was coerced into resigning by the 'war' on the intelligentsia, whether its progenitors were pre-revolutionary liberals or Bolsheviks. TRAM sky-rocketed to fame and was *in* its element, whereas the MAAT, having lost its protector, was completely exposed to the elements. Full of confidence in its immunity from criticism, TRAM mounted for the 1929 anniversary of the October Revolution a protest against 'academic theatres', chanting its signature slogan 'the Liquidation of the MKhAT [MAAT] as a Class'.[65] The MAAT, once it was categorized emblematically as a whole *class* and, by implication, as a *class* enemy, was basically excluded from society. It was precisely this that Stanislavsky had intuited two years earlier: the Art Theatre's central predicament *was* its right to exist.

The burden of history thrust on the MAAT was fearsome, but contemporary history-in-the-making ebbed and flowed again. No sooner had the expanding numbers of skilled jobs been filled and the proletarian cadres set in place to manage them than the leadership turned from the needs of vocational education to the added bonuses of a cultural education. By 1932, TRAM boasted three hundred youth-worker branches in the country, but the exponentially intrusive state machinery would quash them before too long, as had happened earlier with the Proletkult and the Blue Blouse. The militant RAPP, which harboured numbers of the MAAT's 'yapping' critics, was disbanded by the ruling powers from above in 1932.

Policy had already shifted in 1931 in preparation for a public re-evaluation of the Russian literary and artistic traditions. These were to be taken as models, their forms to be filled with up-to-date, politically correct contents. The wave was curling back to the 'old', well-tried genres, forms and moral values with which the MAAT had long been negatively identi-fied; and the wave unfurled the idea that a proletarian culture could be a *culture* if it promoted social responsibility, moral behaviour, strength of character, high-mindedness, and so on, and produced 'good' work (this being the promoted adjective) instead of hackwork. The kernel of what, in a few years' time, would flourish as 'socialist realism' was buried in this

---

[64] *Petersburg, Crucible of Cultural Revolution*, Cambridge, MA: Harvard University Press, 1995, 267.
[65] Ibid., 268.

The Art Theatre in the Stalin Years, 1926–1938

echo, in an entirely different society trading on entirely different meanings, of Stanislavsky's youthful ideals for the Art Theatre at its inception. The big difference lay in how the echo from Stanislavsky's distinguished past had acquired a very specific and dogmatic political voice and a steely political determination that harnessed art to its yoke absolutely – undreamt of by Stanislavsky.

Culture, notwithstanding the dictates of the 'cultural revolution', was still in a thick tangle, but bureaucracy had thrived and forged ahead. For separate reasons, neither Stanislavsky nor Nemirovich-Danchenko was able to fulfil his administrative duties at the MAAT in the eye of this latest storm. Stanislavsky had been a superb manager-administrator from 1925 to 1928 while Nemirovich-Danchenko and his Music Theatre (Chapter 4), the counterpart, in many ways, of Stanislavsky's Opera Studio, were performing in Germany before touring the United States, including Hollywood; and so accomplished was he in the role, while harmony and co-operation reigned, that all the tired clichés about his 'muddle-headedness' and administrative ineptitude vanished into thin air.[66]

Sent off to recuperate after his heart attack, he realized in 1929, as heart failures and influenzas plagued him, that, to help the theatre, it was wiser to pre-empt arbitrary government imposition of personnel on it by requesting a Communist administrator who was not just any bureaucrat, but was sympathetic to the MAAT and the job. Nemirovich-Danchenko firmly disagreed: he had kept abreast of MAAT business in the United States. Olga Radishcheva, the chief archivist of the Art Theatre until shortly before her death in 2013, has suggested that Stanislavsky made an error of judgement in encouraging such a political liaison and in thinking that an administrator sent by the Communist leadership could help to resolve the Art Theatre's internal as well as external problems.[67]

In the event, a Communist administrator was appointed in 1929, obliging Stanislavsky, who was convalescing in Germany but soon to travel for the warmer climate of Nice, to write to senior actor Leonid Leonidov, asking that he communicate his message to the whole company, its juniors not excepted. The upshot of Stanislavsky's message was that 'for us the selection of a Red administrator is a question of the continuing existence of

---

[66] O. A. Radishcheva, *Stanislavsky i Nemirovich-Danchenko. Istoriya teatralnykh otnosheny. 1917–1938* (*Stanislavsky and Nemirovich-Danchenko: A History of Theatre Relations. 1917–1938*), Moscow: Artist. Director. Theatre, 1999, 183–209.

[67] Ibid., 192–4 and 252–6.

76   Context II

the theatre, its life and death'.[68] The political expediency of his proposal was one thing, but Stanislavsky also took the standpoint of administrative expediency, having learned the ropes of administration as the director of a factory. This biographical item of some significance falls by the wayside when the myth of Stanislavsky the political innocent is compounded by the myth of Stanislavsky the administrative incompetent. The latter also obfuscates the fact that during 1931 and 1932, after his return from his cures abroad and when Nemirovich-Danchenko was again absent, now because of illness, Stanislavsky administered completely efficiently and humanly, without antagonizing the Communist bureaucrat who had been appointed.[69]

But this is a jump in time. Here is Stanislavsky's justification to Leonidov while he was still convalescing:

> When questions of a political character arise, we, the non-Communists, cannot speak to that with authority, we are barely heeded, but the picture immediately changes when a Red administrator, a Communist, addresses the question, because he is heeded, matters are discussed with him in a different way than with us, and he speaks with others in quite a different way than we can ... I believe that a Red administrator who has unmediated contact with us, the other administrators [Stanislavsky and Nemirovich-Danchenko], is much better, more useful, or in the case of a bad appointment, less dangerous, if only because he is constantly associating with us, not estranged from us, and because officially he has one vote while we have two if we manage to come to terms.[70]

The government's appointment was Mikhaïl Geytts, whose interest in the theatre had begun with agit-theatre and who, apart from 'running the business' (Stanislavsky, in the same letter to Leonidov), watched over the repertoire and attended rehearsals and performances. He was in office when, in 1930, Bulgakov, whose writings were most definitely blocked, sent a letter to Stalin, asking that he be allowed to write or else to emigrate. The borders were closed, so permission from Stalin was essential. In response, Stalin arranged permanent employment for him at the Art Theatre. Bulgakov started out optimistically by developing a playscript from Gogol's *Dead Souls* and assisting its director Vasily Sakhnovsky. *Dead Souls* resulted in acrimony within the theatre (Stanislavsky became involved late in the piece) and, when it was performed in 1932, in

---

[68] *Stanislavsky – A Life*, 517, letter of 15 September 1929. For the full text in Russian, see *SS* 9, 9, 352–6.
[69] *Stanislavsky i Nemirovich-Danchenko ... 1917–1938*, 277–8.   [70] *SS* 9, 9, 352–6.

The Art Theatre in the Stalin Years, 1926–1938

disapproval from friendly critics and hostility from the usually snarling ones.

Stanislavsky was not happy about the appointment of directors who oversaw the theatre work of the MAAT – it was too much like spying and control – but the repertoire was crying out for viable new productions and he was in no position to cavil. *Othello*, premiered in 1930 in his absence, was his penultimate attempt at mounting a fully fledged production for the Art Theatre, and it was done long-distance, while he was convalescing, as he sent his production notes, thereby repeating the practice of directorial over-intervention that he had repudiated two decades before. Expectations were high, but *Othello* had only limited success with audiences and virtually none with critics. It ran for ten performances, when disaster struck with the injury of one actor and the accidental death of the actor playing Iago.[71] Personal disaster did not spare him, either. In the same year, his nephew's wife and her sister were arrested, separated from their children, and imprisoned. The women were sent to a labour camp shortly afterwards. In January 1931, Stanislavsky wrote to Genrikh Yagoda, the notorious deputy head of the secret police (its head in 1934), and the man in charge of the gulag system in the Soviet Union, asking him to alleviate their situation as much as possible.[72] His petition – heart-rending in its sobriety – was rejected. Stanislavsky subsequently requested permission to adopt the children, which was granted.

Still in search of promising works, Stanislavsky wrote to Stalin on 29 October 1931 for permission to stage Erdman's blacklisted play *The Suicide* of 1928. Describing *The Suicide* as a 'comedy' (not the satire that it was), Stanislavsky carefully explained why he and the Art Theatre thought it to be 'one of the most important works of our era'.[73] (Erdman had asked Meyerhold to direct it, but, although the play had gone into rehearsal, nothing came of the plan.) The play, said Stanislavsky, 'showed the various manifestations and roots of the petit-bourgeois way of life (*meshchanstva*) that resisted the construction of the country' and was 'genuinely innovative' while being 'close to the tradition of our theatre' – Gogol here brought in tow to clinch his argument.[74] Stalin refused, asserting that he did not have a 'very high opinion of the play' and that his 'closest

---

[71] *Zhizn i tvorchestvo*, Vol. 4, 112; *Stanislavsky – A Life*, 538.

[72] *SS* 9, 9, 448, letter of 26 January 1931; in *Stanislavsky – A Life*, 544. For further details, also regarding subsequent arrests of members of Stanislavsky's extended family, see *Alekseyev-Stanislavsky*, 406–8.

[73] Ibid., 463; *Stanislavsky – A Life*, 550.   [74] Ibid., my translation.

78 Context II

comrades' thought it 'rather empty and even harmful'.[75] He suggested, however, that it might do for experimental work under the supervision of a designated senior Party official. Stanislavsky must have baulked at Stalin's imperiousness and its implied slur on his judgement and responsibilities; and he did not follow up. What future was left to him as a director in his own right would be played out, for the rest of the 1930s, in the Opera Theatre named after him and in his Opera-Dramatic Studio at home – with the rare exception of two productions that he worked on from the sanctity of his laboratory research for the Art Theatre stage (Chapter 5).

It is hard, today, even in our catastrophic twenty-first century, to imagine the impact of such misfortunes and the tensions and stresses, conscious and unconscious, that they secreted; or to imagine the erosion of one's own agency by insurmountable obstacles; or to fathom the terror of control, surveillance and 'liquidation', physical and spiritual. Stanislavsky desisted from writing of these traumas, as he experienced them, possibly out of the reserve and discretion usual to him, or out of inhibition and denial, or from a mixture of these responses. But they would have burrowed deeply into the flesh and soul of a man whose 'life in art' soldiered on to complete *An Actor's Work on Himself, Part I*, which was published a few months after his death, and its sequel, which remained unfinished. The wonder of it is that these writings, even considering that they were edited, and at times probably heavily, leave no traces of his and the Art Theatre's battles and pain.

Stress and trauma to come concerned more than one hundred and twenty actors, the number of permanent actors employed by the theatre in 1933, for whom work had to be found;[76] and the problem was persistent, even though the MAAT adhered to the government's policy of touring the USSR extensively, which had the advantage of keeping the actors working. Then there was the mounting dissatisfaction within the company, to which Stanislavsky alluded in a speech on his seventieth birthday, when he also spoke of the value of an ensemble. Understatement hid his anguish over its disintegration: '... when the heart and mind are unsettled by historical events, it is difficult to unite a large group of people with one common idea that will bind them together'.[77] There was, too, the perennial 'bureaucratic chivvying of productions by the industrial-financial plan' (Stanislavsky, now writing in 1934, meant the Second Five Year Plan), and the demands for 'productivity' from [Party] 'people who have

---

[75] *Soviet Culture and Power*, 118–19.   [76] *Stanislavsky – A Life*, 571.
[77] Ibid., 570, letter of 6 January 1933 to Gorky.

The Art Theatre in the Stalin Years, 1926–1938 79

absolutely no understanding at all of our field and specific conditions of work'.[78] Then, in a crescendo of woes, came the debacle over Bulgakov's *Molière* (*A Cabal of Hypocrites*).

Molière was at the epicentre when the Art Theatre imploded in 1935. Briefly. Nikolay Gorchakov, who had been Vakhtangov's student at the Third Studio, was invited to direct, rehearsing with Bulgakov at his side. Stanislavsky, who at first was the production's co-director, disagreed with Bulgakov's view, which focused on Molière's compromise with tyranny. Stanislavsky, in contrast, saw the artist's struggle against tyranny as the heart of the problem. He changed Bulgakov's text (as Nemirovich-Danchenko had done for *Flight*), protracted rehearsals (as was, in any case, his habit when he believed work was not ready to be shown to audiences) and 'interfered', as it was seen to be, in ways that caused further frustration and rage. Nemirovich-Danchenko dismissed Stanislavsky, thereby bringing to a head the festering relations between them, which also exposed the divisions within the company. At the height of the fiasco, but elsewhere in Moscow and by sheer chance, Stalin gave a highly publicized rousing speech on worker co-operation, prompting the actors of the MAAT to hold a general meeting during which they detailed their grievances.

Two days of debate heard complaints about 'the absence of a unified leadership', the lack of a working plan, and the disruptions caused by the two disputatious directors and two quarrelling camps; Knipper-Chekhova stated that 'the atmosphere of joy, love and respect for one another had disappeared from the theatre'.[79] The resolution of the meeting was that 'Stanislavsky and Nemirovich-Danchenko need to be unburdened of administration-organizational work and a director put at the theatre's head'.[80] It was signed by Knipper-Chekhova, Kachalov and Leonidov, among other actors, and by the directors Sudakov and Sakhnovsky. A summary of the resolution went into the memorandum of 3 August 1935 quoted earlier, lodged by the Central Committee of the Russian Communist Party and brought to Stalin's attention. We can only surmise that the situation must have been dire to push Knipper-Chekhova, Kachalov and Leonidov, trusted old hands, into the ambivalent role of ... today we would call them 'whistleblowers'. Stanislavsky and Nemirovich-Danchenko were removed from organizational work, and a Party-approved administrative head was appointed. The two founders of the MAAT remained its artistic directors, when, in truth, they had both

---

[78] Ibid., 588–9, letter of 4 May 1934 to Leonid Sobinov.   [79] *Soviet Culture and Power*, 218.
[80] Ibid.

Context II

lost interest in doing anything of the sort. Nemirovich-Danchenko was to reinvigorate his interest soon enough, but not Stanislavsky who spent his remaining energy on theatre research.

There was no doubt that the MAAT had become a state enterprise from top to bottom. Work on *Molière* continued to its premiere in 1936, but it was banned after seven performances on the grounds that Bulgakov's play was subversive, 'its political meaning ... sufficiently clear, although most viewers may never even notice these hints'.[81] These are Kerzhentsev's words in his memorandum as the key organizing member of the Committee on Arts Affairs to Stalin and Molotov, Stalin's right-hand man and leader of the government. Kerzhentsev's memorandum is dated 29 February 1936, and the 'hints' in question, he explains, are to Bulgakov's analogy between his, 'the writer's status under the dictatorship of the proletariat' and Molière's 'under the "arbitrary tyranny" of Louis XIV'. Kerzhentsev then asks what the theatre had done with this 'poisonous barren flower', answering that it had 'tried not to notice' the 'political hints' and had 'followed the line of least resistance' by making a 'luxurious spectacle', attracting attention to 'the artistry of the players' acting'.[82] After further commentary comes the instruction:

> Let the theatres see from the example of *Molière* that we are trying to achieve not outwardly brilliant productions where the acting is technically clever, but productions that are ideologically saturated, realistically full-blooded and historically accurate from the leading theatres *especially*.[83]

Kerzhentsev's political impetus is clear, and to be noted particularly is his demand for 'ideologically saturated' theatre works – in other words, that they be blatantly tendentious in the sense in which Stanislavsky had formulated his *criticism* of such 'agit-theatre' in 1927. Stanislavsky was now being categorically reprimanded and put sharply in his place. Stalin writes on the memorandum that he agrees with Kerzhentsev's decision to have the production taken out of circulation not by 'formal prohibition' – Kerzhentsev's words – but through pressure from the press (a quintessentially Stalinist tactic) and he passes it on to Molotov to be signed, who then passed it to the rest of the Committee. None of them knew how much effort Stanislavsky had put into deflecting Bulgakov's more than hints about arbitrary tyranny, against Bulgakov's wishes.

However, as is quite evident from the memorandum, Stanislavsky's subterfuge – apart from causing considerable irritation among his

[81] Ibid., 268.   [82] Ibid., 269.   [83] Ibid., 270.

The Art Theatre in the Stalin Years, 1926–1938 81

colleagues – could not have succeeded in covering up the very essence of Bulgakov's play, which was tyranny, with his own interpretation centred on the valiant artist Molière going about his art. Kerzhentsev was not taken in, any more than were Stalin and Molotov, and his purpose, in any case, was to make an example not just of any '*leading*' theatre, but of *the* leading theatre in the country. Kerzhentsev's dispatch to Stalin is a chilling reminder that the state-owned MAAT may have looked privileged to surviving bellicose leftists (and, later, to certain kinds of Cold War warriors), but, in actual fact, it was scapegoated whenever the ruling powers chose to do so.

Much had happened during the two years of *Molière*'s difficult labour and, crucially for literature and the arts, the campaign for socialist realism had begun. The origins of this at first literary category have been debated, and a former Communist Party journalist and administrator claimed that it was invented in 1932 during a meeting in Stalin's study discussing RAPP.[84] Whatever the case may be, the terminology 'socialist realism' did not become common currency straight away. The leadership initiated the campaign, sourcing Stalin's concepts of 'Soviet' and 'anti-Soviet' to drive it, and then devolved it, first of all to the Soviet Writers' Union, which had succeeded the discredited RAPP, at its inaugural 1934 Congress, where the political agenda underpinning literary matters was made patently clear.[85] Socialist realism as a dogma was publicly and officially born here, and it was meant to destroy 'petty bourgeois' avant-garde and generally modernist 'tendencies' in a two-pronged offensive concerning content and form. Its goal was the advancement of proletarian culture: the former chiefs of RAPP brought to heel in the Writer's Union were adamant on this score, the leadership less so since its goal was culture globally speaking, and this meant co-opting the old culture. The starting point for socialist realism was literature, and what applied to literature was transferred to all the arts. Gorky, who had corresponded with Stalin on the direction literature should take – he advocated a 'standardized language for Socialist Realism' devoid of 'subliterary constructions and dialecticisms', in short, a linguistic as well as ideological template – gave the keynote address.[86]

---

[84] Ibid., 162–3.
[85] See the speeches in *Soviet Writers' Congress 1934*, ed. H. G. Scott (no trans.), London: Lawrence and Wishart, 1977, and especially Gorky, 27–69. The Union effectively replaced the RAPP.
[86] *Soviet Culture and Power*, 182.

82   Context II

The date and sequence of political manoeuvres from the mid 1920s to the 1934 Congress show full well that, contrary to the 'received ideas' of myth-making, Stanislavsky was not forced to adhere to socialist-realist dogma as such at the MAAT. This could not be because the dogma had not yet come into existence, and the MAAT's tribulations arose from other, earlier and clearly formulated state political objectives and related political factors discussed in the preceding pages. Most difficult of all to handle, during these years, were the theatre's Bulgakov productions, which were cruelly subjected to objectives that were political through and through; and no critique of them or their formulators – *Molière*, beginning its saga in 1934, was unequivocally understood to be a critique of the latter – was to be tolerated. On the face of it, these objectives were barely concerned with artistic matters of form, style, and so on; or, at least, artistic matters were not primary targets, but collateral damage.

Even assertions like 'Soviet Marxism limited Stanislavsky to ... Socialist Realism' fall outside the evidence.[87] Socialist realism – as ideology, heroics, slogans, formulae or templates – is not what restricted Stanislavsky, but political machinations from the top that incessantly changed tactics and concocted their slogans according to the pressures of the day. Nor, in the run-up to its official formulation and imposition from 1932 to 1934, did his research, teaching and staging during the same years (Chapter 4) succumb to it; nor, building on the achievements of these exploratory years, did his Studio from 1935 to 1938. If anything, his moral aspirations for the Art Theatre, together with its life-rooted plays, productions and acting and their commitment to high standards, *provided*, ironically, the *model* for socialist realism, although this model in its intricate constitution was to be appropriated, bowdlerized and disfigured by a completely different, ideologized language and its different socio-cultural ascriptions. Stanislavsky's motivation was humanist-religious, whereas socialist realism was primarily politically motivated.

The content prescribed by socialist realism consisted of such subjects as life on collective farms, tripled harvests, greater productivity in factories, women dedicated both to their jobs and families, and so forth. It was obliged to mediate normative (also coercive) moral and social attitudes. Thus, for instance, collective farms were happy, factory workers were heroic, and overworked women were tireless. Content reflected the country's social and economic plans, programmes, improvements and successes,

---

[87] Sharon Marie Carnicke, *Stanislavsky in Focus: An Acting Master for the Twenty-First Century*, London and New York: Routledge, 2009, 207.

The Art Theatre in the Stalin Years, 1926–1938

and in this it was considered to be suitably uplifting, as prescribed. The form side of the offensive can be dealt with equally tersely, since its permutations and combinations, like those of content, return to simple base lines. The leading figures of the 1934 Congress resolved the form side of the question by the demand, presumed to have come from the political leadership, that what was written (sung, painted, played, performed) be comprehensible to proletarian citizens. Narrative was comprehensible. Montage was not. A photographic likeness of a face was comprehensible. A triangle for a face was not. The pejorative term 'Formalist' was applied to the 'nots' – to the modernist ways of the Meyerholds, the Eisensteins, the Malevichs and their epigones.

The witch-hunt of the 'Formalists' took off with a vengeance in January 1936, trumpeted by an unsigned article titled 'Muddle Instead of Music' in the newspaper *Pravda*. Its target was Dmitry Shostakovich's opera *Lady Macbeth of the Mtsensk District*, described as 'din' that could do nothing other than bamboozle the 'masses'. Shostakovich, living in Leningrad, where the opera was performed without a breath of scandal, had played the piano in several Meyerhold productions of the 1920s and had composed the music for *The Bathhouse*. Since Meyerhold had been under scrutiny for some time, Shostakovich's past association with him and LEF – after all, Mayakovsky was the author of *The Bathhouse* – was a supplementary, indirect but nevertheless useful, motive for setting him up. Shostakovich was coerced into confessing his errant ways in music, and his public humiliation in the manner of the show trials during the Great Purges of 1936 to 1938 was a warning that art was in the hands of power. It was rumoured that the author of the article was Stalin, which has never been proven.

Stanislavsky, in 1936, was confined to his home under the supervision of doctors and a live-in nurse, having already been virtually housebound by illness for several years. A doctor who had moved into the upper floor of the *kommunalka* was allegedly an agent of the secret police – something that Stanislavsky may have suspected, or even known, but never discussed. He simply went about his artistic work, Tolstoyan to the last in his non-resistance. Nemirovich-Danchenko was now, in practice rather than principle, the sole artistic director at the Art Theatre, staging productions there successfully. Stanislavsky, at home, staged chamber operas and taught his continually evolving System to small and large numbers of actors and directors, many in open sessions that included putative government informers. He incorporated into the System the 'method of physical action' or what he also called the 'method of psychophysical action', which

84

Context II

was a method of rehearsal that he had been working on since the later 1920s but more noticeably and intensively during the 1930s. Maria Knebel, his illustrious student of these late years, coined the phrase 'active analysis' with which, staying close to Stanislavsky's practice, she adjusted his terminology as she absorbed and modified his evolving ideas and disseminated them in her teaching and writing. He read newspapers daily, as he had generally done in the past, outfoxing his nurse, who hid them from him out of concern for his heart condition.[88] In this way, he kept up with official news – the Shostakovich drama was conspicuously official – and listened to the unofficial news of rumour and gossip.

In January 1938, the government closed down Meyerhold's theatre. On hearing this and gauging accurately that he could provide protection where others could not, Stanislavsky immediately rang Meyerhold, inviting him to work in the Opera-Dramatic Studio operating in his home.[89] Meyerhold openly visited Stanislavsky and officially took up the position of director in March, regularly and visibly in conversation with him, rehearsing, preparing to take a Studio opera on tour, and planning, on Stanislavsky's suggestion, a production of Mozart's *Don Giovanni*.[90] The alleged doctor-spy in the household would have kept an eye on the warm relations between the two men during this entire period.

It cannot be forgotten how courageous and principled was Stanislavsky's action during a time of purges in which millions lost their lives. The reign of terror let loose a spate of defamatory articles, making Meyerhold a pariah, shunned by the whole theatre world. Stanislavsky's solidarity was, other than a lifeline to Meyerhold, an unequivocal statement both to the theatre world and the Soviet leadership. On 25 May 1938, before a showing of recently explored opera work at his Studio, Stanislavsky entered with both Meyerhold *and* Shostakovich by his side. He applauded

---

[88] Krechetova in her *Stanislavsky*, 286–7 and 387 (regarding his nurse) refers to Stanislavsky's assiduous reading of newspapers throughout 1937, from which he had deduced the threat to Meyerhold implied by the closure of his theatre. In other words, Stanislavsky had guessed the worst: the 'liquidation', referred to in my text.

Krechetova also notes that the actors Leonidov and Moskvin had commented on how, over the years, Stanislavsky read the Party newspapers *Pravda* and *Izvestia* from cover to cover in the Soviet resorts where they took their summer holidays. It is encouraging to observe that Krechetova contests, as does this author, the myths concerning Stanislavsky's allegedly 'infantile ignorance' (286) of politics and his 'impracticality', which made him incompetent in administrative matters. She shows that he was capable of such ruses as claiming that he knew nothing about politics (215) and 'crafty diplomatic games' (239), and that he stood up to the political regime (231, 238). For her remarks that Stanislavsky was more than capable of practical matters such as administration, see 372, 425–46.

[89] *Zhizn i tvorchestvo*, Vol. 4, 426.   [90] Ibid., 431.

The Art Theatre in the Stalin Years, 1926–1938

the two victims of defamation, requesting by his action and then words of greeting that the crowd should welcome them, and sat one on either side of him, frequently turning to each for consultation and speaking only with them during breaks.[91] Here again, Tolstoyan non-resistance and non-violence had come to his aid to help his extremely vulnerable colleagues. If there were any informants in the crowd, they would have related Stanislavsky's masterful coup to their masters.

All in all, as the conditions surrounding Stanislavsky in his final years were to suggest in time to come – the present could not speak its history – he was most probably not at great risk in helping Meyerhold. He had become an icon of the Soviet Union's fifteen Republics, and this, together with his international fame, had made him virtually untouchable. Whether Stanislavsky was fully aware of it or not, his exceptional status lent itself to state appropriation, essentially making him prized property, whitewashed by the state of any political views he may have had as a man of liberal outlook, and ready to be canonized for future generations. But, in the uncertain circumstances, day by day, he helped for as long as he could. Within a year of Stanislavsky's death in August 1938, Meyerhold would be arrested, imprisoned, tortured, and finally shot in February 1940.

Stanislavsky had begun his journey into 'life in art' in the light of 'the life of the human spirit', and it progressed into the deep darkness shared by millions – a tragic journey in which he was more fortunate than millions. He saw his theatre virtually die in the mid-1930s, and he was not entirely blameless in its demise and reconstruction, the latter essentially by the will of the state, over which, in actual fact, he had no power whatsoever. It is futile to speculate on how he and the Art Theatre may have run their course if the 1930s in the Soviet Union had been different, and if Stalin had been different, or not been at all. Stanislavsky saw his ideal of the ensemble crumble before his very eyes, and its crumbling edifice stared at him as he created an ensemble of another kind, a looser community, with the Opera Studio in 1918 and, after several fluctuations (Chapter 4), with its rebirth as the Opera-Dramatic Studio in 1935.

It is likely that an ensemble of the kind fashioned by Stanislavsky's inner eye cannot ordinarily be of long duration, and not as long as a lifetime. But he knew it was possible for a while, for he had experienced its creative vitality, perhaps most clearly up to and including the Art Theatre's first tour abroad in 1906 and then during its renaissance, in redoubtable conditions, during the second half of the 1920s. He also knew that an

---

[91] Ibid., 445.

ensemble was renewable with fresh hearts, when tired hearts had given up; and, indeed, the Studios, one after the other, not excluding the last Studio, which had come into existence in a terrifying period, had functioned as vibrant young ensembles. At least they did so during varying phases of their respective histories, consolidating even by their temporary unions his belief that an ensemble was not only desirable, but was also possible. It does not really matter that he and the Art Theatre, the founding company of 1897–98, did not embody his ideal 'forever'. What matters is that the ensemble *idea* could and did become flesh, and could and did work its way through varied acting processes and the gestations and compositions of productions, and their living connections with audiences; and it worked its way into the future through its torch bearers, many of them from the Studios, who kept the flame of the Moscow Art Theatre alive, at home and internationally, before and after the seismic devastations of the Second World War. The 'life of the human spirit' was embodied right there in these concrete actions.

CHAPTER 3

Actor

'The Life of the Human Spirit' and Russian Orthodoxy

The System, although a matter of practice, is not lacking in thought, and this thought adds up to what is nothing less than a worldview – a perspective on the world and how to be in it. The actor is emblematic of Stanislavsky's worldview, which has received next to no attention, even though it is vital to the System and illuminates its various elements in their practical dimensions.

The actor, for Stanislavsky, is the human being who is the actor: this is the *chelovek-artist* whom Stanislavsky identifies regularly with a hyphen to accentuate the inseparability of the two components making up one entity.[1] The actor, Stanislavsky observes, is unlike the painter, who works with paints and a canvas, or the musician, who has an instrument on which to play. The actor is his own medium and instrument and thus can only take from himself/herself and from everything that constitutes this person at a particular time in order to *act*; and, even then, Stanislavsky is not sure whether *acting*, when understood simply as *playing (igra)*, is what being an actor and working as an actor is about.

Stanislavsky's uncertainty comes from his critical thoughts on playacting, fake acting, cliché acting and the well-trodden acting routines of theatre convention (*uslovnost*). Peter Brook was to call it the 'deadly' theatre. With time, as Stanislavsky struggled to formulate his practice, he saw that acting was not about adopting masks and 'playing' but about *being* a *chelovek-artist*, who was *doing* rather than pretending to do something on the stage during the imagination-filled process of making theatre.

Stanislavsky combatted whatever was 'deadly' by calling upon 'the life of the human spirit' of the human being-actor who draws on this very node

---

[1] *SS* 8, 2, 310 [*Rabota aktyra nad soboy, Chast I*]. *Chelovek-artist* appears in the same line as *chelovek-rol* (role) to show their relationship. Translations of all sources in Russian are mine. Note that the word 'artist' in Russian is synonymous with 'aktyor'.

87

or 'seed', to use a quintessentially Stanislavskian term, when he/she seeks '"the life of the human spirit" of the [given] role'.[2] The questions of what is engaged in drawing on the 'human spirit', how an actor can find an appropriate 'inner creative state' for doing it, and how this 'state' can help this actor to become a creator rather than an imitator of roles are central to Stanislavsky's ideal of the organic actor liberated from the shackles of standardization. Behind all this lies Stanislavsky's assumption that such liberation cannot come without acquired strong techniques, and techniques are the practicalities that sustain the actor's evolution. Their logical sequence should desirably culminate, after a long process of learning, in the psychotechnique that Tortsov, Stanislavsky's teacher-protagonist in both parts of *An Actor's Work on Himself*, claims he and his students were now 'fortunate' to have at their 'behest' and 'discretion'.[3]

The Russian text is called *An Actor's Work on Himself* and the titles of its two parts translate fully as *An Actor's Work on Himself in the Creative Process of Experiencing* and *An Actor's Work on Himself in the Creative Process of Embodiment*. Jean Benedetti's 2008 translation into English is in one tome, in accordance with Stanislavsky's original intention, although he ultimately decided that one tome would be too long.[4] Benedetti's is the only English edition cross-referenced against the Russian in my book simply because neither the history of Stanislavsky translation nor comparative translation is its task.[5] The first translation into English was Elizabeth Reynolds Hapgood's heavily abridged version in two short volumes of 1936 and 1949. Hapgood had continual contact with Stanislavsky after they met in New York during the Art Theatre's tour and, although he knew no English and so could not check her translation, he willingly entrusted his pages to her excellent Russian – evident in her correspondence with him. They met, in ensuing years, as plans and arrangements would allow, in Moscow, France or Germany, combining rest, health cures and work. In the event, Hapgood was to a large extent hamstrung by the demands of her North American publisher to adapt the material, which seemed singularly Russian and hence difficult to grasp, to circumstances

---

[2] Ibid., 306; Jean Benedetti's translation, *An Actor's Work*, 282.
[3] Ibid., 320; *An Actor's Work*, 295. Note that 'Tortsov' is a scramble of the Russian word for 'creator'.
[4] *SS* 9, 9, 438, letter to Lyubov Gurevich of 23–24 December 1930 and related discussion about the overwhelming quantity of his material overall.
[5] See, however, Jean Benedetti, 'A History of Stanislavski in Translation', *New Theatre Quarterly*, 6, No. 23 (1990), 266–78.

'The Life of the Human Spirit' and Russian Orthodoxy 89

more familiar to an audience that also had little awareness of 'actor training', as it is now widely known.[6]

It is vital to notice the discrepancies between Stanislavsky's titles and Benedetti's English rendition, since titles tell readers what they might expect and how they might be predisposed to it. Starting with the titles of the two parts. Benedetti simplifies and renames them as *Year One: Experiencing* and *Year Two: Embodiment*. His decision to identify Stanislavsky's book immediately as a course curriculum is in line with Stanislavsky's purpose, and it makes for a snappy presentation to readers in English. However, the loss of 'creative' and 'process', which define what *kind* of work the actor is advised to undertake, projects a methodical but somewhat mechanical image of the book's content and approach. Although Tortsov's probing Socratic dialogue with his students often assumes the mask of the all-wise teacher and the subordinate student, the actual subject of this talk-and-do is the 'creative process' in its searching fluidity, in which mechanisms, quick-fix tools and programmed mind-sets and behaviours have no legitimate place. Tortsov can be taken to be Stanislavsky's surrogate.

Second, Benedetti's decision to shorten the title of the whole book (possibly encouraged by his publisher) and render it efficiently as *An Actor's Work* has a similar shortcoming. The word 'work' was accentuated in my Chapter 1 so as to offset Stanislavsky's view of work as an active, consciousness-filled and goal-inspired doing. It is now important to accentuate Stanislavsky's 'on', since his notion of working *on* oneself foregrounds the sense built into the phrase of intentionally and actively becoming, changing, developing, improving, helping and healing oneself. All these meanings disappear in the crisp title *An Actor's Work*. It is not clear why this decision was made, since readers of English would grasp the significance of these meanings perfectly well: they are ubiquitous in contemporary English, thanks to yoga, qi gong and an array of mindful practices by which people work *on* themselves, whether they consider these practices to be spiritual – or to be linked to spiritual practices – or not. The nuances of Stanislavsky's 'on' unfortunately fall away at precisely the initiating point when contemporary readers pick up Benedetti's translation of his book.

The spiritual dimension of a human being is of great consequence to Stanislavsky. He was a religious man by upbringing and habitus, but he

---

[6] Carnicke, *Stanislavsky in Focus*, 2009, 77–93 is an ample account, sensitive to the vagaries of the circumstances in which Hapgood translated, including publisher pressure.

was deeply religious in his blood and bones, one might say, or 'in his essence', as Anatoly Smeliansky put it in his 2012 programme on Stanislavsky for the Russian television channel Kultura. Valery Galendeyev, the acclaimed voice teacher of the Maly Drama Theatre (MDT) in St Petersburg and assistant director to Lev Dodin, used much the same words as he reflected on how completely religious Stanislavsky was 'in himself', which, for Galendeyev, was perhaps most evident in his writings about ethics.[7] Galendeyev added that he had not understood Stanislavsky's religious 'essence' when he published *Ucheniye K. S. Stanislavskogo o stsenicheskom slove* (*K. S. Stanislavsky's Teachings on the Word on the Stage*) in 1990 'because we did not think like that in those days'. This is not so much a reference to national self-censorship regarding religion as an awareness of how religious sentiments were not part of the communist worldview, nor were yet confidently out in the open during 'glasnost' and 'perestroika' as these reforms of the mid-1980s careered into the collapse of the Soviet Union in 1991.

Theatre director Anatoly Vasilyev has, for decades, recognized that Stanislavsky's Orthodoxy was 'in his make-up'.[8] An Orthodox Christian himself, Vasilyev sees Orthodoxy in Stanislavsky's very idea of 'metamorphosis' (Vasilyev's word), that is, the transubstantiation of one substance into another, or, in the language of Stanislavsky's theatre, that of an actor embodied in the not-oneself (which is a role) and of the role embodied in the actor. Embodiment (*voploshcheniye*) achieves transformation (*perevoploshcheniye*) when it crosses over – as indicated by the prefix *pere* – into this highest form of actorly accomplishment. *Pere*, in Russian grammar, always indicates movement, which, in this case, signifies the action towards transformation as it is being accomplished. In other words, transformation is a *process* and not an end result. For Stanislavsky it is, indeed, part and parcel of the 'creative process'.

Such metamorphoses or transformations, symbolic and actual, are in the order of a wide range of religious practices within the many different religions of the world, from archaic times to modern societies, and they include the church rituals about which Vasilyev is thinking at the back of his mind; and, for religious men like Stanislavsky and Vasilyev, there is something sacred above and beyond the secular activity of acting when the

---

[7] Personal conversation with Galendeyev on 6 October 2015, my translation.

[8] Personal conversations with Vasilyev during June 2009 and on 23 October and 19 November 2016, my translation. ('Vassiliev' in French orthography, which is often used in English.) For passages of immediate relevance here, see 328 of the June conversations, 'Studio Theatre, Laboratory Theatre', *New Theatre Quarterly*, 25, No. 100 (2009), 324–32.

'The Life of the Human Spirit' and Russian Orthodoxy

actor 'becomes' someone else. As anthropologist Mircea Eliade argues, for 'many religious human beings' even stones and trees transform into '*ganz andere*' (something other) 'because they show something that is no longer stone or tree but the *sacred* ... something sacred shows itself to us'.[9] Stanislavsky, in quasi-mystical and also sexual language, speaks of that – to him rare – moment when an actor reaches that *ganz andere* which 'shows itself' as 'ecstasy'.[10]

And so back to the 'human spirit', which God breathed into the human beings whom he made in his own image, as Christ was made in his image, in the 'human form divine'. (The latter phrase is from the visionary William Blake's poem 'The Divine Image'.) The spirit, the crowning instance of God's creation of the human being, interconnects with the soul and the body – the corporeal, the 'clay', with which God began. In Orthodoxy, these three 'instances' of a human being – body, soul, spirit – have their specific character, even though they come together as one. The spirit is manifested in humans as conscience (*sovest*) and so in their capacity for moral consciousness and moral actions, which strive upwards towards all that is good.

The distinguished Orthodox prelate Feofan Zatvornik relates this conscience both to a 'thirst for God' and a 'fear of God', which puts a brake on wrongdoing.[11] A faltering conscience descends on this same vertical towards the demonic and Hell – a trope common, of course, to all denominations of Christianity. Galendeyev's recall of Stanislavsky's ethics is important here, not least because its religious base converts, as Stanislavsky was well aware, into social and hence also professional principles. Needless to say, such principles can be understood and acted upon by the theatre profession at large in lay moral terms, without religious inflections or references to the Christian origins of 'lay' morality. This was not so personally for Stanislavsky, for whom morality was always a manifestation of godliness. For a religious person, of course, God is in all things and everywhere, which makes the notion of 'lay' or 'secular' contingent only on socially generated convenience.

The several paragraphs to follow regarding the body-soul-spirit nexus of Orthodoxy refer to Zatvornik's book of religious instruction in the form of

---

[9] *The Sacred and the Profane: The Nature of Religion*, trans. Willard R. Trask, New York and London: Harcourt Brace Jovanovich, 1959, 11–12.

[10] *SS* 9, 5, Part 2, 346 and 348.

[11] *Shto yest dukhovnaya zhizn i kak na neyo nastroyitsya?* (*What Is Spiritual Life and How Do We Tune Ourselves to It?*), Moscow: Otchy dom, 2006, 33–5.

letters to a young woman.[12] The interest of this particular book lies in the fact that Zatvornik's teachings were disseminated at the time when Stanislavsky received his religious education; Zatvornik died in 1894 and so, for half of his lifetime, was Stanislavsky's contemporary. There is no evidence to suggest that Stanislavsky studied these teachings, but they are very much of the era of the first part of his 'split' life, as identified in my preceding chapters, and typical of the religious instruction given across the spectrum of Orthodox believers living in the later nineteenth century. As a consequence, Zatvornik's teachings give us an insight into the thought permeating the System, like a scent rather than a dogma, even as the System accrued the influences of different frames of thought, which were largely scientific and secular. It needs to be noted that this book is not a historical relic but is used for religious instruction in Russia today.

Where scientific frames are concerned, Rose Whyman has thoroughly demonstrated several influences on Stanislavsky that came into play in his thought as of 1908: French experimental psychologist Théodule Ribot's investigations of the 1890s into 'affective memory' (*mémoire affective*), the term he coined and which suited Stanislavsky because the French *affective* encompasses 'feelings', 'emotions' and 'sensations', as does the Russian *chuvstva*, Stanislavsky's key term; William James' theory of the emotions as mental perceptions that excite emotions ('We meet a bear, we are frightened and we run'), to which Ribot's research had introduced him; and the pre-revolutionary Ivan Sechenov's neuro-physiology, which posited that the brain was activated by electric currents and paved the way for the later Soviet behaviourist Pavlov's explorations of reflex responses.[13] All except Pavlov, who died in 1936, were almost exact contemporaries of each other. Sechenov was frequently at loggerheads with the tsarist government, reputedly for having debased Christian morality with his scientific explanations of human behaviour. Imagine – his electric currents supplanted the spirit! Stanislavsky had no patience with such bigotry.

According to Whyman, 'the Soviets increasingly equated Stanislavsky's work with that of Sechenov and Pavlov, distancing him from Ribot'; they also 'persuaded' Stanislavsky to replace 'affective memory' with 'emotion memory' for 'political reasons'.[14] These reason are not specified, but – by

---

[12] Ibid., 9–48. Subsequent quotations are from within these pages.
[13] *The Stanislavsky System of Acting: Legacy and Influence in Modern Performance*, Cambridge University Press, 2008, 52–76, and quotation, 59.
[14] Ibid., 53 and 67.

'The Life of the Human Spirit' and Russian Orthodoxy 93

deduction from Whyman's overall argument – 'emotion memory' presumably co-ordinated better with Pavlov's account of how stimuli operated in tandem with associative memory and triggered responses, which could be demonstrated physically. Pavlov's dogs did just that when they salivated to the same bell ring that they associated, from learned memory, with food. This was provable and measurable, and so was consonant with the reigning ideology of materialism and its emphasis on concrete matter and irrefutable fact. 'Affective memory', on the other hand, embraced, together with feelings and sensations, the ideas of human instinct and intuition which, like 'spirit' (*dukh*), could not be measured scientifically. As Stanislavsky saw it, 'affective memory' was useful for the actor because it was a trigger for his/her *analogous* sensations in the analogous circumstances proposed for performance. He never meant it to be a means for behaviourist replication, as formulated by Pavlov (or, for that matter, by any other behaviourist – physiologist or psychologist).

For reasons of exegetic convenience, the preceding discussion of the Orthodox cosmology started with the spirit. However, Zatvornik's discussion starts with the body and itemizes its organs and muscular and nervous systems so as to point out that the body is the realm of physiological functions, sensitivities (carried through the central nervous system) and wants and desires such as food, water and sex, which require appeasement and fulfilment. The organs of the body are in perpetual invisible motion, but they are in motion, nonetheless, and generate energy which, according to traditional Orthodoxy, is concentrated in the solar plexus. The body, as the creation of God, is to be loved and cherished.

The soul has three 'sides' (Zatvornik's word), the thinking, willing and feeling sides. These are intellect/mind (*um*), will and feeling, which 'house', to put it far more crudely than Zatvornik does, as well as stimulate and nourish the imagination and memory. Neither imagination nor memory can live without the three sides of the soul, whichever side may take precedence over another at a given point. This is of relevance to Stanislavsky's 'affective memory', which he sought to understand better and verify through his scientific reading.[15] The intellectual (thinking) side of the soul is image-full. *Obraz* ('image', although this is not altogether an adequate translation) is the term Stanislavsky uses for what is being imagined and played, for which the translation in English is 'character', but in Russian is also the term for an icon; otherwise Stanislavsky speaks

---

[15] *Affektivnaya pamyat* in MAT Museum K. S. No. 11261 (with Stanislavsky's marginalia) and the remaining Ribot texts, K. S. Nos. 11148, 11263 and 11266.

not of the '*obraz*' but the 'role'. Wants and desires, which reside in the body, grow in the soul and become aspects of it. The will is linked to wants and desires, which are spurs for action, and Zatvornik also speaks of the 'activities' of the soul. Like the internal body, which breathes and moves precisely because the nervous and muscular systems are not static, the soul is perpetually mobile.

The feeling side of the soul envelops the heart and thus everything that settles in the soul passes through the heart. In Zatvornik's words: 'that is why the heart is called the centre of life'. Wants and desires, since they grow in the soul, also pass through the heart, but they need the will in order to be realized. The proposition that the soul has a feeling side indicates to an English reader why the Russian word for 'soul' – '*dusha*' – can also be the word for 'heart', the fount of the emotions.

Of course, Russian culture does not have a monopoly on the heart: it is perceived to be the 'source' of emotions in many if not most cultures, including those well beyond Europe, like the vast Chinese culture. But the link in Russian between the words for 'soul' and 'heart', together with their interchangeability, gives rise to oddities of translation into English – for instance, 'my soul' as a term of endearment (noticeable in translations of Chekhov's plays) when 'dear heart', while old-fashioned and rather 'stuffy', is closer to the required sense; but 'sweetheart' would do just as well. From the same link between heart and soul comes that dreadful, universally exploited cliché of the 'Russian soul' which, when applied to Chekhov's plays, for example, is associated with sensibility, tears, sadness, nostalgia, longing and the depressive state of melancholia – images of emotion (and of Chekhov) that Stanislavsky dismissed with distaste as 'Chekhoviana' (Chapter 2).

Not prone to stereotypes or sentimentalism in the theatre – they were part of the stock-in-trade he disliked – Stanislavsky nevertheless set great store by feelings and emotions, making of them a touchstone for the actor's work on 'the life of the human spirit of the role'. He is quite clear that 'in our language [the language of the theatre] understanding – means feeling'.[16] And while the spirit is of a higher order – 'its strength issues from God' and it 'seeks God', whereas 'the soul is concerned with earthly things' (Zatvornik) – the spirit combines with the soul and with the infinite movements of the soul for which, Zatvornik says, 'we do not have the words in our language'. Put simply, the spirit relates to the soul.

---

[16] *Moya zhizn*, 298.

'The Life of the Human Spirit' and Russian Orthodoxy   95

In sum, the body, the soul and the spirit, together with their aspects and sides (like the feeling side of the soul), are a filigree of holistic interdependences that form the indivisible one of a human being. This filigree is so delicately interwoven that, in order to elucidate this holism, Zatvornik speaks in hyphenated nouns: of spiritual life as being of the 'spirit-soul' and of the life of the soul as of the 'soul-body' to which belong the mind, observation, imagination, memory, bodily sensations and the bodily needs that are wants and desires. Wanting to eat, for instance, is physiologically straightforward, but Zatvornik's idea of wants and desires encompasses the desire for the beauty of art, which is not expressed as a biological function of the organism. Like Stanislavsky, Zatvornik uses the generic term *iskusstvo* and, like him, believes that the desire for its beauty is intrinsic to the 'spirit-soul'. Beauty is a manifestation of God.

Stanislavsky's ingrained Orthodoxy, which could not have departed in any significant way from the doxa of Zatvornik's religious instruction, does not have to be worn on his sleeve to prove its existence. It can just *be* there – implicit or hidden, as it is generally believed to have been during the Soviet era; as were hidden from prying eyes the icons on the inside of Stanislavsky's large cupboard door in the room where he spent the last years of his life. And it can – and does – influence his thought in his theatre practice as well as his writing in the subterranean way of assimilated learning.

Take, for instance, Tortsov's placard heading for one of his classes, 'MIND, WILL AND FEELING' which, he says, are the 'movers [*dvigateli*] of our psychic life'.[17] These three nouns are exactly the nouns Zatvornik uses for the three sides of the soul, and they are placed exactly in Zatvornik's order; and Stanislavsky's adumbrations of how these 'movers' (or 'activators' – this word would also do) move in their valency and coalescence in the processes of acting, have more than a passing similarity with Zatvornik's account of how they motivate and operate 'our psychic life' which, it bears repeating, is representative of Orthodox teaching. However, they reverberate, as well, with Ribot's analyses. This double resonance suggests that what Stanislavsky may have taken in faith was corroborated for him by science, but his faith seeded his desire to check with science. After all, Stanislavsky was neither a prelate nor a monk but a practical and concrete theatre-maker.

Mind, will and feeling also move (activate) the imagination, which is aroused by questions beginning with 'What if?' (Stanislavsky's 'magic if)

---

[17] *SS* 8, 2, 299; *An Actor's Work*, 276, translated as 'inner psychological drives'.

specific to the 'proposed circumstances' of this or that situation.[18] 'What if x was the case in y circumstances, what would you do?' arouses activity, and the actor answers with actions as he/she wishes in the moment of doing them, without reasoning them out beforehand. Imagination is crucial, as Tortsov explains, because 'not a single step on the stage should be made mechanically without being substantiated internally, that is without the participation of the work of the imagination';[19] and the body, excited by the imagination, submits to the will, thereby being able to express what the heart and soul feel. This process is necessary for the actor's 'stage inner creative state', which summons, and consists of, the actor's indivisible oneness in conjunction with the psychotechnique that the actor must muster for embodiment.[20] For Stanislavsky, 'stage creativity' is, before all else, a matter of the 'complete concentration' of the actor's *spiritual and physical nature in its entirety* (Stanislavsky's italics).[21] Note that he uses the adjective 'stage' deliberately so as to distinguish the creative state summoned on the stage from the creative state that can be had in normal life.

It is certainly not my intention to co-opt Stanislavsky for the religious ultra-conservative right that has re-emerged with alarming speed across religions in the early twenty-first century. Stanislavsky denounced religious fundamentalism when he denounced the repression of the state and its collusion with the Church (Chapter 1). There is nothing to be gained, however, from leaving his faith unrecognized and, given the synopsis of the basic premises of Orthodoxy in the preceding paragraphs, two propositions appear questionable. The first is the proposition that Stanislavsky more or less shares, in the words of Sharon Marie Carnicke, 'the Western propensity to see mind and body as two separate realms' and that, try as he might, he 'never fully escapes Western dualism';[22] furthermore, 'despite continual reminders about the indissoluble link between the psychic and the physical'– Carnicke is here referring to An Actor's Work on Himself, *Part I* – Stanislavsky 'creates an endless series of oppositional concepts'. Carnicke cites 'inner/outer', 'mind/body', 'spiritual/physical' and 'truth/lie'

---

[18] Ibid., 318.

[19] Ibid., 95. To be noted is my 'substantiated' instead of the more usual 'justified' in English translation. The latter suggests that the actor needs to prove or to defend what he or she does, which is not at all Stanislavsky's intention. He means the actor to *give grounds for* an action: the nuance is different.

[20] Ibid., 317–20 and 319 for the phrase cited, which is translated in An Actor's Work, 294, as 'the actor's creative state in performance'. Although this is cleaner, I have kept mine for the notion of 'intrinsically belonging to the stage' indicated by Stanislavsky's stsenicheskoye ('scenic').

[21] *Moya zhizn*, 302; *My Life in Art*, 258.   [22] *Stanislavsky in Focus*, 13 and 181, respectively.

'The Life of the Human Spirit' and Russian Orthodoxy

among the 'oppositional concepts' that, she claims, betray 'hidden Cartesian elements in his thinking'.[23]

The second questionable proposition concerns the alleged influence of yoga on Stanislavsky and his

> adaptations to acting from Yoga. Eastern practice allows Stanislavsky to move beyond the Western propensity to see mind and body as two separate realms and to establish the mind-body-spirit continuum for actors who seek to communicate the full scope of human experience through their art.[24]

Now, given that the 'mind-body-spirit continuum' is integral to Orthodoxy, where, however, it is perceived as a knot – an intermesh – rather than a line, Stanislavsky would hardly have needed to turn to 'Eastern practice' to find holistic thinking. Orthodoxy had already provided it for him. And to affirm this does not contradict the fact that Demidov, in 1911, advised Stanislavsky not to continue 'inventing acting exercises yourself', when 'most of your thoughts tally with what was written long ago. I will give you the books. Read *Khatkha-Iyoga* and *Razhda-Iyoga*'.[25] Note especially Demidov's recognition of how Stanislavsky's thoughts 'tally' with those assembled by Yogi Ramacharaka, the pseudonym of the North American writer of spiritual books William Walter Atkinson. *Hatha Yoga* was translated into Russian in 1909, and Stanislavsky's copy exists in the MAT Museum archives;[26] his copy of *Razhda-Iyoga* (Atkinson's *Raja Yoga*) has been lost. His occasional pencilled marks on the available copy, however, are essentially beside references to exercises in breathing and relaxation: relaxed muscles, he had already found from his own vocal blockages as a singer, alleviated tension and so helped actors to enter into a creative state.

Stanislavsky's Orthodox view of the oneness of a human being would have made the holism of yoga congenial and experimenting with its exercises a rewarding experience: his inventions of his own exercises, it must be noted, triggered Demidov's offer of his Ramacharaka books. Stanislavsky was not sectarian, since he, together with Sulerzhitsky, who also privileged the 'human spirit' in artistic as well as quotidian conditions, promoted yoga for the First Studio in an environment that was already far removed from 'Western' Cartesian thought and its emphasis on the reasoning mind. Orthodoxy, which put down its roots deep into Russian

---

[23] Ibid., 181.   [24] Ibid., 13.   [25] Vinogradskaya, *Zhizn i tvorchestvo*, Vol. 2, 291.
[26] MAT Museum, K. S. No. 11262. Ramacharaka's titles are hyphenated in Russian.

98   Actor

culture, was not conducive to Cartesian thought and it was largely impervious to it across the centuries.

As for the group of dichotomies cited above – inner/outer, mind/body, and so on – it is altogether possible to look at them differently: not as traces of Cartesian dualism but as the expression of the methodological – although not conceptual – difficulties that Stanislavsky had already encountered when working with actors; and they were compounded as he struggled to write the sequential course of *An Actor's Work on Himself, Part I* and *Part II*. These difficulties involved knowing where to start with which actors, what to start with, and how to start it; how to follow on; how to build up the receptivity, understanding and sensitivity to what was being explored in practice; how to develop the concrete skills for dealing with the latter; and how to bring the various strands together in some comprehensible and beneficial way. They, as Stanislavsky had compiled them for Tortsov, were probably not all that different from the difficulties faced by teachers of acting today, or, indeed, by actors trying to find their way in a tangle of possible tacks, veers, dead ends and sudden break-through.

Carnicke quotes Tortsov as further evidence of Stanislavsky's dualistic thinking: 'Until now, we have worked with the process of *external, visible, corporeal communication* on stage, but there also exists another more important aspect: *internal, invisible, spiritual communion*'.[27] Yet it can be argued that Tortsov's order of aspects, whereby he starts with the 'external' and proceeds to the 'internal', is not proof of Stanislavsky's division of the 'internal' and the 'external' into 'separate realms', but is his pedagogical solution, at that particular moment in his research, for handling multiple factors that present themselves all at once in the practicalities of work. As for Tortsov's lesson sequence – its first steps could well be seen as necessary preparation for excavating the '*more important* aspect' (my italics), which is the '*invisible, spiritual communion*' that the 'external' techniques of expression make visible. In other words, even Tortsov's qualitative distinction of 'more important' is not a separating device but an evaluative accent, which foregrounds the 'spiritual' precisely because the spirit is the encompassing force that infuses all else (not least externalized actions), holds it together, and crowns it all.

The date of writing at this juncture in Stanislavsky's two-part volume (or, indeed, at any other juncture in it) is hard to pin down because he thought about, wrote and perpetually revised his material over some thirty

[27] *Stanislavsky in Focus*, 181–2.

'The Life of the Human Spirit' and Russian Orthodoxy 99

years. The quicksands of politics and their taboos on thought complicate scholarly research. Lyubov Gurevich, his editor from as early as 1908 until the early 1930s, exhorted Stanislavsky to comply with the Soviet mentality and its vocabulary and to delete such words as 'spirit', 'soul', 'inspiration', 'radiation' (of energy) and others that were disapproved of in society at large for their religious or otherwise metaphysical or mystical ring. She insisted that he replace his exercises involving burning money and finding lost diamond broaches, which evoked wealth and could cause offence to a people who had endured atrocious deprivation for years on end; and the current intelligentsia, she pointed out, could object to his anachronisms with which it had no connection or sympathy.[28] She hinted at, but refrained from directly discussing, the class warfare with which everyone had been bombarded during the 1920s to incite class resentment. Stanislavsky, generally at a loss as to how to comply – and how to abridge and simplify what he knew intuitively as well as from practice – tended to dig in his heels: 'I only need to communicate what I came to know about art during my own [pre-Soviet] era', he wrote, in the Tolstoyan non-resistance familiar to him, now bordering on defiance.[29] Eventually, Gurevich's cup of frustration ran over and, notwithstanding their long friendship, she finally resigned from her duties.

Stanislavsky's inability to handle revisions of his writing with complete confidence regarding matters he knew to be difficult brought out his obsessive streak. However, they became the two-part *An Actor's Work on Himself* and show, sometimes with quite extraordinary flair, the very process of writing utterances. This writing shows, as well, how the word struggles to find form and clarity as it turns around on itself and probes what it says. It is reflexive, like an actor who turns on his/her actions to demonstrate how they are being made, and the Meyerholdian actor of 'theatricality' here springs to mind. The specific character of Stanislavsky's way of writing his book is certainly worth noticing, otherwise its thinking aloud could all too easily be mistaken for mere pedantry.

This having been said, Stanislavsky was on firmer ground when it came to his stage practice, even though his experimentations often appeared ridiculous to Art Theatre colleagues and visitors, especially during their initial testing period, the second half of the 1900s and earlier 1910s. Mikhaïl Chekhov recalls amusing incidents when Stanislavsky asked First Studio students from which 'fool' they had heard x about how to do y, only to discover that he was the culprit. By then, Chekhov observes, he

---

[28] K. S. No. 8058, letter of April 1929 (no day).   [29] *SS* 9, 9, 465, undated letter of autumn 1931.

had already reconsidered this particular proposition for his System and was now examining another.[30] Stanislavsky's continual rethinking of how something might be done differently is a primary feature of his hands-on research, and his openness to challenge and change was an example for successive waves of his students. Chekhov was as inspired by it as the professional practitioners who were Stanislavsky's students in his 1935 Studio.

Yet, no matter what the circumstances and how he turned in them, Stanislavsky never let go of the 'more important' aspect of the actor's work – 'spiritual communion' made visible – to which his fictional Tortsov draws attention. 'Spiritual communion' most definitely refers to that *sobornost* central to Orthodoxy, which Tolstoy cherished, irrespective of how much he vilified the Orthodox Church. Where, for Tolstoy, peasant dance, in its transparent and natural simplicity, epitomized spiritual communion, for Stanislavsky in 1905, it was the dance of Isadora Duncan.[31] The context in which he speaks of Duncan, whom he had only just seen performing in Russia, is revealing for his declaration that the conventional techniques of the theatre had to be cleaned out so as to bring art 'closer to nature (*priroda*), that is, to God'.[32] Stanislavsky's equation of nature with God is logical, since, in the Christian cosmology, God created the world and was in all things. And it is a clue to his lifelong idea that the 'new' type of actor, capable of having a stage creative state and to whom his System was dedicated, had to follow his/her nature. In so doing this 'new' actor was literally natural – untampered with, non-modified, organic – in composition and substance as well as expression. This was the 'natural and simple' of Duncan's dancing.[33]

The System was a means for encouraging what was in an actor's nature. It did not demand that an actor run counter to it, twisting his/her very being to wear what was entirely alien to that nature. The word 'nature' requires a little more attention because, with it, and particularly throughout *An Actor's Work on Himself*, Stanislavsky conforms to the idea in everyday thinking, as in Ribot's scientific treatises and Zatvornik's religious instruction, that there is such a thing as human nature (*priroda*), which is true to its 'laws' of being. It suffices to discover its modus operandi to explain it (Ribot) and to unearth and act with it rather than against it (Stanislavsky) so that acting may be true to the given actor, that is, be true to his or her *particular* 'nature'. In this lies the human being-actor's

---

[30] *Literaturnoye naslediye*, Vol. 1, 151.   [31] *SS* 8, 5, 195, 255–6, and 583.   [32] Ibid., 195.
[33] Ibid., 583.

individuality even as his or her 'nature' partakes of 'human nature' as such; and Tortsov declares the primary significance of individuality:

> It is important that the actor's attitude to the role should lose nothing of his individual sensibility and, along with that, not enter into conflict with an author's plan and ideas. If the actor doesn't invest his own nature as a human being in the role, then what he creates will be dead.[34]

The idea of 'own nature' here recalls Stanislavsky's conviction that 'we are all born with this capacity for creativity', with 'this "system" within ourselves', which 'belongs to our organic nature, spiritual as much as physical' and is thus an integral part of being 'human'.[35]

'Ya yesm': 'I Am' and the Subconscious

Here, in this interface between 'nature' and 'human being' lies the full significance of Stanislavsky's Old Church Slavonic 'ya yesm', which Benedetti translates as 'I am being', but which is more to the point simply as 'I am'. Of crucial importance is the meaning of this phrase, ignored by all commentators in English to date (and in Russian, too, among other languages). Stanislavsky knew from church services, purification rituals and other such religious observances that 'ya yesm' means nothing less than 'I am in God and God is in me' in spirit and body; and the attitude underpinning 'ya yesm' is 'I am attentive to my state of oneness with God'. Knowing this, he would not have randomly used a phrase of such high vibration (always in quotation marks to indicate that he had borrowed it). By saying (or thinking) 'ya yesm', the actor acknowledges his/her acceptance of the 'sacred task' of art (Chapter 1) and his/her readiness to inhabit its 'human form divine'. Stanislavsky is quite subtle in his affirmation that the spirit is *realized* in the actor, and this is of crucial importance, for the spirit does not float on high but is incarnate – in the flesh, in the body, of the human form.

  This is the religious foundation of 'ya yesm'. Its secularized usage in the acting profession was able then, as well as later, to maintain its religious connotations for those who recognized and accepted them, while acquiring the appearance of lay pieces of information, specifically tailored for actors, for those who could not. The Soviet editors of Stanislavsky's works may have taken 'ya yesm' as a 'Stanislavskian' linguistic curiosity for the otherwise practical ends of acting, which may suggest why they left it intact; that

---

[34] *SS* 8, 2, 335; *An Actor's Work*, 309.   [35] *SS* 8, 3, 304; *An Actor's Work*, 611.

is to say, they may have *misrecognized* the language, missing its religious import; or they may simply not have cared to think too hard about it, or not wanted to stir up troubled waters. Whatever the case may have been, the first piece of secular information is that 'It is I, the human being-actor in my individual nature, who am right here, at this moment, concentrated and attentive as I act'. In this sense, the state of 'I am' is the state of 'presence' as actors understand it today. The second piece is that 'I am', which in its religious instance invokes attention-attentiveness (*vnimaniye*) and concentration, calls upon these very same faculties for acting. Stanislavsky devotes a chapter to attention and concentration in *An Actor's Work on Himself, Part I* and relates them consistently to the remaining elements of his System. They recur freely in the editor-compiled miscellany of *An Actor's Work on a Role*.

'I am', then, is manifold. It denotes the actor's attentive 'existence' in the 'very middle of an imagined life', as Tortsov puts it, and his/her 'living it authentically' rather than just playing it.[36] After congratulating an actor, Tortsov explains why he had successfully completed the set exercise. He had demonstrated that 'the logic and sequence of physical actions, feelings and the senses led the actor to truth, truth brought out belief, and all of this together created "I am"'.[37] Further: 'Where there are truth, belief and "I am", there too, necessarily, is sincere human (and not actorly) emotional experiencing' (*perezhivaniye*).[38] 'Truth' here refers to the actor's truthful performance in which he/she believes 'sincerely', as distinct from a perfunctory, competent, over-acted or hammed-up performance in which the actor has no 'internal' (that is, heartfelt) investment; hence Stanislavsky's apposition between 'human' and 'actorly' in his sentence. Tolstoy, whom Stanislavsky saw as his mentor, uses the word '*perezhivaniye*' for unaffectedly felt art, as distinct from imitative or posturing simulations. Stanislavsky's *perezhivaniye* additionally carries the idea that art is a living, changing process rather than a regurgitation of previously established forms and norms, which petrify through constant automatic repetition.

In a parallel context, Tortsov elaborates:

> 'I am' is the actor who is in a relationship with his partner on the stage and not with the spectator [that is, neither playing to the audience nor playing it], and who keeps within the sphere of the play and the role in an

---

[36] *SS* 8, 2, 79 and 202; *An Actor's Work*, 72 and 186.   [37] Ibid., 202.

[38] Ibid., 203. I have added 'emotional' to 'experiencing' to indicate the feeling process undergone, which is intrinsic to the Russian word itself. The parenthesis is Stanislavsky's.

atmosphere that is alive, truthful and believes [in what is being done], 'I am'.[39]

In this particular context, Tortsov also identifies 'I am' as the actor, who 'is genuinely, productively, expediently, and, what is more, continually active' on the stage. Ever-changing activity, which is different in different circumstances, proves to be a significant aspect of 'I am'. Stanislavsky speaks of 'activity' as having 'movement', particularly when he looks for the appropriate tempo-rhythm of a role, a sequence or a whole piece, which is always integral to the relationships between partners in performance.

Fragmented texts added by Stanislavsky's Soviet editors as something of an epilogue to Part II of *An Actor's Work on Himself* include a brief but extremely meaningful dialogue about an etude that went well. Stanislavsky no longer names his protagonists in these fragments, so 'Tortsov' is now simply the 'Teacher'. The Student comments that he 'felt the right to stand there and do what I was doing', and the Teacher replies:

> This is a very important moment of an actor's creative state on the stage. It has its own special name ... 'I am', that is, I exist, I find myself *now, today, here*, in the life of the play, on the stage.
>
> This state is the threshold to another, even more important moment in creativity during which organic nature with its subconscious naturally step into the work, all by themselves.[40]

Note that, by being the first word in Stanislavsky's chain, emphasis falls on '*now*', which attracts attention to this chain's difference from the word order usually cited in English – 'here, today, now'. Stanislavsky most likely accentuates '*now*', because, in this particular context of his thought, the idea of 'this instant' is crucial for defining the state of 'I am' ('I am *present*', glossed above) as the 'threshold' to the subconscious. 'I am' can only be such a threshold when all its energies have gathered '*now, today, here*'.

Stanislavsky's move to the subconscious is of fundamental importance to his System in that it enables him to reaffirm that creativity, while not mindless, does not stem from the reasoning mind. Furthermore, the 'truth' and 'belief' that he foregrounds in the quotations selected above are the truth and belief *of creativity* (my italics) and not of any correspondence to 'reality'; and this needs to be stressed and keenly apprehended since Stanislavsky's 'truth' has been misinterpreted for far too long as verified 'fact' in the concrete real world. 'Truth' and 'belief' are not, in other words, matters of the verisimilitude between x and y, as happens in photographic

---

[39] Ibid., 173.   [40] *SS* 8, 3, 411–12.

104 Actor

likenesses (the creed of French naturalism, which Stanislavsky had abandoned at the turn of the twentieth century). His focus on the indispensable role of the subconscious in creativity prompts him to connect the links between 'truth, belief and "I am"' firmly with the subconscious, giving this lapidary statement: 'and where there is "I am", so too is organic nature with its subconscious.'[41]

Now, today, here is the now of the actor acting in this very moment and not before or after it. This being-in-the-moment does not tolerate the repetition by rote of things previously performed. It must be stressed that, for Stanislavsky, in the persona of the Teacher, 'I am' in this now-and-here is the very doorway of the subconscious. However, once 'I am' is right inside the subconscious, the subconscious works unimpeded, in full swing, and the actor's stage creative state goes into free flow. The Teacher sums up what could be called the faculties that 'together constitute the state of "I am"'. These faculties are: being in the moment in physical and inward actions; a feeling of the truthfulness of these actions; the truthfulness and sincerity of emotional experiencing; and belief in the authenticity of the *now* of action, sensation and feeling.[42] The Teacher concludes: 'As soon as "I am" becomes established, the actor announces with delight that *inspiration* itself has descended upon him.'[43] The point need not be laboured that Stanislavsky's image of inspiration descending evokes the movement of the Holy Spirit becoming incarnate. This is precisely when Spirit/spirit is *realized in* the actor in its recognizable metamorphosis as the 'human spirit'.

Several Problems of Translation

It is most unfortunate that Benedetti's translations of *My Life in Art*, *An Actor's Work on Himself* and *An Actor's Work on a Role* are squeamish about translating *dukh* and *dusha* as 'spirit' and 'soul', which is their exact translation. It would seem that the translator was uncomfortable about using these words in current English, as if embarrassment arose because his allegedly rationally minded readers from allegedly hard-nosed, pragmatic Anglo-Saxon cultures might be embarrassed by such religious terms; or because they recur in 'fey' and 'fashionable' New Age spiritual practices that, outside of institutionalized religions, cannot be taken in the least bit seriously. My remarks are by no means a campaign for pedantic, 'anal' translation, but a question about what is lost – and translation is always a

---

[41] *SS* 8, 4 (*Rabota aktyora nad rolyu – An Actor's Work on a Role*), 360.   [42] Ibid., 412.   [43] Ibid.

Several Problems of Translation 105

matter of losing something to save something else. For, as should by now be clear, losing the 'spirit' and the 'soul' shifts the substance, contours, nuances, inflections and direction of Stanislavsky's thought, reducing its richness concerning the human being-actor, what kind of theatre, precisely, is at stake (it is the theatre of *perezhivaniye*) and, in general, Stanislavsky's worldview, which his religious sentiments encompass. Yet Stanislavsky's worldview is the *binding* component of his life's work. To choose to lose it is a kind of gagging.

Several cases in point may have to suffice. It was observed previously (note 3 to Chapter 1) that Benedetti translates 'spiritual' in *My Life in Art* as 'mental'. It is translated systematically in this way throughout that book and, consequently, *dukh* is translated as 'mind', giving such phrases as 'mind and body' when Stanislavsky unequivocally means 'spirit and body'. 'Spirit', in Stanislavsky's worldview, is the qualitatively highest aspect of a human being and of humanity as such: it is, to repeat, the connection with the divine and the seat (if this term is adequate) of conscience and so of moral knowledge and discernment of what is right and good. This is fundamental for understanding the nuances of Stanislavsky's worldview and how it informs his observations on the theatre. Take, for instance, his evaluation of Ibsen's Stockman – an 'idealist' who acts on his conscience – in terms of the 'motive forces of his spiritual life'.[44] Benedetti's terse rendition of this complete phrase as 'mental drives' entails a considerable loss of Stanislavsky's sense and inflection, and misses, as well, his compassionate perspective on the role, which he first performed in 1900. It sidelines, too, the human understanding he sought when playing Stockman, hoping that such an approach would guide the MAT's work in the future.

Equally, Benedetti translates adjectives derived from *dusha* as 'mental', and occasionally as 'psychological', which at least has the virtue of being related by its root to the ancient Greek word *psyche* (transliterated) for 'soul'. Stanislavsky wrote 'psychological' when he meant 'psychological', although Gurevich may have also suggested it as a replacement for 'spiritual' in certain places of *An Actor's Work on Himself* – a substitution his official editors during the 1930s, as well as posthumously, may well have also made. However, the details of editing, like those of censorship, cannot be known with absolute certainty, any more than can the self-censorship that Stanislavsky is said to have exercised. Smeliansky quotes from Stanislavsky's draft letter to Gurevich (not sent) in which he states:

---

[44] *Moya zhizn*, 296; *My Life in Art*, 254.

'To my mind, the greatest danger of the book [*An Actor's Work on Himself*] is "the creation of the life of the human spirit" (you are not allowed to speak of the spirit)' and, among other dangerous words, he cites 'the word *soul*' (Stanislavsky's italics).[45] Smeliansky states that Stanislavsky was able to write this 'despite his usual display of political naivety' – Smeliansky's customary judgement of Stanislavsky's reactions to events and his ways of dealing with them.

'Naivety' is not the word for Stanislavsky's clear sight on what might cause trouble. In the event, 'spirit' and 'soul' survived in publication, but this vocabulary, just like Stanislavsky's 'psychological', predates his return from the Art Theatre's tours in the United States and Europe in August 1924, a year that was a turning point in the politics of the Soviet Union. Lenin died in January of the same year, after which political positions and agendas hardened considerably, while censorship followed suit. In such conditions, Stanislavsky's ethical obduracy in sticking to what was *true for him* from his old era proved to be his safeguard against the revolutionary new one. Smeliansky's remark that to follow Gurevich point by point would have 'meant the death of his forthcoming book and of his life's work' is astute, but, Stanislavsky's moral stand against persuasion is, still, hardly a matter of naivety.[46] It could be called a matter of principle.

Patterns of translation similar to those cited from *My Life in Art* occur in *An Actor's Work*. Among salient examples regarding 'spiritual' are 'physical and mental sides' (repeated from *My Life in Art*) and 'mental communication' for 'spiritual communion'.[47] Then there are 'mental energy', when Stanislavsky speaks of 'spiritual strength', and 'mental and physical material for the role', which suggests that the actor searches for material closer to the mind and reason than to the 'spirit-soul'.[48] Stanislavsky, by contrast, speaks of the 'spiritual' material for the role because that is where the creation of a role lies. The notion of 'spirit-soul', as Zatvornik's terminology identifies it, is not core exclusively to *An Actor's Work on Himself* but to Stanislavsky's entire train of thought. Of great consequence is how 'communication' for Stanislavsky's *obshcheniye* appears throughout Benedetti's translation, *An Actor's Work*; and it is in the very title of his chapter 10. Whereas *obshcheniye* refers to the personal contacts, connection, interpersonal awareness and the mutual *relations* between people who

---

[45] Afterword to *An Actor's Work*, 689, and also for the quotation following (no date provided for the letter); 687–90 for Smeliansky's incisive commentary on the issue of censorship. See also his preface to the collected letters SS 9, 7, 34–9.

[46] *An Actor's Work*, 688.   [47] Ibid., 147, 239 and 245, also for 'communication'.

[48] Ibid., 461, 584.

Several Problems of Translation

'come together'. *Obshcheniye* also contains the idea of a value-shared, 'spiritual' gathering and communion, which is how Stanislavsky conceives of an ensemble, and he frequently speaks of *obshcheniye* when speaking of ensemble work. 'Communion' is far from being synonymous with 'communication'.

Benedetti translates 'soul' and its cognates with his usual 'mind' and 'psychology' and, rather surprisingly, as 'personality'. Thus, for example, in a discussion of how the 'subjective experiences' of different people playing the same role is of 'great importance for the Supertask' (*sverkhzadacha*), Benedetti translates Tortsov as explaining that the supertask is 'dead' unless it finds 'a response in the actor's personality'.[49] 'Personality' is a considerable deviation from Stanislavsky's sense and meaning. What Stanislavsky writes is not 'personality', for which there is a word in Russian, but 'in the actor's heart' (*dusha*). *Dusha* for 'heart' is interchangeable with 'soul', as was noted earlier, so perhaps 'heart and soul' – a perfectly acceptable expression in English – would have been a solution if 'soul' on its own was cause for discomfort. Or else 'inner life', or 'psychic life' would have adequately conveyed Stanislavsky's meaning, since he uses these words quite frequently when he speaks of the complex entity that is the human being in the actor, who has an 'inner life' from which the role is shaped. He uses them again, when he speaks of the human being in the actor who is in the role.[50] It is this doubling up of actor-in-life and actor-in-role working together that an actor needs to articulate and manifest – make 'external', in Stanislavsky's vocabulary. What the actor makes visible is what the spectator's five senses perceive and seize; and the 'sixth' sense – intuition, which is of such importance to Stanislavsky – seizes what the other senses miss.

To see the nuances of the language Stanislavsky uses is to understand that his practice and thinking are far more supple and subtle than we have been taught. It is relevant to point out an additional factor of translation, which may appear to be only a matter of grammatical fastidiousness, but which really does have an impact on Stanislavsky's meaning. At issue is the

---

[49] Ibid., 308–9.

[50] On the issue of 'psychological' and 'psychic', attention should be drawn to Benedetti's choice of 'psychological' for the titles of chapters 12 and 13 of *An Actor's Work*. The titles of both chapters have 'inner psychological drives'. Stanislavsky, by contrast, writes 'psychic'. There is no denying the particular difficulty of translation in this instance, but there is, nevertheless, a subtle distinction between the two terms. The problems and intricacies of translation evoked in the pages above have been of concern to me for many years. See brief indications in my review of *My Life in Art* and *An Actor's Work*, *TDR*, 54, No. 205 (2010), 172–4.

use of a slash. Benedetti's slash in 'human being/actor' offers an alternative, 'and/or', not introduced by Stanislavsky's hyphen in 'human being-actor'. Stanislavsky's hyphenated noun leaves no doubt whatsoever as to the inseparable connection between the two entities, which cannot negotiate 'or'.

These few examples of a larger problem that concerns not simply the translation of words but of a worldview steeped in cultural subtleties and resonances raise issues bigger than 'translation' alone. Translators, too, have cultural contexts, and necessarily translate from their time (since they live in no other). More precisely, they translate from the vantage point of the social groups with which they are associated (or can sociologically be identified) and whose values they share in their time; and this has a direct bearing on how translators translate. The habitus of social groups, moreover, through which such values are formed and networked, can operate on individuals in them invisibly and can do so, Bourdieu repeats in most of his books, because they are absorbed and become second nature – 'incorporated' is his word to indicate that they are indeed *in carne*, made flesh in social time.[51]

Yet, translating to the letter of contemporary times is not always beneficial to what is being translated. This is so because the risk of traducement is greater when language choices are primarily governed by contemporary *mores*, prejudices and fashions. Bella Merlin cites her conversation with an assistant to Benedetti who reports that decisions regarding the translation of 'spirit' and 'soul' were in part determined by his (their?) desire to 'avoid allusions to ideology that from an English-speaking perspective might seem too religious'.[52] 'English-speaking perspective' is a large claim, given just how many Anglophones there are in England (let alone the United Kingdom), not to mention the Anglophone world. Then, whose perspective among English-speakers is at stake? Is it that of a specific social group, ethnic group, gender group, social class or lone individual who cannot be placed altogether accurately according to sociological criteria? Stanislavsky, we saw, could be socially placed accurately. Furthermore, what if his allusions *were* religious, as is manifestly the case? And when is 'religious' *too* religious?

[51] See *Méditations pascaliennes*, Paris: Le Seuil, 1997, 158–68, for example, the book in which Bourdieu probably most fully articulates this aspect of his theory of habitus.

[52] '"Where's the spirit gone?" The complexities of translation and the nuances of terminology in *An Actor's Work* and an actor's work', *Stanislavski Studies* 1, 2012, 12.

Well... the justification Merlin received might be considered a disservice both to an 'English-speaking perspective' and Stanislavsky's 'Russian' one. It might also be considered somewhat presumptuous, as might several comments from Merlin's interlocutor regarding so-called linguistic justifications for the substitutions of 'mind' and its cognates for 'spirit' and 'soul'. A considerable number of other substitutions, which have not been singled out for attention in this brief discussion, diverge from Stanislavsky's meaning in a similar way. It might be noted that such seemingly minor mishaps as 'mental image' for Stanislavsky's 'visualization' are actually major ones, and they also finish up by underestimating, when not distorting, his meaning. 'Visualization', for instance, is not a flat picture of a finished 'mental image', but the intentional process of making images in sequence frame by frame so as to *see* them, by which they become concrete for the actor as he/she does a series of actions; and this seeing is as vital for acting naturally as it is for helping a partner to *see* how to interact with these actions. Merlin declares that 'Stanislavski's philosophies had already suffered under the knife of Soviet censorship' and expresses her uneasiness 'at the thought that in twenty-first-century Britain we might have added to the strata of censorship.'[53] Indeed.

Yoga; the Superconscious; Inspiration and Orthodoxy

The preceding sections have discussed core aspects of the System as they relate to Stanislavsky's worldview. Now it is time to look at several more in terms of the various stages of its early history. It is all too easy to forget that, with the System, Stanislavsky was inventing a theatre language unlike any other in use in the theatres in Europe and in countries which Europeans had colonized and where Europeans had settled, the United States being the largest of them. His invention of a specific language for wherever it could be adopted was a constituent part of his life's work. And while Stanislavsky feared the word 'system' because it suggested fixed rules and rigidity, whereas he not only envisaged but also practised flexibility and continual change, he was impelled, like any explorer, to articulate and name what he was discovering.

One of the first written signs of his future System appears in Stanislavsky's letter of 1902, where he writes that he wants to 'put together something of a guide for beginner actors ... a kind of grammar of dramatic art'.[54] He had thought, during his days at the Society of Art and Literature,

---

[53] Ibid., 14.   [54] *SS* 9, 7, 458, letter to Vera Kotlyarevskaya.

how he might do something like this to help his fellow amateur actors, but, above all, he wanted to correct himself. What he saw as his failings were the seeds of his 'grammar', nurtured by the lessons he had learned from working *on* himself in the most complete sense of this phrase. It was precisely his capacity to be his own guinea-pig that motivated him to question his and Nemirovich-Danchenko's method of directing actors according to a pre-constructed plan. In 1903, his partner's rehearsals of *The Pillars of Society* precipitated Stanislavsky's outburst on how the directing method they had adopted from the first days of the MAT was stifling the actors' free creativity, exactly as was happening to him as he performed his role in this Ibsen addition to their repertoire. His envisaged 'grammar', while designed for acting 'correctly', was at the same time a means for releasing the creativity that was in all actors, but was different according to each 'nature' in each case.

Stanislavsky's rebellion, as much against his own bad theatre habits as Nemirovich-Danchenko's imposition of a grid for actors, was kept under control up to and including the MAT's successful European tour of 1906. Nemirovich-Danchenko's severe admonishments to Stanislavsky from 1904 to 1906, as Stanislavsky gradually moved away from production plans, about their professional necessity – anything else was amateur – had weighed heavily on his consciousness, concerned as he was about how actors fared when they were subjected to such severe constraints.[55] The giddying acclaim of the tour had temporarily turned his head, but it was unable to cover up his lack of 'systematization' and the need to 'lay down the foundations' of his theatre art.[56] The closure at the end of 1905 of the Povarskaya studio run by Meyerhold – the first exploration of creative principles that might have fed into his potential 'grammar' – only reinforced Stanislavsky's sense of the gaping holes in his theatre project. Meyerhold, sharing Stanislavsky's interest in the creative dynamics of actions in the studio – the germ of his eventual 'method of physical action' – had also abandoned the very idea of production plans in it.

In 1906, painting himself as a Werther from Goethe's gallery of Romantic heroes as he sat on a coastal rock in Finland – such is his opening of the last part of *My Life in Art* – Stanislavsky reflects on his loss of concentration and excitement when performing Stockman in

---

[55] For Nemirovich-Danchenko's somewhat browbeating objections to Stanislavsky's innovation – for that is exactly what it was – see Radishcheva, *Stanislavsky i Nemirovich-Danchenko. 1897–1908*, 270–1.

[56] *Moya zhizn*, 293.

Yoga; the Superconscious; Inspiration and Orthodoxy 111

Berlin – a role unanimously acclaimed, only five years earlier, to be one of his best. He had replaced the 'living memories' that had shaped the role with 'the mechanical signs of non-existent feelings';[57] and this, among related reflections, forced him to reconsider the 'mysterious' spontaneity of inspiration and ask whether there were 'technical ways for establishing the creative state'.[58] Stanislavsky's was not a request for inspiration by 'artificial means', but for the 'soil in myself' and the 'atmosphere' in which the inspiration belonging to the creative state could be prepared rather than happen haphazardly. The actor's mastery of 'technical ways' was important so that the requisite 'soil' could repeatedly grow what had been grown in it once before, although not mechanically, but afresh. The question of how a role could be played, as if for the first time, when it had already been played many times before, was a central question of his System.

By the time of Stanislavsky's crisis of awareness in Finland, his 'grammar' had become rather more than a manual, if ever it was only this plodding ambition. A good number of the MAT actors and also administrative staff who were sceptical of his project right from the start began assiduously to poke fun at his 'system' (Stanislavsky's quotation marks alluded to criticism of it). They had ample opportunity to do so when he experimented in 1907 with what he called 'the devices of inner technique' at the time in *The Drama of Life* by Knut Hamsun and Leonid Andreyev's *The Life of Man*. Unprompted by the scepticism of others, Stanislavsky concluded that the stillness he had forced on the actors in *The Drama of Life* – this device was to control gestures so as to let the actors journey inwardly – had induced very strong tension and constrained their bodies and feelings, while the simplicity that he had hoped to attain was without substance.[59]

Sulerzhitsky was the principal director of these two productions while Stanislavsky worked on himself, with the actors and with Sulerzhitsky, exploring the paths opening up in these early forays into the System. Amused, ironic and at times aggressive criticism (Nemirovich-Danchenko, perturbed by the perceived failure of these productions, tended towards the latter) continued up to and during the rehearsals of *A Month in the Country* in 1909.

Rehearsals of Ivan Turgenev's play proceeded according to Stanislavsky's wishes, but not smoothly. Knipper-Chekhova found adapting to his new way of acting particularly difficult (Stanislavsky coached her independently to allay her fears), while he tried his colleagues' patience by

---

[57] Ibid., 296–7.   [58] Ibid., 299 and 300 for the following citations.   [59] Ibid., 306 and 310.

persisting in directing in a new way, as well, that is, without a pre-established production plan so that director and actor, together, could follow the creative process in its very development. This unprecedented situation ushered in, for the first time, the Stanislavskian actor who was a co-creator both of the role and the production in hand – an ideal to which he kept for the rest of his life in his attempts to oust the old-style 'actor-dependent', borrowing Irina Vinogradskaya's insightful epithet.[60]

The huge public and critical success of *A Month in the Country* when it was premiered in December was seen generally, within the company and outside it, as a vindication of Stanislavsky's System. In effect, congratulations were premature, since the System's 'systematization' was only in its preliminary stages, and the wounds received had to be healed. In January 1910, Stanislavsky wrote a report of seventeen points to Nemirovich-Danchenko and the MAT Board summarizing what had happened and explaining why the System should be officially adopted as the MAT's working method.[61] The System would be a 'compass at the service of the company for many years'. He knew about the hurtful criticisms of him (a 'scatterbrain', a 'madman', a 'dreamer' and 'capricious'), but he should be given a chance to put his ideas into practice. After all, some of his attempts had turned out well and where he went wrong was not wasted, since making mistakes and learning from them 'was the only way forward'. Nemirovich-Danchenko who was known to have been a sceptic, often an especially uncharitable one, and who was unhappy about letting Stanislavsky loose on the company – on top of it he wanted to bring in new, young students for the System – saw an opportunity for a trade-off by which Stanislavsky would cede his managerial 'share', leaving him sole managerial control of the company. Stanislavsky was to find out afterwards that the deal was disadvantageous to him where running what was to become the First Studio was concerned.

The year 1909 was a watershed for other reasons. In June Stanislavsky headed a document 'my system', which appears to be his first recorded use of the term.[62] The handwritten document contains twenty-two points, grouped into two sections. The first starts with the apposition of the 'theatre of representation' (*teatr predstavleniya*, which also contains the idea of 'presentation') and the 'theatre of emotional experiencing' (*teatr perezhivaniya*), followed by three points on 'the correct and incorrect state [of being] for the creative state'. The remaining points titled 'the

---

[60] *Stanislavsky repetiruyet* (*Stanislavsky Rehearses*), Moscow: Moscow Art Theatre, 2000, 17.
[61] *SS* 8, 5, 456–8. [62] Moscow Art Theatre Museum, K. S. No. 628.

Yoga; the Superconscious; Inspiration and Orthodoxy   113

development of the correct state' include the 'relaxation of muscular tension', 'exercises for the relaxation of muscles', 'affective experiencing', 'affective memory', 'circle of concentration', 'relations' (*obshcheniye*), 'concentration of thoughts' and 'transmission of feelings through words'. There is enough in this sketchiest of Stanislavsky's documents to show that his System in embryo was within the same purview as the baggy construction of pages that struggled to grow into Stanislavsky's publications.

With no books yet published to stake his claims to the System and no school that he could really call his own at the Art Theatre – the MAT school, established in 1901, was not under his jurisdiction – Stanislavsky turned for help in 1909 to Sulerzhitsky and the A. I. Adashev school, founded and run by MAT actors, whose most promising students usually graduated to the MAT. Sulerzhitsky taught the System in its preliminary version for three years at Adashev's, piquing his student Vakhtangov's hungry interest in this semi-mythological beast unofficially shunted out of the Art Theatre. The First Studio, when it was opened in September 1912, was in effect an upper-grade surrogate for a school and, better still, the Master Class that the Art Theatre could not provide, for, although Stanislavsky had insisted that his System be taught officially at the MAT, that System, lacking absolute support, moved sideways into the First Studio to seek its full potential.

Here, it flourished under Sulerzhitsky's charge, Vakhtangov hot on his heels as a champion instructor of the System. Stanislavsky gave classes irregularly but with complete commitment, while taking a lively interest in the Studio's activities. After 1916, Vakhtangov taught the System to a group he had gathered around him elsewhere in Moscow, later to become the Third Studio, and at the Habima in 1918, thereby extending the role the First Studio played in the System's dissemination and evolution as it passed from hand to hand. Refinements of the System came through tests of its principles in practice, while its practitioners' individual interpretations additionally modified them. This was to be the case in all the studios that followed as the System continued to grow and change.

Yoga, which was fashionable in Russia in the 1900s and 1910s, was an important activity of the First Studio. Caution, however, is necessary when assessing how much it may have contributed to the System and what, exactly, this contribution was. Sergei Tcherkasski quotes Stanislavsky on muscular tension and refers to his experiments on such tension at the Studio in 1913 as evidence of the influence of yoga; and he cites the independent accounts of two Studio members, Vera Solovyova and Boris Sushkevich, who note that exercises involved sending and receiving rays of energy. Solovyova recalls that Stanislavsky spoke of *prana*, while Richard Boleslavsky, another prominent Studio member, recollects discussion about 'Yogi culture applied to the Art of Acting'.[63] In another of his studies, Tcherkasski cites Yelena Polyakova's claim that yoga exercises had helped First Studio actors to attain 'absolute concentration', to '"lock themselves into a circle"', and to practise '"establishing the creative state"' by training their powers of observation.[64] She detects the influence of yoga in Stanislavsky's notion of the 'circle of attention'.[65]

This is all well and good as far as exercises for training this or that capacity are concerned. However, when it comes to the thought within the System, the danger of overstating the role of yoga in Stanislavsky's practice becomes apparent. Tcherkasski argues that 'yoga gave Stanislavsky a reliable technique for the development of his elements' [of the System];[66] and he selects four 'elements' as cases in point – *obshcheniye*, attention, visualization and '*ya yesm*'. The incongruence here needs to be dealt with in the light of the preceding sections of this chapter where *obshcheniye*, attention, visualization and '*ya yesm*' are shown to be *profoundly Orthodox* ideas that carry their own means of doing within a way of being. Means of doing constitute 'technique' but the 'technique', say, of *obshcheniye* is developed through an understanding congruent with the thought and feeling that shape the doing; and the thought and feeling are not reducible to 'technique', out of context, on its own. The same holds for yoga.

A summary of these ideas, in the order presented, will prevent misunderstanding. *Obshcheniye* is the kindly, loving relation between self and others that binds people together in work and play, and establishes communion between them. *Obshcheniye* in the theatre additionally involves sensitive awareness and responsiveness to a given partner, without losing sight of that partner when a piece of dialogue is finished, and without losing sight of the

---

[63] *Stanislavsky and Yoga*, trans. Vreneli Farber, Abingdon: Routledge Icarus Publishing Enterprise, 2016, 32–4. See Stanislavsky on the emission of rays of energy in *SS* 8, 2, 268–72; *An Actor's Work*, 245–51. Boleslavsky emigrated to the United States in 1922 after a brief stay in Poland, and Solovyova in 1935, after some six years at the Lithuanian National Theatre. Sushkevich remained in the Soviet Union to pursue a noteworthy directing career, first at the Art Theatre and then in Leningrad.

[64] *Masterstvo aktyora: Stanislavsky, Boleslavsky, Strasberg*, St Petersburg: Russian State Institute of Scenic Arts, 2016, 80; Polyakova's book is *Stanislavsky*, Moscow: Iskusstvo, 1977, 302.

[65] *Teatr Sulerzhitskogo. Etika. Estetika. Rezhissura* (*Sulerzhitsky's Theatre: Ethics, Aesthetics, Directing*), Moscow: Agraf, 2006, 184.

[66] Ibid., 81.

Yoga; the Superconscious; Inspiration and Orthodoxy 115

other protagonists in action on the stage.[67] Second, 'attention' is more than individual focus. It is a relational attitude to others that involves thoughtfulness towards them and an awareness of their sensitivities, needs and wants. This kind of 'attention' is the relational I-you essential for communion, as well as for acting with partners in the theatre. It is necessary for ensemble unity. Third, 'visualization' is intrinsic to the practice of painting icons, and so of rendering images concrete. Witness Tortsov's advice to his students in *An Actor's Work on Himself, Part I* to visualize concretely what they are going to do, sequence by sequence, as on a reel of film when it is slowed down and projected frame by frame on a screen.[68] '*Ya yesm*', at the heart of Orthodoxy, defeats, in its plenitude, co-option to yoga 'technique'. It is crucial to place these four elements, as understood by Stanislavsky, in the context of Orthodoxy above all else and not assume that they can be coerced into explanation through yoga.

All four are faculties that can be cultivated through meditation, for which there is a long monastic tradition in Christian Orthodoxy (even though the term 'meditation' is not used). This includes the meditating through breathing intrinsic to Hesychasm, a mystical strand within Orthodoxy, going back to antiquity. 'Meditation' in Hesychasm can take the form of incantatory repetition – often extending into transcendent silence – of the Russian equivalent of the prayer *Kyrie eleison* ('Lord have mercy') in Christian liturgy generally. The incantation 'Lord have mercy' as a single phrase is integral to Orthodox liturgy. Hesychasm was not a secret practice, and devout Orthodox believers like Stanislavsky were well aware of the benefits of the 'wise' prayer, as it is still known in Russian Orthodoxy. Sulerzhitsky reported that the Dukhobors sat for a long time in the morning in silence and then chanted psalm after psalm to prepare for the work of the day.[69] Stanislavsky, who had read his account of the Dukhobor saga, could easily have asked him more about this particular type of meditative practice, derived from old forms of Orthodoxy.

Stanislavsky is known to have taken whatever was useful for helping actors to come to grips with acting. Solovyova observes that, other than

---

[67] See additionally L. N. Novitskaya, *Uroki vdokhnoveniya. Sistema K. S. Stanislavskogo i deystviye* (*Lessons in Inspiration: K. S. Stanislavsky's System and Action*), Moscow: All-Russian Theatre Society, 1984, 319–31. Novitskaya was among Stanislavsky's last director-student-assistants of his Opera-Dramatic Studio, and her fine understanding of *obchsheniye* and the importance Stanislavsky attributed to it for acting and thus his System is backed by exercises taken from or modelled on his own.

[68] *SS* 8, 2, 87; *An Actor's Work*, 76.

[69] *To America with the Doukhobors*, trans. Michael Kalmakoff and introduction by Mark Mealing, Regina: Canadian Plains Research Centre, University of Regina, 1982, 97.

prana emanation and reception of energy rays at the First Studio, classes at the MAT for young company actors were 'in singing, diction, recitation of prose and poetry, fencing and body movement', and the latter 'was of three kinds: classic [*sic*] ballet, Dalcroze and, later on, the Duncan technique, taught by a former student of Isadora's'.[70] Stanislavsky visited Émile Jaques-Dalcroze for the second time in 1913 in Hellerau to understand Dalcroze eurhythmics better at first hand; and Hellerau was an artists' colony cum experimental workers' commune whose utopian foundations he would not have failed to appreciate, given the habitus of his large extended family and circle of close friends. The Hellerau ethos of self-improvement echoed on a boutique scale the visions of perfectibility – self-realization – driving the various social as well as esoteric movements of the Russian Silver Age in different directions. Stanislavsky connected deeply with Tolstoy's idea of spiritual self-realization, and the idea of the actor's self-realization on an ascending scale pervades his System – as mastery of technique ('the more outstanding the actor, the more he is interested in the technique of his art'), but most of all, Stanislavsky emphasizes, in terms of the evolution and transcendence of the 'life of the human spirit', since 'nine-tenths of the actor's activity is to feel his role spiritually'.[71]

Stanislavsky's years of incandescent learning from 1909 onwards are part of what Tcherkasski, in his exposition of the System's development, describes as its 'analytical phase'. Its second, 'synthesizing phase' – also Tcherkasski's words – were set off by two catastrophic events for Stanislavsky-actor:[72] his 1915 monumental failure, in his own judgement, in the role of Salieri in Pushkin's *Mozart and Salieri*; and his humiliating failure in rehearsals during the 1916–17 season in the role of Rostanev in *The Village of Stepanchikovo*. Stanislavsky had played Rostanev splendidly at the Society of Art and Literature in 1891, yet here he was, floundering. Nemirovich-Danchenko, his co-director of the MAT production, took the role away from him without ceremony after Stanislavsky's excruciating but unsuccessful efforts to overcome his various blocks. According to Tcherkasski, 'Stanislavsky paralyzed his mighty creative nature'.[73] The reason? Probably not solely because he had turned himself into the object of analysis of his System, as Tcherkasski suggests, but especially

---

[70] Paul Gray, 'The Reality of Doing: Interviews with Vera Soloviova, Stella Adler, and Sanford Meisner' in *Stanislavski and America*, ed. Erika Munk, Greenwich, CT: Fawcett Publications, 1967, 202.

[71] *Moya zhizn*, 402–3 for both citations. This is an important example of Stanislavsky's 'spiritually', which Benedetti translates as 'psychologically'. See *My Life in Art*, 345.

[72] *Masterstvo aktyora*, 88.   [73] Ibid., 89.

Yoga; the Superconscious; Inspiration and Orthodoxy   117

because he must have done so continually *while he was playing* and this would have been the vital issue. There can be little doubt that, by intervening rationally in this way in the flow of playing, he would have cut the arteries of his imagination and his subconscious and, hence, stopped their flow.

The conclusion to reach might well be this one: the principles of analytical research were possible within the teaching process, but impossible during the very quick of creative composition, when, as Stanislavsky would say, the oceanic depths of the subconscious allowed creativity to well up and surge forth and find itself. He explains to regional directors in 1936 that an actor transits into the subconscious from its threshold in this way: 'It's as if an actor stands on the ocean shore. One wave wets his feet, a second rises to his knees, a third – higher, a fourth seizes him and sweeps him away.'[74] Stanislavsky's poetic image is elemental, from nature – a key point of reference in his worldview, as the preceding pages have shown. And here it is imperative to pause. His notion of the subconscious leaned on yoga in so far as he took up Ramacharaka's image of a sack full of thoughts that was jumbled up and put away so that resolutions could emerge from the subconscious.[75] The Soviet editors of *An Actor's Work on a Role*, among them Grigory Kristi (Chapter 4), the author of the book's explanatory notes, acknowledge Stanislavsky's borrowing.[76] Stanislavsky, for his part, is evasive, speaking generally of the origins of his thinking about the subconscious in the terms just cited in 'Indian yoga' (such as he might have understood it via Ramacharaka-Atkinson).[77]

Ambivalence arises. Stanislavsky intermittently appears to use two other terms, the 'unconscious' and the 'superconscious' (*sverkhsoznaniye*), as near-synonyms for the 'subconscious'. Stanislavsky's Soviet editors imply that his idea of the 'superconscious', which they take as having come from yoga, is that particular part of the subconscious that Stanislavsky refers to as 'inspiration'.[78] Otherwise, they assert, the 'content' of the 'superconscious' and the 'subconscious' is 'the same' and, Stanislavsky, having realized this, dropped the former at the end the 1920s and spoke only of the 'subconscious' thereafter.[79] In actual fact, he did not confuse the two, since the 'superconscious' was, for him, most definitely in the realm of inspiration. Furthermore, he thought of 'inspiration' as the intangible,

---

[74] *SS* 9, 6, 519.   [75] *SS* 8, 4, 158.   [76] Ibid., 496–7.   [77] Ibid., 158.

[78] Ibid., 495. The editors quote Stanislavsky's renunciation of 'inspiration', when he says 'I am not a mystic' in *SS* 8, 3, 314. Stanislavsky's remarks here are nothing if not dissembling, and point to the censorship which Gurevich had advised or which subsequent editors imposed upon him. Or else they indicate his feeble self-censorship. Perhaps all three censorships are involved.

[79] Ibid., 497 and 495.

difficult-to-rationalize aspect of creativity in the 'human spirit' that was close to God, in both art and life, and this came from Orthodoxy, not yoga.

The 'superconscious' needs to be teased out a little more. Stanislavsky's Soviet editors are incorrect in imputing to him the idea that the 'superconscious' was part of the 'subconscious'. There is neither clear nor definitive evidence of just how much Stanislavsky understood about yoga, but it is relatively clear that his 'superconscious' was much closer to his idea of inspiration descending upon the actor when he/she is fully there, 'present', in the moment – Stanislavsky's 'creative "now"' – and in the radiant awareness of '*ya yesm*' – 'I am', discussed several pages earlier.[80] This is the transcendental state of that moment of light and lucidity, or of proximity to the divine 'spirit', which is defined as heightened awareness, enlightenment or ecstasy (Stanislavsky's word). It is that moment when earthly time falls away and the perceiver perceives non-earthly time, or, in yogic terms, non-everyday time. What Stanislavsky was driving at could be put in the following way. Creativity sources its inspirational energy in the superconscious, while it sources its foundational energy and material in the subconscious. This means that, while they are linked, the 'superconscious' is not synonymous with the 'subconscious'. Stanislavsky: 'It seems that a thousand years ago, they [yogis] sought the same thing that we are looking for, only we are going into creativity, but they – into their other world.'[81] His key word is 'creativity'.

What, then, was the third term, the 'unconscious', for him? Whyman points out that the German philosopher Edouard von Hartmann's *Philosophy of the Unconscious*, published in 1869, was 'enormously influential in Russia over the next decades', and that Stanislavsky's notion of the subconscious 'equates to' Hartmann's 'psychological unconscious'.[82] This may have been the case very early in the piece, when Stanislavsky first began to grapple with these issues, but from towards the end of the 1920s or shortly afterwards, he limited 'unconscious' to mean mechanical reflex reactions without consciousness of the kind that Pavlov was studying.[83] His 'subconscious', then, is distinct from the 'unconscious' – in Russian, literally, 'without consciousness'. Galendeyev firmly subscribes to this distinction, as is evident in how he teaches the MDT actors in St

---

[80] See on the 'creative "now"' *Besedy K. S. Stanislavskogo v Studiya Bolshogo teatra v 1918–1922*, 72–3.
[81] Quoted in O. A. Radishcheva, *Istoriya teatralnykh otnosheniya. 1917–1938*, Moscow: Artist. Director. Theatre, 1999, 61.
[82] *The Stanislavsky System of Acting*, 89.   [83] *SS* 8, 3, 496.

Yoga; the Superconscious; Inspiration and Orthodoxy   119

Petersburg as well as from his book cited in my preceding pages. He also affirms this in my conversation with him cited in those pages.

Stanislavsky, always ready to seek verification in science – even if this was contradictory when it came to the non-provable – refers to help from two sources for his thoughts about the subconscious: the North American experimental psychologist Helmar Gates, who argued that the subconscious accounted for 90 per cent of a human being's mental life; and the English psychiatrist Henry Maudsley, who believed that 'consciousness does not fulfil even one-tenth of the functions ascribed to it'.[84] Stanislavsky most probably drew on these statistics when he claimed that nine-tenths of an actor's activity was taken up with feeling his/her role spiritually.

Stanislavsky's paralysis over Rostanev can be interpreted through the shortcomings of 'mental life', suggesting that he would have done far better to trust to his subconscious than to his analytical reason when he performed this role. Demidov was categorical in his judgement that the System suffered from analytical rationalism through and through, and that its division into 'isolated' elements crippled the flow of the creative process instead of encouraging it.[85] Demidov appears not to have discussed Stanislavsky's failure in *The Village of Stepanchikovo* in print, but he recalls Stanislavsky's 1891 success in the same role as that of a quintessentially 'emotional actor' (his other types being 'the imitator' and the 'affective actor'), and asks how an actor of this kind could have come up with a '"system"' that gave such importance '**to reasoning, analysis and imperativity**' (in bold in translation)?[86] As for Salieri – Nikolay Efros, writing earlier on Stanislavsky's failure in the role, had blamed his '"theories"'.[87] Stanislavsky, when reflecting back on this traumatic event, took a practical view: he had miscalculated by speaking Pushkin's verse as if it were everyday speech, thus missing its strength, concision, musicality and precise rhythms.[88] He had missed, in other words, its poetic quality. If Salieri was a blow, Rostanev was a decisive one. Stanislavsky continued to play his old roles in the repertoire, but he never undertook a new role again.

It is clear that Stanislavsky's experimentation on himself in two roles that mattered greatly to him was negative. But these were years of intensive

---

[84] Ibid., 155. Whyman observes that 'these statistics are of doubtful accuracy'. See *The Stanislavsky System of Acting*, 87.
[85] *Nikolai Demidov*, 138–9 and 483–5.   [86] Ibid., 104–5 and 139.
[87] *Zhizn i tvorchestvo*, Vol. 2, 464.   [88] Ibid., 369–71.

exploration of the System which, in 1916, also saw Stanislavsky rehearsing Rabindranath Tagore's *The King of the Dark Chamber*, a symbolic play, in the European terminology of the day, on the soul in conflict that he rated highly. He intended to broaden the MAT's acting range, but Tagore's hieratic expression was unsuited to actors who had become accustomed to the cadences of Chekhov and to the structures of the everyday in the other new-theatre dramatists of their repertoire – Tolstoy, Gorky, Ibsen and Hauptmann. Tagore was to become a friend of Nikolay Roerich, a noted archaeologist who was widely read in the Vedic scriptures as well as in the later Hindu sacred texts, and whose knowledge of Indian religious practices and 'Indian yoga' puts Stanislavsky's dilettantism in that area into perspective. Instrumental in setting up theosophy in Russia, Roerich was a friend and collaborator of Diaghilev's World of Art, co-creating *The Rite of Spring* for the Ballets Russes with Igor Stravinsky, while designing its ethnographically evocative costumes and painting its archaic Russian landscapes; and he designed *Peer Gynt* for Nemirovich-Danchenko's 1912 production at the Art Theatre. Stanislavsky's hopes for employing Roerich as a designer on a more permanent basis did not materialize.

The October Revolution broke out while Roerich was on a cure in Finland with his family. They did not return to St Petersburg, but relocated to London (where he befriended Tagore) and, after a period in New York, to India, settling in the Himalayas whose peaks he painted in a style reminiscent of his maquettes and drawings for *Peer Gynt*. The difference of his Himalayan paintings lay in their much brighter, iridescent colours, which reflected his immersion in spiritual enlightenment. Roerich and his scholar wife Yelena (who believed Ramacharaka was a dilettante) undertook extensive ethnographic expeditions not only throughout the Himalayas and into Tibet, but also into Buryatia and other significant centres of Buddhism in Siberia. They founded Agni-Yoga, whose 'Agni' alludes to the Vedic god of fire. Roerich was to send Stanislavsky greetings through a mutual acquaintance when the Art Theatre was in New York, and Stanislavsky warmly reciprocated by letter.[89] Contact ceased as the borders shut down before the termination of NEP.

---

[89] *Zhizn i tvorchestvo*, Vol. 3, 301.

The Theatre of Emotional Experiencing

A glimpse such as this one of the intelligentsia's interest in India, doubtless fanned by Tagore's receiving the Nobel Prize for Literature in 1913, can only confirm how the adventurous curiosity of the Silver Age brushed off on to the System. However, Stanislavsky also needed to situate the System in terms of the kind of theatre it would shape and serve, and this was the 'theatre of emotional experiencing'. His prescribed task meant differentiating between the latter and the other main 'trends' (Stanislavsky) of contemporary theatre, which Stanislavsky identified as 'stock-in-trade theatre' (*remeslo*) and the 'theatre of representation' (note again that the word *predstavleniye* also carries the idea of *presentation*). He had started his drafts on this subject in 1909, revising them until roughly 1922. In other words, he sifted through these three conceptual categories for a long time before adding the 'last' touches during his years with the Bolshoy Opera Studio from 1918 until the Art Theatre's departure for the United States. The conjuncture was not accidental in that Stanislavsky wanted to test the System with opera singers, who were conditioned even more than actors to act according to *remeslo*, and prove that the System could work for a genre other than spoken theatre.

Stanislavsky reasoned by comparison and elimination. *Remeslo* was not suitable for the System: it would forever stay in its clichés, and was another way of acting altogether. The theatre of representation, on the other hand, was 'on a knife edge', now slipping into *remeslo*, now into the truth and belief of emotional experiencing, which actors feel here and there when they prepare at home or rehearse, and occasionally in very early performances.[90] However, representational actors cannot sustain the living moments of creativity on the stage and have to fall back on performances previously performed hundreds of times, making sure to repeat the prototype skilfully. Consequently, the 'truthfulness' they project is not born in the actual moment of the creative process; it is only 'the *verisimilitude*' of the 'truthfulness of feeling'.[91] These are my italics to mark a distinction, fundamental for Stanislavsky, between verisimilitude, that is, a convincing copy, and the 'genuine, beautiful' moment, as Stanislavsky terms it, of creativity itself. Which is why he calls the verisimilitude type of theatre the 'theatre of representation'.

The third 'trend', the theatre of emotional experiencing, is quite different. Its actors 'feel the feelings [*chuvstva*, which are also 'sensations'] of the

---

[90] *SS* 8, 6, 70.   [91] Ibid., 66, and the following quotation.

role every time that it is created [not regurgitated] on the stage' – 'not only the first or second time, but also the thousandth time'.[92] 'Feeling feelings' is *perezhivaniye* and although the phrase seems to be pleonastic in English, it conveys the sense of the Russian word. These feelings felt on the stage, Stanislavsky insists, are not the same as the feelings of real life: the theatre and life cannot be confused.[93] Yet, in the theatre of *perezhivaniye*, they are truly felt, and this makes them alive. As Stanislavsky sees it, the quality of being alive of any role transcends genres and styles because what is at stake is not this or that theatre 'ism' (he cites constructivism, impressionism, symbolism), but true feeling rather than forced, sham or otherwise fabricated 'feeling'. What Stanislavsky is getting at is that the 'genuine, beautiful' moment of creativity makes it true.

Spectators, he argues, recognize this quality of true feeling, are infected by it and interact with it immediately.[94] In his remarkable pages on spectators, Stanislavsky details how the spectators' subconscious responsiveness brings out 'the most consequential part of the heart and soul' from the subconscious of the actors; and this makes the spectators their collaborators.[95] Collaboration of this kind can only occur in an 'atmosphere saturated with electricity', which both parties create between them. So much for the misbegotten idea that Stanislavsky was not interested in spectators and blocked them off by a 'fourth wall'. In any case – it cannot be harmful to repeat this – the 'fourth wall' in MAT parlance was the image for preventing actors from playing *to* audiences and thereby manipulating easy reactions from them in the manner of vaudevilles, variety shows and clown wizardry in circuses. Playing in such a vein belonged to representational actors.

The theatre of emotional experiencing is not defined solely by experiencing feeling. It is defined by everything engaged in the stage creative process, including, of course, the subconscious, all of which streams towards 'the higher spiritual, creative truth of artistic feeling from which the beautiful and elevated life of the human spirit is established'.[96] Lofty though this may sound, Stanislavsky brings it back to earth, observing that it was not possible for even the most System-developed actors to maintain the dynamics of this most difficult of achievements consistently. Such exceptional actors were obliged to mix the theatre of emotional

---

[92] Ibid., 76.
[93] Ibid. Stanislavsky here recalls the words of Tomaso Salvini. Salvini, Ernesto Rossi, Eleonora Duse and Fyodor Chaliapin are his model actors of *perezhivaniye*.
[94] Ibid., 85–8.   [95] Ibid., 86, and the following citation.   [96] Ibid.

The Theatre of Emotional Experiencing

experiencing with the theatre of representation and, sometimes, even with stock-in-trade.

Having worked so hard to distinguish both the System actor and the theatre of emotional experiencing, Stanislavsky is obliged to declare – he does so dispassionately – that his three theatre categories exist in 'their purest state only in theory'.[97] '*Only*' has to be heard and registered to perceive his awareness that practice is imperfect. *In* practice, the theatre of *perezhivaniye* is in an impure state – bound to be mixed – and this has to be accepted as the condition for its improvement.

Stanislavsky's drafts, when read attentively, show just how much his thinking on his three theatre categories underpins the System. All the points concerning them suggest that, for Stanislavsky, the theatre of emotional experiencing *enabled* the stage creative process and vice versa, and, since the stage creative process was *the* issue, this very process was the System's reason for being. The System, he argued, was 'a guide' to be 'looked over at home' but dropped completely on the stage because the System as such (Stanislavsky writes 'system') did not exist.[98] Reading what looks like a repudiation of his System – this, after so much effort! – may come as a shock, until one realizes that Stanislavsky is here alluding to his usual premise that 'there was only nature', from which the creativity in all human beings springs. Not content with just writing it in his drafts, while not knowing which of them would see the light of day, he makes a formal announcement in 1936 to a group of master actors and directors at the MAAT: 'There is only one system – organic creative nature. There is no other system.'[99] His System's purpose, then, as regards actors, was to coax that creativity out and nurture it, helping it to grow.

The realization that Stanislavsky was in search of neither recipes for actors nor theatre genres or styles but of the creative '*now, today, here*' of acting and performing goes a good way to explaining why he believed that his System was not confined to the psychological realism developed by the MAT, but was of general value across the board – in other words, unrestricted by, or to, theatre 'isms' and similarly partitioned theatre categories, old and new; and this, when taken as a principle, can encompass the 'new' of the twenty-first century, including forms that adamantly evade categorization. Given the terms of Stanislavsky's whole argument concerning the System, it is possible to see how the System could easily extend to dance, and especially to Duncan's (and similar) free-form dance. William Forsythe's 2018 assembly of four pieces called *A Quiet Evening of*

---

[97] Ibid., 89.   [98] *SS* 8, 3, 309.   [99] *SS* 9, 6, 531. See also Chapter 5, 'What Is a Director?'

Dance is an especially pronounced example, from within his choreography, of free-form contemporary dancing that is completely at ease, unforced, simple and natural – organic – and yet, quite evidently, is performed by supremely technically advanced dancers.

By the same token, the System could extend just as well to the highly toned and structured dance form that is ballet, precisely because ballet pivots on the feelings of the creative 'now' and ballet dancers stream the 'now' through their virtuosic technique. Stanislavsky saw the potential of the System for ballet only too well in his work and studies with the Bolshoy Theatre from the mid to the late 1920s and, again, when he resumed his research in the early 1930s, after his convalescence abroad.

An addendum is required. In a short piece, presumed to be from around 1928, Stanislavsky writes that his emphasis in earlier years on feeling and emotional experiencing by no means indicated that he had renounced the 'huge role' of intellect and will in the creative process. (Stanislavsky's word here *is* 'intellect'.) On the contrary, not only did he *not* renounce intellect and will, but he also considered them to be of 'equal value' to feeling and 'inseparable from feeling'.[100] Stanislavsky was possibly responding to the accusations levelled against him during, and after, the Art Theatre's tour in the United States that his work and thought were insufficiently materialist – too much on 'feeling' and not enough on the nitty-gritty of reasoning and reason. But he was also responding to his and his actors' call on the intellect and will without which feeling loses its contours.

Ethics and Discipline

Stanislavsky's understanding of ethics echoes Morozov's Old Believer Orthodoxy and Mamontov's lessons on the 'sacred task of art' in that it absorbs their idea – in his words – that 'we have to look at and see beauty' and that 'the secret of art is in how a thought turns into a beautiful artistic truth'.[101] This legacy was absorbed in the Russian liberal culture of the nineteenth century, and it refined Stanislavsky's view of the actor as a perfectible, educated, morally educated and cultured human being. In such an all-encompassing view, the truthfulness of emotions can be seen to be a moral component of the perfectible actor.

Stanislavsky saw ethics and discipline as part of the System from the very beginning because they were necessary for the actor's creative state, as well as for that of all collaborators. They provided the stable and calm working

---

[100] *SS* 8, 4, 459.   [101] *SS* 8, 6, 89.

Ethics and Discipline

conditions that creativity needed, especially within ensemble theatre and its commitment to harmonious ensemble work. And they encouraged *obshcheniye* in so far as *obshcheniye* mediated a kindly disposition towards others as well as respect for them. Ethics protected the conscience sustained by the spirit and, in this sense, ethics was integral to Stanislavsky's worldview, which saw the theatre bringing spiritual gifts for its makers, spectators and the health of society. Vasilyev takes a tragic view of Stanislavsky's pages on ethics, seeing in them 'the despair' of a man who, after all his great achievements, 'went back to the theatre with his small personal and utopian dream' and 'decided that ethics alone – the ethics of the theatre, ethical convictions – could save these uncouth stars [actors, directors] of the Olympic theatre firmament'.[102]

Vasilyev's touch of bitterness is understandable, given that he was wholly committed to his own ensemble theatre and had experienced his own disappointments, but he knew full well that Stanislavsky's dream was not so small. Furthermore, Stanislavsky's reflections on ethics and what they say obliquely about the conditions of working in the theatre in the 1930s and how people behaved in them suggest a diapason of thought bigger, also in its pertinence to other times and other places – now, too – than whatever 'despair' he may have felt personally about the theatre profession. His unfinished drafts on the subject, intended for a whole chapter in the second part of *An Actor's Work on Himself*, are largely in the dialogical structure of Stanislavsky's book.[103] His Soviet editors affirm that a number of the drafts in a notebook marked 'Ethics' were written around 1930 but were reviewed in 1933, while the sections at the front of their arrangement of the material date from 1937.[104] The latter concentrate on the backstage and workshops of a theatre – the first two areas listed below – with which a student actor as much as a seasoned one must be fully familiar in order to understand just how 'huge and complex an organization' the theatre really is.[105] Needless to say, Stanislavsky was thinking, first and foremost, about the Art Theatre.

Given his premise that ethics and discipline are essential for creativity, it would be a mistake to read these fragmented writings as being little more than sermons or a martinet's commands, even though Stanislavsky is strict about unethical and/or undisciplined conduct. Taken as a whole, they

---

[102] Antonio Attisani and Mario Biagini (eds.), *Opere e sentieri: Testimonianze e riflessioni sull'arte come veicolo* (*Works and Paths: Testimonials and Reflections on Art as Vehicle*), Rome: Bulzoni Editore, 2008, 89; (Vasilyev and Grotowski interviewed by Ferdinando Taviani, 14 July 1991.)

[103] *SS* 8, 3, 237–67; *An Actor's Work*, 552–78, where Benedetti reorganizes the sequence.

[104] Ibid., 474–5.   [105] Ibid., 238.

126   Actor

concern the actor from the various angles of his/her profession, and they cover the following main areas: knowledge of the backstage spaces and the location and dangers of its equipment – lighting rigs, whose heaviness can kill, scenery and how and where it moves, operations from the flies, dark spots, where actors exiting the stage can fall, and so on; knowledge of the location and activities of the carpentry, costume and other workshops; recognition that all those working in a given theatre constitute a team responsible for the success of a production and the welfare of its spectators; responsibility for self and others; obligation to co-workers; acknowledgement and maintenance of ensemble practice; the particular character of actor-director relations; the protection of the actors from theatre managers, accountants and administrators who 'exploit' (Stanislavsky's term) their vulnerable nature and underestimate the cost to their nerves of the long hours and intensity of their work. To top it all, such managers take the credit for the theatre's successes, when credit is due to the actors.

While Stanislavsky principally addresses the actor, either via Tortsov or an anonymous speaker, it is clear that the conversation includes anyone who disrupts the ethics of responsibility, reliability, attentiveness, efficiency and accuracy in the workplace. It could be a careless or lazy dresser, wig fitter, make-up artist or props person who fails to provide the requisite articles or otherwise botches his/her job. Then there is the lighting technician, who under-lights or over-lights an actor or an entire scene, and comparable cases of negligence that throw the contributions of designers, composers, musicians and other artists off course and damage the collaborative work on which an ensemble theatre like the Art Theatre depended. These are all breaches of ethics not only against colleagues, but also against the 'splendid art', which they 'serve'.[106]

Stanislavsky's pages detail the entire cohort of the support staff, from carpenter and doorman to the box-office and front-of-house staff and ushers on whom even the success of specific productions rely at the time of their performance. Spectators are very much at the mercy of the personnel whom they meet the moment they enter the theatre. Any unpleasant treatment affects their mood and, consequently, their receptivity to the performance. They are sensitive to such signs of disorganization and confusion as the late start of a show or noise from backstage. These and related aspects of poor management and uncooperative co-workers have a negative impact all round, most deleteriously of all on the actors tuning up for the stage creative state that lifts a performance to its heights.

---

[106] Ibid., 254.

Ethics and Discipline 127

If a performance does not reach spectators because the theatre is cold, dirty or noisy – failures of support staff – or because the actors are unenthusiastic, or light and sound cues are wrongly given – failures of technicians – then the 'theatre loses its social, artistic and cultural-educative meaning'.[107] In the concluding fragment, where this observation is to be found, Stanislavsky's own voice takes precedence over Socratic dialogue. By 'theatre' he means three things (and the word in Russian is polysemic in this way): a given theatre company, its labour and the 'art' that it makes. This same fragment contains his angriest criticism, unleashed on managers and administrators – those 'office clerks' who throw their weight about and lord it over the actors. These fragments, by shedding some light on working conditions in the 1930s, indicate why Stanislavsky felt compelled to insist on ethics and discipline in the theatre.

Discipline, for Stanislavsky, is not a matter of surface order according to administrative memoranda and other such paperwork which, he argues quite heatedly, stifle the actor's creativity. It is primarily a matter of self-discipline in the regularity, attention and quality of work, on the one hand, and self-controlled and courteous behaviour towards others, on the other, especially when a colleague speaks from a position of authority. There is, as well, the discipline exercised when a colleague breaks the boundaries of what is acceptable and is held to account for the sake of the health and harmony of the troupe as a whole. The third type of discipline, which Stanislavsky scathingly rejects, is the self-congratulatory '"iron discipline"' of stock-in-trade theatre, which imposes rules and exacts fines for pecuniary purposes. Organizations exacting such penalties have a similarly self-seeking outlook on the actors' creative work. The primary interest of this type of discipline is commercial gain, whereas, Stanislavsky thunders, the theatre is neither a market stall nor a bank. Nor is it 'factory' production (in other words, not conveyor-belt production), but 'artisanal' work.[108]

The actor's obligations are many: punctuality in all circumstances and especially for rehearsals; regularity of attendance at rehearsals; cheerfulness in the workplace, which is infectious and stimulates collective joy, while anxieties and depressions have a negative effect and are best kept at home; willingness to try scenes out properly, since helplessness, real or feigned, and demands for attention from the director – Stanislavsky calls such actors 'inert' and 'passive' – impede progress; openness to the director's alterations without smarting from wounded pride or harbouring grudges, hurt and resentment; preparing at home for rehearsals and giving

---

[107] Ibid., 264.   [108] Ibid., 256 and 259.

generously to them, which also means observing the work of colleagues instead of being exclusively interested in one's own. Tortsov's interlocutor quips that, given these high expectations of actors (including of their lives outside the theatre whose 'badge', they are told, they wear in the streets), the theatre might as well only hire saints![109] Tortsov retorts indignantly by asking whether the theatre should be left to uncouth people and ham actors, whose work belittles humanity. Moreover, can an actor, who lives a small, mean life beyond the theatre – 'in the wings', as Stanislavsky puts it – then step onto the stage, thinking he or she is equal to Shakespeare?

Behind such questions is another of Stanislavsky's recurrent preoccupations, that of the 'noble' (Stanislavsky) vocation of acting in the theatre, which can only be compared to a church. Not surprisingly, when referring to the tranquillity of the surroundings and the inward peace necessary for the actor's creative state, Stanislavsky advises a 'liturgical' atmosphere in the actors' dressing rooms. His remarks on the actor's obligation to prepare for rehearsals at home involve a comparison between the actor, who assumes everything can wait until rehearsals, and the singer, dancer or pianist, who trains his/her voice, body or hands every day at home. Yet the actor, who also uses his/her voice, face, body, rhythm and musicality, needs to do more homework than any other performance artist to be ready for collective work; and this is so because intense engagement with each other (*obshcheniye*) demands serious preparation.

Furthermore, training-development, in Stanislavsky's view, does not end in an acting school or in rehearsals, but continues throughout an actor's life.[110] This aspect of the System – continuous work on oneself – seems to have gone under the radar, but rediscovering it in Stanislavsky's pages shows that work on oneself is more than a technical matter, or a matter of rote discipline. It is rooted in an ethical attitude, which is carried through into training understood as perpetual development, and it is carried through into everything else that an actor does as a human being-actor.

---

[109] Ibid., 257.   [110] Ibid., 261.

CHAPTER 4

Studio

A Chart of the Studios

The Povarskaya studio was Stanislavsky's preliminary effort at organizing a place for experimentation. It turned out to be only a 'draft' venture, which is why the reconsidered studio planned for the long haul and to be run by Sulerzhitsky was the one to take the title of 'First Studio' and retain it for posterity. The First Studio was the keystone of a laboratory construct totalling six studios, four of which – First to Fourth Studio – were officially held to be 'of the Moscow Art Theatre. The remaining two, the Opera Studio of the Bolshoy Theatre and the Opera-Dramatic Studio, were not established under the aegis of the MAT. They belonged, nevertheless, to the group of six dedicated in varying ways to the new theatre and the new type of acting required for it. Stanislavsky had no hesitation in including opera in this new theatre, whose actor-singers he was developing in the most comprehensive sense of this word, as explain in the preceding pages.

Stanislavsky declared quite candidly that he and Sulerzhitsky 'dreamed of founding something like a spiritual order of actors'.[1] However, only the First Studio actually set out with such a goal. The remaining Studios, although not devoid of the 'lofty thoughts, broad ideas and wide horizons' desired for the First, were less inclined to spiritual brotherhood.[2] Stanislavsky, for his part, never lost sight of his and Sulerzhitsky's dream as he engaged with these other Studios, and the Bolshoy Opera Studio possibly came the closest to it as it morphed into a theatre. All six Studios put together show the phenomenal scope and reach of Stanislavsky's ideas and aspirations and, as well, the no less phenomenal legacy he succeeded in building up over some thirty years through his studio network.

---

[1] *Moya zhizn*, 355; *My Life*, 304.   [2] Ibid.

The First Studio materialized into a matrix of greater than national importance as its actors on tour in Europe and then its émigrés became international figureheads both of the Studio and the Art Theatre. Sulerzhitsky, who played a decisive role in this matrix, has remained in relative obscurity – a name associated with Stanislavsky and the Moscow Art Theatre, but without a clearly marked working biography. For these very reasons, Sulerzhitsky and the Studio in his care take up the greater part of this chapter. My decision was necessary, although made to the detriment of the five remaining studios, which receive far less space than they need and deserve. Vakhtangov, Sulerzhitsky's closest collaborator, has taken a back seat along with the Third Studio. Fortunately, his work has received due attention within books on the Russian theatre, or on his own, including in English.[3]

Maria Knebel, luminous among Stanislavsky's last group of collaborators in his Opera-Dramatic Studio, is a fitting parallel to Sulerzhitsky in her profound commitment to, and dissemination of, Stanislavsky's System as he developed it, now during his final years. An invaluable witness to more than the System, like Stanislavsky's way of directing, for instance, she too is confined to a few pages of this chapter. Stanislavsky taught her, Knebel says, 'to be a pedagogue and director', and she was both in her own right until her death in 1985.[4]

The following chart provides access to the tangled studio terrain in which Stanislavsky's influence is omnipresent:

First Studio: 1912–24, when it morphed into the Moscow Art Academic Theatre 2. The latter was 'liquidated' in 1936.
Second Studio: 1916–24, when it merged with the MAAT.
Third Studio: 1920–24, based on the group remaining from the Vakhtangov Moscow Dramatic Studio of 1917–20, which had grown out of the Student Studio Vakhtangov had founded in 1913.

1924 – It became the Yevgeny Vakhtangov State Academic Studio.

1926 – Renamed the Yevgeny Vakhtangov State Theatre, known today as the Yevgeny Vakhtangov State Academic Theatre, or simply the Vakhtangov Theatre.

---

[3] See, most recently, Andrei Malaev-Babel, *Yevgeny Vakhtangov: A Critical Portrait*, Abingdon and New York: Routledge, 2013.
[4] *Vsya zhizn*, 277.

A Chart of the Studios

Fourth Studio: 1921–24, based on the itinerant Regional Group of the MAAT (outlying districts of Moscow) organized by Art Theatre actors in 1918. Performed in a stable auditorium 1921–24.

1925 – It became the State Moscow Theatre 'Fourth Studio'.

1927 – Renamed the State Moscow Realistic Theatre under the direction of Nikolay Okhlopkov.

1937 – The Realistic Theatre merged with the Kamerny (Chamber) Theatre under the direction of Aleksandr Taïrov.[5]

The Bolshoy Opera Studio: 1918–22, under Stanislavsky's leadership. It continued during the MAAT's 1922–24 tour; resumed by Stanislavsky on his return.

1926 – It became the Stanislavsky Opera Studio-Theatre (in a building to be renovated for Stanislavsky's purposes at Lunacharsky's request).

1928 – Renamed the Stanislavsky Opera Theatre.

1941 – Renamed the Stanislavsky and Nemirovich-Danchenko Moscow Academic Music Theatre. This was a merger, on Nemirovich-Danchenko's initiative, of the Stanislavsky Opera Theatre and the Nemirovich-Danchenko Music Theatre (see below). It is known as such today, and includes ballet in its repertoire.

Opera-Dramatic Studio: 1935–38, created on Stanislavsky's initiative.

Not to be outdone by Stanislavsky, Nemirovich-Danchenko established the Nemirovich-Danchenko Music Studio in 1919 as a studio of the Art Theatre, generally favouring operettas. In 1926, it became the Nemirovich-Danchenko Music Theatre, primarily staging musical comedies, but also some operas, before merging in 1941, as above. Nemirovich-Danchenko died in 1943.

Note that the Nemirovich-Danchenko Music Studio toured Germany and Prague in 1925 and, having taken the name of Music Theatre, went to New York in December 1926 and, from there, to California and notably Hollywood. Nemirovich-Danchenko, who was signed up as a cinema scriptwriter, stayed in Hollywood until December 1927. A good number of his company remained in the United States, virtually decimating the Music Theatre as such, while Nemirovich-Danchenko returned to Moscow in 1928.

---

[5] Data for these four studios has been checked across various sources (see below), including the *Bolshaya Sovetskaya Entsiklopediya (The Great Soviet Encyclopaedia)*, Moscow: State Scientific Press, 1956, 163–5. For the Fourth Studio, see L. A. Klimenko, 'Chetvyortaya studiya MKhATa – Moskovsky Gosudarstvenny Teatr Chetvyortaya Studiya' ('The Fourth Studio of the MAAT') in *Sovyetsky teatr 1921–1926. Dokumenti i materialy*, ed. A. Ya. Trabsky, Leningrad: Iskusstvo, 1975, 188–94.

Sulerzhitsky and the First Studio

Sulerzhitsky's had been an eventful life and far less carefree than his wholesome appearance would ever have suggested when he first arrived at the Moscow Art Theatre. At his memorial forty days after his death, in accordance with Orthodox ritual, Stanislavsky recalled the descriptions of him that had coursed through the theatre before they were finally to meet: he was kind and cheerful; he was a revolutionary, a Tolstoyan, a Dukhobor, an American, a sailor, an adventurer, a wanderer, a writer, a storyteller, an artist (expelled from an art school for questioning its authority) and an actor who played instruments and had a pleasing singing voice.[6] He sang duos with Chaliapin at 'cabbage parties' or whole operas elsewhere on his own, prompting Chaliapin to encourage him to study with a singing teacher. He spoke some English and so, representing the MAT, he escorted Isadora Duncan during her second tour to Moscow, showing her the sights and dancing with her at social gatherings. She was mightily impressed with his natural talent for movement.

Stanislavsky said that 'all the Muses must have kissed him when he was born', but he might also have added how cruel his youth had been.[7] Sulerzhitsky was a conscientious objector and was imprisoned for refusing compulsory military service. After a visit from Tolstoy and his wife, who found him in good spirits, he was put into solitary confinement as punishment for his connection with Tolstoy. He was sent for a short time to a mental asylum and exiled to hard labour in Turkestan, where, among several jobs of varying severity, he worked as an orderly, subsequently using his limited medical skills when caring for the wounded away from the battlefront of the Russo-Japanese War. On his return from Canada, he smuggled typefaces and a printing press or two into Russia from Switzerland, home of Russian revolutionary exiles. The favour was for Gorky, who in 1901 helped to print *Iskra*, the revolutionary newspaper that Lenin, among other such exiles, directed from abroad. This was the 'revolutionary' to whom Stanislavsky referred – a short-lived deviance for a Sulerzhitsky who adhered to the Tolstoyan credo of non-violence.

Over and above Sulerzhitsky's adventurous temperament, Stanislavsky prized the finer qualities he brought to the theatre: 'the genuine poetry of the prairies, villages, forests and nature, observations of life and art,

---

[6] *SS* 8, 5, 532, 25 January 1917. For other biographical details, see Polyakova's introduction to Sulerzhitsky's writings in *Povesti i rasskazy*, 17–95.
[7] Ibid., 533.

Sulerzhitsky and the First Studio   133

thoughts and goals achieved through suffering, and original philosophical, ethical and religious views'.[8] He brought, as well, his love of people and his excellent organization and teaching. Stanislavsky declared in his deeply felt speech that Sulerzhitsky explained better than he could what his artistic experience told him, and he saluted Sulerzhitsky's indefatigable work in the First Studio, to which he 'gave his last administrative, creative, peda-gogical and moral strength'.[9] Here he fulfilled one of his most important goals – bringing people closer together through shared purpose, work and happiness. Here he served 'love, nature, beauty and God'.[10] Stanislavsky reveals much about himself between the lines, including his own capacity for loving people and his love of nature and freedom, giving fresh insight into why he and Sulerzhitsky were bound together – on the surface, two unlikely friends. Pavel Markov, the MAT's literary advisor, summed up Sulerzhitsky's unique contribution to the First Studio: he was 'a teacher of life and of the stage in equal measure'.[11]

Stanislavsky swiftly understood that Sulerzhitsky's many sides were very valuable for directing, an area in which the MAT was weak because of its too few directors and its methods, as his disagreements with Nemirovich-Danchenko on the subject had revealed. Thus he nurtured Sulerzhitsky as a director – an outstanding one, in his view – while he taught him the System, when and how it unfolded. Stanislavsky's appointment of Sulerz-hitsky was intelligent for another reason. It was a far more effective way of integrating him in the MAT than his role of Stanislavsky's 'personal' assistant would ever allow. After all, Stanislavsky had been paying his salary, and integration also meant employment ratified by the company, which would give him institutional security and status.

Sulerzhitsky's name appeared on the posters as the sole director of *The Drama of Life* (1907) and *The Life of Man* (1907), two 'abstract' and symbolic plays. The third production, Maeterlinck's *The Blue Bird* (1908), credited Sulerzhitsky and, after him, the actor Moskvin, according to the MAT custom of acknowledging secondary directorial contributions. Sta-nislavsky had continually advised on all three productions (his name was not publicized) while he tested his fledgling notions of 'inner techniques' and 'inner process' on the actors. His experiments in design with his collaborators mainly focused on technical problems concerning *The Blue Bird*, but, instead of solving them, they accidentally stumbled upon the

---

[8] Ibid., 535.   [9] Ibid., 537.   [10] Ibid., 535.
[11] *Moskovsky Khudozhestvenny Teatr Vtoroy* (*The Moscow Art Academic Theatre 2*), Moscow: Moscow Art Theatre, 1925, 80.

134   Studio

magic trick of disappearance, when black is on black velvet. Their discovery proved not to be of use in the extended way that Stanislavsky imagined for *The Blue Bird*, but it was perfect for the Silver Age esoteric *The Life of Man*. Stanislavsky commented, with some satisfaction, that 'many principles of staging ... thought to epitomize a new kind of theatre are in fact no more than the result of pure chance'.[12]

Sulerzhitsky was Stanislavsky's emissary to Paris in 1911, sent to stage *The Blue Bird* after the Moscow production at the fundamentally commercial theatre run by Georgette Leblanc, Maeterlinck's wife, and the popular actress Réjane. Where the Moscow original had fairy-tale delicacy, its Paris variant sought gaudy effects. Sulerzhitsky, dismayed by his hostesses' blithe insensitivity to the play, eventually shrugged off the whole 'low-level' (*poshloye*) and 'vulgar' business as being past hope and past care.[13] Vakhtangov, who had come as Sulerzhitsky's assistant, vanished into the streets, leaving Sulerzhitsky to mop up and save face on behalf of the MAT, something he was inveigled into doing more than once as the MAT's dealings with Edward Gordon Craig took twists and turns none of them had bargained for. Duncan had brokered Stanislavsky's invitation to Craig to stage *Hamlet*, and preliminary discussions on how he, director-designer, envisaged the production took place in 1909. Sulerzhitsky returned to Moscow to resume his duties helping Craig, and to a compromised *Hamlet* that had to be saved at all costs, especially as all Europe was watching, as Stanislavsky reminded his colleagues.[14]

Laurence Senelick has admirably detailed the tribulations of *Hamlet*, but of special interest for these pages is the sorry end to Sulerzhitsky's devoted labour for the production and to his affectionate commitment personally to Craig.[15] The difficulties with Craig's frequently high-handed behaviour were many, but Sulerzhitsky cracked when Craig, capriciously, refused to have his name on the posters, although he recognized Stanislavsky as his co-director on them. Stanislavsky prevaricated over the issue, pointing out to a badly wounded Sulerzhitsky, who had every right to be acknowledged for his directorial contribution, that Craig was a 'great artist' and could be excused accordingly, especially because Europe *was* watching.[16]

---

[12] *Moya zhizn*, 317; *My Life in Art*, 272.
[13] *Povesti i rasskazy*, 476–82, letters to Stanislavsky of 21 and 'end' February 1911 (without precise date).
[14] Ibid., 486, letter of 22 December 1911.
[15] *Gordon Craig's Moscow* Hamlet: *A Reconstruction*, Westport: Greenwood Press, 1982.
[16] *Povesti i rasskazy*, 486–7, letter of 22 December 1911.

Sulerzhitsky and the First Studio

Of course, this was like oil on fire. Sulerzhitsky retorted in the equivocal tones of Mark Antony on Brutus the 'honourable man' who killed Caesar for the good of Rome: Craig might be a 'great artist', but Stanislavsky, knowing what kind of man Craig was, had betrayed him by accepting Craig's dishonourable action; worse still, knowing his precarious position in the theatre, he had nevertheless failed him – not for the first time, either, although he had always been successful in protecting the interests of his other friends from injustice.[17] Sulerzhitsky, having made it plain that Stanislavsky took him for granted, concluded his letter on a forgiving note, indicating that any other attitude would not, in any case, change Stanislavsky's. Soon after, Stanislavsky, shamed and repentant, put the situation to rights, registering Sulerzhitsky's name on *Hamlet* (1911) after Craig's and beside his own.

Sulerzhitsky's moral uprightness passed into his teaching at the First Studio, together with his 'spiritual leadership' and 'total selflessness' – in the words of Lidiya Deykun and Serafima Birman, two of the important group of Studio women. Birman notes his combat against 'petty behaviour and injustice' and that he treated his students as equals, but also thought that he had squandered his gifts by caring over-generously for others.[18] Smyshlyayev, in his reminiscences, observes how Sulerzhitsky interconnected ethics with aesthetics, thoughtfully transmitting ideas of morality to the Studio's 'commune of actors' through the way he taught them about the theatre.[19] Thus Sulerzhitsky's 'no aesthetics without ethics' explained that the theatre, which was beautiful to the eye, also gave people the opportunity to understand what concerned them. In this way, it encouraged them to aim 'higher' and 'better', showing their trust in the best in themselves. Such aspects of the 'life of the human spirit' were ethical in their beneficial impact on everybody's daily interaction.

Another of Sulerzhitsky's axioms – the theatre sought God and communed with God (Sulerzhitsky is here in symbiosis with Stanislavsky) – struck a chord with Vakhtangov, who connected it to Sulerzhitsky's dictum that 'being human begins in that moment when ... you pay attention to the individual life of each person.[20] In matters of faith, Sulerzhitsky, of Polish descent and born a Catholic, bypassed the

---

[17] Ibid., 487–9, letter of 23 December 1911.
[18] Ibid., 599, 613 and Serafima Birman, *Put aktrisi* (*The Path of the Actress*), Moscow: All-Russian Theatre Society, 1959, 104.
[19] *Povesti i rasskazy*, 581; 580 for the following citation.   [20] Ibid., 557.

136 Studio

institutional mediation of the Church, like Tolstoy. Yet, not without contradiction, he saw the theatre as a 'monastery'.

Contradictions prevailed. Sulerzhitsky's anti-institutionalism did not prevent the church service at his Catholic funeral, or the Orthodox rites at his burial beside the MAT 'family' in the Orthodox Novodevichy cemetery – on the doorstep of the Novodevichy Convent. Decades later, Birman commented on how the Studio, this 'theatre utopia', was 'beyond time and beyond space, even though it existed in the twentieth century and in the centre of Moscow'.[21] Which was not quite how it was, nor as utopian, when its members began to ignore the Studio's 'higher' laboratory purposes as they questioned Sulerzhitsky's transparent programme of 'only developing scenic material rather than playing plays' – in Sofya Giatsinto-va's paraphrase of Sulerzhitsky's intentions.[22] They wanted to perform more plays than those he had helped them to mount. Sulerzhitsky had pointed out that quantities of stageworthy material were generated in Studio explorations, 'the large part' of which 'remained undiscovered by the public'.[23] In his understanding, this cumulative amassing was greatly beneficial for developing the actors' creativity.

Although a 'theatre utopia' was not to be realized, work in the Studio precincts was, by and large, within its ideational parameters, if not entirely within its tacit code of behaviour, and this gave its members great artistic strengths. Continuity was a significant factor. The same people going from the Adashev School to the Studio guaranteed a degree of cohesion, since they all had some preliminary understanding of the System. This was also true of the additions – Boleslavsky, who was an upcoming young MAT actor, having performed the significant role of Belyayev in the MAT's encounter with the System in *A Month in the Country*, and Mikhaïl Chekhov, of recent date at the MAT. Many of the 'studists' (coined here from the Russian *studytsi*, by which the studio members were known) had heard Stanislavsky map out the differences between stock-in-trade theatre, the theatre of representation and the theatre of emotional experiencing in his 1911 lectures, which had given them a conceptual rationale of sorts for the exercises they had begun at Adashev's and would continue at the Studio. In the gaps between the Adashev School, the MAT and the formalization of the Studio, they voluntarily studied the System with Vakhtangov, to whom Stanislavsky had proposed the idea of teaching it,

[21] *Put aktrisi*, 130.
[22] *C pamyatyu nayedinye* (*In the Solitude of My Memories*), Moscow: Iskusstvo, 1989, 81.
[23] Sulerzhitsky quoted in *Moskovsky Khudozhestvenny Teatr Vtoroy*, 105.

Sulerzhitsky and the First Studio

but without drawing undue attention from those who were against it at the MAT. Vakhtangov's following was sufficiently diligent and enthusiastic to persuade Stanislavsky to risk opening a laboratory-studio, once more.

How the System was taught and modified at the Studio has not been handed down to posterity in course descriptions or books of exercises, but some idea of what they were like can be had from 'studist' memoirs. Birman, a reliable source, reports that the System centred on muscle relaxation, the 'circle of attention', the 'germ' (of an idea, sketch or action), the breakup of tasks, the 'throughaction' of a role and the relations between one partner and another. All these components required concentration so complete that, as Birman puts it, 'anxiety was unable to disturb the most important aspect of the System – [the actor's] creative independence of the spectator [through his/her] immersion in the role' (*obraz*).[24] Immersion, Stanislavsky believed, would prevent pandering to the audience.

Sulerzhitsky had the 'studists' bring in themes from which they constructed exercises for given elements of the System – 'attention', say, and how wide its 'circle' could be in the 'proposed circumstances'. One exercise on the 'circle of attention' concerned a wife who gazes into the window of a tram, from which, meanwhile, her husband had jumped off and broken his leg. The main question appears to have asked whether she was looking at herself or at something in the distance, from which it is possible to infer that the exercise offered two circles of attention for playing, one small, while the other had a wider circumference.

Giatsintova claims that, for Sulerzhitsky, the Studio's 'three main tasks were the psychology of the actor's creativity, the development of the actor's creative state, and bringing the actor closer to an author'.[25] These involved 'developing a taste for initiative and independence'.[26] The 'studists' were asked to choose extracts from literary material for etudes, or to write their own individual scripts from it; and they explored the technical aspects of a potential performance of their scripts – for instance how they would deal with the disadvantages of their space, which was a room without a platform and a lighting rig. When they began to think about mounting plays, Stanislavsky encouraged independence by asking them to decide on actors for roles among themselves instead of relying on him – a responsibility Giatsintova felt was beyond them at that early stage of their development.[27]

---

[24] *Put aktrisi*, 79.   [25] *C pamyatyu nayedinye*, 81–2.   [26] Ibid., 86.   [27] Ibid.

138   Studio

Since Stanislavsky was endlessly busy at the MAT, he sometimes led sessions at night, after his own performances. He gave exercises in believing and naivety – not at all easy, as Giatsintova comments, when you have to believe that the hard floorboards you are walking on are a meadow full of flowers.[28] However, if you do genuinely believe it, she adds, so will your partner and everyone else around you. Stanislavsky's famous 'I don't believe you!' may have resounded more than once through this exercise and its variations in the Studio. They read Anton Chekhov's stories together, and Stanislavsky showed them how to deconstruct narrative, plot and circumstances in order to follow the throughaction [*skvoznoye deystviye*] of each story and, as well, how to construct performable dialogue out of the broken-down material.[29] Both Stanislavsky and Sulerzhitsky taught the 'studists' to train their memory by observing and storing information about the people, situations and objects around them, and their 'inner attitude' (Giatsintova) towards them. Giatsintova states that she hated Sulerzhitsky's etudes on memory, preferring to invent imaginary characters, events and so on, rather than pull items out from her accumulated observations. And she particularly baulked at exercises on personal memory – Sulerzhitsky must have been working on 'affective memory' – arguing that she did not have personal experiences of many of his requests and so could not possibly recall how she felt. She thought that his suggestions to remember how people close to her had felt were just as silly. Giatsintova appears not to have thought of sensations in terms of their importance for triggering memory and so waking up associations to which Stanislavsky continually drew attention.

Overall, Giatsintova's memoirs indicate that the 'studists' were fully aware not only of their experimental value for the System, but also of the pioneering role they were playing in developing acting. She believed that the 'studists' took the System and its terminology 'too literally', as she thought they had done with Stanislavsky's idea of acting 'from yourself'.[30] Giatsintova's remark prompts speculation. Perhaps she is referring to Sulerzhitsky's work on 'affective memory' and her 'too literal' response to it. Sulerzhitsky, for his part, warned actors against whipping themselves up into uncontrollable emotional states of excessive laughter, tears or gesticulation when they were working from 'affective memory', but also when they were not. States of 'hysteria' like these, he argued, had nothing to do with the creative state, but were a matter of overexcited nerves, detrimental to the health of actors, as to that of spectators; and unhealthy

---

[28] Ibid., 83.   [29] Ibid., 86.   [30] Ibid., 85.

Sulerzhitsky and the First Studio 139

behaviours had to do with ethics because they had an impact on every-one.[31] Perhaps by 'from yourself', Giatsintova had failed to grasp that Stanislavsky meant – simplifying from Chapter 3 – 'acting from the whole of yourself, soul-body-mind in the entirety of your being'. Or perhaps she had not realized that Stanislavsky's 'from yourself' also meant 'from *your* imagination'. Whatever the case may have been, she says, just as artlessly, that Stanislavsky 'overestimated their understanding' of the System.

Etudes, although not impromptu, were exercises of the imagination – imagination being *fundamental* to the System (my italics) – just as were the vaudeville and cabaret numbers Sulerzhitsky frequently introduced, either in tandem with etudes or on their own, so as to change the atmosphere and lighten the work. Upbeat skits were conducive to that group spirit vital for a theatre ensemble – the happiest, most creative and most productive kind of theatre possible, as Sulerzhitsky agreed with Stanislavsky. Giatsintova refers to the pleasure of seeing stick-thin Birman beside the diminutive Maria Uspenskaya (founder with Boleslavsky of the American Laboratory Theatre in New York in 1923) developing a funny, captivating etude based on Hanako's showing of her dance theatre.[32] Hanako, the stage name of Ota Hisa, had broken away from more than one Japanese tradition with her free-form constructions and professional travels in Europe, dancing also with Loïe Fuller in Paris; and Stanislavsky had invited her to broaden the students' perceptions of what could be done in the theatre through movement, which was crucial, in his view, for the development of actors. Among Stanislavsky's 'surprises' for them (Giatsintova quotes Stani-slavsky), was a visit from Duncan to watch them work. One of Duncan's former students was a regular dance teacher at the Studio, as noted in the preceding chapter.

Apart from etudes, which were structured events on a motif agreed upon beforehand, Sulerzhitsky used improvisations, which were impromptu events meant to keep the 'studists' on their toes, 'constantly in a creative state', in Deykun's words.[33] The longer-term intention, clearly, was to have them be alert – always imaginative and ready in the 'stage creative state' (Stanislavsky) during a performance. Deykun describes at some length an improvisation sprung upon her in the street by Sulerzhitsky and Vakhtangov. Both men were suddenly 'drunk', falling about in the street and putting her into difficult situations with passers-by before they

---

[31] *Moskovsky Khudozhestvenny Teatr Vtoroy*, 92 and 94. Markov comments that Sulerzhitsky consistently 'kept the seed of the actor's playing clean'.
[32] *C pamyatyu nayedinye*, 110.   [33] *Povesti i rasskazy*, 603.

dived into a café and continued their antics, ending their scene by claiming, still 'drunk', that they had no money to pay the bill. Deykun was obliged to extricate herself from situation to situation – these were certainly challenging 'proposed circumstances' – without letting on that this was all make-believe. Game over, she had her vengeance soon after by walking up to a policeman, as she and Sulerzhitsky were going up the same street on another day, and telling the policeman that the man beside her was bothering her, near as good as molesting her, and would he please help. Sulerzhitsky had to talk himself out of being put in jail, without giving Deykun away.[34] Game over successfully, once again.

Deykun's funny tale of two events which, in the theatre, could have been hilarious, but, in the street, had a very different edge, is unexpectedly instructive. It shows just how much attention, focus, trust, skill, good humour, good temper and ensemble co-operation – not to mention Stanislavsky's 'truth' in the moment rather than 'verisimilitude' after the event – had to be garnered to make something like an artistic success out of a prank, and a piece of theatre that did not look like theatre out of a banal incident. The two improvisations appear to be lessons, even textbook lessons, in the System. But the actor most equipped for the spontaneous inventions of improvisation was Chekhov who, in the Studio productions, and even more so in the years to follow, virtually goaded his partners on the stage with his impromptu variations and shifts of characterization – expressions, movements, actions and anything else his fertile imagination conjured up in the moment – into responding quickly with their own, or else fall flat on their faces and risk bringing the show down with them.

Since those heady days of discovery with Sulerzhitsky (and Stanislavsky, by all accounts, was a master improviser when things went wrong in a performance), the fine distinction between an etude and an improvisation has more or less stabilized in the Russian theatre, even though an etude, once started, requires improvisation within the agreed framework. Dodin, who is in a direct line of transmission from Stanislavsky through his teacher Boris Zon, a participant in Stanislavsky's home research between 1933 and 1935, has clearly marked this distinction with his students, who then became actors of the Maly Drama Theatre. So, too, has Galendeyev in his ongoing coaching of them.[35] However, the terminology for these practices as they were taking root was not altogether clear-cut, as transpires

---

[34] Ibid., 602–4.
[35] Maria Shevtsova, *Dodin and the Maly Drama Theatre: Process to Performance*, London and New York: Routledge, 2004, 49 and 51–2.

Sulerzhitsky and the First Studio 141

in an unpublished letter from Sulerzhitsky to Gorky of 9 March 1913.[36] Gorky, in conversation with Stanislavsky, had launched the idea of writing plays collectively and Stanislavsky had observed that Sulerzhitsky's students were already 'generating their own plays'. Gorky asked for clarification. Sulerzhitsky replied, saying that, when the Studio opened and he had first begun this practice, he called it 'an exercise in your own words'. Normally, the exercise was for two people. He set themes according to what he wanted to get out of the students, citing their concentration, temperament, relations between partners and ability to influence whoever was the object of their attention.

What needs to be noted is that Sulerzhitsky's letter is a detailed document among few documents concerning the actual exercises undertaken by the 'studists'. The memoirs cited above provide scant examples. The allegedly sixty or so large notebooks that Sulerzhitsky kept in the First Studio, filled with his students' commentaries, complaints, suggestions, poems, sketches and cartoons, have not surfaced, and their whereabouts are unknown, with the exception of one, which, resembling thoughtless student frivolity, lacks material for this discussion.[37] Sulerzhitsky's concrete examples are, as a result, invaluable for understanding better how he developed his students and what the First Studio achieved for 'actor training' to this day. Stanislavsky rarely referred to 'actor training', preferring by far the supple notion of growth contained in 'development', but he used 'training' (*trening*), again not often, when talking about necessary exercises and distinguished it from the dutiful repetition of 'drill' (*mushtra*).[38]

Sulerzhitsky's first example to Gorky from his classes of 1912 concerns a young man in a group of visitors to the Tretyakov gallery. He is attracted to the guide and tries his hardest to win her attention. She is attracted to somebody else, and tries her hardest to ignore her admirer. Since the exercise is set rather than spontaneous, it could be called an etude and, as Sulerzhitsky stresses, everything the students did came 'from themselves' – '*from themselves personally*', in his exact, underlined phrase. That is to say, that the words of the students were not a personalized paraphrase of somebody else's language (say, *Uncle Vanya* 'in your own words'), but were their very own invention, specifically for this situation. Sulerzhitsky's

---

[36] Unnumbered document in the Sulerzhitsky archive at the Moscow Art Theatre Museum.

[37] K. S. No. 13771 in the Moscow Art Theatre Museum archives. Polkanova's *V Nov* provides a reproduction, 141–203.

[38] *SS* 8, 3, 364–78, included in the appendix to this volume as 'Training and Drill'; *An Actor's Work*, 641–53.

observation that 'the words were so good that I wanted to write them down' may have been geared to Gorky's interest in collective playwriting, but his remarks on the students' 'vivid and succulent playing' and 'fine psychological gambits' suggest how fully *of* the theatre their execution of the exercise was.

Sulerzhitsky's second example relates to how he used a story, or an episode from a story, when the students' imagination wavered. They performed these in their own words – not to play characters, Sulerzhitsky specifies, but to make the story's thematic content clear, which, presumably, by requiring attention to verbal composition, 'brought the actor closer to the author', as Giatsintova has expressed it. The exercise would also have been extremely useful for learning how to identify components of a story's throughaction– a skill transferable, of course, to plays.

Sulerzhitsky's second batch of examples to Gorky from the work sessions of 1913 was group pieces. In the first, a scene at the barber's, the students emphasized accurate actions – shaving faces, cutting hair and other usual actions in a barber's shop – with dialogue appropriate to its 'working atmosphere'. The second, which Sulerzhitsky thought was possibly closer to what Gorky and Stanislavsky had discussed, was on the theme of a tailor's workshop. The whole group, men and women, performed at the same time and, exceptionally, all roles were fixed and distributed to avoid a muddle because men outnumbered women in the Studio. Small scenes began to grow amid the din. Sulerzhitsky called out the names of the performers in scenes that had 'something alive in them' to keep them on track, while the scenes of groups that had not been marked out were readjusted. During the second round of work, relations between the protagonists began to take shape, as did connections between scenes. Sulerzhitsky's account must have suggested to Gorky that a 'playlet' of sorts was being written collectively with words in action – with the actors' bodies, or their 'nerves and flesh' as Stanislavsky said in 1902, and 'on their feet', as Dodin is fond of saying.[39]

That same year saw the beginning of the Studio's productions, five in all: Herman Hejermans' *The Wreck of the 'Hope'* (1913), directed by Boleslavsky, who introduced the 'studists' to the play and ignited their desire to perform publicly; Gerhart Hauptmann's *The Festival of Peace* (*Das Friedensfest*, 1913), directed by Vakhtangov; Charles Dickens' *The Cricket on the Hearth* (1914), directed by Boris Sushkevich; Vladimir

---

[39] K. S. No. 757. Quoted in Radishcheva, *Stanislavsky i Nemirovich-Danchenko... 1897–1908*, 151; Dodin in conversations during my research for *Dodin and the Maly Drama Theatre*.

Sulerzhitsky and the First Studio

Volkenstein's *The Wayfarers* (1914), directed by Boleslavsky; and Henning Berger's *The Deluge* (1915), directed by Vakhtangov. Sulerzhitsky guided and basically oversaw the young directors' work. Simultaneously, he gave them his tireless moral support, even though he increasingly believed that, with so much effort put into productions, the Studio was losing its laboratory research purpose.

Stanislavsky monitored progress, coming in towards the end with finishing touches, or, as in the case of *The Wayfarers*, going about restructuring the material. He disagreed relatively early with Boleslavsky's monumental heroics for the play's folkloric subject, archaic stylization, choral structure and religious motifs. In any case, monumentalism did not accord with the intimacy cultivated by Sulerzhitsky and Vakhtangov in the Studio. The 'studists' were responsible, on a shoestring budget, for every aspect of production: décor, design, costumes (borrowed from the stack of old costumes at the MAT), make-up, wigs, spatial arrangement (raised seats on the flat floor, amphitheatre-style), serving the spectators tea, and general housekeeping. There were no women directors. Birman was to become Boleslavsky's co-director for *Balladina* by Juliusz Slowacki in 1919–20, but her name went missing from the posters (allegedly Boleslavsky's oversight).

These were disparate productions. Boleslavsky, influenced by Sulerzhitsky's compassionate outlook on the world, pulled back from the strong emotions of *The Wreck of the 'Hope'*, which had initially attracted him, and highlighted the way misfortune brought out the best in people. The characters lost sons, fathers and husbands on an unseaworthy ship knowingly sent to its doom by exploitative ship owners, paid out by an insurance company. The 'studists' had adopted Sulerzhitsky's image of fishing villagers huddled together for comfort and strength, showing what it meant to be a community united in love rather than social vengeance. Love, reconciliation and forgiveness were the themes of *The Cricket on the Hearth* in which Chekhov's slightly 'potty', slightly grotesque Caleb, for instance, and Vakhtangov's openly cruel Tackleton tempered Dickens' sentimentality. As the actors prepared for *The Cricket on the Hearth*, Sulerzhitsky noted that they would probably understand its subject of human kindness better if they went to the monastery nearby to pray, returned to the Studio and read the Gospels by candlelight (and then went back to Dickens).[40]

---

[40] Vakhtangov's recollections in *Povesti i rasskazy*, 554–5.

Vakhtangov's two productions played devil's advocate to the humane optimism that Sulerzhitsky desired for the Studio, focusing on the characters' immovable interest in money and profit: 'They are all wolves to one another. Not a drop of compassion. . . .They have drowned in business'.[41] This was spoken like a man who had erected barricades with the workers of Moscow during the 1905 revolution, and who shared Sulerzhitsky's credo of standing by the dispossessed, albeit, unlike his teacher and friend, his was from a discernible political, rather than religious-moral, perspective.

Markov, when considering what linked the Studio's five disparate productions under Sulerzhitsky's stewardship, decided that they were all concerned, in some way, with the goodness in humanity.[42] The intelligentsia watching the performance had recognized this motif. In fact, it had taken especially warmly to the reassurance and reconciliation that *The Cricket on the Hearth* offered now that Russia was embroiled in war. (Germany declared war on Russia on 1 August 1914. *The Cricket on the Hearth* was premiered in November 1914.) It had recognized, too, that the System had brought about a new 'technique', which Markov identified by such details as criss-crossed gazes, simple movements and barely perceptible changes of position that made acting look organic.[43] This technique also offered impressions rather than replications: hanging fabric gave the impression of a room rather than the copy of a room; and the 'studists' spoke of 'places of action' rather than of 'décor'.[44] A whole assortment of toys that Sulerzhitsky and Chekhov had made by hand designated Caleb's workshop as his 'place of action'.

The counterbalance of the hard creative Studio work was the hard physical exertion in the fresh air, sun and sea of Kanev and Yevpatoria, interspersed with childlike play: pretend sailors, with Sulerzhitsky as captain-with-a-whistle for maritime discipline; pretend 'Indians' and wigwams – his imagination harked back to Canada; and fancy-dress charades, with Sulerzhitsky playing at shaman.[45] His letters to Maria Durasova (Mary Peerybingle in *The Cricket on the Hearth*) refer, as well, to the rural skills learned at Kanev: chopping wood, sawing, cutting grain with a scythe, building, tending to horses and respecting the ecology; and they rowed on the river – Vakhtangov for hours every morning. At Yevpatoria, they built their modest dwellings from the bricks they

---

[41] *Yevgeny Vakhtangov. Dokumenty i svidetelstva (Documents and Evidence)*, ed. Vladislav Ivanov, Vol. 1, Moscow: Indrik, 2011, 389.
[42] *Moskovsky Khudozhestvenny Teatr Vtoroy*, 101–2.   [43] Ibid., 108–9.   [44] Ibid., 106.
[45] Birman in *Put aktrisi*, 113–15; Letters to Maria Durasova, summer 1913 in *Povesti i rasskazy*, 494–7.

Sulerzhitsky and the First Studio

transported in wheelbarrows – Birman remembers lugging stones – and learned how to sail. They swam, sang, ate and read together, like a 'genuine' community.[46]

Sulerzhitsky's regime was strict, but he made allowances for Vakhtangov's severe stomach pain which, as yet undiagnosed, was the growing cancer that would kill him. While Sulerzhitsky worried about Vakhtangov's health, Vakhtangov, in the disgruntled mood of someone who was ill, wrote epigrammatic letters to Deykun every two days in June 1914 from Yevpatoria, reiterating that he was 'bored'; 'it was monotonous'.[47] Sulerzhitsky would have noticed Vakhtangov's mood: they were close, and he had nurtured Vakhtangov's individual creative qualities, encouraged him to develop his artistic will, and stretched him as a human being. And Sulerzhitsky fretted because he was living like a city dweller on holiday (*dachnik*) instead of working the land. In the spring of 1915, when on leave from the Studio, he farmed potatoes with his wife and small sons on land that he was able to buy, at long last.

The summers after 1913 were not unblemished. Sulerzhitsky's letter to Durasova of 4 July 1914 openly expresses his 'confusion'. The young Studio people had been brutal in that year in their ambition and disregard for each other; they were indifferent to the human values of *The Cricket on the Hearth*, seeing in it only an opportunity for mounting a production, as they saw all plays (a sore point for Sulerzhitsky, since he had taught them not to mount a play merely for self-satisfaction, but to ask what their purpose was for doing it); and they overrode what mattered most to him (that is, his faith in community).[48] Sulerzhitsky's feelings were raw – unavoidably so, given that this dystopian situation had arisen in an environment that had fostered equality rather than hierarchy, solidarity rather than rivalry, collective-ensemble aspiration rather than solely individual fulfilment, and discipline as a matter of ethics rather than one of order and control. It took eighteen months and the realities of war – visible in the warships of the Yevpatoria port and by the numbers of injured soldiers in Moscow – for Sulerzhitsky's confusion to turn into bitter hurt, anger and self-blame for not having had the strength to nip the Studio situation in the bud.

This outpouring happened in a letter of resignation of 27 December 1915 to Stanislavsky, which it appears Sulerzhitsky never sent, but whose content, even watered down, he would most likely have discussed with

---

[46] *Put aktrisi*, 113. [47] *Yevgeny Vakhtangov. Dokumenty*, 372–5. [48] *Povesti i rasskazy*, 504–6.

Stanislavsky at some point.[49] Sulerzhitsky explained. The Studio's harmonious first year had turned into the vicious fighting of the second, when it replaced its collective will and shared life with individual will and self-interest. It had lost its idea of utopia for that of business – box-office success, glory, more administration, more involvement with the public and the press, and more concern for power. The Studio's tensions and cruelties were resolved as everybody's heart opened with *The Cricket on the Hearth* and then at Yevpatoria, and this had shown him that utopia *was* possible. He, Sulerzhitsky, had noticed that the Studio had succumbed to the will of a few who, feeling their strength rising, jostled against each other to be 'boss' (reference here is to the three directors, Boleslavsky, Sushkevich and Vakhtangov).[50] He had attempted to solve the problem by widening the membership of the Studio Council, but it was already too late. He should have insisted right from the start that all members of the Studio, and not only the Council, were responsible for running it; this would have caused short-term disagreements and skirmishes, but they would have subsided without damaging the laboratory purposes of the Studio and the quality of its work. He now understood that he was simply not up to the task.

Sulerzhitsky's letter is lucid in its forceful emotions and consciousness of betrayal and failure – the forerunner, on both counts, of Stanislavsky's letter to Nemirovich-Danchenko from New York on the evaporation of the MAT's ideas, ideals and unity (Chapter 1). It precedes, as well, another of Stanislavsky's letters to Nemirovich-Danchenko, not yet encountered in this book, about the three Studios closely affiliated with the MAT: his three 'daughters', modelled on King Lear's daughters, with the First Studio cast as Goneril, the Third as Regan and the Second as Cordelia.[51] This letter of 10 July 1924 responded to the question mooted in Moscow during the MAAT's tour of whether the MAAT should absorb the Studios. Nemirovich-Danchenko firmly opposed their independence, arguing that their initial purpose was to feed into the Art Theatre and eventually to join the company. This would realize the continuity of studio to theatre envisaged from the very beginning.

The First Studio had seen its strength – Sulerzhitsky's assessment had been accurate – as had the Third, headed by Vakhtangov, which Sulerzhitsky, dying prematurely, could not have known. Both of them wanted to

---

[49] Ibid., 379–83.
[50] Sulerzhitsky gives names in an unnumbered variant of the above letter in the Sulerzhitsky archive of the MAT Museum.
[51] *SS* 9, 9, 158 and for following quotations; *Stanislavsky – A Life in Letters*, 434.

Sulerzhitsky and the First Studio 147

remain autonomous as theatres: the First Studio had six 'serious productions' for its 1917–18 season, which 'forced the MAT to give it economic independence'.[52] Lunacharsky had granted it autonomy by decree, which ensured government subsidies, however minimal. The Third Studio was established on the independent Vakhtangov Studio. Nemirovich-Danchenko had pretty well given both studios an ultimatum – agree to his and Lunacharsky's propositions to stay with the Art Theatre, or go – in response to which they dallied a little, the Third Studio declaring that it wanted to wait for Stanislavsky's return and hear what he had to say.[53] Meanwhile, the Second Studio decided to amalgamate with the alma mater, without any reservations.

Stanislavsky, who had always believed in the continuity of studio-theatre, meant it to be the specific continuity of Studio-Art Theatre. His 10 July letter, approving Nemirovich-Danchenko's decision to let the First Studio go its separate way (in any case, it had already gone separately) and to 'cut off' the Third was, in effect, his answer to them. He regretted, however, that the First Studio had bartered for the title of MAAT2 successfully, since it 'had betrayed the Art Theatre in every respect'. Unintentionally, he echoed Sulerzhitsky's sentiment, only his words were different: the First Studio was a 'long-standing disease in my soul'. In Sulerzhitsky's case, the disease was of shorter duration.

On Sulerzhitsky's death, Vakhtangov's authority on matters of art was vital to the First Studio, although he did not formally lead it, and that authority passed to Chekhov on Vakhtangov's death.[54] Chekhov made clear his intentions to run it as a '*theatre*-studio' (my italics for Chekhov's shift of priorities), otherwise he would be obliged to leave and build up a theatre company elsewhere.[55] The majority of his colleagues accepted his conditions (the others, grumbling, put up with them), and the Studio did well, retaining the Art Theatre's endorsement and capitalizing largely, but not exclusively, on its enormously loved early productions: *The Cricket on the Hearth*, for instance, celebrated its five-hundredth performance on 3 December 1922.[56] After striking out into the 'tragic grotesque' with Vakhtangov's production of *Rosmersholm* (1918), it multiplied its stakes in the same direction with Vakhtangov's *Erik XIV* (1921) – Chekhov's tour de force as Erik, and Birman's as the Queen Mother.

'Protected', in a manner of speaking, by the MAT's 'logo', the First Studio did not fall under the weight of the October Revolution. It was also

---

[52] F. N. Mikhalsky and E. S. Kapitaykin, 'Pervaya Studiya' in *Sovyetsky teatr 1921–1926*, 160 and 164.
[53] See notes 59–61 below. [54] 'Pervaya Studiya', 161. [55] Ibid. [56] Ibid., 180.

'protected' by its vibrant work and its varied audiences, who felt its contemporary energy. Then, when *Hamlet* (1924) inaugurated the MAAT2, it proved to be a revolutionary production for its bold, modernist aesthetics, but, above all, because, without ostensibly doing so, it projected, in a modernist oblique fashion, the toughest of immediate problems – generational misapprehensions, political divisions, social and political responsibilities and individual obligations for taking action. All this occurred under the surveillance of the Ghost, the dark spectre of the unknown, which was primarily mystical but was also empirically unknowable because of the ever-shifting turbulence of the post-revolutionary years.[57] *Hamlet* did not reflect but epitomized the early 1920s, while the mystical dimension of Chekhov's vision was atemporal, seeking 'universal' validity. The production's departure from Stanislavsky's principles of evolutionary, organic creativity and the temporal aesthetics of everyday reality –'realism' – was inherent in that vision.

A study of the MAAT2 is not possible within the confines of this book.[58] However, it can at least reference the MAAT2's internal dissensions and power clashes from 1926 to 1928 in which Chekhov was the main protagonist, rejecting his colleagues' interest in staging Soviet plays on Soviet life and their other wishes to do with both art and politics.[59] Chekhov's colleagues gradually distanced themselves from him, while Chekhov was increasingly adamant about wanting his own company. Lunacharsky, who agreed with Stanislavsky on Chekhov's 'genius' and supported Chekhov unstintingly, was unable to procure premises for him. The MAAT2 as good as ousted Chekhov. His letter of 28 October 1928 to Lunacharsky from Berlin, where he had recently emigrated, was a masterful exposition of his views on the Studio situation that had speeded up his exile, and disappointed Lunacharsky's hope that he might return.[60]

In the ensuing years, the MAAT2 worked productively and harmoniously, allowing Platon Kerzhentsev to write to this effect on 20 February 1936 to Stalin and Molotov.[61] Kerzhentsev had become the official

---

[57] Gamlet *na stsene MKhAT Vtorovo* (Hamlet *on the Second MAAT Stage*), ed. Zinaïda Udaltsova and commentary E. A. Kesler, Moscow Art Theatre, 2017. My interpretation of this published script.

[58] See *MXAT Vtoroy. Svidetelstva i dokumenty 1926–1936* (*The Second MAAT: Evidence and Documents*), compiled and ed. Zinaïda Udaltsova, Moscow: Moscow Art Theatre, 2011 and Inna Solovyova, *Pervaya Studiya. Vtoroy MkhAT* (*First Studio. Second MAAT*), Moscow: New Literary Review, 2016.

[59] Confirmed by Udaltsova, personal communication 30 June 2017. See also Nemirovich-Danchenko, *The Moscow Art Theatre Letters*, 324, on Chekhov's lack of full support from his peers already in 1924, when he threatened to leave the Studio.

[60] *Literaturnoye naslediye*, Vol. 1, 341–8.   [61] *MKHAT Vtoroy*, 644.

responsible for the theatre at the beginning of 1936, after a long climb up from the political reshuffle of the end of the 1920s that also saw Lunacharsky's engineered retirement, and he addressed Stalin more cautiously than he would do in nine days' time over *Molière* (Chapter 2). At issue was the 'resettlement' of the MAAT2: Was it to be inside or outside Moscow? Kiev was proposed – offering excellent working conditions – in line with the government's policy of decentralizing culture for the benefit of the regions as well as the Socialist Republics of the Soviet Union. The third solution was 'liquidation'.

Kerzhentsev also wrote that Stanislavsky had telephoned, arguing that, as the first 'branch' of the MAAT, the MAAT2 had to be maintained. He had also argued that the 'whole theatre world' would be 'distressed' by its 'liquidation', and even by its relocation out of the city. Stanislavsky's advocacy was ineffectual. The political leadership shut the MAAT2 down shortly afterwards, handing its venue over to the Moscow Children's Theatre because, being next door to the newly built metro station and so easier for children to travel, it was ideally placed for them.[62] It would appear that this deal was not sealed without some backstage machinations. The MAAT2 actors, among them Giatsintova, Birman, who also directed there, and others from the Sulerzhitsky years, were rehoused in various theatres across Moscow, definitively ending Sulerzhitsky's 'utopia' of collectivity and unity. Birman was to become a director of some standing in the late 1940s and 1950s.

The Second Studio

In 1916, Vakhtang Mchedelov, an energetic young director at the Art Theatre, organized students of the drama school run and taught by three actors of the Art Theatre into the Second Studio. These actors were all called 'Nikolay' – Massalitinov, Podgorny and Aleksandrov – and they had founded the school in 1913. Mchedelov had been rehearsing *The Green Circle* by the contemporary playwright Zinaïda Gippius with their students, and had shown parts of their ongoing work to Stanislavsky in order to win his approval for the formation of a Second Studio. He became the 'heart of the Studio', in Knebel's words (Knebel joined the Second Studio

---

[62] I am infinitely grateful to Udaltsova for pointing me to this and other finer details, which clarify the situation. It is worth noting, for contextual interest, that the director of the Children's Theatre was Natalya Sats, daughter of composer Ilya Sats, greatly admired by Stanislavsky and a close friend of Sulerzhitsky (see note 68, Chapter 1). Natalya was one of the children of the Kanev-Yevpatoria commune.

150 Studio

after first studying with Chekhov in his independent classes);[63] and he co-operated amicably with the three Nikolays, but primarily with Massalitinov, who had spent time at the Kanev-Yevpatoria commune.

There is no evidence to prove that Sulerzhitsky had inspired Massalitinov's quick agreement to the venture – Massalitinov, like Stanislavsky, was one of the friends on rotating bedside duty as Sulerzhitsky lay dying towards the end of 1916 – although the First Studio's growing renown may have been an enticement to try with another kind of youthful talent. Massalitinov left Moscow with the Kachalov group in 1919, stayed abroad with the Prague Group, and then became the chief director of the National Theatre in Sofia (1925–44), where he founded Bulgaria's first professional theatre school, teaching Stanislavsky's System there with outstanding results.

Massalitinov's departure, together with Mchedelov's temporary 'cooling-off' towards the Second Studio in 1919, meant that it did not have a stable presence during its eight years to equal Sulerzhitsky's in the First Studio. Still, the group was well taught, having had, in addition to the three Nikolays, major Art Theatre elders as pedagogues: Yelena Muratova, Nina Litovtseva (Kachalov's wife), Yelena Telesheva (whom Knebel praised highly over the years), Vasily Luzhsky and Leonid Leonidov; with them were the younger teachers Vahktangov, Giatsintova and Birman.[64] Cross-studio co-operation came in plural forms, and so Vakhtangov directed *The Deluge* with the 'studists' in 1919, expressly for the Second Studio's tour to Siberia. (Touring the regions was also a central activity of the First and Third Studios.) He played Frazer, the role he had created in 1915, becoming an embodied lesson in the System, several of whose main principles the 'studists' had already learned. From 1918 to 1920, Mchedelov undertook considerable work with them on what he called 'improvisations', his special interest, which prepared them for long etudes that drew on plays and prose and led to a number of productions.[65] One such prose-based production was the 1918 *Studio Diary*, a compilation of pieces adapted from Nikolay Leskov's novel *No Way Out*, Turgenev's *Lieutenant Yergunov's Story* and Dostoyevsky's *White Nights*.

---

[63] *Vsya zhizn*, 144.
[64] Irina Vinogradskaya, 'Vtoraya studiya Moskovskogo Khudozhestvennogo Teatra' in *Sovetsky teatr. Dokumenty i materialy 1917–1921* ('The Second Studio of the Moscow Art Theatre' in *Soviet Theatre. Documents and Materials 1917–1921*), ed. A. Z. Yufit et al., Leningrad: Iskusstvo, 1968, 387.
[65] Ibid.

The Second Studio   151

Stanislavsky also taught at the Studio, although he did not give it the concentrated emotional energy and time that he had spent on the First Studio. His teaching was of a supervisory-directorial kind, beginning with the final 'many hours' of rehearsals of *The Green Circle*, a play on the young breaking away from the generation before them as they sought their way in uncertain times.[66] Stanislavsky pulled the production together, giving it a wholeness that was lacking, and he whittled away the 'sentimentality and mannerist way of acting' of the 'studists' so as to feed 'healthy optimism, light humour and sincerity of experiencing' into it. His second supervisory teaching was with *Youth* by Andreyev, the author of the Sulerzhitsky-directed *The Life of Man*, who had abandoned Symbolist writing to turn in a play on the conflict between the generations and related daily-life themes similar to those of *The Green Circle*. *Youth* was co-directed in 1918 by Litovtseva and Mchedelov. According to its actors, Stanislavsky put a considerable amount of time into improving their diction and speech, while developing the plasticity of their bodies through intensive movement exercises and exercises in rhythm. He wanted them, above all, to acquire a feeling for rhythm. The results, Markov testifies, were noticeable in that the production was 'light, transparent, clear: as if the youthful studio had grasped that young, democratic and spontaneous writer known to literature'.[67]

During 1919 and 1920, Stanislavsky gave a series of classes on the System, mainly through preparatory work on *The Blue Bird*. Mchedelov directed this production, which the 'studists' performed in repertory at the MAAT as of 1922, when they were asked to stand in for the Art Theatre actors on tour in the United States. Overall, the 'studists' did not so much learn in a classroom situation as 'on their feet', thus absorbing the System's principles directly through performing performances. It could be said that Stanislavsky – constantly at work, constantly short of time – expediently combined tasks, producing teaching of a different, synthesized kind in which teaching, learning and practice were one. The more traditionally structured classes in diction, voice placement, dance and 'rhythmics' (possibly a variant of Jaques-Dalcroze's eurhythmics), with the first taken by Nikolay Podgorny and the last by Stanislavsky's brother Vladimir Alekseyev, provided necessary support. Members of the Second Studio attended Stanislavsky's consecutive course on the System in 1920 and 1921 at the Griboyedov Drama Studio, founded in 1916 by the Art Theatre actress Svetlana Khalutina and a lawyer partner. This Drama

---

[66] Ibid., 384, and the following citations.   [67] Ibid., 386.

Studio was not officially affiliated with the MAAT, although, by teaching there, Stanislavsky clearly encouraged its ambitions.

Direct schooling 'on their feet' was to be had, additionally, from the 'studists' frequent performances on the Art Theatre stage in crowd scenes and small parts. Their attitude to the alma mater, as reported by Anastasiya Zuyeva, a future leading actress of the MAAT, was one of 'sacredness, trembling' and 'quiet' attention because 'they could not separate their faith in their own future from it'.[68] She observes that the theatre's elders instilled in them a sense of modesty and, most important, of ensemble togetherness. They did not teach, but educated them, which resembles Stanislavsky's commitment to educating the whole human being who is the actor, rather than simply teaching/training the actor per se.

The Studio repertoire principally consisted of *The Green Circle*, which saw its hundredth performance in 1919, *Youth*, which was retained until 1925, *Student Diary*, which was broken up to make *Lieutenant Yegurov's Story* a lynchpin for several other dramatized pieces of prose, and *The Rose Pattern*, directed by Luzhsky in 1920. The latter was by another contemporary, the Symbolist Fyodr Sologub, who was closely associated with Meyerhold and whose play replaced the Studio's unsuccessful first choice, Blok's esoteric *The Rose and the Cross*. Riding the crest of the revolutionary wave during 1918 and 1919, the Studio performed parts of *The Green Circle* and *Youth* in factories, workers' clubs and venues of fortune on the outskirts of Moscow. At the same time, it gave 'concerts', the going term for recitations, of Pushkin's, Gogol's and Dostoyevsky's writings in the mass-educational spirit promoted by Lunacharsky of democratizing Russia's cultural heritage. These experiences beyond the Studio's 120-seat theatre and its regular theatregoers would have provided its actors with some insight into audiences of a very different kind.

The critics were positive, giving *The Green Circle* full, if pedestrian, praise in its halcyon days of 1916 for its fidelity to the 'Stanislavsky school' and its realization of 'one whole', according to Stanislavsky's System; Alla Tarasova, who was to become a beacon of the Art Theatre, as of the Soviet cinema, was singled out for her 'wonderful performance' and its 'strong, fresh and young tone'.[69] Efros, the Art Theatre chronicler, complained of the Studio's choice of texts for *Studio Diary*. Leskov's *No Way Out*, he said, was 'so old that it ought to be put into the archives' and 'you really had to

---

[68] Ibid., 388.
[69] K. S. No. 22146 and K. S. No. 22147, 24 November 1916; authors identified as 'I. Zh-n' and 'A. N.'; newspaper titles missing.

The Second Studio

think hard to choose from Turgenev what was least characteristic of him', and more of this ilk.[70] Luzhsky wrote in his diary in March 1920 that Lunacharsky and his colleague Yelena Malinovskaya, who was responsible for state theatres in Moscow, had attended the premiere of *The Rose Pattern* and were happy with the production.[71] The Studio's tenure had become shaky, so their approval would have set Luzhsky's mind at rest regarding continued government support for it.

Only a year before, Mchedelov had harangued the Studio Committee – one of its members was Vakhtangov – saying that there was a 'lack of culture' among the 'studists': they thought 'only of themselves', and all 'wanted to play the main roles', which was 'not normal', nor could the Studio exist in the face of 'an attitude like this to work'.[72] Sadly, his outburst, although less dramatic, sounded like a replay of Sulerzhitsky's letter to Stanislavsky, and at its heart was the same question, although not explicitly formulated: What constituted a *laboratory*-studio? The First Studio had been designed as a laboratory, but the Second started out with a production, which had given its members the false impression that it was a *theatre*-studio: 'false' because, in Mchedelov's view, *The Green Circle* was a matter of research, experiment and exploration – the three features defining a studio's vocation. Serious 'new' theatre, he insisted, was impossible without them.

Mchedelov had perceived the equivocation that had previously beset the First Studio. Did the emphasis fall on *laboratory* or on *theatre*? For Chekhov, it fell on *theatre*-studio, since he itched to act while feeling the pulse of the audience and its breath upon him. In any case, his acting on the stage was ceaselessly explorative of itself, and in this he materialized Stanislavsky's idea of the laboratory actor who was continually researching, continually working on himself. However, the equivocation that germinated in the First Studio was inherent in Stanislavsky's and Nemirovich-Danchenko's initial desire to raise a new type of actor and, simultaneously, revitalize the Art Theatre with fresh blood – effectively on a permanent basis. In other words, they needed free experimentalists *and* actors who would comply with Art Theatre day-to-day routines, the demands of programming, and such public responsibilities as having a specified number of shows ready for every season. What their long-term perspective

---

[70] K. S. No. 22148, 8 March 1918, newspaper unidentified.
[71] 20 March 1920, quoted in Vinogradskaya, 'Vtoraya studiya', 389.
[72] K. S. No. 14312, Committee Notebook, minutes of 12 May 1919.

154 Studio

did not need were studios moving sideways for autonomy and/or personal success.

Fifty and more years later, Grotowski and Vasilyev were to encounter a similar equivocation. Grotowski categorically decided in 1969 that the theatre was dead, but that the laboratory lived, as it was eventually to do, after the painful disbandment of his group and several laboratory-style situations, in his 'closed' research in Pontedera. Vasilyev attempted a fusion of single-minded, 'pure' research in laboratory seclusion with the public dialogue of theatre, this being the nearest to Stanislavsky's conception of the studio-to-theatre continuum that Vakhtangov had realized with the Third Studio. Vasilyev's handling of the 'original' equivocation brought about consequences different to those initiated by Grotowski, as the Epilogue to this book indicates, and Dodin's decision to resolve the dilemma by way of a *school* of practice, which was Stanislavsky's overarching idea of a studio and specifically of the six in question, offers another variation on an issue still vital for the twenty-first century.

It will never be known just how much Stanislavsky may have battled with himself over the equivocation of laboratory-studio/theatre-studio, but, given the Second Studio's beginnings and 'not normal' current situation, as Mchedelov had perceived it, he acted in the only way possible. In late 1919, Stanislavsky took the Studio in hand by directing-teaching Mikhaïl Chekhov's dramatization of *The Tale of Ivan the Fool and His Brothers* by Tolstoy. Tolstoy's tale – essentially a parable – on the great virtue of working the land with one's own hands could not be closer to Sulerzhitsky's worldview, as Stanislavsky would have known; and, for all we know, the production may have been Stanislavsky's secret tribute to his dearest friend. Vakhtangov was to help with the casting, but his absences from meetings suggested the encroachment of his fatal illness.[73]

The production premiered in the 1921–22 season, but neither Stanislavsky's 'solution' nor Chekhov's contribution could save the Second Studio from the critics' dismissal of its 'boring' repertoire, and nor were the 'studists' confident that it was sufficiently attractive. They made a 'sudden change', in Vinogradskaya's words.[74] They devised a new repertoire for their 1922–23 season from Schiller's *The Robbers* (in which Knebel performed) and Ostrovsky's *The Storm*, directed by Sudakov (Chapter 2), performing its old repertoire and the recent *Ivan the Fool* only on regional tours. But the significant 'change' was not so much in the

---

[73] Entries in above Notebook.   [74] 'Vtoraya Studiya', 389.

The Second Studio   155

choice of plays for production as the Studio's imitative constructivist style. Critic Yury Sobolyov's harshest of reviews just about sums up the general opinion. These productions failed in their 'primitive and provincial constructivism', which, in *The Robbers*, 'lacerates the eyes', while *The Storm*, abstracted 'out of time and space ... shows the dilettantism of its makers'.[75]

Taking such tough criticism on the chin, the Second Studio bravely presented Calderon de la Barca's *The Phantom Lady* in 1923 and, in 1924, Dmitri Smolin's *Yelizaveta Petrovna* (its title referring to the daughter of Peter the Great), co-directed by Mchedelov shortly before his sudden death at the age of forty. *The Phantom Lady* disappeared, but *Yelizaveta Petrovna* subsequently enjoyed great popularity on the MAAT Small Stage. During discussions in the 1923–24 season on studio mergers, Sudakov, referring to the Second Studio's constructivist dalliance, declared that the Studio had needed help, but had received very little – churlishly pointing the finger at Luzhsky.[76] Knebel described the Second Studio as 'a severe school demanding a great deal of courage'.[77]

The Second Studio had always been a large studio, and it was still large enough to have thirty-seven of its members merge with the Art Theatre, many to become powerful figures in the Soviet Theatre for the next five decades. Among them, other than Tarasova and Zuyeva, were Nikolay Khmelyov, a formidable actor, who was appointed artistic director of the MAAT after Nemirovich-Danchenko's death; Mikhaïl Kedrov, his successor, and teacher of the polemical Taganka Theatre founder and director Yury Lyubimov; and, of course, Maria Knebel, director and renowned teacher and writer, who became the artistic director of the Central Children's Theatre in 1955 (the very same to which the MAAT2 had lost its venue), and whose students at the famous GITIS (Government Institute of Theatre Art) included Vasilyev and Oleg Yefremov. Yefremov, following the studio tradition, founded the Studio of Young Actors in 1956, which turned into the bold and innovative Sovremennik Theatre, driven by first-rate actors under his leadership. He then became the artistic director of the MAAT in 1970. Anatoly Efros, another student of Knebel who also famously directed at the Children's Theatre, built up a wonderful company at the Moscow Drama Theatre known by the name of its street

---

[75] *Zhizn iskusstva* (*The Life of Art*), 1924, No. 10, 2–3.
[76] Irina Vinogradskaya, 'Vtoraya Studiya Moskovskogo Khudozhestvennogo Akademicheskogo Teatra' ('The Second Studio of the MAAT') in *Sovyetsky teatr 1921–1926*, 186.
[77] *Vsya zhizn*, 146.

Malaya Bronnaya (1967–84). Vasilyev, at one stage, was his assistant. The lineage from the Second Studio, which had never shone as brilliantly as the First, can hardly be accused of being lacklustre or insignificant.

The Third Studio

Vakhtangov was involved in teaching in many studios across Moscow, five and more in a row, including the Second Studio. His very own first studio, the Student Studio of 1913, was a group of Moscow University students, who had asked him to direct them.[78] By then, he had played several minor roles at the MAT, also in Craig's production of *Hamlet*, and was known to be an excellent teacher, not least of the System. He exuded authority from his earliest collaboration with Sulerzhitsky. In the Student Studio, which became a place of exploration and apprenticeship rather than production, he experimented with vaudeville and improvisations inspired by *commedia dell'arte*, fine-tuning the techniques of physical expressivity and the economy of means that were to characterize the Third Studio *Princess Turandot* (1922), the acme of his all-too-short career.

His interest in popular theatre grew with Vakhtangov's critique of bourgeois aspirations, and then with his embrace of the October Revolution – rather like Meyerhold whose theatre achievements he was increasingly to value as he shifted his sights to the theatricality of the theatre, formulating it as 'fantastic realism'. Maeterlinck's *The Miracle of St Anthony*, which he directed at the Third Studio in 1921, dressed social satire in this fantastic realism. *The Dybbuk*, which he directed at the Habima Studio in 1922, was in Hebrew, a language he did not know, but whose rhythms and accompanying gestures he followed, realizing from them the Mystery play that, for some time, he had longed to stage. In this production, he was able to come face to face with the world of spirit – absolute love, possession, exorcism and the passage into the 'other world' of the living whom Vakhtangov juxtaposed against the 'living dead' on earth.

It is difficult to pin down the frequently changing composition of Vakhtangov's Studio taken as a conglomerate entity. The Studio in its 1919 composition broke up, with the large majority leaving and only about four or five members staying to provide the foundations of the

---

[78] Note that the *Soviet Encyclopaedia* cited in note 5 records the Student Studio as lasting until 1917.

The Third Studio   157

Third Studio of the MAAT, which was how Vakhtangov's group was reclassified.[79] Nevertheless, Vakhtangov's Studio left a legacy that had a distinctive identity, as did his productions across studios. Discord must have resurfaced by the time Lunacharsky wrote to the directorate of the Third Studio on 9 May 1924 – with a copy to Nemirovich-Danchenko – commenting that this 'obliges him to think that the Studio had lost its compass after the highly esteemed Vakhtangov's passing away'.[80] Further, given that the Third Studio had economic difficulties, and the Second did not see itself as a 'satisfactory organism', a merger between them would make a stronger laboratory and *the* main laboratory affiliated with the MAAT.

The Third Studio's reply to Lunacharsky on 13 May was a firm 'No'.[81] It was clever in its offensive, arguing that the 'studists' could not merge because they recognized their debt to Stanislavsky and also believed, at the same time, that Vakhtangov's enterprise (*delo*) 'would die with the liquidation of the Studio'. Further, Vakhtangov had created the Studio's 'ideology and culture' on the teachings of Stanislavsky, and 'this thread gave us the right to be a studio of the MAAT' ('right' here meant being affiliated *and* independent). An unexpressed, but implied 'however' gave room for the punchline: 'The Third Studio is the child of the Revolution. It was born and grew up in historical days'. With this, Vakhtangov's students snapped the 'thread' that he had woven assiduously and with affection for Stanislavsky before the Revolution to insist on following their own line by paraphrasing Vakhtangov's assertion that the actor who wants to do what is 'new' must do it 'together with the people. Not "for" [the people] nor because of them, but "together" with them'.[82]

The 'studists'' *coup de théâtre* was a strategy to defend their interests by playing familiar politics. Reclaiming collaboration with 'the people' was music to the ears of a period concerned with the theatre *of* the people, and it possibly echoed leftist accusations that the Art Theatre was unable to handle this kind of 'new'. Then the open bargaining over Lunacharsky's proposed merger began in earnest: The Studio knew that there had been talk of Meyerhold joining Stanislavsky to work on the 'Vakhtangov Studio's territory', and 'this was the only territory on which this unification [could] occur'. Note the assertive 'only'.

---

[79] Malaev-Babel (*Yevgeny Vakhtangov*, 150) specifies that twelve left and 'five of his eldest Studio members remained' with beginner students.
[80] K. S. No. 14539 in the MAT Museum archives.   [81] K. S. No. 14540.   [82] Ibid.

The Third Studio was strategically on the offensive in another way, deciding to write to Stanislavsky rather than wait for his return. The signatories to its letter of 29 June 1924, many of whom were instrumental in founding and running the Vakhtangov Theatre two years later, declare that 'our fate is in your hands' and 'we dare not lose what was given to us to preserve and develop'.[83] They refer to Nemirovich-Danchenko's ultimatum, declare that they cannot agree to the 'liquidation of the Studio' (the implied reason was the preservation of their heritage), stress that Stanislavsky's teaching had provided the foundations of the Studio, recall his and Meyerhold's alleged conversation in 1920, when the two 'colossal theatre artists' discussed the possibility of working together on the 'territory of the Third Studio', and conclude that they want to be the territory of their 'monumental collaboration'. They persevere in their argument, stating that Meyerhold, who was 'providing the "roots" of the theatre's Future', had already agreed to such a collaboration and was waiting for Stanislavsky's reply.

The 'studists' may not have known – or was it a coercive assault, agreed upon beforehand? – that Meyerhold had already written to Stanislavsky about the parlous state of the Studio on 27 June, two days earlier, pointing out that 'only you, Vakhtangov's teacher, can save it'.[84] There seems to be no trace of a reply from Stanislavsky, but he was hardly likely to jump at the offer, given that Meyerhold had been advocating the closure of the 'bourgeois' Art Theatre, along with the leftists. And he was less likely to do so because he was committed to the Art Theatre, however sullied, for life. The Third Studio went on its way to the eventual successes of the Vakhtangov Theatre, a theatre whose stature today is unquestionable.

The Fourth Studio

The Regional Group of the MAAT was the initiative in 1918 of the actors Georgy Burdzhalov and Vasily Luzhsky, a veteran of the Art Theatre's Chekhov and Gorky productions. Luzhsky taught in the Second Studio and, as Knebel warmly remembers, additionally educated its students by walking and talking them through art galleries and lending them books that he thought they should read.[85] The Regional Group was formed with junior actors of the Art Theatre, and Stanislavsky and Nemirovich-Danchenko gave their blessing to use the alma mater's name. Born with

[83] K. S. No. 14543. [84] *Stati. Pisma. Rechy. Besedy*, Vol. 2, Moscow: Iskusstvo, 1968, 63.
[85] *Vsya zhizn*, 146–8.

The Fourth Studio

the Revolution as the youngest of the studios, it was distinguished from its predecessors by two features: it was meant to be a professional theatre from its very inception and it was meant to be an *outreach* professional theatre with a socio-political profile; its only 'laboratory' claims were those of the social 'laboratory' taking place in the country at large. For three years, it followed its star, playing with next to no money in the demanding physical conditions of workers' clubs and makeshift community spaces across greater Moscow. It performed scenes from the Art Theatre repertoire as well as dramatizations of Pushkin, radical poet Nikolay Nekrasov, Anton Chekhov and Tolstoy – all socially engaged writers, in their own way. As soon as the young actors had 'gathered their strength', they offered 'portable stagings' of whole acts of Art Theatre classics, notably Carlo Goldoni's comedy *The Mistress of the Inn* (*La Locandiera*, directed by Benois in 1914) and Molière's *The Doctor in Spite of Himself* (in which Stanislavsky-actor had excelled, directed also by Benois).[86]

The Regional Group's cultural sights, and so also its repertoire, corresponded with Lunacharsky's cultural-educational policy. Politically speaking, its mission politics blended in with the many shades that veered to the Left or were firmly placed somewhere on the Left during this period. Organizationally speaking, it had something of the Proletkult's proselytism, making-do in found conditions, but it lacked the Proletkult's grassroots participatory drive, that is, it did not make theatre with workers. Thus it also lacked the Proletkult's political will to open spaces so that subaltern groups – in this period all categorized as 'proletarian' (Chapter 2) – could find their voice and make it heard. Even so, the Regional Group's broadly social activities favourably reflected back on the Art Theatre, suggesting that this was not, in actual fact, the conservative monolith vehemently denounced by leftist factions: it, too, by lending its reputation and influence to a progressive group, was playing a part in the construction of a socialist society.

A statutory document titled 'From the MAAT Regional Group's Regulations', presumed to be of 5 March 1921, declares its three main objectives: the preparation of a 'good artistic repertoire' to 'serve' the 'broad masses'; the development of future actors and directors from these 'masses' by 'using the MAAT's human resources'; the development of 'principles of portable staging' for venues that had few or no amenities or technical equipment.[87] A note explains that, given the extremely difficult conditions in which work was both prepared and performed, the

---

[86] Quotations from Klimenko, 'Chetvyortaya studiya MKhATa', 188. [87] Ibid., 190–1.

group was very attentive to its 'artistic obligations' and the maintenance of discipline. Another document was signed a few months later under the new name of 'members of the Fourth Studio' – the transition to Studio having occurred in the interim with the added qualification of 'artists' co-operative'.[88] This document stresses the Studio's continuing engagement with 'enlightenment and education' (*vospitaniye*) and the creative principles of the MAAT. To be noticed is the Regional Group's impressive achievement of 325 shows and 150 'concerts' in the three years before it became the Fourth Studio.[89]

The Fourth Studio's intentions were a tall order, and reaching the 'masses' from within the fixed abode that it was granted in 1921 was nothing like going out to them. Undeterred, it celebrated its first season in its theatre in 1922–23 with the topical yet fundamentally bland *The Promised Land* and *Our Own Family*. However, its intensive outreach programme in the Moscow periphery ceded during the ensuing years to touring these productions to the cities of Petrograd, Kazan and Minsk and their outlying regions. A few productions of average merit were added in 1924–25. *The Promised Land* was co-directed by Konstantin Babanin and Nikolay Demidov.

Babanin was one of the signatories to the two documents cited above, indicating that his was already a leading role in the Regional Group, while Demidov's name appears as part of the directorate only in 1922 in a letter from the directorate to Stanislavsky.[90] At this time, Burdzhalov and Luzhsky, the founders of the Studio were with Stanislavsky on the Art Theatre's United States tour. Demidov had been teaching the System at the Fourth Studio since it became such in 1921, as the magazine *Ekran* (*Screen*) had reported;[91] and, according to Andrei Malaev-Babel, he was a co-founder of the Studio and led its artistic matters.[92] At some point before the Studio turned into the Moscow State Theatre 'Fourth Studio' in 1925, fifteen of Demidov's graduates from the Moscow Proletkult Central Studio had entered its ranks, strengthening the Studio considerably.[93]

The Fourth Studio, much like the Second, went in search of contemporary plays with subjects of interest to audiences but also with substance for the creative imagination of directors and performers. By and large, such

---

[88] Ibid., 191.   [89] Ibid., note 9, 195.   [90] Ibid., 191, 10 December 1922.
[91] Ibid., 188 and Vinogradskaya, *Zhizn i tvorchestvo*, Vol. 3, 175.
[92] In conversation of 14 June 2017 and communication of 24 June, detailing source as RGALI (Russian State Literary Archive).
[93] 'Chetvyortaya studiya', 196.

plays were not easy to find and, while critics like Sobolyov complained about the Studio's inadequate repertoire – an affliction common, in his view, to all the studios (Chapter 2 saw the Art Theatre strike the same problem) – a compelling repertoire, let alone a compelling *revolutionary* repertoire, could not be had by command. The aim of the Moscow State Theatre 'Fourth Studio', as announced in 1926, was finding that revolutionary repertoire. The repertoire question had already featured significantly in the discussions between Nemirovich-Danchenko and Lunacharsky about merging the Studios with the Art Theatre, and it was unlikely to be resolved quickly.

The newly renamed Fourth Studio severed its ties with the MAAT, but it did not break contact. In its new capacity, it invited MAAT elders, who had returned to Moscow from their tour, to a showing of its work, which was really an account to its 'fathers' of its achievements. Stanislavsky, Nemirovich-Danchenko (who had helped the Studio greatly during Stanislavsky's absence), Knipper-Chekhova, Kachalov, Moskvin, Luzhsky, Burdzhalov and more praised the work of the former 'studists' in what was, effectively, their rite of passage to adulthood.

The Bolshoy Opera Studio

The Fourth Studio was not close to the MAAT as the Second had always been, but, as an offshoot of the family tree, it nevertheless sheds light on the interconnections between the MAAT extended family and the variety and reach of its activities. The Bolshoy Opera Studio does so as well, although it was not established under the wing of the MAAT. Nor was it Stanislavsky's initiative but Malinovskaya's who, besides holding her political office, backed by Lunacharsky, was the managing director of the Bolshoy and intent on broadening its audiences and appeal.

The idea may have been state-initiated, but it squared with Stanislavsky's view that opera had to be overhauled, as had the theatre twenty years earlier, when he co-founded the Art Theatre. Only when it was reformed could opera survive as a theatre genre – of this Stanislavsky was convinced to his dying day. Most urgent of all, opera needed to be comprehensible in word, diction, musical pleasure and way of singing and acting to the new audiences after 1917. Stanislavsky's unpublished plan of 1919 envisaged teaching singers – soloists and chorus – to expunge bravura declamation and posturing and become natural actors of emotional experiencing.[94]

---

[94] Moscow Art Theatre Museum archives F.3. op. 29. ed. khr. 3.

162   Studio

This meant acting-singing integrally in the moment instead of dredging up pre-played – 'second-hand', one might say – sounds, expressions, gestures and so on. Stanislavsky's reference in his plan to an orchestra studio remained without comment, but he must have been thinking about the confluence between musical, vocal, dramatic and kinetic work, which he set out to accomplish with his opera 'studists' throughout the years.

The Opera Studio was by no means out on a limb on its own. It was kin to the four drama studios through its premise of laboratory research. Similarly to the First Studio, it was intended to be 'like a threshold to the church of art' in which each studio member acquired the necessary 'spiritual baggage' for becoming a 'human being-actor' devoted to his/her 'sacred task'.[95] This was the language of Stanislavsky's formative years, reverberant in his diary entries and other writings that paved his way to *My Life in Art* and *An Actor's Work on Himself*. Although it was unexpected in times of revolution, this was the language he needed as a bulwark against the reductivist utilitarianism that was taking hold of the theatres, much as it had taken hold of society. With it, Stanislavsky was able to educate and develop (the cue, once again, is *vospitaniye*) the Studio's singers as he taught the System in the holistic sense in which he understood it. The System fully inscribed the Opera Studio in the Art Theatre's genealogy, and it also had teachers in common with the Second and Fourth Studios: Zinaïda and Vladimir, Stanislavsky's siblings who, additionally, were assistants for his opera productions, and Demidov, who taught the System and whose practical knowledge of it was probably comparable only to that of Sulerzhitsky and Vakhtangov.

Teaching the System meant instilling a sense of ethics, discipline and self-discipline in the 'studists', and Stanislavsky's determination to succeed in this (perhaps recalling Sulerzhitsky's disappointment in the First Studio as a cautionary example) was behind his decision in 1921 to be especially severe with the people 'responsible for ensuring discipline and the proper flow of work in the Studio'.[96] Demidov was thus fined for having missed a class of waiting students, many of whom, Stanislavsky pointed out, had a long way to walk there and back on an empty stomach and in worn-out footwear during those days of tremendous hardship.

Stanislavsky soon realized that singers employed in the Bolshoy repertoire and who also sang in concert series to boost their income could not

---

[95] Konkordiya Antarova, *Besedy K. S. Stanislavskogo v Studiya Bolshogo teatra v 1918–1922*, 30, 28, 27, 71. All translations are mine.
[96] Vinogradskaya, *Zhizn i tvorchestvo*, Vol. 3, 168.

The Bolshoy Opera Studio 163

manage the commitment demanded by the Studio and, while several of them persisted, the Studio was filled with young singers from the Moscow Conservatorium of Music with whom Stanislavsky could start afresh. Among the Bolshoy singers was the well-known soloist Konkordiya Antarova, whose record in shorthand of Stanislavsky's conversations from 1918 to 1922, from which the citations above were taken, was approved for accuracy by his sister Zinaïda for publication in 1939. When the MAAT went on tour, Stanislavsky's teachers continued their duties, while a Bolshoy soloist took charge of the Studio, apparently with mediocre results. According to Demidov, writing to Stanislavsky in 1923, 'everything in the Opera Studio hangs only by your name – everyone is waiting for your return'.[97]

On his return, Stanislavsky found a depleted group composed primarily of the young, and a government without the resources to support it. Help finally came from the state in 1925, together with that of the rather elusive Association of Friends of the Studio and Nemirovich-Danchenko's Music Studio at the MAAT.[98] It is worth noticing a text presumed to be of this time in which Stanislavsky explained why the Opera Studio mattered. Here he wrote that the 'correspondence between dramatic and vocal-musical art' was important for the dramatic actor, who needed the vocal and musical foundations essential for tragic roles – tragedy being a weakness of the MAAT, which Stanislavsky was careful not to mention.[99]

On the vocal-musical side, the Studio was important for what it could do for opera, aided by the Bolshoy masters. It could stay the erosion of the Bolshoy's 'wonderful vocal-musical-traditions', which were the 'legacy of centuries', before their last traces disappeared; already the numbers of instrumentalists, conductors, soloists and choristers had shrunk due to singers and musicians abandoning music for better pay elsewhere (critical for survival in such straitened times), and to diminished government subsidies, which could barely keep the Studio afloat, let alone sustain the Bolshoy's honourable traditions. Finally, singers needed to be schooled in the acting and related dramatic skills that made opera part and parcel of the theatre and not, as was customarily thought, a separate musical genre that told a story, but was otherwise unrelated to spoken theatre in anything but the most superficial clichés of playacting.

The Studio, then, was both a protector and an avenger. It could protect aspects of a legacy that, in recent decades, had seen Chaliapin weld singing and acting and so opera and drama, and with whose art, Stanislavsky

[97] Ibid., 290.   [98] *SS* 8, 6, 213.   [99] Ibid., 215–16, and following citations and glossary.

164 Studio

pointed out, his own had much in common. Both of them had come from 'Mamontov's circle' (that is, Mamontov's Private Opera and Abramtsevo, where Stanislavsky's practical knowledge of opera had begun). Chaliapin was Stanislavsky's model singer who sang with *perezhivaniye* and acted effortlessly, organically, as System actors and System actor-singers were meant to do. But the Studio was an avenger to an equal degree because, as Stanislavsky was to phrase it in 1927 (the Opera Studio had become a Studio-Theatre), its purpose was to 'reform [opera] at its very roots'.[100] The young actor-singers performed, at this time, Puccini's *La Bohème* according to Stanislavsky's opera-drama integrated approach, channelled through the System.

Stanislavsky explained in *My Life in Art* that he had prepared a syllabus within his System specifically for opera, and had created exercises on 'rhythm and such'.[101] ('Such' must surely refer to breathing, pace, tempo and timing, which are central to the System and crucial for singing.) His System teachers went through these exercises to make sure that the students had a dramatic perspective on the material taught by the Bolshoy specialist vocal, musical and ballet staff – an impressive list of highly competent people.[102] The Bolshoy ballet master taught the actor-singers numerous dances of the opera repertoire so that they, rather than ballet dancers hired in, could perform them. Stanislavsky studied under the Bolshoy teachers alongside his students for the benefit of his 'investigations into words, speech and sound'.[103] What he was exploring was how all three expressed thought and feeling in the registers, timbres, inflections and intonations of the voice.

Learning with these teachers consolidated his own teaching about the desirable harmony between musical, acting and singing rhythms so that they formed one rhythmic composition rather than a 'mish-mash' (Stanislavsky) of competitive strands; and he consistently related breath and respiration to rhythm not only because they were the 'basis of our creative labour' but also to point out that the opera singer was more fortunate than the dramatic actor.[104] Why was this so? Antarova's shorthand notes show Stanislavsky explaining that opera had the advantage of a musical score, which provided the singer with the breath, rhythm, tempo, phrasing and pause necessary for the execution of a piece.[105] Drama, by contrast, had no such guide. It obliged the actor to 'discover the composer within himself'

---

[100] *SS* 9, 6, 505.   [101] *Moya zhizn*, 387–8; *My Life*, 332.   [102] Ibid.
[103] Ibid., 388; *My Life*, 333.   [104] *Besedy K. S. Stanislavskogo*, 87–8 and 61–3.
[105] Ibid., 88, also for the following citation.

The Bolshoy Opera Studio   165

and *compose* a workable score of breathing patterns, rhythms, phrasing and everything else the voice required. This, Stanislavsky averred, was very difficult to do, but opera's advantages over drama were exactly what the dramatic actor could learn from opera and master for his/her purposes.

Antarova's notes are a treasure trove, stored during the insecure revolutionary years, when an Opera Studio might have appeared to be a surreal invention. Judging by them, Stanislavsky was not prepared to compromise his ideas, nor pretend that there was a short cut to them. He thus dispelled any illusions that his students may have had about the exercises of his System with forceful assertions like this one: 'Categorically, it is impossible to do any exercises whatsoever from my System in an automatic fashion, mechanically'; and he categorically warned against spoken and sung words that were devoid of the 'intonations that give them suppleness and worth'.[106] In these two commandments, one against a mechanical implementation or 'application' of the System, and the other against empty, worthless words – what he called 'babble' – must lie the reasons for Stanislavsky's scrupulous attention in his classes at the Opera Studio – at least, as Antarova has recorded them – to the worldview centred on the 'human spirit' underlying the System. The 'human spirit' was the 'heart-soul' of the actor and actor-singer. The System's nuts and bolts were in the exercises that were essential to the practical learning within the Studio.

Pavel Rumyantsev, a baritone who joined the Studio in 1920, wrote down some of the rudimentary exercises practised in it after the Studio moved with Stanislavsky to his state-arranged communal apartment in 1921. These exercises involved walking (for years Stanislavsky had complained that actors did not know how to walk on a stage) and relaxing the muscles of the isolated parts of the body, one by one – neck, shoulders, hands, fingers and so forth – so that the whole body could be fully relaxed.[107] Practice was always his initiating force, as Stanislavsky was to say in *My Life in Art*: 'I endeavoured to have the students assimilate everything through practice, and theory only affirmed it and helped them to be aware of what they had already assimilated'.[108]

By the same token, practical learning involved performing ballads and then prologues and scenes until 'studists' could tackle whole operas. The Studio's first public performances were composed of extracts, and they

---

[106] Ibid., 46–7.

[107] P. I. Rumyantsev, *Stanislavsky i opera*, Moscow: Iskusstvo, 1969, 26–36. Constantin (*sic*) Stanislavski (*sic*) and Pavel Rumyantsev, *Stanislavski on Opera*, trans. and ed. Elizabeth Hapgood, New York and London: Routledge, A Theatre Arts Book, 1998, 5–13.

[108] *Moya zhizn*, 388; *My Life*, 332.

were *A Rimsky-Korsakov Evening* and *A Pushkin Evening* in 1921, both on the MAAT stage. *A Pushkin Evening* comprised the first three scenes from Tchaikovsky's *Yevgeny Onegin* and the prologue to Rimsky-Korsakov's opera *The Tale of Tsar Sultan*, based on Pushkin's eponymous fairy tale.

The same year later saw a complete production, implying that the 'studists' were now ready for such a challenge. The opera was *Werther* by Jules Massenet, based on Goethe's novel *The Sorrows of Young Werther*, which tells of Werther and Charlotte's thwarted love, ending in Werther's suicide. Stanislavsky's advice to the actor-singers reiterated what he frequently said to actors of spoken theatre: not to sing a sad song 'in general' for its sadness, but to sing it within the specific circumstances that made it a specific, unique, sadness;[109] to continue a role out into the wings rather than simply to drop it once it was out of the public eye, only to put the mask back on when the singer-actor had to return to the stage (opera hackwork that killed its drama); to show a protagonist's attitude (*otnosheniye*) towards another protagonist or an object, place or situation. Stanislavsky stopped the actress-singer in the role of Sophie, Charlotte's sister who came with children's gifts for Christmas, handling them without a thought, randomly. He had her construct a whole unspoken, inner narrative that delineated her attitude towards them – where did she buy each one, with what intention, how had she chosen them, what exactly was in each parcel? – which, as she repeated the scene, changed how she handled and treated these gifts and also modified her singing, accordingly. There was now dramatic sense in this bringing of gifts and sense made concrete musically in the notes and phrasing of the music.

Stanislavsky wrote of his progression with the 'studists' from smaller to larger productions, accentuating this cumulative approach to learning in his compact account of *Yevgeny Onegin*, which he staged with his actor-singers in 1922.[110] This production, performed on the minuscule stage in his home, was a chamber piece, adapted to the architectural fixtures of the large room used for rehearsals and performances. It required ingenuity, and Stanislavsky describes how he used the four classical columns, which cut into the already tiny space of the stage, to carve out the multiple spaces where the production's events took place. Just as resourceful was his solution to the problem of showing the opera's two ball scenes: he had several couples dance their way through the fifty spectators – the

[109] Grigory Kristi, *Rabota Stanislavskogo v opernom teatre* (*Stanislavsky's Work in Opera Theatre*), Moscow: Iskusstvo, 1952, 95 and 99, and 100–1 for the next two examples.
[110] *Moya zhizn*, 388–90; *My Life*, 333–4.

maximum number to fit tightly into this intimate setting.[111] The piano normally used for rehearsals had to replace an orchestra.

The disadvantages of the architecturally given space were turned into advantages, none more radical than Stanislavsky's invention of chamber opera for modern times – precisely as Brook was to reinvent it in the intimacy of the Bouffes du Nord in Paris, also a 'found' space, with his wonderful *Tragedy of Carmen* in 1981.[112] Like Stanislavsky, he moulded the space and the dramatic and musical compositions so that they were in symbiosis, doing away, as Stanislavsky had done before him, with the conventions of grand opera in how the singing voice was produced and how the actor-singers minimized and 'naturalized' their singing as well as physical movements. Confined to a small space, Stanislavsky was able to give the audience a close-up of Tatyana's emotions between the pillars of the Studio's stage in *Yevgeny Onegin*'s last scene, when she rejects Onegin's love (as previously he had rejected hers), succumbing to social expectations in the face of conflict between love and duty and love and reason.[113]

Always starting with the musical score for access to the drama of an opera, Stanislavsky-director sometimes went in counterpoint to the music to achieve greater emotional impact, as occurred in an early scene, when Tatyana writes her letter confessing her love to Onegin. The music builds up to a climax, while Stanislavsky has the actress-singer go against this climax by standing still.[114] This too countered grand-opera conventions, and Kristi observes that another of Stanislavsky's innovations concerned light, which he used with remarkable delicacy so that light itself became musical, which suggests that he must have arranged light to capture or complement the tones and overtones of Tchaikovsky's score.[115] Kristi's briefest of comments suggests that Stanislavsky was his own light designer, quoting him on how 'insensitive, inartistic lighting' in the theatre generally was and how 'senseless mechanical lighting' was when done 'without love or care' as to what and why something was being lit. Electro-technology was of such importance, Stanislavsky believed, that it could not be left to those working on a stock-in-trade basis: they were nothing less than 'hack workers', in his terminology, when they should be artists.

Many of Stanislavsky's lifelong themes and preoccupations appear in Antarova's collection of conversations: the nurturing and uniting energy of

---

[111] *Rabota Stanislavskogo v opernom teatre*, 120.
[112] See Maria Shevtsova, 'Peter Brook Adapts *The Tragedy of Carmen*', *Théâtre International*, 2, No. 10 (1983), 38–55.
[113] *Rabota Stanislavskogo v opernom teatre*, 121 and 122.   [114] Ibid., 117.
[115] Ibid., 117, and the citations following.

a studio whose first task is to teach that the creative powers of the actor do not come from the exterior but are all 'within him' (the human being-actor); the pre-eminence of love in work and its activation of what was good in people (strongly echoing Tolstoy, Mamontov and the Old Believers); the necessity of opening the 'creative soul' and enjoying the fruits of creativity; beauty, which lives in every human being and when manifested in the theatre calls up in others their 'responding vibrations to beauty'; brightness and joy in work; truthfulness, which can be brought out of each actor –'actor' at the Bolshoy Opera Studio meant 'actor-singer' – and is transmitted through art; the indispensability, for the actor, of being-in-the-now, in a perpetually transient 'now', which is an incontrovertible principle of creativity; the necessity of visualization; the necessity of close relations (*obshcheniye*) between actors on the stage; total muscular relaxation, which is indispensable for creative freedom; the freedom of the spirit, which is essential for a conducive working atmosphere and impels free physical movement on the stage; courage and happiness, which generate personal and collective well-being; the individuality of each actor, whose unique, 'creative, higher I' – Stanislavsky distinguishes it from the mundane 'I' that 'eats, drinks and thinks about daily-life affairs' – is of primary importance for the theatre.[116]

All these themes were now oriented specifically towards actor-singers who, by singing words instead of saying them, followed the musical lines and the spaces created by musical notes to make opera-theatre that was imbued with the 'life of the human spirit'. Irrespective of the overwhelming revolutionary years, Stanislavsky was not afraid to reiterate his phrase-mantra frequently – perhaps also so as to remind his students that doing opera/theatre meant being fully human even in difficult and unpredictable revolutionary times. Going by Antarova's collection, it would seem – incongruously, since it was published during Stalin's reign of terror – that the censor had left Stanislavsky's vocabulary and its thought untouched.

Stanislavsky offered his actor-singers encouraging maxims of his invention, which also expressed his credo for creativity and living. One of them concerned the processes of work by which 'a difficulty becomes a habit, a habit becomes easy, and what is easy becomes beautiful'.[117] Another, sounding like a motto, should be hung, according to Stanislavsky, at the

---

[116] *Besedy K. S. Stanislavskogo*, 27–8,139, 39, 95, 120; 34, 42; 44, 71; 39; 71–3, 94, 121; 23–5, 85; 54, 93.

[117] Ibid., 42 and 129.

The Opera-Dramatic Studio

entrance of every 'temple of art'. It says: 'simpler, lighter, higher, happier'.[118] He advised teachers of the System to teach lightly and happily, and to avoid 'boring despotism'.[119]

The Opera-Dramatic Studio

All of the points summarized above were stable references for him when Stanislavsky picked up where he left off on his return to Moscow in 1924, and the Bolshoy Opera Theatre transited into the Stanislavsky Opera Studio-Theatre and then into the Stanislavsky Opera Theatre. These three phases laid the foundations of the Opera-Dramatic Studio of 1935, in which Stanislavsky continued his research while his frail body kept him housebound and sometimes bed-ridden for months on end. The Studio-Theatre and the Stanislavsky Opera Theatre were of such importance for Stanislavsky's work at the Opera-Dramatic Studio that they are presented here as its integral parts rather than as separate entities. Yet there was a difference between them, and it lay in the fact that this Studio of the remaining three years of Stanislavsky's life existed for no end other than its own research. In this it was very much a laboratory. Further, the Stanislavsky Opera Theatre had gone through its apprenticeship and, in 1935, was a fully fledged theatre, although its performers still came to the Opera-Dramatic Studio to learn and grow, thereby maintaining their connection with it. The difference between them corresponds to Knebel's distinction between the First Studio, which had purposely sought to become a theatre, and the Second Studio, which had elected to keep its 'studio atmosphere'.[120]

Earlier, during the time of the Stanislavsky Opera Studio-Theatre, thus from 1926 to 1928, Stanislavsky and his assistants mounted the operas that Rumyantsev chronicled with the authority of an actor-singer who had performed the title role of *Yevgeny Onegin* while still a student, and who sang in most of Stanislavsky's opera productions of these years. His operas were single annual events, showing *The Tsar's Bride* (1926), *La Bohème* (1927) and Rimsky-Korsakov's comic opera *A May Night* (1928) after two years of rehearsal, which Stanislavsky had directed from beginning to end rather than delegating follow-up work to his assistants; and he directed it, in Rumyantsev's words 'with all the brilliance, the surprises and the contrasts with which he always astonished the public'.[121] Stanislavsky's

---

[118] Ibid., 23.   [119] Ibid., 44.   [120] *Vsya zhizn*, 143.
[121] *Stanislavsky i opera*, 341; *Stanislavski on Opera*, 269.

slow production of operas in the latter part of the 1920s had to do with his embattled directing schedule at the MAAT and the political interferences that drew him into their vortex (Chapter 2), but also, and no less, with his artistic reasons. A studio, as he had conceived it decades before, gave the gift of time, and his actor-singers needed time to digest what they were learning about System acting in its integration with singing and music. Stanislavsky's attitude to time and gestation was unconventional, going against the ingrained beliefs of opera professionals in a hurry for their careers and, as well, against the predatory attitudes of managers and administrators of the kind he criticized in his writings on discipline and ethics.

Mussorgsky's *Boris Godunov* appeared in 1929 and Tchaikovsky's *The Queen of Spades* in 1930, both in the refurbished theatre named after Stanislavsky and both completed in his absence because of his heart attack and long convalescence abroad. He had rehearsed these operas during 1928 to varying levels of preparation. Moskvin, Rumyantsev and the MAAT director Boris Vershilov, who had directed and taught in the Second Studio, directed *Boris Godunov* as a triumvirate, more or less to Stanislavsky's specifications. Moskvin was tasked with monitoring acting for the emotional logic and truthfulness to which Stanislavsky had carefully led his actor-singers. Rumyantsev also partly directed *The Queen of Spades*, making sure that the opera's action unfolded from the music, Stanislavsky having argued, again unconventionally, that an opera director must start from the score and what its music was 'saying' instead of from the libretto and its story and content.[122] His reason, quite simply, was that music gave the psycho-emotional colouring and resonance of an opera's events and actions and, as a consequence, revealed its throughaction. Furthermore, he explained, music encapsulated feelings, carrying and articulating them with a myriad of intonations built into the score that readily helped to identify both the throughaction and emotional timbre of a work – a distinct advantage over verbal composition to which an actor had to 'add', so to speak, a requisite intonation.

This approach was not necessarily to everybody's liking. The soprano Olga Sobolevskaya, who sang Liza in *The Queen of Spades*, recollected, with hints of dissatisfaction, that Stanislavsky had not stated what the opera was about or what the 'core' of his production would be.[123] She

---

[122] Ibid., 340, 352, and *Rabota Stanislavskogo v opernom teatre*, 141, on music as the leading principle.

[123] *K. S. Stanislavsky rabotayet, beseduyet, otdykhayet* (*K. S. Stanislavsky Works, Speaks, Rests*), Moscow: STD, 1988, 163 and 157 for *Boris Godunov*.

The Opera-Dramatic Studio

seemed to be less concerned about the subject matter of *Boris Godunov*, noting instead Stanislavsky's licence with the libretto – Boris' coronation in a church rather than a public square – and, approvingly, how he had moved choristers into the orchestra pit to suggest the sound of singing from behind the Kremlin wall. Not one for effects for effects' sake, Stanislavsky's unusual manoeuvre was an interpretation of the scene. He placed the common people *behind* the Kremlin wall – not within its walls – to indicate how far Boris' scheming for power had distanced him from his people and his duties to them. The qualities of the music had told Stanislavsky more firmly than any lines of the libretto that the tsar had forsaken his people.

The proposition of starting with the composer and his music to identify what was happening in an opera – its events, counterevents, conflicts, resolutions – was a serious one, and Kristi, who consistently participated in the opera experiments, observed, like Rumyantsev, that Stanislavsky's start mark not only enabled him to pinpoint events in an opera, which he treated as 'music drama', but also made him pay closer attention to 'the word'. Kristi, more analytical than Rumyantsev, explained that this meant treating streams of words as if they were the notes of a score, filled with the qualities of pitch, intonation, accentuation, inflection and so on, that constitute the vocal expression of notes.[124] Notes, like words, embodied the 'inner life' of the role being sung. But words coloured by notes embodied this inner emotional, spiritual and psychological life at a more profoundly articulated level, impelling the actions the singer did with his/her voice together with his/her will, thought and body. Given the particularity of sung words, Stanislavsky worked intensively on diction, arguing that sung words would never reach an audience and be intelligible unless diction was pristinely clear. Kristi declared that Stanislavsky's concentration on diction was 'revolutionary' in itself, diction having been ignored entirely in the Russian operatic tradition. Stanislavsky would have added, 'Chaliapin excluded'.

Action; the Method of Physical Action; Active Analysis

Kristi asserted in a matter-of-fact way that, other than this particular 'revolutionary' innovation, Stanislavsky had overturned the history of Russian opera practice by an approach in which music and dramatic theatre 'could not be separated'.[125] He may not have thought to link the

---

[124] *Rabota Stanislavskogo v opernom teatre*, 152–62.   [125] Ibid.

172 Studio

note-word aspect of Stanislavsky's current research to his failure with Pushkin's poetry in *Mozart and Salieri*, but he certainly thought that *Boris Godunov* – its words were also Pushkin's – was a turning point in Stanislavsky's work on opera as a whole. This was so, according to Kristi, because of what Stanislavsky *did* with notes-words and their qualities to make visible and palpable the 'invisible' inner life of a role. Further, sensitized to the qualities of intonation, accentuation and so on, each different in each particular case, Stanislavsky had heard the conversational tones of Mussorgsky's score, and had begun to look for a technique of verbal action (*slovesnoye deystviye*) capable of showing that speech *was* action. Words, Stanislavsky had come to believe, were not uttered merely for the sake of something else – they were not merely vehicles for the story and content of a play or an opera – but were utterances in their own right. Lidiya Novitskaya, who was on the dramatic 'side' of the Studio with Knebel, teaching and assisting Stanislavsky, echoes Kristi, and recollects how Stanislavsky stressed that speech was made with the tongue and was thus already physical action.[126] Action, Stanislavsky reiterated, was not solely a matter of moving arms and legs.

Furthermore, words acted on people and affected them and, being active in this way, they stimulated people to act. The technique of verbal action, he believed, involved the actor's visualization of his/her inner seeing. When speaking *and* when singing, the actor had to *see* what he/she was speaking or singing out loud. Kristi recalled that Stanislavsky did not tell his actor-singers that he could not hear what they were singing, but frequently told them that he could not *see* what they were singing. With this, as with other explanatory means, he stressed how imperative it was that their partners visualize what they themselves saw in order to be motivated into doing what was wanted of them. Stanislavsky was quite clear: the resultant complicity between partners propelled action and was integral to their interaction (*obshcheniye*) on the stage.

The theatre director Boris Zon, when he travelled from 1933 to 1935 from Leningrad to Moscow to learn from Stanislavsky – carefully taking notes and checking with him anything that was unclear – witnessed a similar conjuncture of Stanislavsky's thoughts: the idea that words were proactive and thus should not be 'just words' in dramatic and music theatre; the importance, for actors, of thinking and feeling in verbs so as to keep action in focus and acting dynamic; the necessity of visualization

---

[126] *Uroki vdokhnoveniya. Sistema K. S. Stanislavskogo v deystvii* (*Inspirational Lessons: K. S. Stanislvasky's System in Action*), Moscow: All-Russian Theatre Society, 1984, 160.

The Opera-Dramatic Studio   173

for the right ('correct') action and close interaction; action in its relation to counteraction, and the necessity of the latter for introducing dramatic conflict and so new layers of action; the vital role played by volition (the 'will' of Stanislavsky's System) when an actor speaks or sings; the will as intrinsic to intellect, thinking and feeling, which are as essential for singing as they are for acting.[127] The latter returns Stanislavsky to his point in earlier formulations of the System that the will, intellect and heart-soul converge in the doing of an action. Recall that the Orthodox prelate Zatvornik refers to the same triadic intermesh in its link with the spirit, which is active.

Zon was struck by Stanislavsky's determination not to part with the word 'soul'. On one occasion in 1934, Stanislavsky was brought a speech that needed proofreading in which he had written that the Soviet writer's main task was to 'show the soul [*dusha*] of the new [Soviet] human being'.[128] Zinaïda Sokolova had commented favourably on 'soul', to which Kedrov, who belonged to the groups soon to merge into the Opera-Dramatic Studio, retorted that 'the soul – is a figurative expression'. Stanislavsky challenged him to find a better word for what he needed to say and, after half an hour of trying to find it himself to satisfy Kedrov (Stanislavsky presumably wanted to drive his point home), Stanislavsky failed to do so, and kept 'soul' intact. It is worth retaining Zon's snapshot of the event because Kedrov became the editor-in-chief of the 1950s edition of Stanislavsky's *Collected Works* and, as far as anyone can be certain, he did not excise '*dusha*' from *An Actor's Work on Himself*. The twist to this anecdote, which neither Stanislavsky nor Zon mentions, is that Kedrov was the son of an Orthodox priest, and consequently was more than able to understand the word in its fullest sense. He was rumoured to be a Communist Party watchdog, but this could not be proved either way.

The period of Zon's visits coincided with the growth years of the Stanislavsky Opera Theatre and so of Rimsky-Korsakov's fantasia-cum-political satire *The Golden Cockerel* (1932), rehearsals of Rimsky-Korsakov's *The Maid from Pskov* (1933), an opera dominated by the sixteenth-century tsar Ivan the Terrible, which was not publicly performed, and Rossini's *The Barber of Seville* (1933), which was billed as

---

[127] 'Vstrechy c K. S. Stanislavskim' ('Meetings with K. S. Stanislavsky') in *Teatralnoye naslediye. K. S. Stanislavsky. Materialy. Pisma. Issledovaniya* (*Theatre Heritage. K. S. Stanislavsky. Materials, Letters, Research*), ed. I. E. Grabarya et al., Moscow: Academy of Sciences of the USSR, 1955, 444–91.
[128] Ibid., 468.

174 Studio

primarily directed by Sokolova but with three others, among them her brother Alekseyev, and with Stanislavsky's input in coaching the actor-singers. Rehearsals of Donizetti's comic opera *Don Pasquale* (1934–35) were the last in this bracket.

Zon remarked on the regular presence of non-singing actors at Stanislavsky's opera rehearsals, and asked questions of special interest to his own work with actors in Leningrad. He asked Stanislavsky about his 'new method': Stanislavsky had spoken to him about his 'new device' alias 'the method of physical action' in 1933. Stanislavsky replied that it was 'the development of what came before' (note 'development') and so not in contradiction with his past explorations; and he replied in the affirmative to Zon's question as to whether he guided the actor towards the role through the 'very process of action'.[129]

Behind their interchange was Zon's recurrent question over the years, and it was to lie beneath their last conversation in 1938, after a three-year gap in Zon's visits. Zon wanted to know at what exact moment Stanislavsky, having had his actors approach their roles through etudes 'on their feet' (Dodin's phrase), actually allowed them to use the text from which the etudes had been devised. Stanislavsky's very first reply in 1933 was still valid for 1938. He had said then that actors, when they began, 'did not know the words, but they knew what to do' and, when a question arose, they checked the text.[130] The process continued in this way, step by step and, by doing, they inhabited their role without forcing it, and gradually learned their script. But the actual moment when the actors began to work with the whole text 'depended on each case'.[131] Presumably – here entering into Stanislavsky's train of thought – it depended on the script and the progress made by its performers as they worked through physical actions. Knebel was to corroborate this in her writings, referring to Stanislavsky as saying that the question of when an author's text should be introduced was 'experimental and needed to be tested in practice', and she adds that Stanislavsky was very much concerned with this question.[132]

The Opera-Dramatic Studio, when it came to staging its opera experiments, showed Bizet's *Carmen* (1935) and Donizetti's *Don Pasquale* (1936) at the Stanislavsky Opera Theatre and, in 1938, *Cio-Cio-San* (Puccini's *Madama Butterfly*) and Otto Nicolai's *The Merry Wives of Windsor* (after Shakespeare's play) in home performances to piano accompaniment. In the latter two, according to Kristi, Stanislavsky tested

---

[129] Ibid., 452–3.   [130] Ibid., 452.   [131] Ibid.
[132] *Slovo v tvorchestve aktyora* (*The Word in the Actor's Creativity*), Moscow: Iskusstvo, 1954, 68.

The Opera-Dramatic Studio

his 'method of physical action' thoroughly, and its impact was very noticeable in the surety and immediacy of their construction and performance.[133] *The Merry Wives of Windsor* was not as strange a sequel to the melodic Puccini operas as might appear, since this German *Singspiel* was composed of musical pieces interspersed with considerable amounts of dialogue – a hybrid suitable for Stanislavsky's research jointly with actor-singers and actors of spoken words. Stanislavsky was rehearsing Verdi's *Rigoletto* in his Studio, another melodic opera, when he died in 1938. Meyerhold, who had been working by his side officially as his co-director – there was nothing covert about it – completed the production for its premiere in 1939. It was then a matter of months before Meyerhold was arrested.

Knebel, arguably the Opera-Dramatic Studio's most significant practitioner-witness, observed that Stanislavsky's lessons were conducted in a 'celebratory atmosphere':[134] his words 'simpler, lighter, higher, happier' as recorded by Antarova would probably have been apt. In retrospect, the Studio's working atmosphere looks like a moral victory in such dark years. Knebel, in closer proximity to her teacher than Zon, who travelled back and forth and also missed three years of Studio work, was able to nuance Zon's remarks (although without reference to him), when she stated that Stanislavsky saw his 'method of physical action' (his 'new device') as a new method of rehearsing.[135] In other words, actors were put in a rehearsal situation of doing right from the start rather than being led by training towards rehearsals, as if rehearsals were an 'advanced' stage. The old MAT had established the principle of reading a play together at a table and discussing at great length the details of 'the life of the human spirit' of its characters and what they might do and why they might do it. However, when the actors got up to play, they were saturated with intellectual talk and so were unable to materialize what they had discussed, often with great finesse. Stanislavsky concluded that the stumbling block was the table work, which exercised only the brain and reason, making actors passive, whereas the antidote was 'immediate action', physically engaging the body from the very start.[136]

'Immediate action' meant that the actors were up on their feet and moving, after having read a play once (twice at most), and they played what they had grasped about its content, characters and motifs 'in their own words'. The actors' own words were 'analogous' (Stanislavsky) 'to

---

[133] *Rabota Stanislavskogo v opernom teatre*, 235–40. [134] *Slovo v tvorchestve aktyora*, 69.
[135] Ibid., 29. [136] Ibid., 39–42.

those of their characters' and, if they were wide of the mark, the actors had
to come back to the text to check what, exactly, their characters had said in
the 'proposed circumstances'.[137] Everything had to come back to the
'proposed circumstances' and be checked against them for the sake of
the coherence of their 'own words' and their relevance to these circumstances. It was imperative that 'analogous' work be accurate.

This process of doing with and in words ('word action' – *slovesnoye
deystviye*), which first only approximated those of a given character and
then gradually became exact through progressive correction, was by no
means anarchical. It was like a controlled experiment in which the vari-
ables, developed by means of etudes, were always controlled by the text.
The actors' lines were not 'just' words. They said their characters'
thoughts, sensations and feelings, and did so in words *and* actions simultaneously in the 'proposed circumstances' verified by the text. Clarity
regarding the 'proposed circumstances' each time was crucial, since they
guided the actors as to what could be done logically in them. At the same
time, their words were active utterances made in the moment, that is to
say – here commenting on Stanislavsky's thought – that they were brought
into being by agents of action or *doers* and, hence, were words-actions.

Most important of all, this approach of letting speech and action come
as they would in the moment – as Stanislavsky's etudes in the early years of
the System had taught and encouraged, and as Sulerzhitsky had practised
them in the First Studio – intended to achieve an organic interconnection
between the 'spiritual' and the 'corporeal' life of a role.[138] Knebel, glossing
Stanislavsky on this very aspect, observes that no amount of intellectual
analysis could achieve this interconnection, nor could learning a role by
heart that did not articulate the role's 'inner life' in physical actions.[139] She
reports one of Stanislavsky's most important findings concerning how
actors learned their roles. When actors had made their roles their own
through their own words-actions, it was not difficult to go back and 'fix'
(or set) a playwright's words into place, since these words, which had once
been 'other' – not theirs – had now become their own and were integrally
part of them. This eventual, beneficial appropriation, Stanislavsky had
pointed out, worked in this way even for the rich, metaphorical language

---

[137] Ibid. See also *Uroki vdokhnoveniya* for Stanislavsky's 'analogous to the role', 147.

[138] Ibid., 29. Knebel quotes Stanislavsky here, since, when speaking in her own person, she says
'*psikhicheskoye*' (of the psyche) instead of '*dukhovnoye*' (spiritual).

[139] *O deystvennom analize pyesi i roli* (*On Active Analysis of a Play and a Role*), Moscow: GITIS, 2014,
28–9. First published in 1959.

of Shakespeare with whose *Romeo and Juliet* and *Hamlet* the student actors in the Studio had been engaging.[140]

Stanislavsky had come to the conclusion, then, that the restrictions of table analysis permitted little more than psychological analysis, and that this approach inevitably broke up a play into small bits and separate episodes that failed to coalesce. The result of such a fragmented approach was a piecemeal composition on the stage, and this, it can be deduced from Stanislavsky's various comments on the subject, had become a directing problem. His new rehearsal method was framed differently and, while it addressed actors, it addressed, at the same time, the problem of composition facing directors. This new method was concerned with events, and it identified the large events, the events that were major turning points in the throughaction, the main conflicts, the main counterevents, and the counter-throughaction that emerged in the course of the entire play. All of them always solicited actions from the actors, that is, made them *act*.

Knebel, when recollecting how Stanislavsky singled out what might be called 'fulcra', quotes him as stating that the issue in this 'new method' was no longer one of 'what I am saying in the role', but of 'what I am doing'.[141] Moreover, it was no longer an issue of 'how' I am to do it, but of knowing 'what' I am to do.[142] Such a shift of perspective was vital, according to Stanislavsky, because it picked out the large events of a play which, more readily than its smaller incidents, revealed the play's throughaction. Large events also more readily identified the throughaction of every role, thereby letting actors see better what they could do for their role. And throughaction was key. The throughaction of the entire play, together with the throughaction of every role, showed the actors the direction that their actions were to take and the direction in which the cumulative actions of the whole play were going. At the same time, the throughaction of the whole play crystallized the play's overarching or governing idea (*sverkhzadacha*).[143]

Behind Stanislavsky's conception of action was his drive to activate actors so that they were not a director's 'puppets' but veritable co-creators – the very same co-creators whom he had begun to seek in earnest in the later 1900s. Knebel, always alert at the Opera-Dramatic Studio, understood this perfectly and, when asserting that Stanislavsky had discovered the 'method of active analysis' in his last years, she in fact slips in her own

---

[140] *Vsya zhizn*, 273.   [141] Ibid. Knebel quoting Stanislavsky.
[142] *Uroki vdokhnoveniya*, 161. Novitskaya's variant on the same idea.
[143] *O deystvennom analize*, 50. My gloss on Knebel re *sverkhzadacha*.

vocabulary, 'active analysis', as if it were his, even if he used it rarely.[144] Stanislavsky appears to have stayed with his own lexicon, using 'the method of physical action'. Knebel's lexical interference is by no means harmful. It is more of a paraphrase of Stanislavsky's discovery than a sleight of hand, or simply a gesture of Soviet-style deference to her teacher by which she modestly did not claim her phrase as her own. However, when developing this method with her own students, she expanded the phrase to say 'the method of active analysis of a play and a role' – reflected in the title of one of her books – so as to be totally precise about what 'active analysis' analyzed, not while sitting but through doing what needs to be done. Doing, in other words, was its own 'analysis'.

Knebel's terminology defined her teaching and directing, but she was as aware as Stanislavsky had been, when he warned his students at the Bolshoy Opera Studio against using his System 'in an automatic fashion', that any 'method' could be exploited mechanically. In her own lifetime, she saw how the pragmatic ring of 'method of physical action' appeared to license the most behaviourist understanding of 'action' when it wiped out, in a trice, 'the life of the human spirit' and its 'creative heart' in every action. Yet Stanislavsky had reiterated, time and again, that 'the life of the human spirit' and its 'creative heart' made action substantial and meaningful. Stanislavsky argued, as Knebel has noted, that there was 'no direct road to feeling', which is why actors needed 'lures' to bring out feelings (and sensations) appropriate to the 'proposed circumstances'.[145] He pointed out during a rehearsal of *The Cherry Orchard* that an action like Varya's looking for galoshes, in the scene when Lopakhin was allegedly going to propose to her, would not automatically bring about feelings appropriate to the role in these very circumstances. Merely searching for galoshes would not elicit feelings of their own accord. Such feelings would have to be coaxed along by psychophysical 'lures'.[146]

Knebel reports how one such 'lure' was of great importance to Stanislavsky, and this was the interior monologue. Stanislavsky asked the student rehearsing Varya to devise spontaneously an unvocalized voice that thought-felt at the same time as the speaking voice with which she addressed Lopakhin.[147] He asked the student to run her/Varya's interior monologue beside the lines that Lopakhin heard, but to say it in a softer voice than her speaking voice for those lines. The subtext, for that is what her interior monologue was, converged with Chekhov's dialogue for Varya,

---

[144] *Vsya zhizn*, 549.   [145] Ibid., 273.   [146] Ibid., 273–4.
[147] *Slovo v tvorchestve aktyora*, 86–9; see also *O deystvennom analize* on the interior monologue, 90–5.

and the appropriate actions and appropriate feelings came together for the student and the role.

The student's subtext had opened up the path to her subconscious, which she entered without inhibition. She had also visualized, all along, what she was doing, frame by frame, as in a film. Visualization, a cornerstone of Stanislavsky's System in its beginnings, remained such in his last contribution to the System at the Opera-Dramatic Studio. Knebel, who was an actor when she joined the MAT, joined the Opera-Dramatic Studio as a director in a group of directors at the Studio, where she taught speech and diction. She marvelled at how Stanislavsky had directed the student. In fact, what emerges very vividly from her writings is just how much Stanislavsky directed as he taught. Or, rather, to put it more accurately, he was a director-pedagogue, which is what Knebel became at GITIS, while this very entity, fashioned first by Stanislavsky, put down its roots in Soviet Russian theatre and is still alive in Russia today.

It transpires, as well, that a good number of Stanislavsky's activities in the Studio made it his first school of directing. He had toyed with the idea of such a school intermittently, placing it within his imagined academy that would unite all the arts necessary for making theatre. His planned fourth book was to be on directing.[148] Knebel certainly saw the Studio as *her* school of directing. She believed that Stanislavsky's principles regarding action, if vital for actors, were indispensable for directors. This is clear in how the synopsis of her practice 'active analysis' addresses directors, first and foremost.[149] And 'active analysis' appears in the title of her book, showing how she recalls Stanislavsky and affirms her voice in one and the same breath.

---

[148] *SS* 8, 6, 319.   [149] *O deystvennom analize*, 21–39.

CHAPTER 5

Director

The Society of Art and Literature

There can be no doubt that Stanislavsky's development as an actor was closely tied to his development as a director, and the one always opened doors to the other, showing him how to tackle difficulties that confinement to only one of these demanding activities would not have been able to resolve. This twinning had great benefits, many coming to fruition in Stanislavsky's opera studios, and they pointed to a third aspect of his directing – his progressive mutation into a director-pedagogue, which he may well never have become had he not been an experienced actor. The Second Studio saw him assuming this role when working with the 'studists' on *The Green Circle* and *The Tale of Ivan the Fool*, but it was not to mature fully until the 1930s, after Stanislavsky's circumstances had radically altered, leaving him freer to explore what directing was and what it could do. As much can be learned about Stanislavsky-director from this third aspect, which is evident in transcripts and several thorough accounts of his rehearsals, as from his production scores and projects as well as details of completed productions.

We have become so used to thinking of Stanislavsky in relation to acting, placed under the glaring lights of '*the* System' and '*the* Method of Physical Action' (the latter, in any case, is part of the former), that the fact of his being a director slips from view. But director he was, and from the outset, directing a vaudeville and a one-act comedy by Pyotr Gnedich in 1889 at the Society of Art and Literature, which he had founded together with Komissarzhevsky and Aleksandr Fedotov, a former member of the Maly Theatre and former husband of Glikeria Fedotova, who mentored Stanislavsky. Gnedich's *The Burning Letters* gave many signs of the director Stanislavsky was to grow into for the Art Theatre ten years later. It showed him striving for fewer clichés, minimal gesticulation (flailing arms, he believed, were an actor's cover-up for a lack of genuine feeling) and, in

180

The Society of Art and Literature

general, a 'quiet, calm performance with long pauses and without raised voices', unseen on the Russian stage.[1]

Stanislavsky confessed that he had not invented this unassuming style but had borrowed it from French theatre. (He had seen it at the Comédie Française, and had taken classes for several months at the Paris Conservatoire in the year preceding *The Burning Letters* so as to understand how it was done.) By contrast, Stanislavsky did not borrow but actually invented a new stage 'look', opening up vistas from an interior setting in Gnedich's play on to roofs of houses and distant buildings and experimenting with various perspectives for other Society productions – spatial juxtapositions within interiors, for example, in *Othello* (1896). He was to explore three-dimensional space further at the MAT, starting with *The Seagull*, where he dispensed with Chekhov's first stage direction – a wide alley symmetrically lined with shrubs that ends at a pavilion, while the lake is hidden behind it. Instead, he envisaged an asymmetrical composition weighted towards stage left in which the pavilion, close up, was at an angle to shrubs and did not hide the lake. Several planes and depths operated in his vision, creating an intimate space without closing it in.

The director in Stanislavsky was already aiming for the sensation of truthfulness in Gnedich's light comedy, which he continued in his next production, Tolstoy's satire *The Fruits of Enlightenment* (1891), performed by a bigger cast to match its ambitious scale. Dismissed by 'reactionary conservatives' for its picture of canny peasants outwitting avaricious landlords over the sale of land, the production concentrated on the psychology of actions and interactions, supported by ensemble playing stronger than the already impressive unity he had achieved for *The Burning Letters*.[2] But the production's socio-political strength was no less of a benchmark and was perceived as such by its audiences. Stanislavsky eventually followed up by directing another explicitly social play, the Austrian Karl Gutskow's 1847 tragedy, *Uriel Acosta*, on the exclusion of Central European Jews from human rights, including their right to citizenship.

Uriel Acosta appeared in all its honesty in 1895, as if a belated response to the pogroms in Russia of the preceding decade and a warning about Russia's present reactionary politics. Stanislavsky directed himself in the title role from the social and artistically daring viewpoints that had earned

---

[1] K. S. Stanislavsky, *Iz zapisnykh knizhek* (*From Notebooks*), Vol. 1, ed. V. N. Prokofiev, Moscow: All-Russian Society, 1986, 50–1.

[2] I. N. Vinogradskaya, 'O postanovkakh K. S. Stanislavskogo v obshchestve iskusstva i literatury' ('On Stanislavsky's productions at the Society of Art and Literature') in *Teatralnoye naslediye. K. S. Stanislavsky. Materialy. Pisma. Issledovaniya*, ed. I. E. Grabarya et al., 504–6.

182   Director

the Society its excellent reputation. Fedotov, from whose directing in the Society's opening season Stanislavsky had learned a good deal, had resigned after heated quarrels with Komissarzhevsky. His departure forced Stanislavsky to recognize that he had no choice but to become a director, regardless of how much he thought of himself as an actor. There was no evidence, at the Society, of a conflict of interest between these two responsibilities. It arose only at the Art Theatre, coming out into the open in 1905, the year when the company had to reassess its priorities. Stanislavsky had ceded some of his most successful roles to his colleagues, with regret but without protest because he was required to direct, and the MAT's needs had to come before his own. He consequently bristled when Nemirovich-Danchenko began to count up grievances and accused him of being jealous of his, Nemirovich-Danchenko's, involvement in directing, writing to his partner:

> There was never any jealousy in my work as a director. *I do not like this activity* and do it out of necessity. . . . My success as a director is needed for the theatre, not me. . . . I cannot refrain from smiling with pleasure when I am praised for my acting, but I laugh when I am praised for directing. . . . Think what it has cost me to relinquish my pride of place as an actor to Kachalov and others.[3]

This anguish over what he believed was a misapprehension about his true vocation was still in the future. So was Stanislavsky's painful avowal to Nemirovich-Danchenko: 'I am crushed by the deterioration in our relationship'. But the time when Stanislavsky liked directing sheds light on how his abilities flourished. Vinogradskaya considers that *Uriel Acosta*, more than any of his preceding productions, revealed Stanislavsky as a director of 'a new type' (intent on coherence between all elements of a production), who was also a 'brilliant organizer of the whole process of putting a production together'.[4] It is not possible to say whether productions following it met similar standards, but they were substantial and varied, and, apart from *Othello*, they included *Much Ado about Nothing* (1897), *Twelfth Night* (1897) and Hauptmann's *The Sunken Bell* (1898), his last for the Society. *The Sunken Bell*, a fairy-tale-drama set in awesome mountains where witches and goblins lived among humans, was Stanislavsky's first co-operative venture with Simov. It allowed him to work fully on the idea that a properly constructed stage environment helped

---

[3] *SS* 9, 7, 586, letter between 16 and 28 June 1905, italics in the original – my translation; *The Moscow Art Theatre Letters*, 225.

[4] 'O postanovkakh K. S. Stanislavskogo', 536.

The Society of Art and Literature

183

actors to inhabit their roles and act accordingly. Nikolay Efros described Stanislavsky's direction as a combination of 'realism with magic fantasy' in harmony with its rocky mountainous landscape, and he positively glowed with praise for this 'master director' – born, it has to be said, out of the wide diapason of work that he had placed at the service of the Society.[5]

Confident in the great success of *The Sunken Bell*, Stanislavsky decided to rerun it in the Art Theatre's first season eight months later. Luzhsky, stepping into the role of director, revamped *Twelfth Night* in the second season, signalling by this that the new theatre on the block, which had mounted *The Merchant of Venice* for its inauguration, intended to keep Shakespeare on its lists. In actual fact, the MAT had a chequered history with Shakespeare, although Stanislavsky regularly drew on Shakespeare in his work with 'studists', notably returning with care to *Twelfth Night* at the First Studio. He took the 'studists' aback – an astonished Vakhtangov, among them – when he suggested they play their dialogue in the aisles of the auditorium as they entered the stage from there. The 'studists' had manifestly underestimated his readiness to try something that he had not done before.

Stanislavsky's unexpected novelty shows that a novelty can have a long life, even when its first incarnation has been forgotten. Indeed, it was the forerunner of a device favoured by the politically radical theatre of the 1960s and 1970s. Thomas Ostermeier has re-used it more recently, a little tongue-in-cheek, in his 2012 *An Enemy of the People* at the Schaubühne in Berlin, citing that radical theatre while offering a razor-sharp debate from within the aisles on contemporary whistleblowing. Occasionally spectators, taking up the cue that the actors offered them, contributed to the debate, raising its temperature higher but without breaking the understanding that this was theatre. Polemics were not to be had from Stanislavsky's Shakespeare scene because it had not been 'set up', as had the scene in *An Enemy of the People*. As for *Doctor Stockman*, the MAT's title for this very play by Ibsen – Stanislavsky perceived a different kind of polemic, not so much on truthsaying as on the truthsayer and what kind of person this could be.

When he performed Stockman in 1901 during the MAT's regular St Petersburg tour, his figure of a modest but rebellious individual became an Everyman, acquiring immense political significance. Crowds of students, who had been arrested that same day, had just been released from jail. They had demonstrated against the implementation of a law allowing the government to expel 'undesirable' elements among them and

[5] *Moskovsky Khudozhestvenny Teatr 1898–1923*, 73.

force them into the army. Fervent admirers of the Art Theatre, they rushed to *Doctor Stockman*. Stanislavsky ordered that they be given tickets and, filling the aisles up to the gods, they brought the house down when Stanislavsky, with the greatest simplicity and without so much as a glance at the students, delivered Stockman's unforgettable line in the last Act about not wearing your new trousers when you 'go out to fight for freedom and justice'. Ever observant, as he taught his actors to be, that extraordinary performative event was possibly at the back of his mind when he experimented with actors who, rather than spectators, performed in the aisles of *Twelfth Night*.

Two Directors

The MAT was formed from fifteen seasoned amateurs of the Society of Art and Literature and twelve of Nemirovich-Danchenko's graduates from the Philharmonic Institute. The first group, which included Lilina, Andreyeva, Sanin, Luzhsky and Artyom, had sound practical experience, while the second – notably Knipper, Meyerhold and Moskvin – had actor training as well as literature and theory behind them, and this combination of different know-how was salutary for the development of ensemble playing. Meyerhold left the company in 1902, as did Maria Roksanova, a former student of Nemirovich-Danchenko whom he had cast as Nina Zarechnaya in *The Seagull* only for everybody to discover that her voice was too weak, her gestures too big and her sentiments too sentimental for the role. Chekhov, for whom a special performance was given in Moscow when his health and the weather had improved, demanded that she be replaced immediately. Nemirovich-Danchenko insisted that she be kept, Roksanova persisted, he coached her, and nobody told her about Chekhov's scornful remarks.

Maria Andreyeva, seen potentially to be of the calibre of Knipper after her performance as Hedda Gabler (1899), left in early 1904, expressing her disappointment in the MAT's change of direction by letter to Stanislavsky: she had expected the MAT to be more politically engaged – more like the 'open' theatre that it had planned to be than the quietist theatre that it had become. Andreyeva had performed in *The Lower Depths* (1902) – Chekhov had persuaded Gorky to write plays for the MAT – and, sharing Gorky's revolutionary views, she had left her wealthy husband to become his companion. Her departure was soon to be linked with the rift between Gorky and the MAT over his *Summerfolk*, which Gorky had read to a group of MAT actors. Stanislavsky, at the reading and, like them, in shock at how 'horrible' the play was, wondered whether 'we were watching a great talent die before our very eyes'.[6] Nemirovich-Danchenko had already declared that the MAT had had too much of Gorky altogether, and trashed the play in a letter to him, stressing its poor structure and overbearing anger, which had produced characters unworthy of being staged.

Gorky, who was aware of his play's shortcomings, was, nevertheless, so insulted that he swore never to co-operate with the theatre again; Savva Morozov, the Art Theatre's patron, resigned from its Board in solidarity with Gorky. In the event, eighteen months later, Nemirovich-Danchenko co-directed Gorky's new drama *Children of the Sun* with Stanislavsky – the repertoire badly needed contemporary plays, and the outspoken Gorky was in vogue with the intelligentsia – while Stanislavsky could not fathom how 'at a time like this' (the 1905 revolution) he 'could be playing and rehearsing this useless nonsense'.[7] However, he respected the person, and they were to remain on friendly terms for the rest of their lives. Gorky, having supported revolutionary students during the uprising, was imprisoned and then exiled in 1906, returning only in 1913 on a general amnesty.

Andreyeva departed in dramatic circumstances, going with Gorky and director Konstantin Mardzhanov (at the MAT 1910–13) to the Russian Theatre in Riga, founded in 1883, for the 1904–05 season where she performed in *Summerfolk* directed by Mardzhanov. Other actors left the MAT in her wake for want of work. Actors who had birthed roles were unlikely to give them up, especially if they had little else to play, and the range of productions was not broad enough to employ the different talents available. Close inspection of the Art Theatre's repertoire in its first seven years shows a concentration of Chekhov, Ibsen, Hauptmann and Gorky; and, although Stanislavsky sought to draw lines of diverse interest through the repertoire, about which he writes in *My Life in Art* ('the historico-realistic line' and 'the line of symbolism and impressionism', for instance), they were not all of equal strength.[8] 'The line of fantasy and imagination', which counted *The Snow Maiden* (a public failure), and the symbolic line with its effete Maeterlinck shorts are cases in point. Aim for variety was hindered, too, by the mixed blessings of *Tsar Fyodor Ioannovich*, whose grand ethnographic character suitably started the 'historico-realistic line' – quite an event, since the play had been banned for thirty years – and of the

---

[6] *SS* 9, 7, 539–40, letter to Lilina 29 April 1904.
[7] Ibid., 670, letter to V. V. Kotlyarevskaya, 3 November 1905.
[8] *Moya zhizn v iskusstve*, 207–27; *My Life in Art*, 181–98.

186   Director

acclaimed Chekhov productions, which were reprised while waiting for another Chekhov premiere. The latter productions marked out 'the line of intuition and feeling'. Inna Solovyova calculates that, by the MAT's tenth anniversary, only fifteen of the thirty-seven actors first signed up remained.[9] Newcomers, in the meantime, had replenished the troupe, Kachalov having been one of them early in the piece.

The Seagull launched both the Art Theatre, as no other production in its first season could do, and the seven-year Chekhov-Gorky period that secured its name. News of the pandemonium of approval at the production's opening night was sent to Chekhov, who was anxiously waiting in Yalta. The play had been misrepresented as a comedy the year before at a benefit for a leading Aleksandrinsky actress in St Petersburg, and Chekhov had suffered deeply from the humiliation of its raucous, even cynical, reception. It took all of Nemirovich-Danchenko's powers of persuasion to convince his friend to release The Seagull to the MAT and to reassure him that Stanislavsky would manage to direct its subtleties – under his watchful eye. According to the terms of their agreement when they founded the MAT, Nemirovich-Danchenko dealt with the play's literary aspects, reading and explaining it to the actors as soon as he received the manuscript. Stanislavsky, who was unable to attend this introduction, read the play by himself a day later, avowing subsequently that he had no idea 'by which end to begin' his plan for the production, so different was it from anything that he had known before.[10] His side of the bargain was to take charge of directing and this, following his practice at the Society of Art and Literature, also meant preparing a production plan.

Stanislavsky retired to the countryside to work in seclusion on what he called The Seagull's 'score' (partitura) – apt, given his musical ear for this play as for Uncle Vanya, which Chekhov had initially contracted to the Maly Theatre, and The Three Sisters and The Cherry Orchard, both of which he wrote specifically for the MAT. On separate pages adjacent to those of Chekhov's text, each page corresponding exactly, were his interpretative commentaries on Chekhov's dialogue, imaginary settings for his stage directions, notes on how the actors might react, or what they could do, and pauses carefully timed and marked for the actors to adhere to.[11]

[9] Inna Solovyova, Khudozhestvenny Teatr. Zhizn i priklyucheniye ideyi (The Art Theatre. Life and the Adventure of an Idea), Moscow: Moscow Art Theatre, 2007, 26.

[10] SS 9, 7, 275, letter to Nemirovich-Danchenko 10 September 1898 – my translation; Senelick, Stanislavsky – A Life in Letters, 110.

[11] See my study of two scenes in Christopher Innes and Maria Shevtsova, The Cambridge Introduction to Theatre Directing, Cambridge University Press, 2013, 68–74.

Two Directors

187

The score shows Stanislavsky counting the seconds for pauses of varied duration (five, ten, fifteen seconds), which helped to shape the rhythmic patterns and tempi of his imagined production. He ignored Chekhov's indication for a pause when his musical phrasing required uninterrupted movement for dramatic urgency, as happened at the close of the last meeting between Zarechnaya and Treplev before he shoots himself.[12]

Nemirovich-Danchenko and the actors were in Pushkino, rehearsing the scenes and acts as they came from Stanislavsky's pen until he arrived to take up his rehearsals. He soon informed Chekhov that Stanislavsky's 'blocking was very bold', but he was disturbed by how Dorn sat with his back to the audience during the performance of Treplev's play.[13] This was actually one of Stanislavsky's boldest directorial innovations and it threw the play-within-the-play into relief by suggesting that Dorn, like other protagonists whose seats had backs to the audience or stood semi-sideways to it, was, in effect, part of the theatre audience. Spatially speaking, the stage and the auditorium were on a continuum. Even later, when Nemirovich-Danchenko changed his tone from condescension to admiration and praised Stanislavsky's 'fiery' imagination, he either ignored or belittled those bold aspects of Stanislavsky's directing that he considered merely fanciful: 'capricious' was his usual term.

Such 'caprice' was Stanislavsky's counterpoint with croaking frogs during Zarechnaya's 'world soul' monologue in the above scene. He justified it to his critical partner:

> Consider that I put in frogs during the play scene to create total silence. After all, quietness in the theatre is not expressed through silence but sounds. You can't achieve the illusion if you don't fill the silence with sounds. Why? Because people back stage (stagehands, uninvited guests, and so forth) and the audience in the auditorium make noise and destroy the mood on the stage.[14]

Stanislavsky's intentions were clear, for, apart from the poetics of the situation – silence, counterpoint, mood – he was trying to solve a practical problem of interfering noise. His practicality had an amusing side: he explained that he 'partly chose the sound of frogs' (compared with the bird-song of *The Sunken Bell*, for instance) because he 'owned a little machine that imitated frogs very well'.[15] The gadget allowed him tricks,

---

[12] Ibid., 72.   [13] Radishcheva, *Stanislavsky i Nemirovich-Danchenko. 1897–1908*, 61.
[14] *SS* 9, 7, 275, letter of 10 September 1898 for both quotations – my translation; Senelick, *Stanislavsky – A Life*, 110.
[15] Ibid.

188   Director

but Stanislavsky was already attempting to convey how Chekhov's writing recalled 'Levitan's landscapes and Tchaikovsky's melodies', which he was to single out as characteristic of the playwright in his speech on the MAT's tenth anniversary.[16] He was also to warn against overemphasis on surface impressions when it was essential 'to absorb the aroma of his feelings and presentiments [and] guess the innuendos of his deep but unfinished thoughts'.[17]

Stanislavsky had begun to sense, as he worked in his musical way on *The Seagull*, that Chekhov's was a totally new dramaturgy compatible with the MAT's understanding of what was 'new', but it was also a gift for the company to realize the 'new' it had not yet articulated, especially its goal of ensemble acting. He perceived fully during the next few years how their respective newness had merged so thoroughly that Chekhov's achievements as a dramatist and the MAT's achievements as a theatre company were interdependent. If Chekhov's fame as a playwright was due to the MAT – this on top of his renown as a writer of short stories – the MAT would not have been as famous without him. It is no wonder, then, that Stanislavsky approached each Chekhov play as a major event, each role he was to play with apprehension – Trigorin, Astrov, Vershinin, Gayev – and each production he was to direct with some fear, even *The Cherry Orchard* whose manuscript he received in 1903, by which time he had grown into Chekhov's dramaturgy and loved this last play unconditionally.

Curiously, Nemirovich-Danchenko went in the opposite direction, first enamoured with *The Seagull* and then disenchanted with *The Cherry Orchard* which, much like Gorky, he thought was essentially a makeover of his preceding three plays. 'There's nothing new here – not a word,' said Gorky;[18] and, while Gorky had singled out the same old 'atmosphere and lack of ideas', Nemirovich-Danchenko specified that 'there was nothing new about the main theme from a social point of view'.[19] Nemirovich-Danchenko's change of heart was blatantly obvious. Having rehearsed Chekhov's preceding play eagerly, to the point of overstepping the boundaries he had agreed with Stanislavsky, he contributed only to the second Act of *The Cherry Orchard*, leaving Stanislavsky to direct and bring it technically to the stage as he saw fit.

Nemirovich-Danchenko had little knowledge of directing before his partnership with Stanislavsky, which is why he relied on Stanislavsky's plans and learned how to write them from him. Directing a production, although Stanislavsky's responsibility, became a division of labour with

---

[16] *SS* 8, 5, 409.   [17] Ibid., 410.   [18] Quoted in *Khudozhestvenny Teatr*, 65.   [19] Ibid., 72.

The Seagull. Nemirovich-Danchenko would normally coach actors in groups or independently, while Stanislavsky rehearsed them with the production in view, ironing out anomalies that had accrued on the way. Permutations and combinations of these arrangements occurred, often for practical reasons tied up with one or the other's obligations to the MAT, like Stanislavsky having to perform nights in a row. So it was that the rehearsals of December 1898 leading up to the premiere of *The Seagull* were unevenly distributed, Nemirovich-Danchenko taking fifteen and Stanislavsky, who was performing most nights, nine of them, the total amounting to some eighty hours of rehearsals.[20] While their arrangements should not have posed any problems in theory, in practice their different accentuations often caused Stanislavsky, who had the director's veto, to modify his partner's modifications of his work – instrumental in Roksanova's being caught between two different interpretations of her role as the premiere approached.

Their directorial system faltered not so much because Nemirovich-Danchenko could not match Stanislavsky's hands-on experience but because, although willing to co-operate, they could not form a collaborative relationship as directors. They were co-directors to varying degrees, more like team individuals side by side than two parts of a convergent whole. Radishcheva rightly points out that, as a director, Stanislavsky was primarily interested in the process of embodiment, often not knowing when it should stop, whereas Nemirovich-Danchenko's interest lay in the completion of the thing, in its 'redaction', as she puts it.[21] Stanislavsky's concern with embodiment and exploration – already foreshadowing his laboratory-studios – meant that, if he thought a production was seriously not ready, he would postpone it, refunding tickets. On such occasions Nemirovich-Danchenko behaved more like a managing director than an artistic one, although his annoyance at the loss of credit, financial and symbolic, had little leverage against Stanislavsky's wishes.

Still, much was achieved in their co-direction, and they offered an alternative to the model of the solo director controlling a production. Whatever its disadvantages, this model was largely followed at the MAT other than by Nemirovich-Danchenko and Stanislavsky, who stopped directing together in 1917. Responsibilities were swapped at different preparatory phases, and *répétiteurs* were occasionally added. Stanislavsky would often be called in to oversee work in progress. Having three directors with varying input was not uncommon – the case, we saw, of

---

[20] *Stanislavsky i Nemirovich-Danchenko. 1897–1908*, 62.   [21] Ibid., 103.

190   Director

Hamlet – but there was also room for directing individually without a 'co-'
of any kind, which occurred more often by design than by default, like the
default that passed *The Cherry Orchard* to Stanislavsky. During the Soviet
period, blurred responsibilities ceded to clearer lines of demarcation,
distinguishing the director in charge from an assistant director, as
happened with the Bulgakov productions discussed in Chapter 2.

Production Scores and Musicality: Chekhov and Gorky

Irrespective of the Art Theatre's complex arrangements, Stanislavsky
played a major role in directing all the Chekhov productions and, of the
four, both Radishcheva and Solovyova claim, *Uncle Vanya* was the only
perfectly synchronized work by its two directors, the result of true unity
between them.[22] Meyerhold had said as much about their 'fusion' to
Chekhov at the time, while pointing to Stanislavsky's 'great imagination
as a director-actor' and to Nemirovich-Danchenko's watch over the
'author's interests', as a 'director-literary man'.[23] Fusion was achieved,
but not without Nemirovich-Danchenko objecting to the imaginary mos-
quitoes, which Stanislavsky-Astrov noticeably swatted. Stanislavsky must
not have owned a mosquito-buzzing instrument (!), so sight had to convey
sound, which was the intention, also, of the knotted handkerchief around
Stanislavsky-Astrov's head for protection against mosquito bites!

Stanislavsky claimed that the handkerchief helped him to enter creatively into the role, but it incensed Nemirovich-Danchenko, who wrote
to him saying this was a 'detail I simply cannot take' and, since he could
not find 'one serious argument of any kind whatsoever' for it, the handkerchief had to be removed.[24] Nor did he see any reason for Stanislavsky's
directing Knipper-Yelena to react with fear to a drunken Vanya, which was
out of kilter with her usually languid tone, or to have her sing at the end of
the second Act and wail 'hysterically' at the end of the third. The latter two
details, he wrote in his letter to Chekhov about the opening night, were
debris of the 'noise and external effects' that Stanislavsky favoured as a
director ("his fondness for underlining things") but which would 'go after
the second performance'.[25]

Both directors agreed, however, that 'mood' and 'tone' were key to the
production. 'Mood' was generated by the sight and sound of rain dropping

---

[22] Ibid., 100 and Solovyova, *Khudozhestvenny Teatr*, 44.
[23] Quoted in Konstantin Rudnitsky, *Russkoye rezhissyorskoye iskusstvo 1898–1917* (*The Russian Art of
    Directing*), Moscow: GITIS, 2014, 102.
[24] *The Moscow Art Theatre Letters*, 60–1.   [25] Ibid., 64.

in varied intensity and rhythm on windowpanes, or by the clatter of horses' hooves when Serebryakov and his wife drove away on the wooden bridge in front of the family home. Far from 'underlining things', Stanislavsky's soundscape, like his visual environment, supported both the actors and the motifs that ran through the whole production. Silence – then the chirp of a cricket, the sound of 'They've gone' and the tinkling of the horses' bells in the distance were his gentle 'external effects' to offset, as Sonya and Vanya settled down to their neglected bookkeeping, the massive inner turmoil that they had undergone. The scene's elegiac mood lingered as the abacus clicked their calculations in a steady rhythm until the swell of Sonya's monologue turned the initial polyphony into a polyphony of pain, stoicism, compassion and hope of the kind that Astrov had evoked in his impromptu lecture to Yelena in Act Three on the dire social and ecological condition of the countryside.

'Tone' in *Uncle Vanya*, as Rudnitsky has argued, was not a matter of the 'intonation of the voice, but a precursor of the impulse behind it; nor was it a way of speaking, but a way of living'.[26] The directors' purpose, in Nemirovich-Danchenko's words, was 'to go into the deepest depths of each character's tone separately and – even more importantly – together so as to have a shared mood ... a shared whole'.[27] Rudnitsky observes that the idea of the ensemble was here conceived as an 'emotional ensemble', which Stanislavsky's score had turned into continuous scenic action. Years later, Knipper-Chekhova was to remember Stanislavsky-Astrov walking up to the map of Africa at the end of Act Four and commenting on how hot it must now be there; his tone was filled with the bitter taste of everything Astrov had lived through that summer and during the grey, hard life to which he was returning.[28] Here, indeed, was Rudnitsky's 'tone' as a 'way of living'. Knipper-Chekhova recalled, as well, how loving Stanislavsky-Astrov's gaze was in Act Three, and his voice full of affectionate irony when he told Yelena she was 'cunning'.

Affectionate it may have been on the stage, but Astrov does not appear to be so in Stanislavsky's score for this scene; and, throughout the score, he is a vigorous man with a sense of humour. The fragment below comes straight after Astrov's first 'cunning', and it follows Astrov's monologues on the ecological damage to the countryside that Yelena had interrupted to broach the subject of his feelings towards Sonya. Shortly before, the two women had agreed that Yelena would speak with Astrov to find out where he stood:

---

[26] *Russkoye rezhissyorskoye iskusstvo 1898–1917*, 104.   [27] Ibid.

[28] *Chast pervaya. Vospominaniya i stati. Perepiska s A. P. Chekhovym (1902–1904)* (*Recollections and Articles; Correspondence with A. P. Chekhov*), Part I, Moscow: Iskusstvo, 1972, 102–3.

Director

Chekhov's text	Stanislavsky's directions
YELENA: What do you mean? **109**	**109** Yelena has stopped reading. She looks at Astrov with surprise; he comes closer, laughing rather loudly.
ASTROV: (*laughing*): You're cunning! **110** All right, I'm willing to accept that Sonya feels pain, but what is the point of your cross-examination? (*Briskly, preventing her from speaking*)	**110** Astrov is leaning with his elbows on the back of the sofa and is looking at her suspiciously.
111 Come on, don't give me that surprised face. You know perfectly well why I come here every day. Why and who I come to see – you know it perfectly well. **112** and **113** Sweet bird of prey, don't look at me like that, I am an old sparrow.	**111** Ironically shaking his hand at her. He sits beside Yelena, looking boldly and persistently into her eyes. She cannot withstand his gaze – moves along. He continues with greater force. **112** He boldly clasps her hand, preventing her from moving. Yelena, taken aback, looks at him. **113** Astrov shakes his head ironically.
YELENA: **114** Bird of prey? I don't understand a thing.	**114** Yelena, a little frightened, tries to free her hand, looking at Astrov with astonishment.[29]

Note that Stanislavsky, unlike Knipper-Chekhova, does not write 'loving' for Astrov's gaze. He focuses on its ironic, bold and even predatory quality, and this suggests that his score was not taken as a dictation for the living actors who made the production. In other words, it cannot be assumed that the actual production replicated the imagined one in all its aspects. Press articles of the period lack detail and so cannot help. We are left, then, with Knipper-Chekhova's memory and Stanislavsky's score, and Yelena's 'astonishment' in it is ambiguous. Astrov leads spectators to agree with his assumptions as to why Yelena had called him in. Yelena's behaviour denies his assumptions, but she had confessed to Sonya that she found Astrov attractive. Is Yelena playing the role of an ingénue, like those to be found in farces? Or is this a comedy of total misunderstanding in which Yelena is a genuine ingénue? Or is she simply caught out by her subconscious desires? Is she 'a little frightened' because she begins to realize,

---

[29] *Rezhissyorskiye ekzemplyary K. S. Stanislavskogo 1898–1930. Dyadya Vanya (Production Plans ... Uncle Vanya),* Moscow–St Petersburg: Atheneum–Feniks, 1994, 80–1. All translations here and afterwards are mine.

Production Scores and Musicality: Chekhov and Gorky 193

however vaguely, what really is at stake in the teasing game Astrov plays with her? The balance between these possibilities is delicate, and Stanislavsky appears to hold it, suspended, even at the end of the scene when Vanya enters unexpectedly with his bunch of autumn roses, catching two people in the act that never happened.

One can only speculate on how Stanislavsky and Knipper actually played this scene and how Stanislavsky-director regulated their 'tones' and its 'tone' so that they did not clash with the colours – shades, tonalities – that guaranteed the production's 'wholeness'; that guaranteed, as well, the 'fusion' of its directors that Nemirovich-Danchenko told Stanislavsky they had achieved. As for the social views impregnating the production – the intelligentsia listened attentively and heard in it the ominous rumblings around them. V. A. Telyakovsky, the director of the Moscow Imperial Theatres, declared that, if *Uncle Vanya* was really an account of contemporary Russia, then the Russian situation was 'a rotten business' (*delo dryan*) and 'such a state of affairs would inevitably lead to catastrophe'.[30] Tolstoy, who had seen *Uncle Vanya*, concluded in his harsh way that Vanya and Astrov were 'rubbish people' (*dryan lyudi*).[31]

Neither man comments on Sonya's lyrical – and biblical – flight into the cosmos where she and Vanya 'will hear the angels and see the sky filled with diamonds'. Given the religious innuendos of Sonya's peroration, Stanislavsky's last stage direction for Sonya is 'she barely whispers some sort of prayer'. Stanislavsky thus makes it impossible to ignore the counterpoint of Sonya's prayer to the 'sky filled with diamonds' with Astrov's lamentation on the decaying earth.

The Three Sisters *and* The Cherry Orchard

Stanislavsky took musical construction further in *The Three Sisters*, and far enough for Gorky to exclaim that this was 'music, and not acting'.[32] By the same token, he used his music to lift out from behind and beneath the words what Stanislavsky called 'unfinished thoughts' but which are also unspoken feelings as well as shadows of actions that have been screened from view. Such is the love affair between Masha and Vershinin. Three years and some have passed between Act One and the end of Act Three since they first met. Their love had had time to develop – unseen by

---

[30] Quoted in *Khudozhestvenny Teatr*, 35.   [31] Ibid.
[32] Quoted in Inna Solovyova's introduction to *Rezhissyorskiye ekzemplyary K. S. Stanislavskogo*, Vol. 3, Moscow: Iskusstvo, 1983, 23.

spectators – into the intimate silliness of lovers, into his 'Tram-tum-tum' from somewhere outside the room in which she had confessed her love to her sisters, and her reply with 'Tra-ta-ta' to say that yes, she was coming: this was their secret code in musical phrases – wisps of a melody that functioned as dialogue perfectly understood. Stanislavsky writes in his score that 'Vershinin's voice is totally unexpected (a question)' and corroborates its unexpectedness by noting that Masha 'shoots out from behind the screen like an arrow and answers'.[33] For these two, action is concrete.

For the most part, however, shadow actions are hinted at or hoped for but never realized. Consider Olga's longing for marriage, which could be patter unless you 'guess' (Stanislavsky) the colourations of that longing as they flow not only into the multiple undertones of what is not said – the 'subtext' that has stuck to Stanislavsky – but also into the overtones of words that, like musical notes, accumulate from start to finish and resonate and reverberate as they go, as in a symphony. But 'subtext' is understood incompletely unless, besides unspoken words and feelings, it includes the actions not done whose enormous subconscious reservoir is yet another musical level, the deepest, for the director to work on. Precisely, Stanislavsky-director structures his production symphonically into four movements that, to all intents and purposes, can be identified as allegro, andante and scherzo, while the fourth was still unidentified when he sketched it out to Chekhov in January 1901:

Act One – joyful, lively.
Act Two – Chekhovian mood.
Act Three – terribly nervous, fast, moves on tempo and nerves. Towards the end, their strength strains and the tempo slows down.
Act Four – isn't clear enough yet.[34]

His score shows that Stanislavsky perceived the fragmented quality of Chekhov's writing as duos, trios, quartets and even quintets and sextets that he eventually streamed into his symphony, even into the end of Act Three whose fragments are the most disconnected from each other of Chekhov's entire play. Chekhov implies his protagonists' extreme exhaustion after the fire that had threatened to burn down the town, and Stanislavsky picks up his hint by a tempo that 'slows down' to Andrey's unheard apology to his sisters, which disintegrates into his weeping, and to Irina's resumption of the refrain about going to Moscow, which

[33] Ibid., 235. [34] *SS* 9, 7, 389 – my translation; Senelick, *Stanislavsky – A Life*, 137.

anticipates, as never before until then, the sisters' trio on this very refrain that closes Act Four.

Great tragedies occur in the quietest of ways, not excluding Tusenbach's death, and this may well explain why Knipper complained to Chekhov that Meyerhold was 'dreary' in the role. Meanwhile, the Old Believer actor (and sculptor subsidized by Morozov) Serafim Sudbinin was 'heavy' in the role of Vershinin. Neither, then, could provide the vigour with the lightness of touch that Stanislavsky envisaged for the 'life of the human spirit' played in its highs, lows and innermost recesses. Stanislavsky thus directed Knipper away from her highly charged confession of Masha's love towards calm statements in which love was deeply rooted rather than defended; and, following Nemirovich-Danchenko, who agreed with him about Knipper's overacting, he reduced the nervous tension of the preceding small scenes to prepare her for finding a voice weary from the night. Perhaps this was also the voice of Masha's internal dialogue with herself that had finally settled its conversation. Nemirovich-Danchenko replaced Meyerhold with Kachalov, and Sudbinin with Stanislavsky, which stalled rehearsals but brought the work closer to Stanislavsky-director's idea that an 'inner state' should be anything but dull.

Stanislavsky's score provides inventories of objects for the props manager, some with sonic annotations, like the 'sound of broken glass'. It occurs when Chebutikin drops the small china clock once owned by the sisters' mother, tempting Stanislavsky to 'clutter' the scenic action. No sooner broken than the clock becomes the focal point of fuss and bother. Vershinin picks it up to fix it; Irina gives him glue; he reaches into his pocket for cigarettes; remembers he is not allowed to smoke in the house and puts them back; she picks up pieces from the floor and carries them to the table; and so forth in Stanislavsky's score (but not in Chekhov's text) whose minutiae of gestures, movements and the sounds that go with them accompany Chebutikin's incongruous, fake-philosophical lines on how 'we might not exist at all'.[35]

Stanislavsky's personal notes offer plenty more sounds, over thirty for Act Two, for instance, and twenty for Act Three, and they range from the sounds of nature in the howl of wind in the chimney and the light fall of snow on windows to the domestic sounds of banging doors, creaking floor boards and the shuffle of tired feet and frequent washing in Act Three.[36] Stanislavsky must have used an overabundance of sounds, judging by Nemirovich-Danchenko's insistence on cutting them back, as he did with

---

[35] *Rezhissyorskiye ekzemplyary*, Vol. 3, 213.   [36] *Iz zapisnykh knizhek*, Vol. 1, 149–53.

196   Director

superfluous props – 'clutter' that, he believed, obscured the author's text. Visual encumbrance there must surely have been, but of interest here is the thought that Stanislavsky's domestic detail suggested a comfortably lived-in hearth and home meant to protect its inhabitants, but which failed to do so. More compelling still is the thought that he was directing what he saw as intimate tragedies, tragedies on a domestic scale in domestic surroundings where the fire was not outside, visibly ferocious, but in the soul-heart.

Such a modest notion of tragedy co-exists with Stanislavsky's belief that the characters were not melancholic but sought joy, laughter, cheerfulness: they 'wanted to live'.[37] Vershinin, having found love, bursts, in Act Three, with the desire to live. ('Oh, God, how I want to live!') His earlier speeches on humanity's steps towards a better future sound like prepared speeches by comparison, but even they, combined with Tusenbach's reflections on the steadfast course of life, provide an optimistic melodic line to Stanislavsky's symphony. The critic Leonid Andreyev, writing under the pseudonym of James Lynch, declared that he was reluctant to see the production because 'Chekhovian protagonists were intolerable for their lack of an appetite for life'.[38] Having seen it, however, he disagreed that the production was 'pessimistic'. His own response of wanting to live after he had left the theatre tallied with the swell he felt in the audience which, on that night, was not a select gathering but a 'grey throng': these were the testimonials of the production's bracing impact after the tears shed on the stage and off it had been washed away. Stroyeva calls this 'grey' public the 'democratic intelligentsia and student youth' which, she claims, received the production as a call for freedom and 'the reconstruction of life'.[39]

The Three Sisters enjoyed success, while Chekhov wrote that the production was 'going along magnificently, with brilliance, and better, by far, than the written play'.[40] This may have been one of his double-edged swipes, a slur, perhaps, on Stanislavsky's added 'noises' to his plays: frogs, dogs, crickets, birds, bells – horses' bells, church bells – and all sorts of peripheral voices nearby or in the distance, which were especially richly imagined for Act Three of *The Three Sisters*. Stanislavsky's sonosphere for the latter had a stereophonic effect, while his eye travelled cinematically, picking up details or taking in long shots, as he was soon to do again for the opening of Act Two of *The Cherry Orchard*. Here, in addition to

---

[37] M. N. Stroyeva, *Rezhissyorskiye iskaniya Stanislavskogo 1898–1917* (*Stanislavsky's Research in Directing*), Moscow: Nauka, 1973, 75.

[38] *Moskovsky Khudozhestvenny Teatr v russkoy teatralnoy kritike 1898–1905*, ed. Yu. M. Vinogradov, O. A. Radishcheva and E. A. Shingaryova, Moscow: Artist. Director. Theatre, 2005, 232.

[39] *Rezhissyorskiye iskaniya Stanislavskogo*, 78.   [40] Quoted in *Rezhissyorskiye ekzemplyary*, Vol. 3, 55.

Chekhov's telegraph poles and the imprecise shape of a large city on the horizon, Stanislavsky drew rolling waves of rye in the fields in the distance and, closer, a forest and then a mist rising from a dip in the earth after the heat of the day.[41]

So persistent were Chekhov's objections to Stanislavsky's embellishments for the first three productions of his plays that, when it came to *The Cherry Orchard*, the director, on tenterhooks, respectfully asked his permission to run a toy train with smoke through Act Two.[42] The writer joked that he could, providing it did not make the slightest sound.[43] Stanislavsky took the joke at his expense without a flutter, and crossed the train out, written in pencil and thus indicating that it was tentative in his score.[44] His wish was not granted until Giorgio Strehler, remembering Stanislavsky's letter to Chekhov, showed a toy train running in a circle – with a light sound, but without smoke – in his 1974 production with the Piccolo Teatro in Milan. It was one of those wondrous moments of inter-theatre citation which, operating like a finely etched palimpsest, illuminated both Strehler's and Stanislavsky's vision of this pivotal scene between the past and the future, between rural fields and the trains carrying holidaymakers to Lopakhin-built holiday homes.

Chekhov famously complained that Stanislavsky's production of *The Cherry Orchard* had ruined his play.[45] However, frogs were not the main reason for his accusation but tuberculosis, which made him anxious and cantankerous. Being a doctor, he knew that death was imminent, while he, like Vershinin, wanted to live and love. So he argued testily not only against Stanislavsky and Nemirovich-Danchenko but also against his wife and the entire company that his play was a comedy, even a farce. Putting up a front against his worst fears about himself, he placed it on the funny end of the spectrum, possibly near Balzac's idea of the '*comédie humaine*' rather than on its tragic end. (Chebutikin might name Balzac randomly in *The Three Sisters*, but not Chekhov.) Chekhov had attended four or five rehearsals and had disrupted them with criticisms of the actors' tear-stained approach – to the point where Nemirovich-Danchenko banned him from them, muttering to his face that writers had little to no idea about the theatre.[46] Stanislavsky, although shy to contradict the author, wrote saying

---

[41] Ibid., 339.
[42] *SS* 9, 7, 518, letter of 19 November 1903 – my translation; *Stanislavsky – A Life*, 175.
[43] *The Moscow Art Theatre Letters*, 186.   [44] *Rezhissyorskiye ekzemplyary*, Vol. 3, 363.
[45] *Stanislavsky i Nemirovich-Danchenko. 1897–1908*, 222.   [46] Quoted in ibid., 229.

198 Director

that Chekhov, an intellectual, might think it was a farce, but 'to the ordinary person – it was a tragedy'.[47]

The issue was not theatre genres but textual interpretation, which had far-reaching consequences for how the director would direct and the actors would act. The second major contention was the structure of the play and its core interest. Chekhov insisted that Lopakhin was the central character – a peasant boy who had learned how to become rich, but who, for all that, was neither boorish nor vulgar; and he wanted Stanislavsky in the role because he was a man of peasant origin, like himself (albeit several generations ahead), who had come up in life and understood what this meant. Stanislavsky, on the other hand, did not conceive his production in terms of central characters, but, if a central interest had to be defined, then it would be Ranyevskaya and Gayev (whom he ended up playing) and their loss of house, home, land, orchard, social status and personal reason for being. Such loss was enough for the ordinary person to understand that Chekhov's play was tragic. And while Lopakhin was a decent man and would live well, and the younger generation, Trofimov and Anya, would take up a productive future, the swan song of the gentry, such as it might be represented by two hapless figures, was also the swan song of feudal Russia confronted with huge uncertainties about her future. Stanislavsky could see nothing comical, let alone farcical, in any of this.

The following scene from Act Three concerns Ranyevskaya and Lopakhin after Lopakhin returns with Gayev from the auction where he bought Ranyevskaya's estate. Stanislavsky-director writes: 'I advise the actor to forget, for the moment, all expressions of happiness – it is more powerful to convey [Lopakhin's] embarrassment and the awkward situation.'[48] Stanislavsky comments that Lopakhin is embarrassed 'to the point of being ridiculous, almost pitiful' and shows him running his hands through his hair, followed by other gestures that exteriorize his discomfort. When Ranyevskaya asks: 'Who bought it?' Stanislavsky writes: 'Pause. Barely audible.' Then to Lopakhin's 'I did', he writes: 'Pause. Even more quietly and more embarrassed still': and he reverts Chekov's 'pause' from the end of Lopakhin's sentence to its beginning. In this prelude to the protagonists' 'inner state', Stanislavsky-director sees the generations of serfdom behind Lopakhin's discomfort in which, during the brief exchange above, he also notices Lopakhin's 'feeling of guilt' over his victory. Mixed with his ancestral memory of social inferiority is his 'feeling of guilt' towards Ranyevskaya personally.

[47] *SS* 9, 7, 506, letter of 22 October 1903.
[48] *Rezhissyorskiye ekzemplyary*, Vol. 3, 419, then 420–1.

Production Scores and Musicality: Chekhov and Gorky   199

Stanislavsky brings the two contested dramatic centres together and follows the throughaction without engaging in further debate with Chekhov and without prejudice to either Ranyevskaya or Lopakhin. He describes the second pause for Lopakhin as an 'excruciating pause' during which 'Lopakhin feels bad and, because of it, the beast within him stirs'.[49] Varya interrupts the pause by throwing down the house keys, which causes him to lose patience. Then Stanislavsky builds up a counteraction. Lopakhin 'becomes angry and almost shouts, bitterly and impudently: "I bought it"'. This, Lopakhin's second acknowledgement of ownership, is a high pitch in his 'feeling bad' about himself and the situation, and it prompts Stanislavsky to write many more meticulous stage directions, which involve Ranyevskaya, whom he has immobile, staring stupidly at the floor, and Pishchik, whom Stanislavsky casts more or less as a self-appointed servant to a new master, who follows Lopakhin around, or closes doors so that no one else will hear. Among Stanislavsky's directions for Lopakhin, who moves away from Ranyevskaya, is his crescendo of 'feelings of happiness and a merchant's pride, which overcome the good feeling of embarrassment, and he begins to boast as a business man might to his fellow merchants or landowners'. Lopakhin's gesticulations, which Stanislavsky describes as 'posturing', are not downgraded but are attributed to a 'strong temperament and an unbridled nature'.

As Lopakhin becomes vehement about his childhood, Stanislavsky notes:

> Now he knows no mercy. Intoxication has hit him over the head – he feels no compassion for the unfortunate Ranyevskaya. The anger and bile stored up within him against the degradation he had known when he was young have woken up in him. He may be saying this ['I bought it'] straight to Ranyevskaya. Everything will be comprehensible if the performer makes bigger sweeping gestures, is mighty [and] is more of a knight [*bogatyr* – from Russian folktales] than a small-time wealthy peasant (*kulachok*).[50]

By the end of his monologue, Ranyevskaya has 'sunk into a chair and is weeping bitterly' (Chekhov's stage direction, which Stanislavsky retains). Lopakhin, oblivious to her until then, falls to his knees and shows his 'tender love for her family, but especially for her' (Stanislavsky's stage direction). Stanislavsky asks why, with such a soft heart, does Lopakhin not save her? And answers: 'Because he is a slave of merchant prejudice, because the merchants would ridicule him. Business is business.' The latter

---

[49] Ibid., 422–3, and following citations.   [50] Ibid., 425 and following.

phrase is in French to indicate the complicity of a habitus in which it is commonly used – the habitus of merchants like Stanislavsky's father but not yet that of the newly risen businessmen of Lopakhin's kind. Stanislavsky had caught the social nuance nicely in his commentary, summed up concisely in his concluding phrase in French.

Stanislavsky's musical direction takes Lopakhin through a diminuendo to bring the scene to a close. From the scene's opening gambit until its conclusion, he identifies the attitudes and actions of all its characters, but does so most precisely for Lopakhin, who is finally able to assume his social mobility not merely as a social fact but *psychologically*. 'Attitude' (*otnosheniye*) always means, for Stanislavsky, the way a character looks at and feels about the world and the people and situations in it; 'attitude' is part and parcel of 'the life of the human spirit of the role'. Its embodiment in his Chekhov productions, together with that of the psycho-emotional motivations for actions and their manifestation in actions – noted precisely, once again, for Lopakhin – made his reputation as a director of realism and, specifically, of psychological realism. He was this director but was certainly more in that his 'psychological' was of the heart-soul played in multiple motifs by actors who all had their individual sounds and reverberations in relation to each other – the attitudes that Stanislavsky always talked about – and they performed listening to each other, as do the instrumentalists of a musical ensemble.

Thus to Rudnitsky's 'emotional ensemble' can be added another nuance 'musical' for what constituted the MAT ensemble which blew the theatre milieu of Europe away in 1906 and again in 1922 when the company was en route to New York and performed at Jacques Copeau's Théâtre du Vieux Colombier in Paris. This dimension of Stanislavsky's directorial achievement in his early years of founding a new theatre is one of paramount importance for understanding his growth as a man of the theatre, which enabled his international impact and influence during his lifetime, and the scale and ramifications of that growth. His musicality – probably not less than that of Meyerhold (a violinist, Stanislavsky, a pianist) – inevitably led him to the theatre of music in opera and its different but related challenges to those of spoken theatre, and he cross-pollinated both of them. Strehler, the most musical director of the later twentieth century (he was also a violinist), rubbed shoulders with Stanislavsky not only in his *Cherry Orchard*, and even more so in his beloved Goldoni productions, but also in his opera productions to which Stanislavsky would doubtlessly have bowed deeply, in the old Russian manner.[51] Strehler's prose theatre and music productions, it must be acknowledged, were also discussed in terms of realism, the nuance aptly introduced by the adjective 'poetic'.

'Reality' and *The Lower Depths*

The notion of 'realism' has been contested ever since Stanislavsky's productions brought it to the forefront of theatre practice and theatre history. Among these voices are such prominent dissenters from 'realism' (in effect, essentially understood by them as 'psychological realism') as Ariane Mnouchkine, Eimuntas Nekrosius, Valery Fokin and Frank Castorf and, of course, directors who define themselves in terms of 'realism' in some particular way.[52] Most prominent among the latter group from a generation or two younger than the preceding directors is Thomas Ostermeier, who has approached the notion in a thought-provoking way. He has pointed out that realism comes in various shades according to the changing times, as does his own 'capitalist realism' developed in the late 1990s (dubbed 'brutalist realism' or just 'brutalism' by the German press).[53] Looking back to Stanislavsky, Ostermeier's approach questions the doxa that Stanislavsky had provided a 'realist' template, which has been applied willy-nilly in all times and all places without serious modification or adaptation to local socio-cultural and political circumstances – or without outright reconstruction because of them.

Second, Ostermeier has proposed the idea that all reforms brought about in twentieth-century theatre were attempts by their reformers to 'reactivate the umbilical cord between theatre and reality'.[54] His alteration of the vector from 'realism' to 'reality' frees theatre from the paradigm of 'realism' (recall Stanislavsky's rejection of all 'isms') and lets it breathe in 'reality', that is, in the boundless energy of life from which, as Stanislavsky saw it, the theatre took its creativity in time and place, regardless of how theatre works were composed and identified aesthetically. Ostermeier's image of the umbilical cord elucidates how Stanislavsky approached directing – in fact, on a par with how he envisaged and taught acting – and this means that, although with time he developed a director's 'language' and signature, he continually attempted to reactivate how he was directing in terms of the 'proposed circumstances' of this or that material

---

[51] See my account of Strehler's *The Cherry Orchard* in *The Cambridge Introduction to Theatre Directing*, 189–91.

[52] See my discussion of these directors in ibid., 77–115.

[53] *Le Théâtre et la peur*, trans. Jitka Goriaux Pelechová, Paris: Actes Sud, 2016, 60–4.   [54] Ibid., 45.

202 Director

and the wider world – 'reality' and the 'times' – in which the given material made sense.

The difficulty of maintaining his resolve to reactivate instead of iterate and replicate 'reality' struck Stanislavsky when, in 1902, he directed Gorky's first play, *The Petty Bourgeois* (also known as *The Philistines*, neither being the best translation for *Meshchanye*). The play forced him to confront the problem of reconciling his dislike of tendentiousness in the theatre (of which Nil, the machine operator, was virtually a proto-type) with his perception that 'reality' in respect of Gorky's play had to do with the daily grind of disenfranchised people – in effect, with *byt* understood, in Stroyeva's words, as 'obtuse and harmful to humans'.[55] Gorky saw his petty bourgeoisie as wedged somewhere slightly above the peasantry, and he profiled it by its aimless talk, brusque manners, loud whispering and violent quarrels. Stanislavsky was less interested in social stratification than in this 'obtuse' type of daily life which, because of his overemphasis on the latter, undermined the political meaning of Nil's speeches – recognized and praised by liberal and left-wing theatre critics but lost completely on audiences. His groupings of characters were impressive, but their picturesque appearance also deadened Gorky's social critique.

These same critics, in both Moscow and St Petersburg, unanimously panned the production for having taken the revolutionary bite out of Gorky's play. Efros, for instance, spoke of the MAT's 'emasculation of Gorky'.[56] The censor, who had excised 'unfit' passages, had undoubtedly hampered Stanislavsky, but he had considerably shortened the second half of Act Four anyway to foreground his 'genres', as Efros called his concentrated daily-life pictures and 'epic' crowd scenes. The production limped to the end of the season and never returned thereafter.

Nine months later, the triumph of *The Lower Depths* compensated for the failure of *The Petty Bourgeois*. Knipper wrote to Chekhov that it was almost like the premiere of *The Seagull* – uproar, frenzied spectators climbing onto the stage, repeated curtain calls.[57] 'Reality', this time, took form in the squalor of doss-houses whose inhabitants had hit rock bottom – the most accurate words in English for the title of Gorky's play (*Na dnye* – at the bottom). Gorky's 'reality' was authenticated by the excursion Stanislavsky had organized for the company to Khitrovka, the

---

[55] *Rezhissyorskiye iskaniya Stanislavskogo*, 89.   [56] Quoted in ibid., 95 and following.
[57] *Vospominaniya i stati; perepiska s A. P. Chekhovym*, 155.

'Reality' and The Lower Depths 203

market area of central Moscow notorious for its slums. The purpose, even of limited immersion in this milieu, was to stimulate the actors' imagination so that they could come to grips with characters out of their normal range of experience. Stanislavsky also had an inkling of the importance of such immersion for a director, who could guide by allusion to shared impressions instead of imposing his/her own. Slowly but surely, the immersive principle that he had hit upon entered the consciousness of Russian directors, without necessarily becoming part of their practice. But it certainly became a major principle for Dodin's 1986 *Brothers and Sisters*, the first of several of his outstanding productions to use immersion for garnering ensemble memory and awakening sensations to be stored psychophysically for reactivation when actors needed them.[58]

Rudnitsky remarks that Art Theatre productions had gone down the social ladder from the aristocracy, the intelligentsia, the peasantry and the petty bourgeoisie, to reach, with Gorky's second play, 'the dregs of society, the lumpen [proletariat], the thieves, the prostitutes' – the 'bottom, beyond which there was nowhere to go'.[59] This is all very well, but it is essential to add that here, in this nether world, Stanislavsky had discovered the 'naturalism' that went with the territory of abject poverty, human depravation, social degradation and social indifference, as Émile Zola had identified 'naturalism', that is, socially, which pre-empted Zola's use of the term as an aesthetic category. At the same time, Zola had turned 'naturalism' into a class aesthetic capable of depicting the lower social classes in the hard truth of their existence without either sentimentalism or moralizing. Efros called Stanislavsky's amassed details of human misery in *The Lower Depths* 'coarse truth', while other Russian critics called it 'naked naturalism';[60] by now, Zola's writings, and not least his theory of naturalism, were widely known in Russia. Amassed detail appears to have been Stanislavsky's only instrument for nailing a particular 'reality' that he must have felt had to be *seen* to be believed. He had taken a comparable approach with Tolstoy's grim *The Power of Darkness* in the same season but immediately before *The Lower Depths*, finding the former's 'crude truth' (Stanislavsky), which included infanticide, among the peasantry. What cannot be ignored, however, is

---

[58] *Dodin and the Maly Drama Theatre*, 44–6. See also my interview with Dodin regarding immersion in Norilsk in Arctic Russia and Auschwitz for *Life and Fate* (2007) in Maria Shevtsova and Christopher Innes, *Directors/Directing: Conversations on Theatre*, Cambridge University Press, 2009, 46–7 and 58–9.
[59] *Russkoye rezhissyorskoye iskusstvo*, 204.   [60] Quoted in ibid., 203.

that 'truth' for Stanislavsky, as for Tolstoy but also Gorky, was not merely a matter of knowledge acquisition or circumstantial information. It was for the promotion of *action* – of moral and social action for social *change*.

Stanislavsky-director slipped into the trap of 'external effects', which he warned against for Chekhov on the MAT's tenth anniversary and, relying too heavily on pictorial truthfulness – Repin rather than Levitan was now his reference – he found that entries into 'inner' being were blocked. The more earnestly his actors sought the 'inner' of Gorky's characters, the more ponderous their characterization became. Furthermore, Rudnitsky points out, mundane doss-house speech could not accommodate Luka's 'sentimentality', Satin's 'loud-mouth tirades', the Baron's 'philosophical maxims' and the Actor's 'pathos'.[61] Nemirovich-Danchenko pulled rehearsals out of their stalemate with, as he wrote to Chekhov, a 'brighter, faster, more forceful tone' not 'weighed down by unnecessary pauses'.[62] And he advised Artyom, Stanislavsky, Kachalov and Moskvin in these four problematic roles in the order just given to stand beside their roles as if they were outside, looking at them, and deliver their speeches like reports or lectures: this would enable them to distance their characters and present them at face value, without bothering about 'inner' substance. As a result, the production acquired the sharpness indispensable for its socio-political intent. Note how closely several of Brecht's techniques for *Verfremdungseffekt* resemble Nemirovich-Danchenko's instructions so much earlier in 1902.

Stanislavsky wavered between a liberal humanist view of Satin and the upbeat revolutionary one taken by audiences, and his oscillation between the two mirrored, in fact, this very ambiguity in Gorky's text, without his consciously trying to reflect it. Stanislavsky's score captures his initial response to Satin's monologue in Act Four whose centrepiece 'What is a human being?' evokes a question important to Hamlet, whom the Actor cites persistently, suggesting Gorky's interest in humanism in and for his play. Satin's monologue below is abridged from Stanislavsky's score. The Baron has just told Satin he was always kind and clever when he drank. Stanislavsky writes that snoring, a quiet accordion, and the Tartar's praying accompany Satin's speech:

Note Stanislavsky's 'drunkard' for Satin which, given Nemirovich-Danchenko's turn-about and change of direction for the work and his subsequent control over rehearsals, is possibly not how he or his

---

[61] Ibid., 199.   [62] Ibid., 200.

Gorky's text	Stanislavsky's directions
SATIN: When I'm drunk ... **176** So – he's praying? Fine! A person can believe, or not believe, that's his business! A human being is free [and] pays for everything himself: **177** for believing or not believing, for loving, for thinking. A human being pays for everything himself, and that's why he's free! A human being – there's your truth! What is a human being? It isn't you, or me, or them – no! It's you, me, them, the old man [reference to Luka], Napoleon, Mahomet – all rolled into one! (*He draws the figure of a man in the air.*) ... It's tremendous! ... A hu-man be-ing! It's magnificent! It rings – proudly! ... Baron let's drink to the human being! **178**	**176** Quietly, glancing at the Tartar [who has rolled out his prayer rug and is praying.] **177** Satin, holding a bottle in one hand, pours Kleshch, who has pushed his glass forward, a generous drink. Kleshch tries to pick out some kind of tune on his harmonica. The Baron is quietly snoozing. The Tartar is praying in the Eastern way. Satin continues speaking happily. He is a sincere and good-natured drunkard. He has a great deal of love and the sense of beauty in people. One feels the artist in him. **178** Satin is full of joy. Pours the alcohol, drinks, pours, gives the Baron and Kleshch some more. The Baron drinks lazily; no longer pesters him.[63]

grandiloquent speech was performed. Gorky soon echoes Satin's words in *Children of the Sun*, which pits a utopian view of humanity against ugly manifestations of humanity, and Gorky insisted that the MAT respect this play's farcical elements, of which there were many, revealing an ingrained ambivalence towards high-minded aspirations, largely of an ethical rather than a political order, and low-minded, vaguely 'political' villainy, alike. Stanislavsky may have thought it was 'useless nonsense', but it attracted audiences, playing twenty-one times over six weeks.[64] The audience's interest was a clue to how 'democratic' society was divided between a humanist-universalist approach to its ills and a socialist-revolutionary one. This division could only grow as the forces heading for 1917 gathered apace.

Rehearsal Notes: *Cain* and *The Marriage of Figaro*

The end of this foundational period, crowned by the accolades of the 1906 European tour, saw Stanislavsky return to his complaints about directing 'puppets' instead of co-creators of the production process. A February entry in his 1908 notebooks shows how he broached the travails of MAT directors first:

---

[63] *Rezhissyorskiye ekzemplyary*, Vol. 4, 1988, 484–5.   [64] *Khudozhestvenny Teatr*, 91.

They say that the directors in our theatre are despots. What a joke! Our directors are miserable horses, driven to the end of their tether. Not only is their labour not valued, but no one actually understands it. They are mocked and insulted until the director, worn out, begins to yell hysterically or to curse everybody at the top of his voice.[65]

Then he criticized the MAT actors. He and Nemirovich-Danchenko had established the model of the director as the production centre when the company was finding its feet, but the actors, having grown artistically since then, had not learned how to be independent. They continued 'to wait for handouts from the directors like beggars or, like spoiled children, to demand them'.[66] They had learned to reap what the directors had planted in them and to share this with audiences, but they had failed to learn to seed creativity within themselves.[67] His notebook entry was probably a draft, if not the verbatim text, of what he had said at a meeting with the MAT shareholders, also in February, when he was held to account for the company's recently low productivity. Stanislavsky held his ground, pointing out with his critique of ingrained stultifying practice why work had been slow; and he argued forcibly for the remedies he was offering, which he presented as rights. These were the rights of the System, which was to help actors, and the rights of his new way of directing by which actors were not made to be dependents but helped the director.[68]

If only it was as simple in practice as it was on paper. *A Month in the Country* in 1909 was the first MAT production to test the System adequately and to be tested adequately by it (Chapter 3), but his insistence that the actors work with System principles encountered more of the mockery and insult to which Stanislavsky-director had referred the year before his 'pilot' run with this production. And his System-related co-operative approach to directing raised the problem of authority, which he must have deployed at times to oblige an unwilling group to do as he directed. Where was the dividing line between authority and authoritarianism? Stanislavsky's concise summary of what he calls the 'history' of the production indicates that this line was very thin: that, if the actors had a hard time, he, Stanislavsky-director, did not have it any easier; that Stanislavsky-actor also had to buckle under his co-director Moskvin so as not to undermine the latter's authority with the group and, as well, to preserve the group's cohesion.[69] This, as transpires from his summary, was fragile in the given situation of conflict. He notes that the transfer from

---

[65] *SS* 9, 5, 347. [66] Ibid. [67] Ibid., 348. [68] *SS* 8, 5, 634–5.
[69] *Iz zapisnykh knizhek*, Vol. 1, 368–72.

Rehearsal Notes: Cain *and* The Marriage of Figaro

table work to rehearsals on the stage was 'hell' because what had looked fine in the one revealed its weaknesses in the other, the greatest being stock-in-trade acting. And, while Stanislavsky's score for *A Month in the Country* was sparse by comparison with the Chekhov and Gorky scores, thus suggesting the director's resistance to top-heavy leading from the front, it was only too obvious that the MAT's primarily director-led and table-talk habits would not shift overnight.

Stanislavsky was taking the steps he thought necessary and he trod carefully up to and including 1917, when he fine-tuned Sushkevich's direction of *Twelfth Night* for the First Studio shortly before its premiere in December, featuring a dazzling Mikhaïl Chekhov as Malvolio. However, for the next two years, Stanislavsky-director went into retreat. He helped with *Balladina* at the First Studio in 1919, but his energies were mostly spent on the Bolshoy Opera Studio and his new goal to unite the First, Second and Third Studios with the MAT in a 'Pantheon', which would afterwards spread further afield.[70] Stanislavsky had calculated that the existing institutions were now made up of four generations of System students, each familiar with its different stages.[71] They would retain the working methods that suited them best, but the System would remain their core theatre language within shared perspectives on why theatre mattered to society. The 'Pantheon' – with the Art Theatre as its 'cupola', as Radishcheva observes – would protect their achievements (Stanislavsky was thinking of current enemies at the gate), but, more than a fortress, it would continue to develop them.

As Stanislavsky mused on its potentiality (in fact, the Pantheon never happened), the MAT reprised its old repertoire, while the First Studio came to its aid, performing *The Cricket on the Hearth*, *The Deluge* and the recent *Twelfth Night* on its main stage to fill out the MAT's seasons. All of it was taken as evidence by the miscellaneous political Left of the company's uselessness to revolutionary society. To make matters worse, Stanislavsky, in liberal-entrepreneurial fashion, spoke out in 1919 against Lenin and Lunacharsky's project for nationalizing theatres, capitulating, despite himself, to the state protection of 'academic theatres' in which the MAT was included, the only formerly private theatre to be granted this relative security. Lenin had made it his business during 1918–19 to see *The Village of Stepanchikovo*, *The Lower Depths* and *Uncle Vanya*, and he disagreed with Gorky's remark at the time that 'the new proletarian

---

[70] *SS* 8, 6, 34–41, in a speech of 22 May 1918.
[71] Radishcheva, *Stanislavsky i Nemirovich-Danchenko. 1917–1938*, 24–6 and 26 for 'cupola'.

208 Director

spectators only needed heroics on the stage', retorting that 'lyricism was necessary, life truth was necessary... Chekhov was necessary'.[72] The old repertoire thus turned out to have its uses recognized in more ways than one.

The Art Theatre's reprieve from closure meant that a new production had to be shown as quickly as possible. Stanislavsky had wanted to stage *Cain* in 1907, probably as part of his symbolic line, but it was banned by the Synod and released only when the revolution dismantled the Orthodox Church – a situation that allowed Lunacharsky to announce, as he planned nationalization, that art imperatively had to be accessible to all and, to boot, to replace religion.[73] The novelist Ivan Bunin (who emigrated to Paris in 1920) had translated Byron's Mystery with the flourish of the Silver Age. But Stanislavsky was no longer tempted by Silver Age esotericism. *Cain* interested him in 1919 because its Mystery concerned fratricide, in which he saw 'a parallel' with the Civil War raging in Russia; and he asked how the Bolsheviks, who had opposed the First World War in the name of high principles (Stanislavsky cites 'work, goodness, beauty'), could have instigated, in the name of the same principles, a war that was worse than the first.[74] Stanislavsky extended his 'parallel', pairing Lenin with Lucifer and Trotsky with God, that is, with Byron's Jehovah, a God not of love but of wrath who, ruling by fear, had initiated prayer that came of fear.[75] Cain rebels against this God who subjugates the fallen Adam, Eve and their children unto eternity through fear and through all the other earthly imperfections that he had created. Cain shares Lucifer's point of view: God had created mortality by creating a snake in Paradise (the only place where immortality was possible), and this imperfection was evidence of God's imperfection.

Stanislavsky's notes on *Cain* were not pre-arranged for rehearsals. They were mostly written during them, and they indicate that his references to Bolsheviks, in general, and to Lenin and Trotsky, in particular, were not intended for an explicitly political production; at most, given his aversion to 'tendentiousness', the production could be allegorical. These references were associative so as to give a face to supernatural figures and render them less abstract than their long philosophical deliberations permitted (which

---

[72] Quoted in M. N. Stroyeva, *Rezhissyorskiye iskaniya Stanislavskogo 1917–1938*, Moscow: Nauka, 1977, 28.

[73] Ibid., 26.

[74] *Stanislavsky repetiruyet* (*Stanislavsky Rehearses*), ed. I. N. Vinogradskaya, Moscow: Moscow Art Theatre, 2000, 174.

[75] Ibid., 178.

Rehearsal Notes: Cain *and* The Marriage of Figaro   209

Stanislavsky ruthlessly abridged in his copy of Bunin's translation).[76] The central struggle of Byron's drama, as he saw it, was not between Cain and Lucifer, but between Lucifer and God; Cain was Lucifer's pawn in this struggle. Stanislavsky and his actors used 'lures' for the imagination to envision such entities as concrete characters, and his aphorisms 'Lucifer is an anarchist. God – a conservative' (here his parallel with Trotsky dissolved!) were like memory aids when discussions became too abstract.[77]

The actors asked whether it was possible to embody disembodiment and Stanislavsky replied that, since they had bodies, they could only imagine spirits from within themselves as humans;[78] and, since Spirit was within them, they could grasp the 'astral' in themselves intuitively and realize it corporeally in theatrical form. How important this 'astral' was for Stanislavsky-director – a priority equal to his 'human', which on no account would he allow to be reduced to banality – can be glimpsed in his ironic remark to himself on paper that Leonidov-Cain greeted Lucifer 'as if Ivanov had come in' (that is, in a banal, everyday way; 'Ivanov' is a surname as common as 'Smith').[79] He notes his 'personal' (Orthodox) disagreement with the idea of God's imperfection, but the director in him approved Aleksandr Shakhalov's justification of Lucifer's view of God because it meant that this First Studio actor could believe in Lucifer's claim to innocence in the fall of humanity and thus act the part convincingly.[80]

The rehearsal notes show the actors, the director and Stanislavsky's assistant director Aleksandr Vishnevsky discussing what Cain's throughaction might be; and the actors appeared to have mooted the reasons for Cain's fratricide at length. Stanislavsky returned to his initial proposition that Cain always asked the question 'Why?' Moreover, the reiteration of his fundamental question made it the kernel of the role and a reliable guide to Cain's throughaction, which, Stanislavsky suggested, was Cain's thirst for life. Here he was following Byron's text closely: Cain had to know death to know life, and this, precisely, was his contradictory reason for killing Abel. All the collaborators searched for the throughaction of each character. Stanislavsky writes, for instance (with patriarchal reasoning), that Adah's role had an ideal *woman's* point of departure (my italics for his gender distinction) in that she radiated joy.[81] Her throughaction, then, was to give joy. Eve's, by contrast, was self-punishment for her sin, the origin of that death which suffering humanity would know eternally.

---

[76] Moscow Art Theatre Museum Archive, K. S. No. 18893.   [77] *Stanislavsky repetiruyet*, 187.
[78] Ibid., 186–9 and 194.   [79] Ibid., 171.   [80] Ibid., 188.   [81] Ibid., 170.

'Throughaction' was the main term, although far from the only one taken from the System for rehearsals, and the ease with which the group seems to have used its vocabulary suggests that the System had become a common language and a common culture to some degree at the Art Theatre.

Stanislavsky speaks in his rehearsal notes of the necessity of putting together the play's 'pieces' and the 'logical bridges' that linked them, and he challenged the actors to pinpoint their 'wants' for each piece by thinking in verbs rather than nouns – a practice mistakenly considered to have come into effect in the 'method of physical action' but which was already apparent here.[82] He worked on crystal clear diction and the sobriety but also the musical rhythm of words. These were the essential qualities of tragedy, and *Cain* was, for him, a tragedy above all else.[83] Various notes refer to the lateness or absences of actors and technicians, which held up rehearsals. One, written in a resigned tone, records a delay of two hours because the sets were not in place. Such details of inadequate care and its repercussions on self and others and the work in hand indicate why Stanislavsky thought it necessary to include his observations on ethics and discipline in his publications.

How he saw *Cain* scenographically is vividly outlined in *My Life in Art*.[84] He first imagined it in the interior of a Gothic Cathedral, with high vaults and stained-glass windows through which varied light from the sun and the moon would fall. The theatre's stage and auditorium would be rearranged accordingly, transforming actors and spectators into one congregation. Monks dressed in black would carry burning candles, their myriad lights creating the illusion of stars in the cosmic space that Lucifer opens up to Cain's gaze, while lanterns carried at the end of sticks (allusions to medieval procession and pageantry) would intimate the fading planets and the ghostly grey spirits floating past Cain in infinity. Stanislavsky's architectural space for 'astral'-spiritual space in which the 'human' was embedded provides a marvellous example of his pioneering understanding of stage design in its integral relation to dramatic meaning. As usual, his imagined sonosphere, which incorporated an invisible choir and instrumentalists, was in synergy with the spatial and dramatic whole. Stanislavsky commissioned such a score from Pavel Chesnokov, the esteemed composer and choirmaster of sacred music at the Moscow Conservatorium.

Stanislavsky's magnificent vision was way beyond the means of the times, although it was probably conceived in its grandiose proportions already in 1907, when finance was still available. He was forced, now, to

---

[82] Ibid., 191–3.   [83] *Rezhissyorskiye iskaniya Stanislavskogo 1917–1938*, 32.
[84] *SS* 8, 1, 378–83; *My Life in Art*, 324–8.

Rehearsal Notes: Cain and The Marriage of Figaro

propose an alternative: a stage covered entirely in black velvet against which numerous lit candles were stars in the heavens (quite likely Stanislavsky's subliminal cross-reference to Sonya's 'sky filled with diamonds'). His designer Nikolay Andreyev shaped sculptures – huge heads, shoulders and arms on poles draped in canvas – to look hallucinatory against the velvet, as were supposed to do equally huge sculptured columns alluding to a cathedral. A podium built high above the stage floor from which Lucifer and Cain would float into the cosmos was to be covered in black velvet to create the illusion of their flight. Stanislavsky soon discovered that there was not enough black velvet in all of pauperized Moscow, but the solution to use supplementary fabrics dyed black destroyed the effects intended by his light design.

Theatre critic Zagorsky (Chapter 2) blasted the production's crude visual devices, music that would hardly inspire angels to sing, acting that produced unimpressive, banal characters, whereas stylization was key to tragedy, and directorial incompetence in the 'formlessness' of the entire work.[85] Meyerhold, in his article on Stanislavsky's isolation cited previously, agreed entirely, while bemoaning the waste of Stanislavsky's gift for theatricality, so evident in *Cain* and so unfulfilled in it. The considerably late start of the opening night on 4 April 1920 due to a wildcat strike of electricians and other stage workers exasperated the spectators and disoriented the actors, sending *Cain* off into perdition.

The documentation for *Cain* is of a different order from the production scores and it differs again from the documentation for the production of Beaumarchais' *A Mad Day or The Marriage of Figaro*. This production was part of a discernible 'line' of French comedy plus one melodrama that Stanislavsky had introduced into the repertoire starting from Molière's *The Imaginary Invalid* (1913, directed by Benois). *The Merchants of Glory*, written in 1925 by Marcel Pagnol and Paul Nivoix, which Stanislavsky directed with Sudakov in 1926, had preceded *The Marriage of Figaro* and the melodrama *The Gérard Sisters* after the 1875 *Two Orphans* by Adolphe d'Ennery and Eugène Cormon followed it in 1927. Stanislavsky had selected these texts not only to maintain variety (the purpose of his repertory 'lines', as discussed earlier) and to weaken the perception that the Art Theatre was stuck in the rut of 'naturalism' and 'psychological' theatre (both, to his mind, inadequately understood or downright misrepresented by critics of the MAAT), but also to keep the company agile,

---

[85] *Moskovsky Khudozhestvenny Teatr v russkoy teatralnoy kritike 1919–1943. Chast pervaya. 1919–1930*, ed. O. A. Radishcheva and E. A. Shingaryova, Moscow: Artist. Director. Theatre, 2009, 19–23.

212   Director

vigilant and, precisely, not fall into any rut whatsoever. His youthful experiences of French light comedies and operettas did not go amiss in how he imagined *The Marriage of Figaro*.

Beaumarchais' was another play from which Stanislavsky, in collaboration with Golovin his stage and costume designer, did not wish to make a tendentious or, worse still, an 'agitprop' production (Chapter 2). Nikolay Gorchakov, a young Third Studio director who had joined the MAAT during the merger negotiations of 1924, was a skilled stenographer, and his records of Stanislavsky's rehearsals from 1924 to 1936 are invaluable for understanding how Stanislavsky's directing developed after *Cain*; and just how flexible his directing was in its adaptation to varying material, not least to such ideologically transparent plays as *The Amoured Train 14–69* out of which he made a production with a human face.

It was not that Stanislavsky was incapable of dealing with political subjects. The cardinal issue was how he, as a director, could not believe in directing that used the theatre as a political platform. Nor could he believe in a theatre that was explicitly ideological. Ideology was not, for him, the same as having a political position. Judging from his comments, he must have seen it as the *imposition* of a position, and he never appears to have acknowledged that Meyerhold's overtly ideological theatre – much of it being his Constructivist theatre – was construed from a *chosen* and not an imposed set of ideas. In a personal conversation of 1922, he told Gorchakov, in response to Gorchakov's questions on directing, that a director 'had to be independent in his/her thinking' (which also meant independence from coercive dogmas) and had to have 'the ability to observe, to think and to build work so that it aroused thoughts needed in contemporary society' – something, he added ruefully, that he had tried but failed to do in *Cain*.[86] The question that Stanislavsky omitted was, of course: '*Who* "needed" *what* thoughts in which particular *sector* of contemporary society'?

It is absolutely clear from Gorchakov's records that Stanislavsky did not fudge the political aspects of *The Marriage of Figaro* (written in 1778), nor the political climate that had influenced Louis XVI's decision to ban a play openly critical of aristocratic privilege. (It was finally performed in Paris in 1783.) When Stanislavsky met with his assistant directors Telesheva and Vershilov (Chapter 4), he referred to Beaumarchais' subterfuge of situating the play in Spain (when the author had France in mind) and

---

[86] Nikolay Gorchakov, *Rezhissyorskiye uroki K. S. Stanislavskogo* (*K. S. Stanislavsky's Lessons in Directing*), Moscow: Iskusstvo, 1952, 42.

Rehearsal Notes: Cain *and* The Marriage of Figaro 213

his use of comedy to highlight Figaro's triumph over Count Almaviva whose permission he needed to marry Suzanne. Almaviva's permission depended on his satisfying his seigniorial rights to bed the bride first on her wedding night. Stanislavsky's historical exposition to his assistant directors entailed a correction: Figaro's throughaction was not simply 'I want to marry Suzanne' – but 'I want to marry Suzanne and gain my freedom'.[87] Freedom meant depriving Almaviva of his feudal rights and achieving his, Figaro's, democratic rights as a human being.

The Marriage of Figaro's reputation as a forerunner of the 1789 French Revolution was not lost on Stanislavsky, who stressed that Figaro was, 'first and foremost, a man of the people' [*narod*] and 'a democrat, protestor and rebel' against the aristocracy.[88] He was, in other words, the very emblem of the 'Rights of Man' written into the French Constitution of 1791. Stanislavsky conceived of Figaro as a representative of the people and not as a maverick rebelling on his own account. Stanislavsky: 'The hero of our production is the people'; and the 'people' were also Suzanne, Cherubino and the crowd of forty local peasant and domestic workers (Stanislavsky's interpolation) who were invited to the wedding and anticipated with Figaro their future freedom as citizens.[89] Although Stanislavsky had helped to translate Beaumarchais' French into vernacular Russian, he was firm in his intention not to update the play and 'make it contemporary'. The production would remain in the play's time and place, in France rather than Spain, with costumes to match. Figaro was to have a mixed French-Spanish 'temperament', its French traits being lightness, alertness, insolence and wiliness, which he was to deploy fully in outwitting the Count.

Above all, the production had to take its cue from the first half of Beaumarchais' title *A Mad Day* – a day whose events occurred at top speed, demanding swift and precise action from all performers. Stanislavsky and his co-translator-dramaturge restructured the play from five Acts to eleven scenes and a wedding finale with song and dance. These scenes, which he sometimes called 'episodes' to emphasize that something was happening in them, turned rapidly on the Art Theatre's revolving stage, allowing characters to appear or disappear from one situation to the next without any pause. The revolve also solved the problem of delays in scene changes, which were unusually numerous because of the intricacies of Beaumarchais' plot and its various subplots whose comic energy had to be vivaciously sustained from start to finish. Stanislavsky described the play as 'a comedy-

---

[87] Ibid., 375. Vershilov quoted in *Rezhissyorskiye iskaniya Stanislavskogo 1917–1938*, 169.
[88] Ibid., 364 and 368. [89] Ibid., 364.

satire' full of 'the froth of champagne';[90] and he patiently, painstakingly made sure the actors kept up their tempi and sparkle over the eighteen months of rehearsals (end 1925 to April 1927) so that the dynamics of the production would become second nature to them and emerge spontaneously on the stage.

What is particularly striking about Stanislavsky's approach to rehearsals of *The Marriage of Figaro* is their qualitative continuity with the production as artefact, that is to say, rehearsals were not treated as preparations for performances or as preambles to them, but as performances in their own right; and this meant that players had to give their all in every rehearsal, as if they were playing the real thing in front of audiences. This was another of Stanislavsky-director's most innovative practices, and it was passed down to generations of Russian directors among whom, in the circuit of living directors, Dodin and Vasilyev – and the younger Yury Butusov to be met in the conclusion to this book – are probably the most consistently exacting heirs, each in his singular way. The thinking behind this qualitative continuity is straightforward in its belief that actors who work with no holds barred during rehearsals incorporate their effort to such a degree that it becomes effortless in staged productions. Ballet dancers provide the appropriate comparison: studio jumps in rehearsals can never be at halfmast; they are jumped as high as they need to be in performances – or higher – so that the very real effort invested in them does not look like 'effort' on the stage. It is no wonder that Stanislavsky paid careful attention to the ballet dancers at the Bolshoy, seeing what he could learn from them (as he did from opera singers) for the theatre. By the same token, it had occurred to him that the dance-acting in ballet could benefit enormously from the System;[91] and, as Kristi recalls, he referred to his idea of establishing a ballet studio 'if he could live till he was at least one hundred' so as to study the melding of action and movement in ballet as he was doing in his research on opera.[92]

Stanislavsky frequently worked with individual actors, but especially with Nikolay Batalov, a broad-faced, fresh-faced Russian lad whom he had to inspire to become fleet-footed and swift-tongued – in short, become what Stanislavsky thought of as 'French'. (Batalov was to have a major role as a morally upright Russian revolutionary in *The Armoured Train*.) Almost without exception, the cast was made up of young actors with

---

[90] Ibid., 375. Vershilov quoted in *Rezhissyorskiye iskaniya Stanislavskogo 1917–1938*, 170.

[91] Moscow Art Theatre Museum archives F.3. op. 29. ed. khr. 3.

[92] *Rabota Stanislavskogo v opernom teatre*, 261.

Rehearsal Notes: Cain *and* The Marriage of Figaro

the stamina to keep up with Stanislavsky's fast-paced demands. Yury Zavadsky, Vakhtangov's former student, played a slim and trim Almaviva who gave Batalov-Figaro a run for his money, as was required for a 'mad day' in which all social norms were overturned together with the play's plot and sub-plots. Comedy was one of Stanislavsky's strengths, also as an actor. Once, when he was playing Argan in *The Imaginary Invalid*, his fake nose fell off. Stanislavsky had the audience in stitches as he ostentatiously attempted to glue it back on, mumbling all the while that so sick was he that even his nose had fallen off his face. It was a masterstroke of invention of the kind that delighted Meyerhold in his former director's work, and actor improvisation of the kind that enraptured Vakhtangov and Mikhaïl Chekhov.

Much can be learned from Gorchakov's documentation of rehearsals about how Stanislavsky-director achieved the actors' co-creative input in the production process – Dodin calls it 'co-authorship'.[93] Take, for example, the crowd of forty local people who rush through the gates for the wedding of the finale. Stanislavsky, contra Beaumarchais, situates the wedding not in an elegant room within the château, as conventionally done, but in a small and neglected inner courtyard of the château whose corner was piled up with discarded furniture, boxes, barrels and ladders. Golovin had provided a richly coloured drawing of an exquisite room, which Stanislavsky sent back for revision. Stanislavsky-director's point regarding the courtyard was that the Count was putting Figaro back in his place and, of course, punishing him for his victory in the battle over Suzanne. The point of the piled-up discarded objects was to stimulate the actors' co-creativity as they worked out how to deal with them in the 'proposed circumstances' of the play and the production.

In the first rehearsal, the crowd stood about the stage, waiting for Stanislavsky's blocking, whereupon he called the actors into the auditorium to say that they had to make do as best they could with the junk and fit into the tight space. After their first successful attempt, he suggested that they laugh, shout, sing and jostle in the wings before they rushed onto the revolving stage: this would be much more dynamic, and would excite them as well as alert the audience to the festive occasion. The scramble for something to sit or stand on – or just to press against a wall – made for a lively scene composed spontaneously and multifariously by the actors. Almaviva and the Countess arrived to find there was no room for them, and all the actors had to find a way of fitting them in.

[93] *Dodin and the Maly Drama Theatre,* 51–2 and 58–60.

216   Director

Solutions to the task that Stanislavsky had seemingly innocently set
varied from rehearsal to rehearsal until the best variations were 'fixed' (set)
into the production. This included a leg breaking on a scruffy armchair,
which was pulled out from somewhere and placed on a plank across two
chairs. Zavadsky-Almaviva, who was obliged to climb up onto the plank,
had accidently broken the armchair's leg the first time he sat in it. When
Zavadsky demurred, Stanislavsky, in a state of immersed director co-
creativity, retorted that he only had himself to blame for punishing Figaro
by having a wedding in such a location! Swept away again, Stanislavsky
asserted that he was only following Beaumarchais' text, whereas there was
no reference whatsoever to a courtyard wedding in it. Knebel, who played
an old woman in this scene, noted the actors' sheer delight in composing
it, adding various observations on how Stanislavsky encouraged his actors'
co-creativity, including by inventing two more scenes so that she could
have more scope for developing her character.[94] Hers was a minor character, it has to be said, but Stanislavsky's proactive measure was in line with
his conviction that there were no small roles, only small actors.

A second example of actor co-creativity concerns Batalov in the eleventh
scene, the garden scene, where Figaro, suspecting that Suzanne was dally-
ing with the Count, goes in search of her to denounce her. Suzanne,
however, had set a trap for the Count by dressing the Countess in her
clothes, while she wore those of the Countess. Stanislavsky rehearsed this
scene with Batalov in his *kommunalka* apartment, urging the actor to run
from small room to small room and into the corridor and up and down the
stairs and improvise in whichever way he could, displacing whichever
objects were in his way in his drive to find Suzanne. Batalov was to create
his role by charting his own actions but without saying his lines, prompted
only by Stanislavsky's calls, as if he had just sighted Suzanne. Stanislavsky
aimed to develop quick reflexes and deft, light movements, and the words
were not added until Batalov had come closer to this goal. Stanislavsky
additionally sang out 'Figaro here, Figaro there' as a trigger, an impulse, to
sharpen Batalov's reactions. He took this catch-phrase on Figaro's ubiquity
from Rossini's well-known opera *The Barber of Seville* whose libretto was
based on Beaumarchais' first play of his Figaro trilogy. After many delays
and Golovin's death in 1930 (Golovin was to be the designer of the opera),
Stanislavsky eventually staged it in the energetic, laughing spirit of *The
Marriage of Figaro* in 1933 at the Stanislavsky Opera Theatre (Chapter 4).

[94] *Vsya zhizn*, 240–9.

Rehearsal Notes: Cain *and* The Marriage of Figaro

Progress was slow. An impromptu visit from Gorchakov inspired Stanislavsky to ask for his help by hiding from Batalov, which he (Stanislavsky) had been doing. Gorchakov as his replacement would free him to speed up calls and to trick Batalov with false alarms, all of which revved up the actor's reactions and finally gave him a feel for the allegro of his actions as a whole. Batalov retained the quality of his movements, spurred on by Stanislavsky's urgent direction – fortunately recorded by Gorchakov – so that they became Batalov-Figaro's 'muscle memory' (Stanislavsky), in reserve for subsequent rehearsals and performances.[95]

The actor's work with his body had set off a whole range of emotions in him logically suitable for the actions of his role, and Stanislavsky continued this particular aspect of the method of physical action by encouraging Batalov-Figaro to shave Almaviva as if he was going to cut his throat. The director went so far as to give Batalov a genuinely sharp barber's shaving knife so that his movements – how he wielded the knife (angling it to 'show the audience how its sharpness glistens'), pushed back Zavadsky's collar, tilted his head, and so on – built up within him Figaro's hatred of the Count.[96] Stanislavsky-director kept nudging Batalov by recounting the Count's sexual escapades so as to have him feel and embody this smouldering hatred and convey it so clearly in his actions that the audience would fear he might really cut Zavadsky's – not the Count's but Zavadsky's – throat.

Stanislavsky had declared at the very beginning of the production process that the production was to have unbridled 'theatricality', and he certainly crossed the line between reality and theatricality in the shaving scene – on the face of it, a bread-and-butter realistic piece. Theatricality generated the carnivalesque atmosphere of the production as a whole, recalling *Princess Turandot.* Perhaps, like the latter, its wit, warmth and carefree impetuous rush had healing power for audiences battered by incessantly onerous socio-political conditions.

The Marriage of Figaro may have been taken as a temporary respite – indeed, as a liberating carnival moment of the kind Mikhaïl Bakhtin studies in *Rabelais and His World*;[97] and although Bakhtin gathered his material from 1934 until the end of the decade, unable to publish it until 1965, the relation between the 'popular' and even the 'populist' worldview emerging from Stanislavsky's production and the one permeating Bakhtin's book is

---

[95] *Rezhissyorskiye uroki,* 394–402.   [96] Ibid., 383.
[97] Trans. Hélène Iswolsky, Bloomington: Indiana University Press, 1984.

218   Director

striking.[98] So too is their respective focus on the 'people' perceived as 'folk' (*narod*), that is, a 'people' preceding the industrial proletariat, whereas the mid-1920s and, even more so, the 1930s, were the growth years of that proletariat. Evident, as well, is their utopian dimension in their vision of communal unity and communion. Stanislavsky referred in rehearsals to the necessity of creating *sobornost* in the production and *sobornost*, as discussed in this book, is far from the ideological closing of ranks prevalent in Soviet society in these years. He most definitely did not want to make an 'agit' production, but he had made one that, pivoted on Figaro, subverted agitprop tenets and tactics and it did so through laughter.

Director-Pedagogue: *Othello, Romeo and Juliet, Hamlet*

Three more examples give further insight into the range of Stanislavsky's explorations in the field of directing: *Othello*, which is linked temporally with *The Marriage of Figaro*, and two pedagogical projects at the Opera-Dramatic Studio in 1937 during the surge of Stalin's reign of terror against which Stanislavsky managed to barricade the Studio. These cases also show the advances he made for theatre directing in the twentieth- and twenty-first centuries. My reader will keep in the back of his/her mind the advances he made specifically as a director of operas, as discussed in the preceding chapter, and the part they played in stretching his directorial horizons and practical capabilities as a director *tout court*.

Batalov's outline of his physical actions *as if* he were in Figaro's circumstances, mastering them before he added Beaumarchais' dialogue to his actions, coincided with Stanislavsky's few preliminary rehearsals in 1926 with Leonidov playing Othello. Knebel, who was present, remembers Stanislavsky tackling what he understood to be the play's turning point – a section of five repartees from the third scene of Act Three, after Iago had poisoned Othello's heart and mind with his insinuations that Desdemona was unfaithful.[99]

The section begins in Shakespeare with Othello's 'Ha, ha, false to me?', which yields, when translated back into English from the Russian, 'Aha, false to me! To me!' The inserted exclamation marks and repeated 'to me' change the inflections in that they stress Othello's incredulity that he could have been betrayed, and this must be taken into account in Stanislavsky's

---

[98] For further discussion of Bakhtin's 'popular', see Maria Shevtsova, 'Dialogism in the Novel and Bakhtin's Theory of Culture, *New Literary History*, 23, No. 3 (1992), 760–2.

[99] *Slovo v tvorchestve aktyora*, 112–16; 114 for Knebel's personal response to Leonidov's performance.

Director-Pedagogue: Othello, Romeo and Juliet, Hamlet   219

direction of Leonidov. Stanislavsky asked Leonidov, whom he considered to be a great tragedian, to play, without words, a man whose pain was so overwhelming that he simply did not know which way to turn. Leonidov did so – according to Knebel 'one of the most powerful impressions made on me in my life' – and then he performed the part again with Shake-speare's text, Stanislavsky having stressed how vital the 'author's thought' was to an actor's psychophysical realization of what he/she was doing. It should be noted that Stanislavsky's directorial technique of wordless playing, as in *The Marriage of Figaro*, was not a substitute but a support for playing in words. It was advantageous for releasing the feelings in and behind words *and* in actions, which the director coaxed out of actors as part of his/her responsibility to the actor. This feeling-body fusion would be described in the twenty-first century as psychosomatic, and the term sits well with the process of *perezhivaniye* as Stanislavsky understood it.

The Glavrepertkom (Chapter 2) had rejected Stanislavsky's application for permission to stage *Othello* in 1925, at the time of a blitz on classics. (*The Marriage of Figaro* had escaped censure, but not the subsequent ire of theatre critics.) A lull in the blitz allowed Stanislavsky to resume work in 1928 on his favourite Shakespeare play, which Salvini's performance as Othello had revealed to him and which he had directed, apparently with little success, at the Society of Art and Literature. Moreover, Leonidov had longed to play Othello for decades. The rest is known: Stanislavsky's heart attack; his enforced convalescence in Nice in 1929; his handover of the production to his assistant director Sudakov; his mistrust of Sudakov and consequent reliance on Leonidov to follow his guidance by correspondence; Sudakov's abandonment of Stanislavsky's production plan, sent in instalments to Moscow from December 1929 to March 1930; Sudakov's considerable alterations to Golovin's scenography; the MAAT's 'red administrator' Geytts' interference, and Sudakov's decision, out of fear of political recrimin-ations, to show the work before it was ripe. Stanislavsky, who had envisaged a year of rehearsals – Sudakov took less than three months – was not consulted. Geytts wrote to inform him of the premiere *after* it had happened.

Stanislavsky had unwillingly fallen back on writing a production plan, but he was stuck in Nice and either he sent his imaginings or gave up his cherished production. The penalty of returning to a method that he had discredited was heavy. Not only did he not recognize his vision (as accounts from his MAAT friends of the production's makeover had made plain) but also he, a managing director of the MAAT, was left to play 'a fool's part' not knowing what everyone else knew about Sudakov's raiding

220 Director

his work and going against the timetable he had estimated for it; meanwhile, his name was advertised on the posters as its principal director.[100]

Then there was the calamity of Vladimir Sinitsyn – Iago – who had accidentally fallen four floors to his death, and Leonidov's agoraphobia, which had ruined his performance. (Stanislavsky fully empathized, having experienced similarly paralytic fear of the black space of the audience at the time of *The Village of Stepanchikovo*.) Zagorsky saw a fascinating Iago, who had overshadowed a Leonidov maimed, he argued, by the Art Theatre's infatuation with daily life and robbed, by the System, of the great emotional depth and breadth required of tragedy.[101] And 'What was *Othello* without Othello?' sneered fellow theatre critic Vladimir Blyum, that other undisguised enemy of the MAAT. Well, after such devastation all round, there was no *Othello* for Stanislavsky to see on his return. Although there was talk of a rehabilitated production, Stanislavsky did not have the heart to do it.

What remained was his incomplete but thorough plan, a subtly inflected conversation with individual actors within a dissertation on ideas and working principles of importance to all. Stanislavsky establishes with Leonidov that Othello is not a jealous but a trusting man whose excruciating pain stems from shattered faith in love compounded by his shattered trust in humanity. Iago's hints about Desdemona contradict everything that Othello perceives to be beautiful both in her and the world, throwing his emotions into turmoil.[102] Iago destroys Othello's 'trusting nature'– here, for Stanislavsky, is the very heart of Othello's tragedy – and in being capable of doing so, he proves that he is not simply a foil for Othello but a protagonist level with him. By realigning the positions, Stanislavsky challenges conventional assumptions about Iago's secondary status in the play, and by accentuating Othello's 'trusting nature' he minimizes Othello's jealousy. Iago is the one who is consumed by jealousy, enraged against Othello for having passed him over for military promotion in favour of Cassio; Iago who has an inflated sense of his own importance in his services to Othello and to the wars waged by Venice in which, in reality, he was not a warrior but an opportunist. Iago, in Stanislavsky's perception, victimizes and scapegoats Othello to an extent inconceivable in established interpretations of the play.

---

[100] *SS* 9, 9, 408, letter of 9 April 1930 to Ripsime Tamantsova, his secretary.

[101] *Moskovsky Khudozhestvenny Teatr ... 1919–1943. Chast pervaya. 1919–1930*, 319–20; 316 for Blyum.

[102] *Rezhissyorsky Plan Otello*, ed. N. Zograf, Moscow and Leningrad: Iskusstvo, 1945, 9–18 and 262–5.

Director-Pedagogue: Othello, Romeo and Juliet, Hamlet   221

Stanislavsky returns to the section of Act Three that Knebel had seen him rehearse with Leonidov and to his idea of the 'line of physical and elementary psychological tasks and actions' which, when followed accurately, lures feelings out of the subconscious. He affirms, as he had done in the past, that a direct approach to feelings frightens them away.[103] His analogy is the hunter who uses decoys to lure game out of the thicket, and he takes up this image for Othello's 'Aha, false to me! To me!'[104] Leonidov's task, he specifies, is 'I have to decide why Desdemona is unfaithful to me', and his accompanying actions – the decoys – tease out Leonidov's feelings 'today, here, now' (in Stanislavsky's present order of these words) in their aptitude for the role.

As Stanislavsky continues along Leonidov's and Sinitsyn's respective line of tasks and actions, he observes that, beneath the former's line, which in the selected section ends in English with 'Farewell! Othello's occupation's gone', Othello seems to be saying to Iago: 'See what you have done to me [and] what you have taken away from me'.[105] What have gone besides trust, faith and love are the glories and social recognition of a General victorious in war. As Othello comes towards the end of his speech, Stanislavsky imagines for Othello and Iago a series of small but very clearly articulated actions that control reaction and condense intense internal psychological action. Stanislavsky's was a virtual pedagogy, intended to nourish the actors' imagination so that they could find independent solutions to their questions. Thirty years had passed since *The Seagull*, when the Art Theatre actors had their hands firmly held by two directors.

The idea that solutions were always defined by well-identified 'proposed circumstances' had become axiomatic for both directors and actors of the Stanislavsky school and it served as an organizing frame, as did other such frames as 'task', 'action' and 'line of physical actions', in terms of which productions were directed. Stanislavsky's conversations with Zon from 1933 to 1935 indicate that he already had a vocabulary for his 'new' method by the time he got his laboratory going in the Opera-Dramatic Studio. But the Studio was where he wanted to pull together the principles with which he had been experimenting in the interface between opera and dramatic theatre for a considerable period and to formulate them in something like a theory of what he had been learning through his evolving practice. Keep in mind that Stanislavsky's opinion in 1936 of theory as 'boring' or even as outright 'rubbish' is based on his premise that everything in the theatre is and must be 'done concretely'.[106]

---

[103] Ibid., 266.   [104] Ibid., 274–5.   [105] Ibid., 268 and 276–7.   [106] *SS* 9, 6, 534 and 536.

222 Director

If Stanislavsky's endeavour to pull his principles together ('theory' in this sense) risked falling into the 'rationalism' for which Demidov had criticized his System, then so be it, for he kept showing right through the three years of the Studio that his practice was devoted to the 'life of the human spirit' – in this respect Sulerzhitsky was always with him – and that the very purpose of tracking the 'line of physical actions' was to reach this very 'life of the human spirit' concretely. Novitskaya (Chapter 4), who directed *Romeo and Juliet* at the Studio under Stanislavsky's supervision – this was her director's apprenticeship – cites her directing teacher, who became the teacher of her students when they demonstrated what they had done under her supervision: '"One of the most important tasks of our art" – Stanislavsky continually claimed during the days of our meetings – "is the creation of the life of the human spirit".[107]

The vocabulary of the spirit, not least *'ya yesm'*, the most religiously saturated of its terms, is a consistent feature of his language as recorded directly by Novitskaya or when she reports the main points raised and discussed during rehearsals.[108] This indicates that Stanislavsky did not renounce the worldview integral to his System (Chapter 3) as the Terror began to peak, however slim the margins of tolerance for non-hegemonic thinking may have been. Novitskaya, with her students, followed Stanislavsky's advice to take notes during and after rehearsals, although never while they were playing; nor were they to analyze what they were doing while they were doing it. Stanislavsky may here have been silently referencing his traumatic blocks during performances of *Mozart and Salieri* and rehearsals of *The Village of Stepanchikovo* where he most probably had analyzed himself continually while he was performing.

Stanislavsky had suggested to Novitskaya in April 1937 that she direct *Romeo and Juliet* with first- and third-year students, and her colleague V. A. Vyakhireva, *Hamlet*. Their preliminary discussion revolved around the question of what a director should first do with a play. Novitskaya's answer – break it up into large pieces so as to outline the play's through-action – recalls an unpublished, related conversation in which Stanislavsky graphically explains with the example of a chicken: large chunks of a chicken 'contain' the form of the bird, whereas small bits cannot visually suggest that form; the same holds for a play.[109] Stanislavsky offered, in reply, what he believed was a more logical sequence: first find the play's overarching idea (*sverkhzadacha*), even if it is only an approximate idea,

---

[107] *Uroki vdokhnoveniya*, 214. [108] Ibid., 145–218.
[109] Moscow Art Theatre Museum Archive, K. S. 21162/1–2.

Director-Pedagogue: Othello, Romeo and Juliet, Hamlet 223

and then divide the play into large pieces according to episodes; then, after that, gather the facts that go with them. An episode – Stanislavsky was now quite clear what he meant by this term – consists of a *main* event. When all main events are identified, they reveal throughaction and give it form. By doing this, it might be added, they help the director to envisage potential form for the production in waiting.

Once the director has deconstructed a play, the work with actors begins, and does so with etudes on their feet, following lines of physical actions, which correspond with the episodes-events of the play. Stanislavsky asks why an actor needs to go through a role with physical actions and the two women reply that physical actions are more accessible than elusive inner sensations; they can be fixed into place more easily; they are material and visible. It is worth recounting most of the rest of their reply, since Novitskaya cogently sums up the essential points. Thus, physical actions are tightly bound up with all other necessary elements: wishes and wants that the actors determine, tasks (Stanislavsky describes tasks as 'rational' and actions as 'intuitive'), actor incentive and will, and the fundamental question 'What if?' And physical actions develop a feeling for truth, faith, logic and sequence (Chapter 3).

Stanislavsky approvingly continues: they also help to secure emotional memories and other characteristics of the human being-actor, which are unique to him/her but are made to be analogous to the role. Batalov, who was active *as if* he were in Figaro's 'proposed circumstances', is an eloquent example of what Stanislavsky means by an actor's being analogous with a role and acting analogously with it. Analogous acting, as Stanislavsky sees it, releases the actor to do and feel freely precisely because this actor is not trying hard to be someone else.

The human being-actor has an existential 'I'. When watching Vyakhir-eva's students rehearse *Hamlet*, Stanislavsky stresses again and again that there is no Hamlet or Ophelia or any other character but only 'I' who act *in relation to* acting partners (my italics). The young woman cast as Hamlet (I. A. Rozanova), whom Stanislavsky reminded to rehearse analogously 'from herself' rather than from a fictitious character named 'Hamlet' that would generate fake acting, had been First Studio Serafima Birman's student at the MAAT2 before it was shut down. She had requested this role, and Stanislavsky saw no reason why a woman should not play a man, unlike a few young men in the *Hamlet* group who at first were doubtful about his agreement. Of course, he had seen Sarah Bernhardt perform *Hamlet* in breeches in Paris and he was hardly likely to let social conform-ism cloud his judgement as to what was possible and effective in the theatre. Furthermore, he believed that actors should follow their heart and try out roles that they desired.

It was decided that the overarching idea (*sverkhzadacha*) of *Romeo and Juliet* was 'love triumphs' in a play entirely focused on the conflict between love and enmity.[110] The students, guided by the director, who had trekked through the play beforehand so as to guide them accurately, determined its episodes in co-ordination with its overarching idea, while keeping in mind that each event yielded a creative task, 'that is, the main action of each participant in each episode'.[111] Here, it is clear, Stanislavsky's equation-like 'that is' aligns 'task' and 'main action', even though he claimed that their nature was different, the one being rationally decided, while the other was intuitive. Vasilyev's insightful remark in another context that *zadacha* ('task') cannot be understood other than as 'practice' (which is doing) illuminates Stanislavsky's alignment exactly.[112]

Further breakdown at the Studio was into smaller 'events-facts' that make up the main action. Stanislavsky's leading term was now 'episode-event', and Novitskaya's compilation of episodes for each Act of *Romeo and Juliet* is straightforward, illustrating how a director might proceed with this type of deconstructive method that Stanislavsky sees as being the first stage of the director's work. Novitskaya's simplest but nonetheless representative list concerns Act One:

Episodes:
1. The fight is to the death – the argument is between two warring families;
2. Romeo's secret is revealed – he is in love with Rosalind;
3. Juliet's mother tells her that her life is about to change – she is to marry Paris;
4. Despite their presentiments and doubts, Romeo and his friends go to the ball;
5. Romeo and Juliet meet – love at first sight (flight and fall).[113]

Irrespective of such neat lists, their objective is not a tidy intellectual deconstruction of a playtext but a dynamic performance. Novitskaya maps out the two stages that follow and she highlights further work that develops out of the third stage, which is when directors and actors fully

---

[110] *Uroki vdokhnoveniya*, 181. [111] Ibid., 209.
[112] Personal conversation with Vasilyev on throughaction after his Director's Workshop, Wrocław Cultural Capital of Europe, 21 October 2016.
[113] Ibid., 212.

Director-Pedagogue: Othello, Romeo and Juliet, Hamlet   225

interconnect the actors' various 'lines'. Her principal point regarding this crucial third stage reads as follows: 'the unification of the physical line with the lines of organic processes, with the logic of thought (the author's thoughts + interior monologues) and with the line of imaginative vision (active by means of etudes)'.[114] Items like this one in Novitskaya's schema are dryly expressed, cerebral, but then she is here putting her directorial procedures schematically into order on paper. Her schema details, as she affirms, 'what is done', and she uses Stanislavsky's key word 'organic' to suggest that the 'what-is-done' of directing, like that of acting, is not a matter of mechanics.

Not to be overlooked is Novitskaya's reference to 'interior monologues', for they are fundamental to Stanislavsky's method, as demonstrated in the actress-student's work on Varya in *The Cherry Orchard* in Chapter 4. Just the same, she omits Stanislavsky's constant reminder that physical actions and feelings are organically interdependent and intertwined. Stanislavsky reiterates, when working concurrently on *Hamlet*:

> Physical actions are necessary precisely because they activate our feelings and our subconscious. Further on, as we create, our adaptations [to what we do] have to come from our subconscious'.[115]

All along Stanislavsky had stressed that feelings were volatile, fleeting, and could not be set; physical actions brought them out in their integral organic nature. It is imperative to note this and scotch the myth that Stanislavsky's method of physical action/active analysis had done away with the feelings that were vital to his System in its earlier years. Crucial to Stanislavsky's view is his argument, cited earlier, that feelings could not be approached directly because they were easily frightened away, and in their stead appear imitations or copies of feelings amenable to hackwork and 'acting', but antagonistic to *perezhivaniye*.

There is little difference in how Stanislavsky treats questions of method in the two groups, but the substance of *Romeo and Juliet* and *Hamlet* is decisive for what he says to them. *Hamlet* presented greater difficulties, which, as far as can be judged from the stenographic records, obliged Stanislavsky to provide extensive exegesis, starting with the opening episodes. He explained that Hamlet's father's Ghost imposes a task upon Hamlet beyond his powers, which is the crux of his tragedy, and that Shakespeare's 'big thoughts' cannot be discussed like 'sausages at breakfast' (a quip similar to Stanislavsky's on Lucifer being taken for Ivanov);[116] that,

---

[114] Ibid., 210.   [115] *Stanislavsky repetiruyet*, 462.   [116] Ibid., 480; 489.

226   Director

confounded by an insoluble dilemma, Hamlet tries to understand the meaning of life and why he is alive;[117] that Hamlet is like the Messiah and his throughaction is 'to cleanse the world';[118] that only by Hamlet's 'reconstruction of life on earth' can the Ghost be at peace 'over there' [among the shades]. Stanislavsky's religious reading of Hamlet is not surprising, and it recalls his view of Hamlet as a Christ-like figure (which Sulerzhitsky shared) in the years of *Hamlet* dominated by Craig. Yet the kind of insight into what physical actions can achieve and mean for a role thus perceived, as available in the rehearsal records of *The Marriage of Figaro*, is scant in the merely six, mostly short, stenographic records of the beginning rehearsals of *Hamlet*. And Vinogradskaya is right to point out that the forty-eight stenographic records in total of the Opera-Dramatic Studio are far from a full representation of what happened in Stanislavsky's lessons.[119]

Of the two student productions in preparation, only *Romeo and Juliet* was brought to full term after Stanislavsky's death and shown to an examining committee headed by Kedrov. It was praised highly and was to enter into the Studio's repertoire as a fully mounted production in June 1941, but the plan was cancelled after Nazi Germany's invasion of the Soviet Union in that month. The last production that Stanislavsky directed for the Art Theatre, with Litovtseva (Chapter 4), was Ostrovsky's *Talents and Admirers* in 1933.[120] He was rehearsing, also for the Art Theatre, Molière's *Tartuffe* with Kedrov in the title role, when he died. *Tartuffe* became Kedrov's production and it was dedicated to Stanislavsky's memory when it was premiered in December 1939.[121] Novitskaya was to become an assistant to directors at Moscow's Maly Theatre, the 'university' of Stanislavsky's youth.

What Is a Director?

Having denounced the director-tyrant, Stanislavsky appears not to have thought too much about what defines a director until the 1910s, when his notebooks intermittently sketch a few features. A director is a midwife who gently steers the course of a birth.[122] He or she is an administrator, a leader

---

[117] Ibid., 481; 509.   [118] Ibid., 508 and 508–10 for following.   [119] Ibid., 441.
[120] Rehearsal notes Ibid., 214–50.
[121] Rehearsal notes in V. O. Toporkov, *Stanislavsky na repetitsii. Vospominaniya*, Moscow: AST-Press SKD, 2002, 161–239. In English as *Stanislavski in Rehearsal: The Final Years*, trans. Christine Edwards, New York and London: Routledge, A Theatre Arts Book, 1998, 152–201.
[122] *Zapisnye knizhki* (*Notebooks*), Moscow: Vagrius, 2001, 196.

of an artistic process, a visual artist, a literary person and playwright, and a psychologist, critic and teacher.[123] A director has to have enough 'sensitivity and imagination to bring even the smallest of details not indicated or only sketchily shown by an author into the work, but going in the same direction as this author', and this 'director's obligation' applies as well to the 'genius Shakespeare'.[124]

By the time Gorchakov asked him in 1922 what a director was, Stanislavsky had come to realize that, when politics were an indelible part of everybody's life, a director had a greater social responsibility to think independently, referring, as we saw, to his failed *Cain*. Most important of all was Stanislavsky's understanding that a director's principal work was with actors and that it must grow together with the actor.[125] The sense of his emphasis is clear since it was with these actors, together with all other collaborators, that a production was indeed 'co-created' and became a harmonious whole. A director's responsibility was to see the making of a production to its end, and ensure that its component parts held together not only through its first season but also through its life in the repertoire. Inseparable from this artistic responsibility was a director's responsibility for watching over the ensemble. All of Stanislavsky's points also concern the director of opera – evident in Rumyantsev's and Kristi's accounts of how he works in opera rehearsals – with the additional specific factor that 'an opera director has to be a musician and occasionally a conductor'.[126] The reverse is just as necessary: an opera conductor has to work on the musical score like a theatre director works with actors.

Stanislavsky defines the director's role in artistic processes in the article 'The Art of the Actor and the Director' finished in 1928 for the *Encyclopaedia Britannica*.[127] After swiftly demolishing his earlier way of directing with production plans, he affirms that a 'director's creative work must be carried out together with the work of the actors'.[128] From here follows a brilliant summary of his main principles and procedures at the time of the article – identification of the *sverkhzadacha* and the throughaction of roles, breakdown of roles into pieces and concrete tasks, use of verbs for tasks ('I want x so will do y') and related points as discussed in my pages, including

---

[123] *Iz zapisnykh knizhek* (*From Notebooks*), Vol. 2, 140–1.
[124] Quoted in Radishcheva from Stanislavsky's notes of 1899–1902, *Stanislavsky i Nemirovich-Danchenko. 1897–1908*, 100–1.
[125] *SS* 9, 6, 526. 'Discussion with Regional Directors' of 1936.
[126] Kristi, *Rabota Stanislavskogo v opernom teatre*, 264.
[127] *SS* 8, 6, 232–42 and 421 for the note re the *Encyclopaedia Britannica*, and note 18 of Chapter 1.
[128] Ibid., 240.

228 Director

Stanislavsky's explanation to his readers that a director helps the actors to feel their way towards the throughaction of their role when they have difficulties in finding it.

There are hints here of Stanislavsky's director-midwife, but he is emphatic that on no account can a director intervene directly, least of all to instruct actors as to what to do, since this comes from the director's point of view and stifles the actors' initiative. Only by asking further questions beginning with 'What if?' can the director facilitate the actors' explorations as they gradually fuse their score of actions for their role with their organically generated experiencing of it. Stanislavsky takes his readers through the way actors creatively own, deepen and interconnect their roles and their feelings, conveying to spectators the 'spiritual substance of the drama', which is neither visible nor capable of being expressed in words but, all the same, is the very essence of the art of the stage.[129] Stanislavsky implies that the director, who is active throughout the process of growth, fades into the background at that moment when the actors encounter their spectators. The fact that Stanislavsky is silent about the director in this encounter suggests that he or she disappears when the actors are perform-ing because their performance is *theirs*.

Stanislavsky concludes his article by saying that the director is respon-sible for ensuring that the sets and music of a production 'illuminate the drama' and are subordinate to the needs of the actors. There can be little doubt that, for Stanislavsky, actors are the prime movers of the theatre, and this hardly makes him a candidate for the 'director's theatre' said to dominate the twentieth century – a debatable issue, in any case, regardless of this cliché's popularity in recent decades. Recall Stanislavsky's disagree-ment with Meyerhold in 1905 on Meyerhold-director's hegemonic role *at the expense of actors* (my italics) in the pilot Povarskaya Studio.

Stanislavsky's theatre hinges on actor-director co-creativity. He felt early in his career that a director needed to know how to act in order to direct and it re-emerged in a published article of 1931 in his idea of a 'faculty of directing' where future directors would be obliged to learn to act to some degree.[130] In such a faculty, director-pedagogues would teach students in small groups to guarantee individual attention and these, having become directors, would teach their students in a relay of practice that Stanislavsky would soon establish in his Opera-Dramatic Studio rather than in a grander-sounding 'faculty'. In an article of 1937, he draws attention to what he claims was currently the predominant style of teaching in theatre

[129] Ibid., 242.   [130] Ibid., 285–8.

schools – the bad teaching of demonstrating how roles 'are played'.[131] Stanislavsky admonishes this type of 'inspirer-director' (a description he had not come up with before) who demonstrates roles to actors superbly, but woe betide these actors when such directors go elsewhere, leaving them helpless. New kinds of directors were needed in faculties of directing to form independent young actors. In the longer term, his advice did not fall on deaf ears. Faculties of directing more or less modelled on Stanislavsky's ideas were institutionalized on a wide scale across all the Republics of the Soviet Union after the Second World War, Knebel becoming one of the main teachers of directing at GITIS, as was noted previously.

Officially the Russian Academy of Theatre Arts since 1991 but still spoken of as GITIS, this venerable institution consolidated in the mid-to-later 1930s also boasted Gorchakov within its directing faculty. Gorchakov taught Pyotr Fomenko, the multi-award-winning director in various theatres in Moscow and Leningrad/St Petersburg who taught directing at GITIS, forming from his students graduating in 1993 his internationally renowned Pyotr Fomenko Workshop Theatre. He and his troupe were particularly admired in France where they were invited frequently – this included the Avignon Festival – until his death in 2012. 'Workshop' (*masterskaya*), a modernized variation on 'studio', nigh replaced the latter term during the 1990s, although the entity operated on the principles of a studio as Stanislavsky had understood it, emphasis falling on 'theatre' or 'laboratory' differently in each case. Fomenko's *Masterskaya* started out as a *theatre*-laboratory.

True to Stanislavsky's idea of a directing faculty, Fomenko taught Sergey Zhenovach who, in his turn, taught at GITIS, where he directed acclaimed productions while also directing at the Malaya Bronnaya Theatre (1991–98), which Anatoly Efros had lifted to a generally recognized high level. He occasionally directed afterwards at the Moscow Art Theatre, named after Chekhov in the wake of the MAT's split into two in 1987 during the troubled days of perestroika, which ushered in the collapse of the Soviet Union. The MAT's second half, torn away by personal and political acrimony, became the Moscow Art Theatre named after Gorky in a separate venue. Stanislavsky must have turned in his grave at this breach of faith in unity, which he would have considered with greater trepidation than the breakaway of First Studio 'studists' in search of independence, although the young MAAT2 had also been divided largely by political disputes.

---

[131] Ibid., 346 and for following.

In 2005, Zhenovach founded the generously subsidized Theatre Art Studio located in an impressively refurbished part of the old Alekseyev golden thread factory, the historical significance of which escaped nobody. It was, after all, the factory where Stanislavsky had worked, first for his father and then as his heir, and where he had built a theatre for its workers. The founding of a new theatre, to boot under the name of 'Studio', appeared to be paying homage to Stanislavsky. Expression of esteem could be discerned elsewhere, but especially in Zhenovach's choice of *The Suicide* after Erdman (2015), the play denied to Stanislavsky-director in 1931 and which Zhenovach directed as a comedy, as Stanislavsky had described it to Stalin. Which is not to say that he tailored his production to fit an imagined 'Stanislavskian' rendition. On the contrary, the work looked as if it had been shaped by biomechanics in its pronounced angularity and stark juxtapositions. Zhenovach's itinerary as a director in its various connections to Stanislavsky came full circle when, in March 2018, he was appointed artistic director of the (Chekhov) Moscow Art Theatre.

The genealogical links Stanislavsky–Gorchakov–Fomenko–Zhenovach show quite cleanly how a directing faculty run along Stanislavsky's envisaged lines of relay (or close enough to them) operated at its best. The links Stanislavsky–Knebel–Vasilyev or Stanislavsky–Zon–Dodin lack, to date, an obvious fourth, but they would do as well to demonstrate how the development of directors took hold in Russia and became a twentieth-century tradition. Zon taught Dodin at the Theatre for Young People (TyuZ), a nursery of considerable standing in then Leningrad for the theatre profession; and Dodin taught actors, among whom were students of directing engaged to take their extra year at the Leningrad State Institute of Theatre, Music and Film, renamed in 2013 as the Russian State Institute of Scenic Arts (RGISI).

The idea of tradition here is pertinent since the director as a defined professional person who exercised a profession identified and recognized by its specific practice, like, say, a doctor is identified by the practice of medicine, not only barely existed in Russia before the Art Theatre but also barely existed as a 'director' in all of Europe in the modern sense in which this word is still used in the twenty-first century. 'Actor-managers' there were in the nineteenth century (Henry Irving resplendent in Britain), and before them, in modern history (*pace* the Greeks), were the towering figures of Shakespeare and Molière with their companies. But 'profession: director' is decidedly modern of the modernist age.

This having been said, the *development* of directors as a given tradition (courses are usually over four years, Dodin extended his to five) is very specific to Russia – not unique to Russia, as Germany most visibly shows in Europe – but specific to the theatre culture of this country, and both Stanislavsky and Nemirovich-Danchenko played a decisive role in establishing it. But the tradition of development may well have not occurred to such an extent and with its tenacity without the group of modern directors that grew together with Stanislavsky – Meyerhold, Vakhtangov, Sulerzhitsky, Chekhov and many lesser known directors like Birman – and, in the next generation, Gorchakov, Knebel and Kedrov. Furthermore, in the longer term and largely, though not exclusively posthumously, Stanislavsky proved to have been highly influential in the formation of directing faculties which, like all institutions the world over, have their drawbacks as well as advantages, one of the former being 'tradition' understood as the oppressive weight of established practices. Another drawback is the dead weight of decaying practices and still another is the exertion of authoritarian behaviour and political control through tradition.

Caution. Established practices on the side of institutional advantages do not automatically bring about conformity of doing and perception, even though they entail the reproduction of institutional structures and value-laden ways of doing to a certain degree – and even this 'to a certain degree' is no longer quite so evident in the protean societies of the late 2010s. Looking at the genealogy and DNA of director development in Russia through the three examples given, it is clear that, when at their best, directing faculties have not been cloning machines. Zhenovach's work is distinctly different from that of his teacher Fomenko. Mindaugas Karbauskis, another of Fomenko's well-known students, who first studied in Lithuania and graduated from GITIS in 2001, crafts productions distinctly different from those of both Fomenko and Zhenovach. Karbauskis retains Lithuanian citizenship and was appointed artistic director of the Mayakovsky Theatre in Moscow – the site of Meyerhold's revolutionary theatre – in 2011 at the tender age (for a director in Russia) of thirty-nine.

What deserves to be noted as well is that the tradition of development at issue here has person-to-person transmission at its core – 'transmission' not being a term commonly used in discussions of Russian theatre outside Russia, having become closely associated with Grotowski. The Russian phrase for the notion of such transmission is 'from hand to hand' and hand-to-hand-person-to-person transmission cannot be confused, as neither Stanislavsky nor Grotowski did, with learning from documentation and wise books.

Stanislavsky had two conversations in April 1936 about his recent work as a director, published as 'Masters of the Art Theatre'. Among these masters were directors Litovtseva, Gorchakov, Kedrov, Sakhnovsky and Sudakov, the actor Vasily Toporkov, whom Stanislavsky would soon rehearse as Orgon in *Tartuffe*, and his old friends and colleagues Knipper-Chekhova, Kachalov and Leonidov.[132] In the course of these conversations, Stanislavsky declared that 'a director is not made but born'; teaching of itself cannot create a director, but a good atmosphere can be established in which both 'born' directors and other directors can be developed and be seen to grow.[133] A director has to have multiple identities rolled into one – actor, administrator, artist, teacher, literary person and a sociable person aware of what is happening in society.[134] And a director's thoughts have to be open while an actor is acting because learning from an actor who is playing genuinely is 'more powerful by far than sitting in an office and thinking about a play'.[135]

A director has to know how to 'knead the clay' of an actor to bring this actor into the state of 'I am', whereas working with hard clay is an 'act of violence'.[136] The director-potter has to co-exist with the director-prompter. The latter must be capable of prompting the 'thoughts of a play' as the actor is thinking them when he/she acts without words until this actor is ready to take up the words 'and put them in his[/her] heart, the place from where he [or she] strives to reach the overarching idea' (*sverkhzadacha*).[137] Think of Stanislavsky prompting Batalov in the shaving scene of *The Marriage of Figaro*, or of Leonidov, prompted in earlier rehearsals to find the feelings for Othello's destroyed 'trusting nature' without words but 'in his heart'; observe, as well, the immediate relevance here of Stanislavsky's direction of opera whose music, he said, was to be 'taken not as sounding outside me (the actor) but within me as the movement of my heart'.[138]

Stanislavsky's sketch of a director is compelling, but what is most compelling in his 1936 conversations is that he is looking specifically from a director's perspective. He confirms to the directors present that, when they work with an actor in this way, they will feel that, effectively, the actor does have the line of the role and his/her inner line. These lines could not have been had if the throughaction (*skvoznoye deystviye*) had not been identified. Stanislavsky:

> This throughaction is present and it is certainly right, but it may not be brightly outlined, or may be of little interest, or may not excite. Here is

---

[132] *SS* 9, 6, 518–69.   [133] Ibid., 532.   [134] Ibid., and 571.   [135] Ibid., 542.
[136] Ibid., 535 and 552.   [137] Ibid., 541.   [138] *Rabota Stanislavskogo v opernom teatre*, 233.

What Is a Director? 233

where the director has a huge amount of work – clarify, deepen the throughaction, make it resound [and] be interesting.[139]

Stanislavsky-director is what he calls a 'root director' as distinct from a 'result director' who rejects the painstaking work of process or just does not know how to do it.[140] In a conversation in May 1937, recorded in shorthand but not published during his lifetime, Stanislavsky thinks about such master actors of the old Maly Theatre as Fedotova who, in the absence of competent directors, worked together so sensitively attuned to each other that they directed themselves. Their profound understanding and respect for their art enabled them to make productions collectively, without a director;[141] and here Bourdieu's wonderful image of the 'conductorless orchestra' for the workings of habitus springs immediately to mind.[142] The Maly actors, working conductorless within the practices, knowledge, know-how, expectations and so forth of their social-professional group habitus, were merely overseen by an efficient theatre manager and administrator who paid attention to blocking for immediately practical staging reasons. Their 'conductorless orchestra' was made up of the co-creators whom Stanislavsky wished to see replacing actor-dependents. Stanislavsky reflected on the case of the Maly because he was concerned about the dearth of directors at the MAAT and, given his preoccupation with the development of directors, he was possibly also worrying about the quality of the directors available.

Here was Stanislavsky, thinking about the future, when he declared that all actors needed to be masters because, when they *were* masters and worked as masters with each other, they no longer needed a director. In a flash, Stanislavsky sees the same dream as Mnouchkine, whose Théâtre du Soleil began with collective directors made out of all the company actors in a collectivity of equals in all areas of their common enterprise. When her experiment – of several years – was no longer tenable because the desire of each to become *the* master pushed out the collective goal, she assumed her responsibilities of director on the basis that collaborators should do what they are best at doing. Stanislavsky sees, as well, the dream

---

[139] *SS* 9, 6, 541.   [140] Ibid., 532.
[141] Ibid., 569. Published under the title 'Beseda s Stanislavskim' ('A Conversation with K. S. Stanislavsky').
[142] *Le Sens pratique*, 99.

of young devising groups in the twenty-first century – and this includes dancers – who, without using his language or even without knowing of his existence, assume a role analogous with that of the masters in Stanislavsky's idea of an ensemble of master creators. Stanislavsky: 'When an actor knows everything, he or she will be a director. . . . When heights are envisaged, art will exist'.[143]

[143] *SS* 9, 6, 572.

Epilogue
Legacy

Which Stanislavsky?

The question of Stanislavsky's legacy and of which of its aspects and where, when, how and why they were appropriated, adapted or refashioned in differing social and artistic contexts is so vast that it cannot be handled in a chapter of one single book, let alone in an epilogue of the kind I am writing here. This epilogue is a panorama, a *tour d'horizon* of various landmarks that the eye can grasp while others recede in the distance simply because sight cannot seize them all at once, or even on a third or fourth round. Furthermore, in the manner of certain types of epilogue, mine has no claim to being other than a personal view (and certainly not exhaustive), although it is not casual but comes from the terrain I know and can speak from; to call it a 'construction', even a subjective one, would be far too grand an appellation for what is essentially a lighter, more lyrical, venture.

My eye thus hovers over several promontories on the European and North American cultural landscapes, which is necessarily where it must start because the Art Theatre's very first, seminal tours were on these continents and had a direct and immediate impact, generating what is termed 'influence', which is integral to cultural legacy. Russia, a part of the European continent, has its very own history of legacy involving the studio practice and the studio and much other documentation of Stanislavsky's ever-changing approaches to his work. Sulerzhitsky and Demidov stand beside the more familiar figures of Meyerhold, Vakhtangov and Mikhaïl Chekhov and, in their vicinity, Sushkevich, Boleslavsky, Birman, Uspenskaya and Giatsintova from the efflorescent First Studio. Sushkevich, the only one of this group named but not given even the shortest of biographies in Chapter 4, became an Art Theatre stage director, the director of the Aleksandrinsky Theatre in Leningrad in 1933 and then,

235

236   Epilogue

in 1936, the director of the Leningrad State Theatre Institute, now RGISI (Chapter 5).[1] From the Second Studio, Tarasova, Knebel and Kedrov stand tall on the horizon among more also cited in Chapter 4. Kristi, a colleague of Knebel and Kedrov in the opera studios, was an astute note-taker and publisher of Stanislavsky's opera rehearsals, a director and an editor of the 1950s collected works. He finds his place in the panorama of Stanislavsky's legacy.

Sushkevich provides another excellent example of practitioners who, having worked with Stanislavsky, became disseminators of his principles within pedagogical structures. For, in Leningrad, as both a teacher and an important administrator, Sushkevich was influential in the construction of the Institute's curriculum and how it was taught. The extent to which the curricula of centres of learning pass down and shape (or deform) a legacy cannot be underestimated. Chapter 5 indicates how state institutions of learning in Russia passed on Stanislavsky's legacy, much of it from hand to hand, starting also from the first generation of great teachers of directing at GITIS – Birman, Sakhnovsky, Sudakov, Sushkevich, Zavadsky, among them – although many more exist than the few pre-eminent ones cited in those pages. Similar transferrals occur in theatre institutions and drama schools, colleges and universities throughout the world, whether they are government sponsored or have private or mixed sponsorship.

Stanislavsky's legacy has spread widely, and my terms below are simply geographical. It has spread to the Caucasian and the Turkic-speaking countries, the Middle East (notably Israel, not least because members of the Habima settled there), the Indian subcontinent, China, Japan and Korea (the countries usually cited, although others in Asia might be included), Australasia, South America and Africa, not to mention the Nordic and Baltic countries.[2] My focus in this epilogue – narrow, in respect of the globe – has nothing to do with Eurocentrism and everything to do with the impossibility for one person to cover the whole world.[3]

---

[1] A conversation about Sushkevich with my old friend and remarkable scholar Aleksandr Chepurov after I had completed this Epilogue prompted him to observe that the Committee of Artistic Affairs in Moscow sent Sushkevich to Leningrad for the express purpose of teaching the System to this city steeped in the St Petersburg tradition of theatricality. This fact reinforces my point here, as in Chapters 2 and 5, about how institutions transfer attitudes and values and transferred Stanislavsky's legacy across the world in general and the Soviet Union in particular, especially when government-led directives like the one involving Sushkevich were (and are) concerned.

[2] See Jonathan Pitches and Stefan Aquilina (eds.), *Stanislavsky in the World: The System and Its Transformations across Continents*, London: Bloomsbury, 2017.

[3] For reasons of similar impossibility, the editors above have relied on the specialist knowledge of their individual contributors, and one is hardly likely to quibble because they have missed Korea, Georgia and Azerbaijan (not to mention more countries), where Stanislavsky's teachings, and not only

With the limits common to all scholars acknowledged, it is instructive to consider that Georgia as well as the Turkic-speaking countries have generally benefited mostly from hand-to-hand transmission and that this transmission occurred mostly during the 1930s and for three or so decades after the Second World War. The Georgian director Georgy Tovstonogov graduated from GITIS in 1938, directed in Tbilisi until 1946, returned to Moscow, and took charge of the Bolshoy Drama Theatre in Leningrad in 1956, where he established his legendary status and was known to have a particular affinity with Stanislavsky. The younger Robert Sturua, taught in the Russian way in Tbilisi, launched his internationally acclaimed career as a director from this city in 1965. That the Turkic-speaking nations at issue were largely of the Russian Empire and were amalgamated in the Soviet Union is a significant factor in a transmission starting, more often than not, at GITIS and often with Knebel but also Aleksey Popov, a member of the MAT First Studio and, in 1923, a Third Studio director, with whom she regularly taught directing.

Take, as a representative figure, the Tatar director Rifkat Israfilov, who was Knebel's student and who subsequently directed at the Bashkir State Drama Theatre in Ufa, highlighting local-language priorities and making it a major artistic centre of Bashkiriya, whose renown went beyond the borders of a territory renamed the Republic of Bashkortostan in 1992. Now the director of the Orienburg Maksim Gorky State Drama Theatre, Israfilov, as a transmitter of the Stanislavsky school of acting and directing, can be compared with Azerbaijani leading director Israfil Israfilov (no relation). Israfil Israfilov, by comparison, is once removed from the GITIS 'source' in that he was the student of Tofik Kazimov (known in history books of Soviet theatre as Kyazimov), who was a student of Popov in the same hand-picked group as Efros. Taught in Azerbaijan, Israfilov is an example of generational transmission going down the chain of time, or along it, if a horizontal image is preferred. In these cases, hand-to-hand generational transmission involves ethnic-cultural-linguistic issues and issues to do with tsarist and then Soviet hegemony and subordination as well as individual desire, volition and allegiance within this network. The two directors discussed, while fully aware of these complexities, harnessed them to their desire to direct.

---

concerning the System, have made a powerful impact and continue to be powerful in various quarters. And it is necessary to remember that 'Stanislavsky' is not only the Stanislavsky of the System. Indeed, *Which* Stanislavsky? is a question of importance.

238   Epilogue

Generational transmission of legacy can be described as mediated legacy whose instances accumulate practical adjustments and necessary socio-cultural 'interferences', since transmission is a living process between people; anything else would be carbon-copy reproduction. Another form of mediated legacy exists in the traces of varying strength that sometimes appear in unexpected places like the rebellious, highly theatricalized Théâtre du Soleil with its ensemble, actor-as co-creator principles evoked in Chapter 1, or the no less rebellious, no less actor-generated but smaller Odin Teatret, which Eugenio Barba established in 1964 as a company of amateurs in the spirit, like the Soleil, of the counter-cultural 1960s. The studio-laboratory practice that Stanislavsky had fostered was especially appealing to Barba for the Odin, and he frequently recalls that Stanislavsky was himself an amateur when he co-founded the MAT.[4] In such cases, notions of 'influence' seem inopportune. The connection might be better perceived as a meeting of goals and views – albeit in dissimilar socio-cultural and political contexts – in which long-echoing cultural memory and the aspirations that reside in memory as well as inspire those who discover it also play their part. The question that arises immediately concerns what Stanislavsky, referring to the actor, calls the 'soil' in which a seed can grow. Put differently, it asks under what conditions connection can occur and how readiness for connection is prepared and sustained.

Time and timing are critical for legacy in so far as they determine which particular aspect of Stanislavsky – indeed, *which* 'Stanislavsky' – is selected, accepted and put into practice. The vital example here is Boleslavsky, who settled in New York shortly before the MAT's first tour and who, with Uspenskaya, created and taught at the American Laboratory Theatre (1923–29), drawing substantially on the principles of affective memory, concentration and the individuality of the actor central to the First Studio. (Uspenskaya came with the tour and stayed.) Dodin, in several conversations over the years and even as recently as 16 February 2018, referred to Boleslavsky as a salient case of legacy rooted in a particular moment of Stanislavsky's research, which, when displaced, was inevitably confined to the moment when it was received, while Stanislavsky moved on to new research, significantly modifying the old.

Temporal set of the kind that Boleslavsky experienced is not an incidental but a *constitutive* factor of Stanislavsky's legacy as such. This means that misunderstandings are intrinsic to relations among Stanislavsky's

---

[4] For example, Eugenio Barba in conversation with Maria Shevtsova, 'Reinventing Theatre', *New Theatre Quarterly*, 23, No. 2 (2007), 100–1.

followers, all of whom claim exclusive authenticity, which turns out to be the authenticity of their particular piece of a heritage that is bigger than the sum of its parts. Hence the 'incomplete' Stanislavsky streamlined into Method acting as developed by Lee Strasberg, who was Boleslavsky's and Uspenskaya's student together with Stella Adler. Hence, too, Adler's feud with Strasberg over whether, to put it crudely, emotion had priority over action in acting or the other way around. Adler had gone in search of Stanislavsky in Paris in 1934 and had taken lessons with him (Stanislavsky remembers it as being one month), returning to the United States with another angle on Stanislavsky's teachings from another time in his ceaseless explorations.[5]

Rhonda Blair's incisive introduction to Boleslavsky's 1933 *Acting: The First Six Lessons* points out that 'Boleslavsky's view was adamantly holistic in its recognition that action and emotion are inseparable' and that Adler and Strasberg, regardless of their disagreements, 'ultimately held holistic views'.[6] It suffices to compare Boleslavsky's collection of lessons and lectures with Strasberg's 1987 *A Dream of Passion* – a summary of *his* legacy accrued over many decades – to understand that Strasberg was an apple that had not fallen too far from the tree, even though student and teacher had quite different voices and accentuated different aspects.[7] Sanford Meisner joined the fray on the issue of action. He had not been Boleslavsky's student but, at the theatre collective known as the Group Theatre founded in 1931, he had absorbed from Strasberg as well as Adler what Boleslavsky and Uspenskaya had taught them, stressing, from his side of the ring, the primacy of action, which was *doing*. He offered, accordingly, another method for dealing with how to do. Yet, as Blair observes: 'Meisner, with his focus on concentration, doing and observation, is part of the Boleslavsky "family"'.[8] Meisner, then, was in an indirect line from Boleslavsky and at two degrees of separation from Stanislavsky but within his orbit, nevertheless.

Many have written about Stanislavsky's heritage in the United States, including Christine Edwards riding the crest of the wave of resurgent interest in him during the 1960s and well into the 1970s.[9] The distinguished authors of Erika Munk's edited volume *Stanislavski and America*

---

[5] See Carnicke's excellent summary of their meeting in *Stanislavsky in Focus*, 65–6.

[6] *Acting: The First Six Lessons. Documents from the American Laboratory Theatre*, ed. Rhonda Blair, Abingdon and New York: Routledge, 2010, xv.

[7] *A Dream of Passion: The Development of the Method*, ed. Evangeline Morphos, London: Bloomsbury, 1988.

[8] *Acting: The First Six Lessons*, xviii–xix.   [9] *The Stanislavsky Heritage*, London: Peter Owen, 1966.

240   Epilogue

are on that same wave.[10] In more recent years, there are Mel Gordon's expansive *Stanislavsky in America* and, sharper and more analytical, Sharon Marie Carnicke in the relevant sections of her *Stanislavsky in Focus* and David Krasner, who has carried the discussion further into the arena of active analysis.[11] Such writings have so thoroughly covered the ground that nothing would be served by going over it again except to highlight the fact that 'active analysis' is a marker for another time in Stanislavsky's practice – the time of the method of physical action, which, as Chapter 5 shows, started earlier and developed over a longer period than previously thought. The prominent names of this period are Kristi, Kedrov, Gorchakov, Zavadsky (who also taught at GITIS), Toporkov, Zon, Knebel and Novitskaya. Their particular dissemination of Stanislavsky's legacy was nurtured by their time of close encounter with him, revealing just how great was the scope of Stanislavsky's body of work during his lifetime.

Which Stanislavsky? The very importance of the method of physical action has given rise to the assumption that it deviated from Stanislavsky's earlier research or had indeed replaced it, creating a 'second-life' Stanislavsky who erased the first. Whereas Stanislavsky argued consistently – this book has substantiated his position – that his 'new method', although correcting or shedding what he subsequently saw as mistakes (affective memory obfuscating the importance he placed on the creative imagination, protracted table discussion), was, in effect, a continuation, on another path, of his preceding work. Dodin puts it differently, saying that 'there was always a new Stanislavsky . . . and, when he rejected something, he left it in his baggage'.[12] The differences of emphasis and accent that mark Stanislavsky's research are inseparable from the whole of it. They need to be recognized and acted upon when practitioners solve difficulties in their own way, but they are by no means reasons for beating the heirs of the younger Stanislavsky with a stick. Boleslavsky and Strasberg are such heirs and managed very well in their territory with what they had taken, or thought they had taken, from him.

---

[10] Greenwich, CT: Fawcett Publications, 1967.

[11] Abingdon: Routledge, 2010; especially 41–75; 'Stanislavsky's System, Sense-Emotion Memory, and Physical Action/Active Analysis: American Interpretations of the System's Legacy' in *The Routledge Companion to Stanislavsky*, ed. R. Andrew White, Abingdon and New York: Routledge, 2014, 195–213. See also David Krasner (ed.), *Method Acting Reconsidered: Theory, Practice, Future*, New York: St Martin's Press, 2000.

    For an account in Russian of Stanislavsky's early legacy in the United States, see Sergey Cherkassky, *Masterstvo aktyora: Stanislavsky, Boleslavsky, Strasberg* (as cited in note 64 of Chapter 3).

[12] Conversation of 16 February 2018. My translation.

Perspectives: France, Britain, Germany

It would be myopic to assume that the System alone constitutes Stanislavsky's legacy, for it was not the System but the ensemble that left its lasting traces in France. Stanislavsky was conscious of the country's national pride in its theatre tradition and its deference to Diderot's theory of the actor and acting, revivified in modern times by the acclaimed actor Constant Coquelin. He consequently was cautious about how French audiences might react to a company coming out of Moscow. But he had something like national pride of his own to defend when the sets and costumes for the Art Theatre's debut in Paris in December 1922 were lost in transit, eventually found, held up, and then said again to be on their way as spectators filled the theatre. Stanislavsky's cliff-hanger account shows that a legacy is hard won, whatever shape it takes.[13]

The 'soil', however, was more ready than not. Jacques Copeau and André Antoine met him with open arms, and neither was a stranger. Stanislavsky had written to Copeau in 1917, inviting him to join his proposed Pantheon for the protection of theatre of high artistic quality, making it sound like the endangered species he thought it was. Copeau, of a similar mind, had founded Le Vieux Colombier in 1913 on the idea of a brotherhood, striking a chord with the one envisaged by Stanislavsky and Sulerzhitsky. Antoine was familiar from his battles for a new theatre at the Théâtre Libre (a private, that is, non-state-subsidized theatre) whose financial losses had forced him to close down in 1894, and then from 1897 at the Théâtre Antoine, which closed in 1906. In 1923, after the Art Theatre had set sail for New York, Antoine published an article in which he states that 'it is Stanislavsky, prompted by his firmness, his lucidity and faith to carry the task to its end, who remains our teacher and model'.[14] The operative phrase is 'to carry the task to its end', since Antoine had just referred to the disappearance of his own theatres and the 'hope for the future' offered by the 'newcomers already appreciated' – Copeau and

---

[13] *SS* 8, 6, 148–55 and as an Appendix to *My Life in Art*, 400–5. Note Stanislavsky's 'Copeau who considers himself our disciple spoke with ardour' [after Antoine] (150; 401 in Benedetti's trans.) and his reference to Jacques Rouché, director of the Grand Opéra de Paris, who was present at the Art Theatre opening and 'had been in Russia many years before and had gone to our theatre many times and visited me in my dressing-room' (155, my translation; 405).
 The point is that personal artistic connections with France were significant and cannot be ignored in any discussion of legacy.

[14] In English in Sergey Melik-Zakharov and Shoel Bogatyryov (compiled), *K. Stanislavsky, 1863–1963: Man and Actor; Stanislavsky and the World Theatre; Stanislavsky's Letters*, trans. Vic Schneierson, Moscow: Progress Publishers, 1963, 177, and all citations from Antoine.

242   Epilogue

Charles Dullin at L'Atelier (also a private theatre) – against a situation where 'our past work seems to have been defeated, and we have returned to our old routine'.

Antoine urges the 'newcomers' to go back to the drawing board where he had started in 1887 and pursue the revival of the theatre that they had 'dreamed of'. Their respective attempts, like his, acted on the belief that an ensemble raised the quality of productions and the standards of the theatre, although none was able to reach the goal in the comprehensive way of the ensemble established by the MAAT. A *repertory* ensemble was missing from their projects, as was longevity, elided by their 'combat [against] financial obstacles', the 'tyranny of the money bags' and 'the selfish official art' – combats, Antoine stresses, that Stanislavsky also had had to fight, yet his mission had prevailed. The MAAT, then, was a revelation to Paris (despite the 'official' Comédie Française, whose stability had to do with state patronage since Louis XIV). And it was a repertory ensemble of impressive duration – twenty-four years, by the time the MAAT performed at the Théâtre des Champs-Elysées – and not outwardly showing that it actually *was* in need of renovation.

Copeau shut down Le Vieux Colombier in 1924, at the height of its achievements as the premier art theatre in France, and this happened for several reasons, among them the pressure and fatigue of mounting numerous productions and his yearning to return to his research on the actor and the new theatre. He had spent 'several intimate conversations' with Stanislavsky in Paris discussing what the theatre opposed to the 'old routine' should be, with reference to the latter's reborn project of defending this alternative theatre in Europe:[15] Stanislavsky had proposed an 'international society and studio' for this very purpose, and it is quite likely that the exchange of ideas had reactivated Copeau's innermost desires.[16] Stanislavsky is just as likely to have watered, if not planted, the seeds of Copeau's decision to retreat to the countryside in Burgundy with a group of thirty-five people dedicated to theatre research, forming a 'studio' in the style of the First Studio, and a utopian community of the Yevpatoria kind dotted around Europe (Hellerau, Monte Verità).

The venture foundered and sank after three months, leaving twenty hardy survivors, dubbed '*les copiaus*' by the local farmers, who remained as an ensemble company in Burgundy until 1929. Among them were Étienne Decroux (teacher of Jacques Lecoq of 'physical theatre' fame) and

---

[15] Vinogradskaya, *Zhizn i tvorchestvo*, Vol. 3, 249.
[16] SS 8, 6, 157–8; Appendix to *My Life in Art*, 407.

Copeau's nephew Michel Saint-Denis, who was to carry its foundational aspirations, tinted by its affective association with Stanislavsky and the Art Theatre, to London and the Royal Court Theatre. Its direct descendent in France can be none other than Mnouchkine, who studied for a short period with Lecoq and counts Copeau among her 'masters', as she does Stanislavsky, the studio-researcher and defender of actors, who is *her* Stanislavsky. It is not insignificant that *Une Chambre en Inde* (2016), although hardly likely to be her very last production, gives the impression of being an artistic testament and a farewell, notably in a fast and playful scene where her masters are named – Stanislavsky with mild irony regarding his 'realism'. There is an aura of sanctity about this roll call, as if her masters were the guardian angels of the community and 'family' that she had created with the Théâtre du Soleil. Whether the Soleil had willed it or not, its embrace of community and family linked it to the Art Theatre tradition.

Copeau, when he wrote the foreword to the French translation of *My Life in Art* in 1934, spoke affectionately of Stanislavsky whom 'I should like to name as my dear teacher', thereby claiming his right as a student to partake of Stanislavsky's legacy.[17] Firmin Gémier, who promoted the idea of '*théâtre populaire*' in France – closer to a French socialist understanding than to Stanislavsky's liberal notion of an open and accessible theatre – did the same in a letter to Stanislavsky after he had visited him in Moscow in 1928 by addressing him as his 'great teacher and friend'.[18] Gémier was at the Paris meeting just mentioned. Aurélien-Marie Lugné-Poe, founder and director of the Théâtre de l'Oeuvre and advocate of Symbolism, was also present at this meeting, having established cordial relations with Stanislavsky by correspondence (inviting the MAT to tour Paris in 1908) and during his visit to Moscow in 1915.[19] He did not claim a special relationship with Stanislavsky, but clearly recognized the affinities mediated by their mutual faith in art theatre.

Jean Vilar, Gémier's successor and so director of the Théâtre National Populaire from 1951 to 1963 (Gémier had established it in 1920), coined the phrase '*service public*' for this theatre whose democratic tenor, commitment to service for the social good and educative aims were similar to those of the Art Theatre. He authored the introduction to the first French edition of *La Formation de l'acteur* in 1958 (the first part of *Rabota aktyora nad soboy*), warning his reader of 'the endless labyrinth of the "system"',

---

[17] *K. Stanislavsky, 1863–1963*, 173.   [18] Ibid., 183.
[19] *Zhizn i tvorchestvo*, Vol. 2, 126 and 459–60.

244 Epilogue

but also pointing out that 'no real actor ever fails, sooner or later, to assume, consciously or not, some paths of analysis so thoroughly worked out by Konstantin Stanislavsky'.[20] It cannot be said with certainty which of Stanislavsky's 'paths of analysis' he may have taken himself as an actor, but what is certain is that his pared-back directing of the French classics and Shakespeare brought out their contours, subject matter and emotional underpinnings so clearly as really to be accessible across all social sectors; and he shared with Stanislavsky a belief in institutional clout, which the TNP had, as it was meant to.

Harley Granville Barker also participated in that significant 1922 Paris meeting, even though its pan-European goal failed to materialize for want of the sizeable finance it required. The ensemble principles of the Art Theatre were a great attraction for Barker since he opposed the commercial theatre dominating England and its competitive grooming of 'stars', which he thought prevented other actors from growing artistically and taking their profession seriously. A friend of George Bernard Shaw, an actor in his plays at the Royal Court and his colleague in the Fabian Society, Barker strove for a theatre community not unlike the large community of co-operation rather than competition envisaged for society by the Fabians. The interconnection between Barker's Fabianism and his theatre object-ives cannot be underestimated, including his roles of writer and director (both soon took precedence over his acting), for which theatre critics punished him when the political wind blew in their direction.

Barker spent two weeks at the MAT in 1914 observing, conversing with Stanislavsky, arranging for two of his students to come and study under the supervision of the First Studio and seeing performances, among others, of *The Cherry Orchard* and *The Three Sisters*.[21] He was to say in 1923, having quit the theatre not so long after his return from Moscow: 'It was when I saw the Moscow people interpreting Chekhov that I fully realized what I had been struggling towards and that I saw how much actors could add to a play.'[22] One of his aims had been to achieve creative harmony among actors and between them and the plays they were performing – said, in his case as a dramatist, passably to resemble in their ellipses those of Chekhov.

Interest in England in the results achieved by the MAT ensemble had helped Barker to prepare his creative probing in Moscow. Negotiations

---

[20] *K. Stanislavsky, 1863–1963*, 205.   [21] *Zhizn i tvorchestvo*, Vol. 2, 423.

[22] Cited in Jan McDonald, 'Chekhov, Naturalism and the Drama of Dissent: Productions of Chekhov's Plays in Britain before 1914' in *Chekhov on the British Stage*, ed. and trans. Patrick Miles, Cambridge University Press, 1993, 41.

Perspectives: France, Britain, Germany

had begun in 1908 to bring the company to London; actor-manager Herbert Beerbohm Tree had sent an emissary to see *The Blue Bird*; Herbert Trench offered to present the production at the Haymarket and, when Stanislavsky refused because his terms were unacceptable, he requested copies of its sets and costumes for his own direction (1909), to which Stanislavsky agreed.[23] Negotiations continued in 1911 (Stanislavsky doubted the repertoire was travel-worthy) and then in January 1913, when Beerbohm Tree saw Craig's *Hamlet* with Duncan[24]; Duncan danced at the reception afterwards, accompanied on the piano by Scriabin. H. G. Wells, who had travelled to Russia on several occasions since 1908, saw *The Three Sisters* in 1914, and he too resumed the conversation about playing in London.

The First World War put an end to any further discussion. As events would have it, the Art Theatre never came, although, Alexei Bartoshevich argues, the 'mere existence' of these 'unrealized plans' indicated the English theatre's 'genuine, indeed, passionate interest in what was happening on the Russian stage'.[25] Even so, 'the crucial fact remains that London saw no [MAT] productions in the original. It did not experience [the] MKhT [MAT] at the height of its powers'.[26] Barker had had that first-hand experience in Moscow, enlarging his idea of what an ensemble was and how it nurtured ensemble playing. And here might be the crux of the matter where 'legacy' is concerned: the strength of an *idea* of ensemble affected those, most notably Barker, who found confirmation in the MAT of what they were trying to find themselves. Moreover, the steps that he took for the development of actors and his own development as a director were 'rewarded' as well as legitimated by an inspiring legacy that *enveloped* them since, after all, that legacy *was* bigger than the sum of its individual legatees; and, because this legacy was supra-individual, it was ample and generous enough to cover all kinds of individual cases. Such must be more or less the situation of the various teaching institutions that, today, teach their own variations on the System in Britain. The absence of a direct transmission thins out the legacy but does not destroy its reach. What condition it might be in as it spreads is another question.

The Moscow Art Theatre Prague Group performed in London in 1928 and 1931 and, while not ersatz, it was understood not to be the 'real

---

[23] Alexei Bartoshevich points out that Trench's exact scenographic copying was accepted practice. See 'The "Inevitability" of Chekhov: Anglo-Russian Theatrical Contacts in the 1910s' in *Chekhov on the British Stage*, 24.

[24] *Zhizn i tvorchestvo*, Vol. 2, 365.   [25] *Chekhov on the British Stage*, 24.   [26] Ibid., 24–5.

246   Epilogue

deal'; Stanislavsky and Nemirovich-Danchenko, for their part, took a litigious attitude towards what they saw as an unlawful exploitation of the MAT 'brand' (Stanislavsky's word). However, the Prague Group was certainly closer to the MAT than Theodore Komisarjevsky, who became a staged Chekhov 'expert' in England but whom Bartoshevich correctly describes as being 'as far from Chekhov as he was from the Moscow Art Theatre'.[27] Komisarjevsky had never studied with Stanislavsky, but had kept in touch with him about the possibility of directing at the MAT as he established his name as a director, primarily in St Petersburg. A position he hoped would be his was offered to Mardzhanov (Chapter 5), who eventually returned to Georgia to contribute to the glory of its theatre. ('Mardzhanov' was a Russification of 'Marjanishvili'.) Although convinced of the virtues of ensemble theatre, Komisarjevsky tended to favour hierarchical relations within it, and his was a 'theatre of philosophic essences';[28] a theatre, one could add, of general 'world' perceptions framed by bold visual configurations that recalled German expressionism and were far removed from the elisions of Chekhov. Much as Komisarjevsky believed in 'inner technique', it was not imbued with spiritual content in the comprehensive sense in which Stanislavsky conceived of the 'spirit'.

If he inflamed Stanislavsky by his 1917 book published in Russia for wrongly asserting that his senior had little respect for the creative imagination, he did himself a disservice in England by his sales-pitch, evoking Stanislavsky's name in the hope of furthering his career.[29] His was an immigrant's self-protection and, outspoken and uncompromising, he railed against the stale Victorian theatre he had come into with the licence of a foreigner who was also stigmatized as a 'foreigner'. This imprecation, as Victor Borovsky's detailed study of Komisarjevsky's trajectory shows, was especially nastily thrown at him when his modernist approach to Shakespeare was not seen in terms of artistic innovation but as a matter of an outsider meddling with a national icon.[30]

Borovsky indirectly and Bartoshevich directly have warned from their respective perspectives against making Komisarjevksy a representative of

---

[27] 'Theodore Komisarjevsky, Chekhov, and Shakespeare' in *Wandering Stars: Russian Emigré Theatre, 1905–1940*, ed. Laurence Senelick, Iowa City: University of Iowa Press, 1992, 106.

[28] Ibid., 108.

[29] *Tvorchestvo aktyora i teoriya Stanislavskogo*, Petrograd (n.p.), 1917. The book is ill judged in various areas.

[30] *A Triptych from the Russian Theatre: An Artistic Biography of the Komissarzhevskys*, London: Hurst and Company, 2001, 402–25; 423 for James Agate's review titled 'Anton and Cleopatrova, A Tragedy by Komispeare'.

Stanislavsky in England – and Stanislavskian he was not. There was little chance of this confusion happening in the United States, where he emigrated before the outbreak in 1939 of the Second World War. He and Chekhov did not meet, and one wonders how Chekhov, who had been an integral part of the Art Theatre 'family', its dysfunctions included, and who was moored at his Studio at Dartington Hall from 1936 to 1938, might have fared – rather, how *his* legacy might have fared – had he stayed permanently in England.

Conjecture aside, what cannot be minimized in either Chekhov's or Stanislavsky's legacy is Chekhov's debt to Stanislavsky, his roots going deep into the System even though by 1938 he had established his own method for actors. He had written two enthusiastic articles on the System in 1919, sternly criticized by Vakhtangov on ethical grounds because Stanislavsky had not yet done so himself.[31] However, his later disagreement with Stanislavsky on the role of affective memory in the creative process was the subject, together with the imagination, of their five-hour conversation in Berlin in 1928, not long after Chekhov had left Russia.[32] It was central to Chekhov's method because he worked on the principle of distance between 'self' and 'role' for the creation of figures that could be said to be closer to archetypes than to particularized entities. The two men agreed to disagree, parting, according to Chekhov, as friends; Chekhov also remarked that the discussion had helped him greatly to clarify his theoretical propositions.[33]

His last contact with Stanislavsky was a note conveying seventy-fifth birthday greetings from himself and his students 'with love and admiration', postmarked 25 January 1938.[34] Chekhov, who was sensitive to symbols and signs, may have seen this message in English as a sign that affirmed continuing heredity and the positive link between his past and future; and, after all, Dartington Hall, like the First Studio, was founded in the spirit of utopian communities.

The belief in ensemble theatre upheld by both men was slow on the uptake in England in the 1920s and 1930s, where the very term 'ensemble' was rarely heard unless it was uttered by another 'foreigner' like Saint-Denis, backed by his loyal English entourage. Barker, its vociferous

---

[31] Mikhaïl Chekhov, *Literaturnoye naslediye*, Vol. 2, 31–58.

[32] *Literaturnoye naslediye*, Vol. 1, *Life and Encounters*, 157–9 (most unfortunately not included in the selected extracts of the English *The Path of the Actor*).

[33] Ibid., 337–9; letter no later than 19 September 1928 [editor's date] to his close friend V. A. Podgorny in Moscow.

[34] Ibid., 439.

248 Epilogue

publicist, had departed first to France and then to the United States, leaving a gap into which stepped, more fiercely, Joan Littlewood and Ewan MacColl, founding the Theatre Union in 1936 on ensemble principles, hand in glove with their temporarily communist politics. They and their colleagues combed Manchester public libraries for information on Stanislavsky and the Art Theatre. Already with the Union Theatre and then with its successor the Theatre Workshop, Littlewood worked mainly via Hapgood's translation titled *An Actor Prepares*, adapting Stanislavsky's ideas of the 'magic if', the 'circle of concentration' and the player's and the play's 'throughaction' while she 'trained' actors not individually but as a composite group in order to sustain the appointed ensemble ethos.

The silhouettes of a laboratory studio and a school were visible enough in her 'actor training' to suggest her deep insight into how such *practices* ('school' and 'studio' being more than 'entities') were formative in the very tissue, attitude and atmosphere of ensemble unity and ensemble playing, even when they covered a limited time span. In her explorative drive to learn and teach can also be seen Stanislavsky's imprint, pressed with energy into the indigenous socio-political textures specific to Littlewood's social time and place-space within which she inserted her theatre and against which – establishment habitus, practices, mentality and institutions – she sought to preserve its life force. Brecht's influence was to be seen there as well, although his appeared to have followed Stanislavsky's. It is instructive to remember that the Berliner Ensemble first performed in London in 1956, providing the first-hand viewing of high-level ensemble practice that the MAT had not been able to offer in person.

Peter Hall, who recognized how much Littlewood had accomplished and who was in contact with Helene Weigel after Brecht's death, answered unequivocally, when asked if he 'was more influenced by the Brechtian or by the Moscow Art Model', that it was '[the] Moscow Art': it was 'the Stanislavski books and the Magarshack Chekhov books' that had had an 'enormous influence' on him in adolescence, and he 'desperately wanted to run a company, to make a company'. Which in a sense had never really been done in this country.[35] One composed 'of Shakespearean actors' – the Royal Shakespeare Company that he headed from 1960 to 1968 – 'was terribly necessary' at the time, he observed, although in 1991, the year of the interview, he was no longer sure that this would be 'wise'.[36]

---

[35] Peter Hall interviewed by Patrick Miles, 'Chekhov, Shakespeare, the Ensemble and the Company', *New Theatre Quarterly*, 11, No. 2 (1995), 204.
[36] Ibid.

His was the first ensemble company in England to be subsidized by the public purse.

Hall's sense of ensemble, which in this interview he pretty well equated with 'company', was acute: ensembles were 'about that spirit of sharing, and support, and understanding of a common goal, and actually assisting each other on the stage in performance, just that'.[37] His echoes of Stanislavsky's thoughts on the subject are unmistakable (Chapter 1), as is his conviction: '*I fervently believe in ensemble*' (italics in the original). Yet it is important to note two particularities of this fervour, which distinguish it from Stanislavsky's. For Hall 'the reality of an ensemble is about three years' (whereas for Stanislavsky it was much longer), and he envisages a core of 'twelve crack actors' surrounded by 'people coming and going' (which is antithetical to Stanislavsky's 'spirit of sharing').[38] Not unexpectedly, this is precisely the variation that Trevor Nunn continued as the incumbent director of the RSC (1968–86) before he led it like a company of 'people coming and going' minus a core – the situation predating Hall, which has become the British standard.

A model closer to Stanislavsky's idea of the ensemble (without, however, a repertory base) was Brook's ensemble for the first six or so years at the Bouffes du Nord, which he founded in Paris in 1974. This fresh, vibrant group, resplendent in the energy of its inaugural *Timon of Athens*, as this spectator still remembers, was largely composed of the actors involved in the years of experimentation carried out under the rubric of the Centre International de Recherche Théâtrale established in 1970. Their shared research and daily close proximity during their travels (the Middle East, Africa) made it a cohesive group, nurturing the artistic ease and strength that shone through Bouffes productions. Finding the upkeep of a brick-and-mortar theatre plus an ensemble too heavy a load to bear – and it took time away from his research – Brook turned to working with a core group and then increasingly on a project basis with new actors each time, thus letting go in the twenty-first century the threads of ensemble drawn together with varying degrees of fulfilment in France and Britain in the twentieth.

Brook acknowledges his indebtedness to Stanislavsky in the associative and allusive manner characteristic of his productions and, in his 1995 dramatized discourse *Qui est là?*, he places Stanislavsky among Artaud, Brecht, Craig, Meyerhold and Zeami as the director-thinkers who mattered to him. However, in his elusive way, he manages to avoid

---

[37] Ibid., 207–8.   [38] Ibid., 208 and 204.

telling either his spectator or his reader (when it comes to his books) just how deeply linked to Stanislavsky he actually is; just how Stanislavskian is his central emphasis on the actor 'being there', 'present', 'in the moment' and 'true' in that moment, and how much he shares Stanislavsky's abhorrence of fake playing, seeking, instead, the simple, unaffected organic actor who plays attentively with his/her co-actors. In this 'creative state', as identified by Stanislavsky, they are 'alive' and 'in the quick' of feeling, as described by Brook. 'Organic' is taken as quintessentially Brook when it might just as well be taken as quintessentially Stanislavsky (Chapter 3).

These are the actorly qualities together with Brook's evocative rather than expository directing that Declan Donnellan admired, and they were in some respects akin to his own aspirations for the ensemble company Cheek by Jowl that he and his partner Nick Ormerod founded as a touring company in 1981. Cheek by Jowl took a two-year sabbatical in 1999, showing its *Homebody/Kabul* in London in 2002. *The Winter's Tale* (1997), which Donnellan staged with Dodin's actors in Russian in St Petersburg, was a major turning point in that he experienced directly what a comprehensively trained, co-authored ensemble could give. The attentiveness such work required, which Donnellan found increasingly beguiling in the Russian school of acting (rooted as it was in Stanislavsky, like it or not), proved to be the binding power that instantly made an ensemble out of the collection of 'independent stars' and 'strangers' whom he had called together.[39]

This Russian ensemble, this Russian arm of Cheek by Jowl, became the collectivity that he had seen fall away in his British company as much for cultural-historical reasons, which had been counter-productive to 'ensemble', as for contemporary ones, which were tied up with the 'entertainment industry', including its disruptive and comparatively lucrative offers from television and cinema. The Russian troupe premiered its splendid *Boris Godunov* in Moscow in 2000 (in Britain a year later), beginning the continuity that Donnellan cherished: 'I am a big one for continuity in my life and the actor continuity in my life is exclusively Russian'.[40]

Donnellan's is the unique case of a British director who works regularly in Russia (Craig's *Hamlet* was a one-off), rehearsing in 2018 Francis Beaumont's *The Knight of the Burning Pestle* in the immersive conditions

---

[39] Interview with Donnellan (who speaks of 'attention' contra my 'attentiveness' above) in Maria Shevtsova and Christopher Innes, *Directors/Directing: Conversations on Theatre*, 80–1. See, as well, my working 'portrait', 66–71.
[40] Ibid., 81.

of a peaceful wooden studio in a forest outside Moscow, where he had already made preliminary preparations for other of his Russian productions. A director of Shakespeare (twenty-two Shakespeare productions by 2018), he ran a one-year acting Academy for leavers of drama schools at the RSC in 2002, culminating in a production of *King Lear*. It was meant to be an experimental 'school' and, possibly, something of a prelude to the renewed ensemble orientation of the RSC led by Michael Boyd (2003–12). Boyd is the only other British director to have had a working connection with Russia, having studied directing with Efros at his theatre, the Malaya Bronnaya. His lineage was visible to the discerning eye in the pace, timing and momentum of his *Shakespeare Histories* (2007), the close interconnection between the actors, and their clustered, undulating groupings in scenes of war. Recall that Knebel and Popov were Efros' teachers, and what Efros had absorbed of Stanislavsky through them was there for the taking for Boyd.

There was another ensemble venture, earlier and shorter than Boyd's, at the Newcastle Playhouse. This was Alan Lyddiard's two-year project, the Northern Stage Ensemble, inspired directly by Dodin and the Maly. Dodin conducted a three-day workshop on *Uncle Vanya* at the beginning of the project in June 1999, in the village of Allenheads in County Durham.[41] Dodin, being 'big' on immersion, and bigger, by far, than its innovator, Stanislavsky, took the opportunity of this country sojourn for a slowly evolving, delicately fragrant (numerous burning candles, the scent of leaves on branches of trees decorating the room) and deeply atmospheric induction into the opening scenes of *Uncle Vanya* – improvisations played quietly, autumnally, in a cold British spring by a few Maly actors.[42] Dodin's textual commentaries (interpreted into English) initiated several table discussions, and Northern Stage actors were also interpreted.

This event was dovetailed with performances of *The Winter's Tale* in Newcastle, watched over by Donnellan, thus bringing together key figures, actors and directors, in what, in retrospect, turns out to have been a historical moment. As the money ran out so the Ensemble ran down, but no account of Stanislavsky's legacy in Britain can be made without the inclusion of Dodin. Nor can an overview, let alone a history, of ensemble formation and practice in Britain.

---

[41] *Dodin and the Maly Drama Theatre*, 34–5.
[42] This account is written from my insights as a participant-observer in the workshop and as a member of the audience of *The Winter's Tale* in Newcastle.

252   Epilogue

The third British director to have privileged experience inside Russia is Katie Mitchell, although hers is not hands-on experience but short-term contact and close observation. In 1989, she received a grant from the Winston Churchill Memorial Trust to research what she called 'director training' in Russia, Poland, Lithuania and Georgia.[43] In St Petersburg, she concentrated on Dodin and in Moscow on Vasilyev. Consequently, Dodin, by enabling Mitchell as a live source of Stanislavskian know-how, by contrast with her knowledge of Stanislavsky through books, appears again on the panorama of Stanislavsky's legacy in Britain.[44] Vasilyev captivated her by his aesthetics, but his debt to Stanislavsky via Knebel has yet to belong to this localized legacy. Another live, albeit indirect, source for Mitchell was the little-known Sam Kogan, a British resident from Soviet Russia, who, in Mitchell's words, 'combined a training in Stanislavsky at GITIS ... with work as a psychiatric nurse before coming to the UK in the 1970s'.[45]

In fact, Kogan had studied with Knebel (which Mitchell does not mention) and he established the School of the Science of Acting in London in 1991. The main thesis of this modest but self-sufficient school claiming to be teaching Stanislavsky was that actors had to be aware of their own consciousness in order to understand the states of mind of their characters. Mitchell, who had learned from Kogan's student Elen Bowman about his similar approach to directing – this over two and a half years in one-on-one lessons – cites Bowman as saying 'you have to study yourself in life. This helps you analyze a character and makes you learn how to help an actor to get into the skin of a character'.[46] Mitchell's interest in what she has consistently called 'behaviour' and, more specifically, in its psychophysio-logical motives, physical manifestations and the mechanisms by which they are manifested, has taken her to 'forensic' (Mitchell) textual analysis and complementary 'forensic' stage breakdown of actor and character behaviours within precisely located events in the identified 'proposed circumstances' of every event.

The thought contained in Stanislavsky's phrase 'proposed circum-stances' underpins Mitchell's method. She is a rigorous director who teaches her actors to pinpoint the situations and circumstances that give rise to the behaviours laid bare on the stage, frequently looking like a

---

[43] Interview with Maria Shevtsova in *Directors/Directing*, 181.
[44] See her *The Director's Craft: A Handbook for the Theatre*, Abingdon and New York: Routledge, 2009, and 227–30 for her report on one of Dodin's classes.
[45] *Directors/Directing*, 189.   [46] Ibid.

Perspectives: France, Britain, Germany

demonstration of behaviours rather than lived behaviours. Perhaps this impression is due to what might be called a 'transplantation' of her research in neuroscience into stage action, which marks her productions in Germany and France, most recently *La Maladie de la mort* after Marguerite Duras (2018, made at the Bouffes du Nord). The same rigour is evident in how thoroughly her actors prepare the 'back histories' of their characters to be guided by these detailed imaginings in rehearsals.

Which is Mitchell's Stanislavsky? For her live-cinema theatre (how else to call it?) of the second decade of the twenty-first century, he is the 'behavioural' (but not 'behaviourist') Stanislavsky who, in the first decade of the twentieth, sought a backup for his insights into acting through practice in the psychological and physiological research of Ribot and others. Mitchell said in the later 2000s that Stanislavsky's 'writings still outline an enormously useful and practical working process for people working in the theatre now – especially directors'.[47] Her recognition of the much forgotten contribution Stanislavsky's writings have made to theatre directing is salutary, although his contribution came above all else and first of all in Russia from his *practice* as a director and a director-pedagogue.

Since 2010, Mitchell has directed primarily in Germany. By coincidence, Ostermeier, who has been supportive of her various tacks as a director at the Schaubühne, is knowledgeable and surprisingly unprejudiced about Stanislavsky: 'surprisingly' because Ostermeier emerged from the dissenting German avant-garde of the 1990s, which was as angry about capitalism and complacent politics as it was about the well-heeled bourgeois theatre into which it lumped the 'outmoded' and 'emotional' Stanislavsky. However, Ostermeier, who was born and bred in the former West Germany, is a directing graduate of the prestigious Ernst Busch Academy of Dramatic Art in former East Berlin, where he had learned to approach Stanislavsky independently of the ideological encasements of both East and West.

This meant that he was able to use Stanislavsky's 'magic if' to develop his actors' imagination for works as surreal as his *Hamlet* (2008) and *Richard III* (2015). 'Etude' is not a term Ostermeier uses, but etudes are, in fact, what he and his actors do on the premise of 'What if?' and such etudes generated many of the zany and outlandish mini-scenes that he stacked up for paroxysmal effects in these two productions. By the same token, Ostermeier speaks of the value of 'storytelling' for which his actors rely on personal 'emotional memory' as they explore situations that

[47] *The Director's Craft*, 225.

correspond to those of the play they are performing.[48] Storytelling also entails inventing biographical events, which prompt actions that unfold facets of 'what a human being is' – something that nowadays 'interests few directors', in his view, but is invaluable for the creativity of actors.[49] Stanislavsky used this type of biographical-social fleshing-out device for the precision and dynamics of action and characterization.

Following Stanislavsky, Ostermeier works within the parameters of the 'proposed circumstances' of a play – his device for preventing even the most delirious of stage actions from disintegrating into chaos, like Lars Eidinger-Hamlet's hysterical ranting and physical abandon in the mud, which he eats at his mother's wedding, while Claudius' face falls into his food. The stage can look chaotic, but the 'proposed circumstances' contain the actors' invention of chaos, giving it an artistic logic that does not have to square with common-sense logic; and this artistic logic is right there in the mud and the unseemly bridal party (which includes Hamlet), encapsulating Hamlet's disgust at Gertrude's marriage to Claudius in the circumstances of that marriage. Four of Stanislavsky's cardinal principles in Ostermeier's hands – 'proposed circumstances', the 'magic if', emotion memory and biographical and other contours – argue in favour of Stanislavsky's claim that his System was not confined to this or that 'ism' (nor could it be dictated to by any 'ism') but would be beneficial to actors across all kinds of creative processes, including ways of directing.

How to create a permanent repertory ensemble was not one of Ostermeier's worries. The Schaubühne fits into German ensemble history, pushed along not exclusively but notably by Reinhardt and Brecht, becoming today a bastion of unquestioned rights that include lavish government and municipal subsidies. Furthermore, this theatre's eminent head, who had left it in 1985, was Peter Stein, world renowned for keeping together its ensemble on egalitarian lines and, with a good knowledge of Russian, for his 'Stanislavskian' Chekhov productions (psychophysical articulation of 'inner life', beautiful tempo-rhythm, fine and telling detail, believable motives for action, credible reality in actor interaction), the first of which was *The Three Sisters* (1984). The most famous was *The Cherry Orchard* (1989) in which a massive, hyper-real tree trunk – an apocalyptic symbol of an oncoming era – crashed into the abandoned house.

---

[48] Gerhard Jörder, *Ostermeier Backstage* [interviews], trans. Laurent Muhleisen and Frank Weigand, Paris: L'Arche, 2015, 92–3. My translation.

[49] Ibid., 95.

Ostermeier is by no means beholden to Stein, but what appears to have captured his imagination is how, in the twenty-first century, practical approaches drawn from Stanislavsky can actually operate in a theatre culture that appears to have little affinity with him and, further, that rejects the 'emotional', 'empathetic' and 'mystical' Stanislavsky, along – obligatorily – with his alleged 'naturalism'. These words, while currently disparaging words in Germany, are Brecht's very words for criticizing Stanislavsky in the 1920s and 1930s. For Brecht's 'mystical', understand 'spiritual', 'religious' and even 'humanist': the latter, when he was at his most caustic, referred to a generalized 'humanity' papering over the realities of class war and the necessity for socialism (Chapter 2 for comparable views in the Soviet Union). The platitude might as well be repeated that Brecht's put-down, especially of Stanislavsky's alleged prioritization of 'empathy', was a build-up of 'epic theatre', which he, together with Erwin Piscator, saw as being indubitably political theatre and, perforce, anti-dramatic theatre.

This is not to imply that socialism is, these days, a going concern in German theatre generally (far from it), but to suggest, once again, the role historical change and changing social attitudes and personal convictions play in whether and how a legacy is considered congenial and/or acceptable. In 1952, Brecht made a list titled 'Some of the Things that can be Learnt from Stanislavsky' and, silent on religion and politics, it summarizes, in John Willett's words, 'the characteristics which he [Stanislavsky] and Brecht had in common'.[50]

Now: The 'Human Being'

The religious line went to Poland through Juliusz Osterwa whom Grotowski identified as the third of his touchstones for the theatre, the first and second being the Eleusinian Mysteries and Stanislavsky.[51] Stanislavsky had seen him acting at the Polish Theatre in Moscow in 1916 and, according to Osterwa, he had immediately asked him to join the MAT.[52] Osterwa declined and returned to Poland with Mieczyslaw Limanowski to establish Reduta, the first laboratory theatre in the country. Limanowski had spent a few months at the First Studio and shared

---

[50] *Brecht on Theatre: The Development of an Aesthetic*, trans. and ed. John Willett, London: Methuen, 1964, 236–7 and 38 for Willett's note.

[51] Antonio Attisani and Mario Biagini (eds.), *Opere e sentieri: Testimonianze e riflessioni sull'arte come veicolo*, Rome: Bulzoni Editore, 2008, 94–6. My translation, as for all below.

[52] *Zhizn i tvorchestvo*, Vol. 2, 484.

256 Epilogue

Stanislavsky's and Sulerzhitsky's views on the theatre's 'holy' mission for which an actor had to undergo continual training: this, for Limanowski, was part of the self-sacrifice required for the task. Osterwa's idea of the theatre in the service of God was steeped in his Catholicism and prompted him to model Reduta on a monastery, with actors dressed as monks. Sulerzhitsky, who also thought of the theatre as a monastery, had never attempted to transform the First Studio literally in such a way. In Grotowski's words, Osterwa's was a 'theatre of mysteries' and so of rites and rituals in which he not only proved his mettle as an actor but also as a 'great spiritual guide'.[53]

Grotowski's first laboratory theatre in Opole, which resettled in 1965 in Wroclaw, was styled more or less after Reduta (minus monks' habits), and this could be done easily, given that Catholicism had entered Grotowski's bloodstream – witness the insistent Christian iconography of *The Constant Prince* (1965), even as a critique of institutionalized and intolerant Catholicism – just as Orthodoxy had entered Stanislavsky's. Grotowski's parallel to Stanislavsky's 'theatre-church' was not without its 'derision' (Grotowski), but it nurtured the 'holy actor' whose inner spiritual journey became a public event without becoming a public confession of what was in and behind that journey personally for the actor. The journey was charged by visceral energy and its impact went back into the actor's 'inner life' while, at the same time, it resonated with, and vibrated within, the spectator. Grotowski recognized this double motion as much as Stanislavsky had. Like Stanislavsky, he believed that the actor could not progress on the 'vertical' of enlightenment unless he/she had the technique and training (Grotowski's 'craft') attained through rigorous work.

Let us take a step backwards to situate briefly the Stanislavsky-Grotowski connection to which Grotowski drew attention with 'gratitude' throughout his life. Already as a student at his drama school 'in the faculty for actors, I founded the entire basis of my theatre knowledge on the principles of Stanislavsky. As an actor I was possessed by Stanislavsky. I was a fanatic'.[54] Stimulated by the thought that he had discovered in Stanislavsky 'the key that opens all the doors to creativity', Grotowski went

---

[53] *Opere e sentieri*, 92.
[54] 'Risposta a Stanislavskij (1980)' ('An Answer to Stanislavsky (1980)') in *Opere e sentieri: Jerzy Grotowski Testi 1968–1998*, ed. Antonio Attisani and Mario Biagini, Rome: Bulzoni Editore, 2007, 47–8, and the following quotation. See also 'Odpowiedź Stanisławskiemu' in *Teksty zebrane: Grotowski*, ed. Agata Adamiecka-Sitek et al., Wrocław and Warsaw: The Grotowski Institute, The Zbigniew Raszewski Theatre Institute and The Political Critique Publishing House, 2017, 469. My translation.

Now: The 'Human Being' 257

in 1955 to study directing at GITIS for ten months, serendipitously falling into the hands of none other than Zavadsky with whom Stanislavsky had worked on Count Almaviva (Chapter 5). Not only did Zavadsky offer insider information on Stanislavsky's laboratory-studios, but he was also superbly placed to disclose the finer points of the doing that constituted Stanislavsky's method of physical action, Grotowski's special interest.

Zavadsky additionally gave him access to Meyerhold's materials on biomechanics from which, after derivative attempts in the later 1950s, he fashioned the singular body language of *Akropolis* (1961) – the master code, so to speak, of the aesthetics of his subsequent productions; Stanislavsky's aesthetics were not to his liking. Furthermore, Zavadsky recommended that he go for a cure for his kidney ailment to the dry climate of Soviet Turkmenia (now Turkmenistan), the crossroads for centuries of many civilizations.[55] The experience further whetted his appetite for the 'archaic' cultures and the 'East' – India notable in his dispositions – that, together with his inherited Catholicism, albeit selectively sifted, formed the worldview guiding his work. Stanislavsky's worldview, we saw, was integral to his System.

The link between Grotowski and Stanislavsky provided the former with strengths against which he could test his own and from which he could also push away, knowing that 'you are somebody's son' and are thus indebted to what precedes you, but knowing too that, to be worthy of this heritage, you have to be your own person and supersede it.[56] This is no different from Stanislavsky's telling his pupils that, teach them as he might, they had to find their own solutions according to their own light. And so Grotowski continued his research, eventually eschewing the actor and what he termed the 'theatre of presentation', by which he referred to the theatre that was intended to have audiences. Rejection of theatre was his embrace of research of the kind that Stanislavsky, in his rehearsals, had dared to do as 'creative processes without spectators', that is, creative processes per se.[57] He recalls Stanislavsky's observation that willpower cannot summon or otherwise conjure up feelings, adding that it can, however, muster action, which he perceives, via his short commentary on Stanislavsky's experiments on memory, as emerging from 'corpo-memory'.[58] Grotowski could only be referring in these pages to

---

[55] Dariusz Kosinski, *Grotowski: Przewodnik* (*Grotowski: A Guide*), Wroclaw: The Grotowski Institute, 2009, 42–5.

[56] 'Tu es le fils de quelqu'un' in *The Grotowski Sourcebook*, ed. Richard Schechner and Lisa Wolford, London and New York: Routledge, 1997, 294–305.

[57] 'Risposta a Stanislavskij (1980)', 52; 'Odpowiedż Stanisławskiemu', 472.   [58] Ibid., 58; 476.

Stanislavsky's practice in his last two Studios, where Stanislavsky had taught that actions stimulated deeply embodied emotions and prompted them to be remembered and felt corporeally in the very doing of action.

Grotowski was to go further and extend his dialogue with Stanislavsky by progressively replacing 'actor' with 'performer' and the latter with 'doer' in his exploration of action. In so doing, he confirmed his departure from Stanislavsky, which he had identified in 1980: Stanislavsky's 'end' was the theatre (theatre understood as drama, according to Grotowski), whereas for him 'there was only the Act' which yielded 'living existence as it evolved'.[59] Grotowski's passage into 'the Act' entailed intensive research on 'corpomemory', which was a matter of visceral energy and how this energy facilitated the doer's return to his/her ancestral sources. It could be argued, in fact, that Grotowski's idea of the performer/doer's inward journey to the sources replaced Stanislavsky's idea of the actor's journey to the subconscious. This aspect of Grotowski's research segued into his research on 'impulses' which he defined as being both 'physical' and 'pre-physical' and which he believed was the point where Stanislavsky had left off, but he, Grotowski, had continued, independently.[60] Grotowski progressively whittled down his selected collaborators, focusing his energies after 1986 on Thomas Richards and Mario Biagini in Pontedera.

Within his own charged journey was Grotowski's search for the potential and even the 'hidden' substance of the human being, the *człowiek* whom he invoked in all the different phases of his work and who carried within him/her the germ of another order of being altogether. Selected spectators – 'witnesses'– were invited not to co-create the performance but to allow the performers/doers to test what they were doing up against them. Here indeed were people who worked *on* themselves body and soul in ways unknown to Stanislavsky and which he could not even conceive of, since his work on himself, as his actors' work on themselves, led him back to the public theatre. Was this intense practice Mystery, keeping in mind Grotowski's first touchstone in the Eleusinian Mysteries? Peter Brook put it brilliantly when he called it 'art as vehicle' and pointed out that 'the vehicle which is the strongest in all the forms of theatre is the human being'.[61]

Brook continues: 'Right from the first moment when one begins to explore the possibilities of the human being, one must face up squarely to

---

[59] Ibid., 60–1; 478. [60] Ibid., 59; 477.
[61] *With Grotowski: Theatre Is Just a Form*, ed. Georges Banu et al., Wroclaw: The Grotowski Institute, 2009, 33.

Now: The 'Human Being'

the fact that this investigation is a spiritual search'[62]; and he explains that he 'mean[s] "spiritual" in the sense that, as one goes towards the interiority of man, one passes from the known to the unknown' and that 'spiritual traditions of the whole history of mankind have always needed to develop their own specific forms'. In another essay, Brook returns to how his and Grotowski's 'deep friendship' had to do with their shared aims, although their 'paths were different'.[63] For the sake of clarity, the following remarkable passage should be quoted in full:

> Grotowski's work leads him deeper and deeper into the actor's inner world to the point where the actor ceases to be actor and becomes essential man. For this, all the dynamic elements of drama are needed so that every cell of the body can be pushed to reveal its secrets. At first, director and audience are necessary to intensify the process. However, as the action goes deeper, everything external must wither away until at the end there is no more theatre, no more actor, no more audience – only a solitary man playing out his ultimate drama alone.

There is something tragic about this image of solitude, and it casts its shadow on Vasilyev after the loss in 2006 of his magnificent theatre on Sretenka Street in Moscow, opened in 2001. 'Sretenka' was part of his School of Dramatic Art founded in 1987 in a basement in Povarskaya Street, familiar to my reader from Chapter 1. Vasilyev had co-designed it to look and feel in its translucent arches and high white walls like a sacred space.[64] It was, effectively, a material realization of the 'theatre-church' favoured by Stanislavsky whom Vasilyev never tired of acknowledging as his compass, and its 'liturgical' atmosphere (to borrow Stanislavsky's term for the ideal dressing-room for actors) enveloped the building and penetrated the skin of those who entered its precincts. Vasilyev's altar to beauty, constructed from a Russian Orthodox viewpoint on the proximity of beauty to God, saw a whole array of productions grown out of the laboratory conditions in which ample time for creativity was a priority. Vasilyev chose the 'laboratory-theatre' option discussed in Chapter 4.

His sublime liturgical work was *The Lamentations of Jeremiah* (1995), the double winner in 1996 of the Golden Mask Award for best production as well as scenography – a controversial choice in those early years after perestroika because it seemed to the more cautious critics that the piece was religious choral singing rather than theatre, and a musical

---

[62] Ibid., 34.   [63] Ibid., 26, and the following quotation.
[64] Anatoli Vassiliev (French transliteration) in conversation with Maria Shevtsova, 'Studio Theatre, Laboratory Theatre', *New Theatre Quarterly*, 25, No. 4 (2009), 324–32.

rendition of the Old Testament rather than a proper drama. Music was by the composer Vladimir Martynov, by no means an unknown figure. The Golden Mask jury had the sense to see that the production certainly was theatre and theatre of another kind, completely sincere in its sacred calling and exquisite in its sonic, spatial and visual structures and configurations.

Ten women and ten men sang in ritual motion with short silences but for the sound of spluttering candles and cooing pigeons flying in the upper space. Vasilyev let eighteen pigeons loose in the second half of the performance – symbols of love (like the dove, which, in Christianity, represents the Holy Spirit) but also of the links between the heavenly powers and earth. In 2016, several pigeons were released towards the end of the last section of his *La Musica et la Musica deuxième*, a combination of two separate pieces thus titled by Marguerite Duras and performed in the Vieux Colombier. Of course, *colombier* in the name of Copeau's old theatre means 'dovecote', as Vasilyev knew, allowing him, in addition to his symbolic allusions, to pay a discreet tribute to the space of performance as well as to his key production of twenty years earlier.

The 1990s were the years of Vasilyev's binding friendship with Grotowski, sustained by his and several of his actors' visits to Pontedera; and he saw Grotowski as his mentor precisely because Grotowski's research stretched the boundaries of spiritual exploration through inner, *visceral* energy, on which he was also working; simultaneously, it provided Vasilyev with a sounding board for his 'ludic structures' – his playful, stylized, highly formal and evocative theatre that had turned its back on the theatres of stock-in-trade, presentation/representation and, *as well*, of *perezhivaniya* to explore action.

Vasilyev's study of Stanislavsky's method of physical action, mediated by Knebel's teachings on verbal-textual structuring, re-examined Stanislavsky's practice with this method, and, in doing so, liberated it not from its psychophysical processes but from its psychophysical sense. Sense came from action itself which, first of all, was inner action, and from the constructed composition of actions emergent from their visceral but subtle energy field; feeling emanated from this composition when and how it came, but it was neither meant to lead nor to be the endpoint of action. The three-part *La Musica et la Musica deuxième*, each part a variation on the same text and its situations and events, was a master class in the distinction between the theatres of presentation/representation, *perezhivaniya* and the third, embodied in the third part of the production, which was Vasilyev's very own 'play'. It can be deduced, from this apposition,

Now: The 'Human Being'

that Vasilyev sees the latter as his reconstruction of Stanislavsky's systemic work on action and, too, of how it interlinks with text.[65]

Vasilyev's 1990s concluded with magisterial works that, here and there, delicately echoed the spiritual quality of *The Lamentations of Jeremiah*. This quality reverberated especially powerfully in *Mozart and Salieri* (2000 – Stanislavsky's nemesis), an elegant blend of words, uttered not as mundane speech but in the intonations of Mystery – something Stanislavsky had intuited, but was unable to realize – choreographed movement, instrumental music and solo and choral singing, with a singer on every step of an ornamental staircase only wide enough for one person. This staircase went up and then down on the other side to add to the multiple architectural perspectives on which the entire production depended. Halos, standing just above the heads of the singer-angels, drew attention to their fabrication as an aspect of 'ludic' performance. Vasilyev had seized with a gentle touch the poetry of Pushkin that had eluded Stanislavsky. Hybrid blending and apposition, with a religious aura, constituted the breath-taking *Iliad. Chant XXIII* (2001) whose circular dance evoked the movements suggested on Ancient Greek vases (the source of Duncan's imagined Greek dance) and, as well, the light, repetitive and slightly rocking treading of the trance dance of mystical ceremonies. That these works were constructed from Vasilyev's use of Stanislavsky's principles of physical action does not take anything at all away from Vasilyev's individual approach.

Also within this group was Heiner Müller's *Medea-material* (2001), a solo piece whose words Valérie Dréville hewed and spat out like rocks in what can only be called a ritualistic fashion, making the Word sacramental, as *Mozart and Salieri* had made it earlier in a more sensual context. Dréville had left the comforts of the Comédie Française to travel over three years on the cusp of the 1990s to Moscow for prolonged periods of study with Vasilyev, and she continued to work with him after he had relocated to Paris in 2006. She performed in 2018 in the sculpturally shaped and slowly paced *Récit d'un homme inconnu* (*The Story of an Unknown Man*), Vasilyev's rendition of this novella by Chekhov, in a mode that he no longer saw as 'ludic' but 'metaphysical' because, among other things, its energy was located at the end of the performance from where it continued outwards into the ambient space and beyond it into what can only be called cosmic space.

---

[65] For some of his principles on this subject, see *The Cambridge Introduction to Theatre Directing*, 204–9.

262   Epilogue

Vasilyev had worked with another of the three actors before, so coaching
them as a director-pedagogue was straightforward. The process began with
weeks of laboratory exploration through etudes related to the text, but
without saying the text as such – Stanislavsky's opening gambit. The actors
concentrated on inner action, moving from their internal energy field as
they wished in relation to each other, gradually developing a score for the
actions of their role. The next stage was playing this role silently with
scored actions. Finally, the spoken text was layered over the top of the
layering that had already taken place. Text was not instrumentalized for
this or that purpose, nor was action forced into a mechanical relation to
text, illustrative or otherwise. The whole process followed the steps that we
saw Stanislavsky follow in Chapter 5 (Batalov playing Figaro and during
preliminary 1926 rehearsals with Leonidov playing Othello), but the actual
doing inevitably rendered its very own particular colouring and unique
qualities.

A 'spiritual search', understood as an exploration 'of the possibilities of
the human being' (Brook above) is the case of director Luk Perceval, a
Buddhist who teaches yoga and practices it every morning with his actors
before rehearsals begin. Perceval's key benefits of yoga (his form is related
to Zen Buddhism) are focus, attention, concentration and freedom from
external circumstances, which, he observes, is essential for creativity to
begin.[66] These are the very terms that we saw Stanislavsky use for his
burgeoning System several years before Demidov introduced him to yoga,
their inspiration coming from Russian Orthodoxy (Chapter 3). Perceval
speaks of the 'moment of enlightenment' that theatre can provide, and,
where Perceval equates this moment with the 'catharsis received by
spectators' through a performance, Stanislavsky speaks of the 'cleansing'
undergone by spectators and their 'communion' with each other and the
actors in the co-creative act. His 'enlightenment' is related, on the one
hand, to Perceval's 'conscious awareness', which yoga precipitates in
Perceval's actors, and, on the other hand, is close to Tolstoy's idea of
enlightenment as a catalyst for right action in life.

However, it is not so much the nuances of meaning that matter here as
the religious bases of Perceval's and Stanislavsky's thoughts – a different
religion in each case, but each providing a grounding for an attitude
towards theatre and theatre-makers and for a way of doing theatre that,
palpably, is not mundane but does not advertise itself as 'religious' or

---

[66] Notes taken from Perceval's open meeting at the Cultural Forum in St Petersburg, 17 November
2017. All quotations below are from this event.

Now: The 'Human Being' 263

'spiritual'. For Perceval, 'theatre is above all the human being' and its centring on the human being is the precondition for theatre being 'one of the rare places where truthfulness is to be found'. Perceval does not see Stanislavsky as his teacher, but thinks that 'we all owe him' for 'liberating the actor'.

Of significance in this context is how Perceval's primary questions to the theatre, which he puts as 'Where is the human being?' and 'Where is the substance?' are profoundly Stanislavskian questions, and they shed light on both men's respective projects. It is impossible to watch Perceval's six-hour trilogy *My Family* in three two-hour parts – *Love, Money, Hunger* (2015–17) – derived from Zola's twenty-volume *Les Rougon-Macquart* (*Hunger* is based on *Germinal*), without realizing just how much his 'conscious awareness' of contemporary times sustains his two primary questions to these times, and not exclusively as regards his native Belgium and adoptive Germany, where, at the Thalia Theatre in Hamburg, the trilogy was created. This awareness precipitates the non-sentimental compassion taught in Buddhism, which, for Perceval as much as for Stanislavsky's 'feeling with' others, is in the gift of being human.

Concern with what is human may be less rare among the prominent European directors on my panorama than Ostermeier's current experience implies, and the best example in relation to him might be Oskaras Korsunovas who, nearly fifty, is the same age as Ostermeier and younger, although not by a generation, than Perceval. Korsunovas' 'trilogy' (my description, with his approval) is composed of *Hamlet* (2008), *The Lower Depths* (2010, in which he pointedly showcases Hamlet's speech 'To be') and *The Seagull* (2014, with its unmissable references to *Hamlet*). *Hamlet* starts with the actors' dressing-room, which, Korsunovas observes, is where Stanislavsky's ethics for the theatre begin ('with the coat-hanger', Korsunovas adds), and this dressing-room becomes the driving metaphor both visually and substantially for *Hamlet* and, in terms of substance, for the 'trilogy' as a whole.[67] This is so because the dressing-room is the threshold from which actors enter 'illusion' in its relation to 'reality' and the actor has to be truthful on both counts. Korsunovas: 'Stanislavsky talked about the actor not losing himself/ herself in the role', and 'truthfulness had to be in the actor' for the human being-actor and the role to operate simultaneously.

Korsunovas' remarks indicate that, although he was not consciously thinking about Stanislavsky when he was working on these three

---

[67] With Shevtsova in an unpublished interview 15 November 2018. My translation from the Russian.

productions and their ontological and existential questions, together with questions about the actor (Who and what was the actor?), they simply showed their relation to a few strands of Stanislavsky's practice by themselves. Rehearsals of *Hamlet* started from the idea of analogy (analogous situations, and so on), which Stanislavsky had implemented to avoid confusion between the human being-actor and the role. And the actors worked, especially in *The Seagull*, on the edge of the 'rubicon' (Korsunovas) between the person and the role in the 'natural' organic way that Stanislavsky had advocated. Given that the Oskaras Korsunovas Theatre of the City of Vilnius is an ensemble and repertory company, the actors could carry over their shared method from one production to the next and let it go completely freely in *The Seagull*. Note that, early in his career, Korsunovas had rebelled against a lingering 1950s Soviet-style doxa in Lithuania concerning Stanislavsky (not unlike Peter Sellars fleeing a similarly stifling US doxa that he identifies below), and, by rejecting it, found a truer part of Stanislavsky's legacy for his own purposes.

Sellars, akin to Korsunovas in his escape from a sterilized legacy, 'absolutely located' himself in the work of Stanislavsky *and* Meyerhold when he was a student-director at Harvard University. He believed that both had created a 'mystical zone of their own' in Russia's 'extremely mystical period' of the turn of the twentieth century.[68] They dealt with it differently but, he argues, 'their metaphysics were identical', seeking for the theatre the 'spiritual energies' and spiritual channels that the visual arts and music had already navigated. The musicality of their productions was a case in point, and so the sound of crickets, in Stanislavsky's case, 'had nothing to do with realism' and everything to do with the 'placing of human beings in a cosmology'. Sellars suggests that human beings within a cosmology 'yearn to reach beyond their limits', the salient example of which, as he sees it, is *The Cherry Orchard*. Meyerhold's 'musicality and form', with their comparable sense of cosmology, is 'behind' (my extrapolation) what Sellars perceives as the 'historically fulfilled prophecy' of Meyerhold's finally working together with Stanislavsky on opera. Sellars is here referring to 1937 (Chapter 2).

It is striking that Sellars closely connects Stanislavsky and Meyerhold on the 'edge' between 'the known and the unknown' and 'the visible and the invisible' – the 'pivotal point', he says, 'on which they placed their theatre'. No less striking is his early realization that there was a Stanislavsky unlike the one 'stuffed down everybody's throat in America in the 1950s',

---

[68] With Shevtsova in an unpublished interview, 15 January 2017.

including by a 'bizarre Actors Studio', which he compares negatively with Harold Clurman's writing of the 1930s, and by a 'certain type of American theatre' trading on the stereotypes socially imposed on it. The image of an 'obnoxious' Stanislavsky, presented as having a 'high-handed way of working', was exploited, Sellars appears to suggest, to excuse similarly high-handed behaviour in the dominant sector of theatre practice. He rebuffed this Stanislavsky as he set out to find 'something that was organic and visionary' in another Stanislavsky, looking also towards Meyerhold for help. It is totally in the order of things, given Boleslavsky's importation of the younger Stanislavsky into the United States, that Sellars' alternative Stanislavsky should be the early visionary one of the Silver Age. Saying this does not minimize Sellars' very own, distinctive, spiritual quest.

Speaking in 2017, Sellars still places himself in this twin lineage, unspoiled by the fame of his wide diapason of operas, some of which are in the scenic languages of street violence and urban decay (Mozart's *Don Giovanni*, 1987), while others (Tchaikovsky's *Iolanta*, 2012) tackle fantasy and magic, occasionally in a celestial key. Where Stanislavsky is specifically concerned, Sellars values his attention to 'highly crafted detail' (since 'truth is in the detail') and how he scraped away layers gathered on top of works so as to 'look and listen all over again', just as he understood that people, no matter how 'small', needed to be noticed and listened to. Such care and observation are completely necessary in the present historical time: they are 'humane in an inhumane world'. '*That*', for Sellars, 'is the heart of the Stanislavsky practice ... and it is the only justification for theatre continuing to exist'.

These details regarding the foremost contemporary directors make 'legacy' a matter of a living legacy rather than a dusty archive; they also provide greater insight into how the theatre of our time was enriched as it established its strength and diversity. The purpose is not to seek Stanislavsky here, there and everywhere to prove that he is 'contemporary', but really to see him where he is present or where traces of his presence are visible or palpable today. Noticing his presence is not the same as forcing correspondences between aspects of a twenty-first-century director's work with something in Stanislavsky. Nor does it uphold the scholastic or dogmatic modes that Dodin believes are alien to the 'yeast' that gives rise 'here, today, now' to the 'living moment of the theatre'.[69] Dodin spontaneously quotes Stanislavsky while he reflects on 'scholasticism', which is a 'rational account', whereas actors in the living moment are alive to that

---

[69] Conversation of 16 February 2018, as all quotations below.

266 Epilogue

moment, unconcerned by rational thought. Dogmatism is fixated on rigid conceptions and terminology and wants to check whether x piece of work, acted or directed, is 'according to Stanislavsky'. Dodin argues that the very notion of 'according to Stanislavsky', which he still hears in Russia, is unacceptable for directing, since a director can only work in his/her own way. He was Zon's pupil (at the Leningrad State Theatre Institute, today's RGISI) and he had absorbed Stanislavsky 'as an infant imbibes its mother's milk'; Stanislavsky 'is a parent', but he, Dodin, can be nothing other than independent of this parent.

Yury Butusov, almost one generation younger than Dodin, speaks from within the same trope. He had studied at the Theatre Institute with Irina Malochevskaya, who, as a pupil of Tovstonogov, was 'very adept at the Stanislavsky method', leaving 'marks' on him that made him part of the same 'family'.[70] He was offered a dialogue with Stanislavsky, which freed him to find a path for himself. Like his teacher and Dodin, he rejects 'dogmatized Stanislavsky' but observes that 'it is impossible to overestimate him': 'Nothing is better than an ensemble' and 'What could be more to the point today than Stanislavsky's writings on ethics?' Butusov's is a case of mediated legacy, and the words most important to him are 'atmosphere, space, air, energy and time'. He needs time in order to slow time down and become immersed in his material as well as 'wake up' his subconscious whose role in creativity Stanislavsky had understood well; this alone makes him 'a great theatre person'.[71]

Butusov's productions could hardly be more different from Dodin's. Their array of virtually non-stop contemporary popular music and dance sequences – stomp, twist, rave, club dance, rock-star pyrotechnics – in collages formed also with dialogue break all generic boundaries. *Macbeth. Cinema* (2012), for instance, is five and a half hectic hours with masses of invented text and two discernible lines from Shakespeare while the rock band Nirvana pounds away. Yet all of Shakespeare's themes – passion, murder, power, dynasty, morality and its transgressions – are right there, prismatically refracted as spectators as much as performers sweep into this extraordinarily energized marathon (with, nevertheless, three intermissions). That Butusov has captured large audiences up to two generations younger than himself shows how accurately he has felt the social pulse, combining its desire for free flow – and his young actors' desire for the same flow – with plays that captivate him, attract his actors and will

[70] Conversation of 8 October 2015. My translation. [71] Conversation of 18 November 2017.

Now: The 'Human Being'

attract, he hopes, his upbeat spectators, who probably had not encountered them before.

Butusov: 'I always work through the text. We stretch the text. We do not illustrate an author but try to have more interesting relations with him.'[72] Indeed, he has often said that he prefers discovering his actors' attitudes and relation to plays to watching them interpret lines. What he means is evident in his rehearsals, where his actors invent seemingly endlessly on the basis of etudes. They try on roles as they try on costumes, make-up and hairdos. They play games with texts, improvise on them, extrapolate from them, repeat passages in unexpected places, and add their own or borrowed words from various sources. They 'stretch' in ways that are often totally surprising. Butusov constructs his productions from these etudes, keeping their etude spontaneity and atmosphere and encouraging the actors to create them afresh in successive performances. *The Three Sisters* (2014) is more transparent about its method of composition than its stunning, complex predecessor *The Seagull* (2011), which celebrates creativity while recognizing its mortal wounds and closes with a dancer who had appeared and reappeared during the performance and now sheds tears of diamonds that scatter across the stage and into the audience.[73] Could this be a recall of Sonia's 'sky filled with diamonds' but tuned to our world more than a hundred years later?

A whole generation younger than Butusov, Dmitry Volkostrelov, who is in his mid-thirties and was a student of Dodin as well as an actor at the Maly, also refers to the importance of Stanislavsky's writings on ethics for him.[74] It may be unexpected to hear a young director close in age to the 'me generation' speak with such earnestness about the imperative of ethical relations in the theatre profession and how this Stanislavsky is more meaningful to his work today than any other. And, if he was alluding to his teacher Dodin's directorial approach and so to artistic issues and Dodin's concentrated psycho-emotional characterization, then it is clear how his work differs. As he seeks his voice, he veers between the two poles established by his mysterious and imagistic *Lecture on Nothing* by John Cage (2015) and the equally minimal but coolly rationalized *The Field* (2017) by Pavel Pryazhko, his collaborator dramatist since he founded Teatr Post in St Petersburg in 2011. Volkostrelov began with impartial,

---

[72] Conversation of 8 October 2015.
[73] Maria Shevtsova, 'Alive, Kicking – and Kicking Back: Russia's Golden Mask Festival 2015', *New Theatre Quarterly*, 31, No. 123 (2015), 232–40 for the pages on *The Three Sisters*.
[74] Conversation of 2 April 2017.

268   Epilogue

frequently documentary-'objective' productions as practised especially in Moscow at the turn of the twenty-first century, and he appears to perceive in this phenomenon glimmers of a reassessment not so much of Stanislavsky but of how the theatre has habitually used him.

Dodin, for his part, is more vocal on the subject. He has increasingly felt that, in order to be a 'living' presence, Stanislavsky has to be rethought with the changing times. His view of *An Actor's Work on Himself* (both volumes) is unequivocal: it is a 'rather unsatisfactory book, but with wonderful things in it' and, although Stanislavsky wrote it while he was trying to work out 'laws' [of acting, creativity, nature], 'they may possibly not be solvable because laws may not exist'.[75] Musing on his thoughts, Dodin observes that Stanislavsky was the first to understand that 'live feeling had to have very precise expression'; the first to make models of his stage settings; the first to light his own productions; and the first in many other areas. Scholars, however, tend to rationalize his achievements and concentrate on definitions.

Consequently, when they read Knebel and read her practical extrapolations from Stanislavsky, they invariably forget that 'life is more varied and complex than any scholarly definition'. Dodin speaks highly of Knebel's seminars, which he had attended in various cities ('a marvellous pedagogue' and 'a very young, lively person' in advancing age). But he believes that life circumstances are so complex today that it is very difficult to follow in her footsteps and say what an event is, or to choose one of many as the decisive 'event'. There are many events that occur together and many factors that tangle situations. He simply does not use the idea of 'event' with his actors, preferring them to try out scenes in a less structured and more fluid and open-ended way with etudes and improvisations on a particular piece of text.

Working 'on their feet' has remained a characteristic of MDT actors. However, Dodin has come to realize that a text is a complex business for 'contemporary young people', and he 'can hear when they do not understand what they are saying'. The odds are against them in a world of short-sentence text messaging, short sentences generally, daily fast pace and pressure, and other instantaneous demands on them in which 'it is difficult for them to find time to read'. He is currently working with his young actors (2018) on *The Brothers Karamazov*, which, devised from Dostoyevsky's novel, will enter the 'theatre of prose' he has created over the years with earlier generations of actors whom he had developed.[76]

[75] 16 February 2018.   [76] *Dodin and the Maly Drama Theatre*, 63–100.

Now: The 'Human Being'

But Dostoevsky's prose is particularly challenging for this present generation, obliging him to rethink Stanislavsky and why Stanislavsky had abandoned reading together at a table. Contemporary circumstances have pushed him to return to the table, 'where you have to sit and work out the meaning' so that the young actors 'actually do understand what they are saying'. The process, Dodin specifies, entails breaking down and deciphering the text, but does not require much talking about it. *That*, it is worth adding, the actors can do afterwards with their feet.

Where Stanislavsky's legacy is concerned, Dodin's commentary indicates that this legacy finds its just value only when those who turn to it view it from the prism of the time contemporary to them. This means that whatever resonates with them in Stanislavsky's work will have its impact and leave its traces in varying depths and degrees within their time; and the part of the legacy that they have absorbed is bound to mutate with the changing times and their differing conditions, energies and questions. Stanislavsky's motto for the theatre 'simpler, lighter, higher, happier' may be taken as a note to his legacy and a reminder that, while all things pass, they can pass with grace.

Bibliography

WORKS BY K. S. STANISLAVSKY

Besedy K. S. Stanislavskogo v Studiya Bolshogo teatra v 1918–1922, recorded in shorthand and transcribed and compiled by Konkordiya Antarova (general ed.), with an introduction by L. Ya. Gurevich, Moscow and Leningrad: All-Russian Theatre Association, 1939

Rezhissyorsky Plan *Otello*, ed. N. Zograf, Moscow and Leningrad: Iskusstvo, 1945

Sobraniye sochineny v vosmi tomakh, ed. M. N. Kedrov et al. (with explanatory notes by G. V. Kristi), 8 vols., Moscow: Iskusstvo, 1954–61

Sobraniye sochineny v devyati tomakh, ed. O. N. Efremov, V. Ya. Vilenkin, A. M. Smeliansky, I. N. Soloyova et al., 9 vols, Moscow: Iskusstvo, 1980–99

Iz zapisnykh knizhek, 2 vols., ed. V. N. Prokofiev, Moscow: All-Russian Society, 1986

Rezhissyorskiye ekzemplyary K. S. Stanislavskogo, 6 vols., ed. V. Ya. Vilenkin and I. N. Solovyova (Vol. 2 co-ed. I. N. Vinogradskaya), Moscow: Iskusstvo, 1980–94; *hors série, Dyadya Vanya*, ed. I. N. Solovyova, Moscow–St Petersburg: Atheneum–Feniks, 1994

Stanislavsky repetiruyet, ed. I. N. Vinogradskaya, Moscow: Moscow Art Theatre, 2000

Zapisnye knizhki (no ed.), Moscow: Vagrius, 2001

WORKS BY OTHER AUTHORS

In Russian

Note: English translations of Russian titles are given in the body of the text.

Balukhaty, S. D., *Chayka* v postanovke Moskovskovo Khudozhestvennogo Teatra, Rezhisserskaya partitura K. S. Stanislavskogo, Leningrad: Iskusstvo, 1938

Birman, Serafima, *Put aktrisi*, Moscow: All-Russian Theatre Society, 1959

Bolshaya Sovetskaya Entsiklopediya, Moscow: State Scientific Press, 1956

Brodskaya, G., *Alekseyev-Stanislavsky, Chekhov i drugiye. Vishnyovosadnaya epopeya*, Moscow: Agraph, 2000

Bibliography

Bryusov, Valery, 'Realism i uslovnost na stsenye' in *Teatr. Kniga o novom teatre*, Moscow: GITIS, 2008, 202–14

Chekhov, Mikhaïl, *Literaturnoye naslediye*, ed. Maria Knebel et al., 2 vols., Moscow: Iskusstvo, 1995

Chepurov, A. A., *Aleksandrinskaya Chayka*, St Petersburg: Aleksandrinsky Theatre Library, 2002.

Cherkassky, Sergey, *Masterstvo aktyora: Stanislavsky, Boleslavsky, Strasberg*, St Petersburg: Russian State Institute of Scenic Arts, 2016

Dodin, Lev, *Puteshestviye bez kontsa. Pogruzheniye v miry Chekhova*, St Petersburg: Baltic Seasons, 2010

Dodin, Lev, *Puteshestviye bez kontsa. Pogruzheniye v miry Tri sestry*, St Petersburg: Baltic Seasons, 2011

Dodin, Lev, *Puteshestviye bez kontsa. Pogruzheniye v miry Vishnyovy sad*, St Petersburg: Baltic Seasons, 2016

Efros, Nikolay, *Moskovsky Khudozhestvenny Teatr 1898–1923*, Moscow and St Petersburg: State Publishing House, 1924

Evreinov, Nikolay, *Teatralizatsiya zhizni*, Moscow: Vremya, 1922

Feldman, Oleg (documents compiled and ed.), *Meyerhkolda naslediye*, Vol. 3, Moscow: Novoye Izdatelstvo, 2010

Galendeyev, Valery, *Ucheniye K. S. Stanislavskogo o stsenicheskom slove*, N. K. Cherkasov Leningrad State Institute of Theatre, Music and Film, 1990

Giatsintova, Sofya, *C pamyatyu nayedinye*, Moscow: Iskusstvo, 1989

Gladkov, Aleksandr, *Teatr. Vospominaniya i razmyshleniya*, Moscow: Iskusstvo, 1980

Gorchakov, N., *Rezhissyorskiye uroki Stanislavskogo*, Moscow: Iskusstvo, 1952

Kalashnikov, Yu. (ed.), *Stanislavsky, reformator opernogo iskusstva: Materialy, Dokumenty*, Moscow: Musyka, 1988

Kalugina, O. V., *Skulptor Anna Golubkina*, Moscow: 'Galart' Publisher, 2006

Klimenko, L. A., 'Chetvyortaya studiya MKhATa – Moskovsky Gosudarstvenny Teatr Chetvyortaya Studiya' in *Sovyetsky teatr 1921–1926. Dokumenti i materialy*, ed. A. Ya. Trabsky, Leningrad: Iskusstvo, 1975, 188–228

Knebel, Maria, *Slovo v tvorchestve aktyora*, Moscow: Iskusstvo, 1954

Knebel, Maria, *Vsya zhizn*, Moscow: All-Russian Theatre Society, 1967

Knebel, Maria, *O deystvennom analize pyesi i roli*, Moscow: GITIS, 2014

Knipper-Chekhova, Olga Leonardovna, *Chast pervaya. Vospominaniya i stati. Perepiska s A. P. Chekhovym (1902–1904)*, Part I, Moscow: Iskusstvo, 1972

Komissarzhevsky, F. F., *Tvorchestvo aktyora i teoriya Stanislavskogo*, Petrograd (n.p.), 1917

Krechetova, Rima, *Stanislavsky*, Moscow: The Young Guard, 2013

Kristi, G., *Rabota Stanislavskogo v opernom teatre*, Moscow: Iskusstvo, 1952

Markov, P. A., *Moskovsky Khudozhestvenny Teatr Vtoroy*, Moscow: Moscow Art Theatre, 1925

Meyerhold, V. E., *Stati. Pisma. Rechi. Besedy*, 2 vols., Moscow: Iskusstvo, 1968

Bibliography

Mikhalsky, F. N. and E. S. Kapitaykin, 'Pervaya Studiya' in *Sovyetsky teatr 1921–1926. Dokumenti i materialy*, ed. A. Ya. Trabsky, Leningrad: Iskusstvo, 1975, 160–87

Nemirovich-Danchenko, Vladimir, *Iz Proshlogo*, Moscow: Moy2ovek, 2003

Novitskaya, L. N., *Uroki vdokhnoveniya. Sistema K. S. Stanislavskogo v deystviye*, Moscow: All-Russian Theatre Society, 1984

Paston, Eleonora, *Abramtsevo. Iskusstvo i zhizn*, Moscow: Iskusstvo, 2003

Polkanova, Maria (compiled and ed.), *I vnov o Khudozhetsvennom. MXAT v vospominaniyakh i zapisyakh 1901–1920*, Moscow: Avantitul, 2004

Polyakova, Yelena, *Stanislavsky*, Moscow: Iskusstvo, 1977

Polyakova, Yelena, *Teatr Sulerzhitskogo. Etika. Estetika. Rezhissura*, Moscow: Agraf, 2006

Radishcheva, O. A., *Stanislavsky i Nemirovich-Danchenko. Istoriya teatralnykh otnosheny. 1897–1908*, Moscow: Artist. Director. Theatre, 1997

Radishcheva, O. A., *Stanislavsky i Nemirovich-Danchenko. Istoriya teatralnykh otnosheny. 1909–1917*, Moscow: Artist. Director. Theatre, 1999

Radishcheva, O. A., *Stanislavsky i Nemirovich-Danchenko. Istoriya teatralnykh otnosheny. 1917–1938*, Moscow: Artist. Director. Theatre, 1999

Radishcheva, O. A. and E. A. Shingaryova (eds.) (Vol. 1 with Yu. M. Vinogradova), *Moskovsky Khudozhestvenny Teatr v russkoy teatralnoy kritike 1898–1943*, 4 vols., Moscow: Artist. Director. Theatre, 2005–10

Rudnitsky, K. L., *Russkoye rezhissyorskoye iskusstvo 1898–1917*, Moscow: GITIS, 2014

Rumyantsev, P. I., *Stanislavsky i opera*, Moscow: Iskusstvo, 1969

Smeliansky, A., *Mikhaïl Bulgakov v Khudozhestvennom Teatre*, Moscow: Iskusstvo, 1986

Smyshlyayev, Valentin, *Teoriya obrobotki stsenicheskogo zrelishcha*, Izhevsk: Proletkult Publication, 1921

Sobolevskaya, O. C., *K. S. Stanislavsky rabotayet, beseduyet, otdykhayet*, Moscow: STD, 1988

Solovyova, Inna, *Khudozhestvenny Teatr. Zhizn i priklyucheniye ideyi*, Moscow: Moscow Art Theatre, 2007

Solovyova, Inna, *Pervaya Studiya. Vtoroy MkhAT*, Moscow: New Literary Review, 2016

Stroyeva, M. N., *Rezhissyorskiye iskaniya Stanislavskogo 1898–1917*, Moscow: Nauka, 1973

Stroyeva, M. N., *Rezhissyorskiye iskaniya Stanislavskogo 1917–1938*, Moscow: Nauka, 1977

Sulerzhitsky, Leopold Antonovich, *Povesti i rasskazy. Stati i zametki. Perepiska. Vospominaniya o L. A. Sulerzhitskom*, ed. Yelena Polyakova, Moscow: Iskusstvo, 1970

Toporkov, V. O., *Stanislavsky na repetitsii. Vospominaniya*, Moscow: AST-Press SKD, 2002

Tovstonogov, G. A., *O professii rezhissyora*, St Petersburg: The Planet of MUSIC, 2017

Bibliography

273

Udaltsova, Z. P. (compiled and commented), *Khudozhestvenny Teatr. Tvorcheskiye ponedelniki i drugiye dokumenty 1916–1919*, Moscow: Moscow Art Theatre Press, 2006

Udaltsova, Z. P. (compiled and ed.), *MXAT Vtoroy. Svidetelstva i dokumenty 1926–1936*, Moscow: Moscow Art Theatre, 2011

Udaltsova, Zinaïda (ed.) and E. A. Kesler (commentary), *Gamlet na stsene MKhAT Vtorovo*, Moscow: Moscow Art Theatre, 2017

Vakhtangov, Yevgeny, *Yevgeny Vakhtangov. Dokumenty i svidetelstva*, Vol. 1, ed. Vladislav Ivanov, Moscow: Indrik, 2011

Vasilyev, Anatoly, in conversation with Zara Abdullayeva, *Parautopia*, Moscow: ABC design, 2016

Vinogradskaya, I. N., 'O postanovkakh K. S. Stanislavskogo v obshchestve iskusstva i literatury' in *Teatralnoye naslediye. K. S. Stanislavsky. Materialy. Pisma. Issledovaniya*, ed. I. E. Grabarya et al., Moscow: Academy of Sciences of the USSR, 1955, 495–552

Vinogradskaya, I. N., 'Vtoraya studiya Moskovskogo Khudozhestvennogo Teatra' in *Sovetsky teatr. Dokumenti i materialy 1917–1921*, ed. A. Z. Yufit et al., Leningrad: Iskusstvo, 1968, 384–9

Vinogradskaya, I. N., 'Vtoraya Studiya Moskovskogo Khudozhestvennogo Akademicheskogo Teatra' in *Sovyetsky teatr 1921–1926, Dokumenti i materialy*, ed. A. Ya. Trabsky, Leningrad: Iskusstvo, 1975, 182–7

Vinogradskaya, I. N., *Zhizn i tvorchestvo K. S. Stanislavskogo. Letopis*, 4 vols., Moscow: Moscow Art Theatre Press, 2003

Zatvornik, Feofan, *Shto yest dukhovnaya zhizn i kak na neyo nastroyitsya?*, Moscow: Otchy dom, 2006

Zolotinsky, D., *Zori teatralnogo oktyabrya*, Leningrad: Iskusstvo, 1976

Zon, B. V., 'Vstrechi s K. S. Stanislavskim' in *Teatralnoye naslediye. K. S. Stanislavsky. Materialy. Pisma. Issledovaniya*, ed. I. E. Grabarya et al., Moscow: Academy of Sciences of the USSR, 1955, 449–91

In English

Adler, Stella, *The Technique of Acting*, New York: Bantam Books, 1990

Bakhtin, Mikhaïl, *Rabelais and His World*, trans. Hélène Iswolsky, Bloomington: Indiana University Press, 1984

Barba, Eugenio, in conversation with Maria Shevtsova, 'Reinventing Theatre', *New Theatre Quarterly*, 23, No. 2 (2007), 99–114

Bartlett, Rosamund, *Chekhov: Scenes from a Life*, London: The Free Press, 2004

Bartoshevich, Alexei, 'Theodore Komisarjevsky, Chekhov, and Shakespeare' in *Wandering Stars: Russian Emigré Theatre, 1905–1940*, ed. Laurence Senelick, Iowa City: University of Iowa Press, 1992, 102–15

Bartoshevich, Alexei, 'The "Inevitability" of Chekhov: Anglo-Russian Theatrical Contacts in the 1910s' in *Chekhov on the British Stage*, ed. and trans. Patrick Miles, Cambridge University Press, 1993, 20–8

Bibliography

Benedetti, Jean, 'A History of Stanislavski in Translation', *New Theatre Quarterly*, 6, No. 23 (1990), 266–78

Benedetti, Jean (selected, ed. and trans.), *The Moscow Art Theatre Letters*, London: Methuen Drama, 1991

Benedetti, Jean, *Stanislavski: His Life and Art*, London: Methuen Drama, 1999

Boleslavsky, Richard, *Acting: The First Six Lessons. Documents from the American Laboratory Theatre*, ed. Rhonda Blair, Abingdon and New York: Routledge, 2010

Borovsky, Victor, *Chaliapin: A Critical Biography*, London: Hamish Hamilton, 1998

Borovsky, Victor, *A Triptych from the Russian Theatre: An Artistic Biography of the Komissarzhevskys*, London: Hurst and Company, 2001

Bowlt, John E., *Moscow and St Petersburg, 1900–1920: Art, Life and Culture of the Russian Silver Age*, New York: The Vendome Press, 2008

Braun, Edward (trans. and ed.), *Meyerhold on Theatre*, London: Methuen Drama, 1969

Brecht, Bertolt, *Brecht on Theatre: The Development of an Aesthetic*, trans. and ed. John Willett, London: Methuen, 1964

Brook, Peter, *With Grotowski: Theatre Is Just a Form*, ed. Georges Banu et al., Wroclaw: The Grotowski Institute, 2009

Carnicke, Sharon Marie, *Stanislavsky in Focus: An Acting Master for the Twenty-First Century*, London and New York: Routledge, 2009

Chekhov, Michael, *To the Actor*, London and New York: Routledge, 2002

Chekhov, Michael, *The Path of the Actor*, ed. Andrei Kirillov and Bella Merlin, London and New York: Routledge, 2005

Clark, Katerina, *Petersburg, Crucible of Cultural Revolution*, Cambridge, MA: Harvard University Press, 1995

Clark, Katerina and Evgeny Dobrenko with Andrei Artizov and Oleg Naumov, *Soviet Culture and Power: A History in Documents*, trans. Marian Schwartz, New Haven and London: Yale University Press, 2007

Clurman, Harold, *The Fervent Years: The Group Theatre and the Thirties*, New York: Da Capo Press, 1983

Deak, Frantisec, 'Blue Blouse: 1923–28', *The Drama Review*, 17 (1972), 35–46

Edwards, Christine, *The Stanislavsky Heritage*, London: Peter Owen, 1966

Eliade, Mircea, *The Sacred and the Profane: The Nature of Religion*, trans. Willard R. Trask, New York and London: Harcourt Brace Jovanovich, 1959

Figes, Orlando, *Natasha's Dance: A Cultural History of Russia*, London: Allen Lane, 2002

Fitzpatrick, Sheila, *The Commissariat of Enlightenment: Soviet Organization of Education and the Arts under Lunacharsky, October 1917–1921*, Cambridge University Press, 1970

Fitzpatrick, Sheila (ed.), *Cultural Revolution in Russia, 1928–1931*, Bloomington and London: Indiana University Press, 1978

Fitzpatrick, Sheila, *The Cultural Front: The Proletkult in Revolutionary Russia*, Ithaca and London: Cornell University Press, 1992

Gillett, John, *Acting Stanislavski: A Practical Guide to Stanislavski's Approach and Legacy*, London and New York: Bloomsbury Methuen Drama, 2014

Bibliography

Golub, Spencer, *Evreinov: The Theatre of Paradox and Transformation*, Ann Arbor: UMI Research Press, 1984

Gorchakov, Nikolai M., *Stanislavsky Directs*, trans. Miriam Goldina, New York: Limelight Editions, 1985

Gordon, Mel, *Stanislavsky in America*, Abingdon: Routledge, 2010

Gray, Paul, 'The Reality of Doing: Interviews with Vera Soloviova, Stella Adler, and Sanford Meisner' in *Stanislavski and America*, ed. Erika Munk, with an introduction by Richard Schechner, Greenwich, CT: Fawcett Publications, 1967, 201–18

Granville Barker, Harley, *The Exemplary Theatre*, London: Chatto and Windus, 1922

Grotowski, Jerzy, *Towards a Poor Theatre*, ed. Eugenio Barba, Holstebro: Odin Teatret, 1984

Hall, Peter, interviewed by Patrick Miles, 'Chekhov, Shakespeare, the Ensemble and the Company', *New Theatre Quarterly*, 11, No. 2 (1995), 203–10

Hosking, Geoffrey, *Russia: People and Empire, 1552–1917*, London: Fontana Press, 1998

Innes, Christopher and Maria Shevtsova, *The Cambridge Introduction to Theatre Directing*, Cambridge University Press, 2013

Kogan, Sam, *The Science of Acting*, ed. Helen Kogan, London and New York: Routledge, 2010

Komisarjevsky, Theodore, *Myself and the Theatre*, London: William Heinemann Limited, 1929

Krasner, David (ed.), *Method Acting Reconsidered: Theory, Practice, Future*, New York: St Martin's Press, 2000

Krasner, David, 'Stanislavsky's System, Sense-Emotion Memory, and Physical Action/Active Analysis: American Interpretations of the System's Legacy' in *The Routledge Companion to Stanislavsky*, ed. R. Andrew White, Abingdon and New York: Routledge, 2014, 195–213

Leach, Robert, *Vsevolod Meyerhold*, Cambridge University Press, 1989

Leach, Robert and Victor Borovsky (eds.), *A History of Russian Theatre*, Cambridge University Press, 1999

Leyda, Jay, *A History of the Russian and Soviet Film*, Princeton: Princeton University Press, 1983

Lieven, Dominic, *Towards the Flame: Empire, War and the End of Tsarist Russia*, London: Allen Lane, 2015

Likhachev, Dmitry S., 'Religion: Russian Orthodoxy' in *The Cambridge Companion to Modern Russian Culture*, ed. Nicholas Rzhevsky Cambridge University Press, 1998, 38–56

Magarshack, David, *Stanislavsky: A Life*, London: Faber and Faber, 1968

Malaev-Babel, Andrei, *Yevgeny Vakhtangov: A Critical Portrait*, Abingdon and New York: Routledge, 2013

Malaev-Babel, Andrei and Margarita Laskina (eds.), *Nikolai Demidov: Becoming an Actor-Creator*, trans. Andrei Malaev-Babel with Alexander Rojavin and Sarah Lillbridge, London and New York: Routledge, 2016

Bibliography

Mally, Lynn, *Culture of the Future: The Proletkult in Revolutionary Russia*, Berkeley and Oxford: University of California Press, 1990

Maude, Aylmer, *A Peculiar People: The Doukhobors*, New York: Funk and Wagnalls Company, 1904

McDonald, Jan, 'Chekhov, Naturalism and the Drama of Dissent: Productions of Chekhov's Plays in Britain before 1914' in *Chekhov on the British Stage*, ed. and trans. Patrick Miles, Cambridge University Press, 1993, 29–42

Melik-Zakharov, Sergei and Shoel Bogatyrev (compiled), *K. Stanislavsky, 1863–1963: Man and Actor; Stanislavsky and the World Theatre; Stanislavsky's Letters*, trans. Vic Schneierson, Moscow: Progress Publishers, 1963

Merlin, Bella, *The Complete Stanislavsky Toolkit*, London: Nick Hern Books, 2007

Merlin, Bella, '"Where's the Spirit Gone?" The Complexities of Translation and the Nuances of Terminology in *An Actor's Work* and an Actor's Work', *Stanislavski Studies*, 1 (2012), 43–86

Miles, Patrick (ed. and trans.), *Chekhov on the British Stage*, Cambridge University Press, 1993

Mitchell, Katie, *The Director's Craft: A Handbook for the Theatre*, Abingdon and New York: Routledge, 2009

Nemirovich-Danchenko, Vladimir, *My Life in the Russian Theatre*, trans. John Cournos, London: Geoffrey Bles, 1968

Pitches, Jonathan and Stefan Aquilina, (eds.), *Stanislavsky in the World: The System and Its Transformations across the Continents*, Bloomsbury: London, 2017

Rudnitsky, Konstantin, *Meyerhold, the Director*, trans. George Petrov, Ann Arbor: Ardis, 1981

Sayler, Oliver, *The Russian Theatre under the Revolution*, Boston: Little, Brown and Company, 1920

Schechner, Richard and Lisa Wolford (eds.), *The Grotowski Sourcebook*, London and New York: Routledge, 1997

Scott, H. G. (ed.), *Soviet Writers' Congress 1934*, no trans., London: Lawrence and Wishart, 1977

Senelick, Laurence, Gordon Craig's Moscow *Hamlet*: A Reconstruction, Westport: Greenwood Press, 1982

Senelick, Laurence (ed.), *Wandering Stars: Russian Emigré Theatre, 1905–1940*, Iowa City: University of Iowa Press, 1992

Senelick, Laurence and Sergei Ostrovsky (eds.), *The Soviet Theatre: A Documentary History*, New Haven and London: Yale University Press, 2014

Senelick, Laurence (selected, trans. and ed.), *Stanislavsky – A Life in Letters*, London and New York: Routledge, 2014

Senelick, Laurence, 'The Accidental Evolution of the Moscow Art Theatre Group of Prague', *New Theatre Quarterly*, 30, No. 118 (2014), 154–67

Shevtsova, Maria, *The Theatre Practice of Anatoly Efros: A Contemporary Soviet Director*, Devon: Theatre Papers no. 6, Dartington College of the Arts, 1978

Bibliography

Shevtsova, Maria, 'Peter Brook Adapts *The Tragedy of Carmen*', *Théâtre International*, 2, No. 10 (1983), 38–55

Shevtsova, Maria, 'Dialogism in the Novel and Bakhtin's Theory of Culture', *New Literary History*, 23, No. 3 (1992), 747–63

Shevtsova, Maria, *Dodin and the Maly Drama Theatre: Process to Performance*, London and New York: Routledge, 2004

Shevtsova, Maria, *Sociology of Theatre and Performance*, Verona: QuiEdit, 2009

Shevtsova, Maria, in conversation with Anatoly Vasiliev, 'Studio Theatre, Laboratory Theatre', *New Theatre Quarterly*, 25, No. 100 (2009), 324–32

Shevtsova, Maria and Christopher Innes, *Directors/Directing: Conversations on Theatre*, Cambridge University Press, 2009

Shevtsova, Maria, 'Book Review of *My Life in Art* and *An Actor's Work*', *TDR*, 54, No. 205 (2010), 172–4

Shevtsova, Maria, 'Stanislavsky to Grotowski: Actor to Performer/Doer', *New Theatre Quarterly*, 30, No. 120 (2014), 333–40

Shevtsova, Maria, 'Alive, Kicking – and Kicking Back: Russia's Golden Mask Festival 2015', *New Theatre Quarterly*, 31, No. 123 (2015), 232–40

Shevtsova, Maria, 'Revolutions Remembered: The Golden Mask in Moscow 2017', *New Theatre Quarterly*, 33, No. 131 (2017), 288–98

Smeliansky, Anatoly, *Is Comrade Bulgakov Dead? Mikhail Bulgakov at the Moscow Art Theatre*, trans. Arch Tait, London: Methuen Drama, 1993

Stanislavsky, K. S., 'Direction and Acting' in *Encyclopaedia Britannica*, Vol. 22, London: Encyclopaedia Britannica, 1929–32, 35–8

Stanislavsky, Konstantin, *Stanislavsky: On the Art of the Stage*, trans. David Magarshack, London: Faber and Faber, 1950

Stanislavski, Constantin (*sic*) and Pavel Rumyantsev, *Stanislavski on Opera*, trans. and ed. Elizabeth Hapgood, New York and London: Routledge, A Theatre Arts Book, 1998

Stanislavsky, Konstantin, *My Life in Art*, trans. and ed. Jean Benedetti, London and New York: Routledge, 2008

Stanislavsky, Konstantin, *An Actor's Work: A Student's Diary*, trans. and ed. Jean Benedetti, London and New York: Routledge, 2008

Stanislavsky, Konstantin, *An Actor's Work on a Role*, trans. and ed. Jean Benedetti, London and New York: Routledge, 2009

Strasberg, Lee, *A Dream of Passion: The Development of the Method*, ed. Evangeline Morphos, London: Bloomsbury, 1988

Sulerzhitsky, Leopold Antonovich, *To America with the Doukhobors*, trans. Michael Kalmakoff and introduction by Mark Mealing, Regina: Canadian Plains Research Centre, University of Regina, 1982

Tcherkasski, Sergei, *Stanislavsky and Yoga*, trans. Vreneli Farber, Abingdon: Routledge Icarus Publishing Enterprise, 2016

Thomas, James, *A Director's Guide to Stanislavsky's Active Analysis*, London and New York: Bloomsbury Methuen Drama, 2016

Tolstoy, Sofia, *The Diaries of Sofia Tolstoy*, trans. Cathy Porter, Surrey: Alma Books, 2009

278 *Bibliography*

Toporkov, Vasily, *Stanislavsky in Rehearsal: The Final Years*, trans. Christine Edwards, New York and London: Routledge, A Theatre Arts Book, 1998
Trotsky, Leon, *Literature and Revolution*, trans. Rose Strunsky, Ann Arbor: University of Michigan Press, 1960
White, R. Andrew (ed.), *The Routledge Companion to Stanislavsky*, Abingdon and New York: Routledge, 2014
Whyman, Rose, *The Stanislavsky System of Acting: Legacy and Influence in Modern Performance*, Cambridge University Press, 2008
Worrall, Nick, *The Moscow Art Theatre*, London and New York: Routledge, 1996

In French

Autant-Mathieu, Marie-Christine (ed.), *Le Théâtre d'Art de Moscou: Ramifications, voyages*, Paris: CNRS Editions, 2005
Bourdieu, Pierre, *Le Sens pratique*, Paris: Le Seuil, 1980
Bourdieu, Pierre, *Méditations pascaliennes*, Paris: Le Seuil, 1997
Dréville, Valéry, Face à *Médée:* Journal de répétition, Paris: Actes Sud-Papiers, 2018
Dusigne, François, *Le Théâtre d'Art: Aventure européenne du xxième siècle*, Paris: Editions THEATRALES, 1997
Jörder, Gerhard, *Ostermeier Backstage*, trans. Laurent Muhleisen and Frank Weigand, Paris: L'Arche, 2015 [interview with Ostermeier]
Mojenok-Ninin, Tatiana, *Vassili Polenov: Chevalier de la beauté*, Rouen: Editions points de vue, Association Vassili Polenov, 2013
Ostermeier, Thomas, *Le Théâtre et la peur*, trans. Jitka Goriaux Pelechová, Paris: Actes Sud, 2016
Poliakov, Stéphane, *Anatoli Vassiliev: L'Art de la composition*, Paris: Actes Sud-Papiers, 2006
Vassiliev, Anatoli, *Sept ou huit leçons de théâtre*, trans. Martine Néron, Paris: P.O.L., 1999

In Italian

Attisani, Antonio and Mario Biagini (eds.), *Opere e sentieri: Jerzy Grotowski Testi 1968–1998*, Rome: Bulzoni Editore, 2007
Attisani, Antonio and Mario Biagini (eds.), *Opere e sentieri: Testimonianze e riflessioni sull'arte come veicolo*, Rome: Bulzoni Editore, 2008
Strehler Giorgio, *Per un teatro umano*, ed. Sinah Kessler, Milan: Feltrinelli, 1974

In Polish

Kosinski, Dariusz, *Grotowski: Przewodnik*, Wroclaw: The Grotowski Institute, 2009
Teksty zebrane: Grotowski, ed. Agata Adamieck-Sitek et al., Wroclaw and Warsaw: The Grotowski Institute, The Zbigniew Raszewski Theatre Institute and The Political Critique Publishing House, 2017

Index

Abramtsevo Circle, 23–5, 52–3
    Private Opera Theatre and, 26–7
Abramtsevo commune
    collective goals of, 23
    cross-arts explorations in, x
    Mamontov and, 22–4
    Stanislavsky at, 23
acting. *See also* System of acting
    analogous, 223
    as noble profession, 128
Acting: The First Six Lessons (Boleslavsky), 239
active analysis, 171–9
    restrictions on, 177
actors. *See also* System of acting
    co-creativity with directors, 216, 227–9, 233
    discipline for, 127
    in First Studio, 137
    inert, 127–8
    in MAT, 9–10
    method of physical action, 83–4, 171–2,
        174–5, 178, 217
    obligations of, 127–8
    passive, 127–8
    stage creativity of, 96
    Stanislavsky as, 1–2, 116, 119, 154–5, 188,
        215, 222
    in theatre of emotional experiencing,
        121–2
An Actor's Work on a Role (Stanislavsky), 8–9
An Actor's Work on Himself, Part One
        (Stanislavsky), 8–9, 78, 88, 99
    English translation of, 89, 104–9
An Actor's Work on Himself, Part Two
        (Stanislavsky), 8–9, 88, 99, 125
    English translation of, 89, 104–9
actor-singers, at Bolshoy Opera Studio, 168
Adashev, A. I., 113
Adashev School, 136–7
Adler, Stella, 239
'advocates of the people.' *See narodniki*
affective memory, 138–9

Agitprop (agitational propaganda) groups, xi, 57
    Stanislavsky on, 65–6
Aleksandrov, Nikolay, 149–50
Alekseyev, Georgy, 49
Alekseyev, Konstantin. *See* Stanislavsky,
        Konstantin
Alekseyev, Sergey, 1–2
Alekseyev, Vladimir, 151–2
Alekseyev Circle, 1–2
All-Russian Theatre Association, 9
American Laboratory Theatre, 238
Andreyev, Leonid, 111, 133, 151, 196
Andreyev, Nikolay, 211
Andreyeva, Maria, 184–6
Antarova, Konkordiya, 163–5, 167–8
anthroposophists, 37–40
    First Studio and, 37–8
    yoga and, 38
Antoine, André, 20, 241–3
    Théâtre Libre, 21
The Armoured Train 14-69 (Ivanov), 70, 72
art. *See also* System of acting; *specific topics*
    cross-arts explorations, in Abramtsevo
        commune, x
    Stanislavsky on, 33–4
    Tolstoy, Lev, on, 33–4
    World of Art, x
Association of Friends of the Studio, 163
audiences, for theatre
    ensemble theatre and, relationship with, 12
    in US, Stanislavsky on, 16–18
The Avenger (Pletnev), 47

Babanin, Konstantin, 160
Bakhrushin, Aleksey, 30
Bakhtin, Mikhaïl, 217–18
Bakst, Leon, 27
Baliyev, Nikita, 14, 58–9
Balladina (Slowacki), 143
ballet masters, at Bolshoy Opera Studio, 164–5
Ballets Russes, x, 27

Index

Barba, Eugenio, 238
The Barber of Seville (Rossini), 173–4, 216
Barca, Calderon de la, 155
Barker, Harley Granville, 244
Bartoshevich, Alexei, 245
The Bat cabaret, 58–9
Batalov, Nikolay, 214–17
The Bathhouse (Mayakovsky), 64
Beaumarchais, Pierre, 211–18
Beaumont, Francis, 250–1
Benedetti, Jean, 3, 21, 88
  translation of Stanislavsky's works, 89, 104–9
Benois, Aleksandr, 27, 159, 211
Berger, Henning, 142–3
Bernhardt, Sarah, 223–4
Bessalko, Pavel, 47
Biagini, Mario, 258
Bill-Belotserkovsky, V. N., 69
biomechanics, 48
Birman, Serafima, xi, 135, 137, 139, 144–5, 147,
  149–50, 223, 235
Blair, Rhonda, 239
Blake, William, 91
Blok, Aleksandr, 39–40
'Bloody Sunday,' 5
The Blue Bird (Maeterlinck), 133–4
Blue Blouse theatre groups, xi, 56, 64–5
Blyum, Vladimir, 220
Bogdanov, Aleksandr, 46–7
Boleslavsky, Richard, 113–14, 142–3, 239
Bolsheviks, 44–6
Bolshoy Opera Studio, 131, 161–9
  actor-singers at, 168
  architectural limitations of, 167
  Association of Friends of the Studio and, 163
  ballet masters at, 164–5
  First Studio and, 162
  musical tradition in, 163–4
  Opera-Dramatic Studio transition from, 169
  teachers at, 164–5
Bolshoy Theatre, 2
  after October Revolution, 6
Borovsky, Victor, 246–7
Bourdieu, Pierre, 28
  on conductorless orchestra, 233
bourgeois culture, 56
Boyd, Michael, 251
Brahm, Otto, 20
Brecht, Bertolt, 19, 204, 248–9, 255
The Bricklayer (Bessalko), 47
Brook, Peter, 87, 167, 249–50, 258–9
brutalism, 201
Bruysov, Valery, 39–41
Bulgakov, Mikhaïl, 68–70, 72–3, 79–82
Burdzhalov, Georgy, 158–61. *See also* Fourth Studio

The Burning Letters (Gnedich), 180–1
Butusov, Yury, 214, 266–7
Byron, George Gordon (Lord), 60–1, 205–11

cabbage party. *See kapustnik*
Cain (Byron), 60–1, 205–11
  throughaction in, 209–10
Carnicke, Sharon Marie, 96–7, 240
Castorf, Frank, 201
Chagall, Marc, 41
Chaliapin, Fyodor, 25, 122
  Art Theatre and, x–xi, 102–3, 163–4, 171
Cheban, Aleksandr, 39
Chekhov, Anton, 3, 12–14, 138, 159, 186–7
  Stanislavsky and
    musicality and, 190–201
    production scores by Stanislavsky and,
      190–201
    works directed by Stanislavsky and,
      187–201
Chekhov, Mikhaïl, xi, 19, 37, 99–100,
  136–7, 154, 181, 184–5, 207, 215,
  246–7
  artistic legacy of, 246–7
  psychological gesture theory of, 39
Chepurov, Aleksandr, 236
Cherevichki (Tchaikovsky), 28
The Cherry Orchard (Chekhov, Anton), 13–14,
  186–201
Chesnokov, Pavel, 210
Children of the Sun (Gorky), 45, 185, 205,
  246–8
Children's Theatre, 149, 155
Chronegk, Ludwig, 20–1
Civil War, in Russia, 45, 53–4
Clark, Katerina, 73–4
Claudel, Paul, 47
collective creation, through ensemble theatre, 10
collective creativity, through ensemble theatre,
  10
Communist Party
  criticism of Meyerhold, 63–4
  MAT and, 56
  newspapers controlled by, 84
conductorless orchestra, as metaphor, 233
Constructivism, 19, 54–5, 61–3, 122, 155, 212
Copeau, Jacques, 200, 241–3
Coquelin, Constant, 241
Cormon, Eugène, 211–12
Craig, Edward Gordon, 134–5, 156, 226, 245,
  249–51
creation. *See* collective creation
creativity. *See* collective creativity
The Cricket on the Hearth (Dickens), 142–5, 147
Crommelynck, Fernand, 55, 61

Index

D. E. (Podgayetsky), 62
The Dawn (Verhaeren), 67
The Days of the Turbins (Bulgakov), 68–70, 72–3
Dead Souls (Gogol), 76–7
The Death of Ivan the Terrible (Tolstoy, Aleksey), 24
Decroux, Étienne, 242–3
The Deluge (Berger), 142–3
Demidov, Nikolay, xi, 38, 97–8, 119, 160, 162, 222, 235
d'Ennery, Adolphe, 211–12
Deutsches Theater, 20
Deykun, Lidiya, xi, 135, 139–40
Diaghilev, Sergey, 26–7
  Ballets Russes, x, 27
  Stanislavsky and, 28
  World of Art, x
Dickens, Charles, 142–3, 145, 147
directors, 180–234
  co-creativity with actors, 216, 227–9, 233
  definition of, 226–34
  development traditions for, 230–1
  at MAT, 184–97
  Meyerhold as, 61–3
  Nemirovich-Danchenko as, 182–97
    with Stanislavsky, 187–90
  result director, 233
  role in artistic process, 227–8
  root director, 233
  Stanislavsky as, 180–4. *See also* Chekhov, Anton; Gorky, Maksim; Shakespeare, William
    of *A Mad Day or The Marriage of Figaro*, 211–18
    with Nemirovich-Danchenko, 187–90
    realism for, 201–5
    of *The Sunken Bell*, 182–3
    of *Uriel Costa*, 181–2
discipline, 124–8
  for actors, 127
  in System of acting, 124–5
  types of, 127
The Divine Image (Blake), 91
The Divine Poem (Scriabin), 41
The Doctor in Spite of Himself (Molière), 159
Doctor Stockman (Ibsen), 183–4
Dodin, Lev, x, 140, 142, 154, 174, 203, 214–15, 230–1, 238, 240, 250–2, 265–9
Don Pasquale (Donizetti), 173–4
Donizetti, Gaetano, 173–4
Donnellan, Declan, 250–1
Dostoyevsky, Fyodor, 26, 119, 150
The Drama of Life (Hamsun), 111, 133
A Dream of Passion (Strasberg), 239
Dréville, Valérie, 261

Dukhobors ('spirit wrestlers'), 34–6
Dullin, Charles, 241–2
Duma, establishment of, 44
Duncan, Isadora, xi, 100, 115–16, 123–4, 132, 134, 139
Duras, Marguerite, 253
Durasova, Maria, 144–5
Duse, Eleonora, 122

Earth Rampant (Tretyakov, Sergey), 62
Edwards, Christine, 239–40
Efros, Anatoly, 155–6, 229
Efros, Nikolay, 24, 119
Eidinger, Lars, 254
Eisenstein, Sergey, 47–8
Eliade, Mircea, 91
Elizabeth I (Empress), 2–3
emotional experiencing. *See* theatre of emotional experiencing
An Enemy of the People (Ibsen), 183–4
ensemble theatre
  audience relationship with, 12
  collective creation through, 10
  collective creativity through, 10
  framework for, 8–9
  MAT as, 7–21
  mission of, 7–8
    permanence of ensemble as element of, 10
  Nemirovich-Danchenko on, 8
  organic processes of, 13.
  Pushkino and, 22
  as repertory company, 11
  Stanislavsky as influence on, 7–21
  star system as distinct from, 7
  System of acting in, 13–14
  as 'theatre-church,' 10–11
  under USSR regime, 17–18
  as Utopian community, 21–37
'epic theatre,' 19
Erdman, Nikolay, 62, 77–8
Erik XIV (Strindberg), 39, 147
ethics, 124–8
  disruptions of, 126
  in System of acting, 124–5, 162
etudes, in System of acting, 10–11, 49, 137, 139, 150, 174, 176, 223, 225, 262, 268
eurhythmics, 116, 151
Evreinov, Nikolay, 57–9

The Fairground Booth (Blok), 40
'fantastic realism,' 19
  of Vakhtangov, 60
Fedotov, Aleksandr, 180–1
Fedotov, Glikeria, 1, 233
The Festival of Peace (Hauptmann), 142–3

Index

The Fiery Angel (Bruysov), 40–1
Figes, Orlando, 37
First Five Year Plan, under Stalin, 57, 73
First Studio, xi, 113, 132–49
 actor's creativity in, 137
 Adashev School and, 136–7
 anthroposophists and, 37–8
 Bolshoy Opera Studio and, 162
 greater than national importance of, 130
 MAAT2 and, 38–9
 student training at, 141–2
 System of acting in, 113–14
 timeline for, 130
 as Utopian community, 136–7
 yoga and, 113–14
Fitzpatrick, Sheila, 47
Flight (Bulgakov), 69, 72, 79
Fokin, Valery, 201
Fomenko, Pyotr, 229
The Forest (Ostrovsky), 62
Forsythe, William, 81
Fourth Studio, 131, 158–61
 formation of, 158–9
 political mission of, 159
 theatrical objectives of, 159–60
The Fruits of Enlightenment (Tolstoy, Lev), xi, 33, 154, 159, 181
Fuller, Loïe, 139

Galendeyev, Valery, 89–90
Gandhi, Mahatma, 34
Gas Masks (Tretyakov, Sergey), 47
Gates, Helmar, 119
Gémier, Firmin, 243
Gest, Morris, 14
Geytts, Mikhaïl, 76–7
Giatsintova, Sofya, xi, 136, 138–9
Gippius, Zinaïda, 149–51
Gnedich, Pyotr, 180–1
Gogol, Nikolai, 17, 62–3, 76–7
The Golden Cockerel (Rimsky-Korsakov), 173–4
Goldoni, Carlo, 159
Golovin, Aleksandr, xiii, 27, 70–1, 212, 215–16, 219
Golubkina, Anna, 29, 31
Gorchakov, Nikolay, 79, 212
Gorky, Maksim
 Children of the Sun, 45, 185, 205, 246–8
 The Lower Depths, 13–14, 24, 45, 184–5, 202–4
 The Petty Bourgeois, 202
 Stanislavsky and, works directed by
  musicality of, 190–201
  production scores by, 190–201

The Government Inspector (Gogol), 17, 62–3
Granovsky, Aleksandr, 65–6
The Green Circle (Gippius), 149–51
Griboyedov Drama Studio, 151–2
Grotowski, Jerzy, 19, 154, 256–8
Group Theatre, 239
Gurevich, Lyubov, 99, 105–6
Gutskow, Karl, 181–2
gymnastic theatre, 64–5

Habima theatre, 65
habitus, 28, 32–3, 108, 199–200, 248
Hall, Peter, 248–9
Hamlet (Shakespeare), 148, 223–6
Hamsun, Knut, 111, 133
Hanako, 139
Hapgood, Elizabeth Reynolds, 88–9
Hauptmann, Gerhart, 142–3, 182–3
Hejermans, Herman, 142–3
Hellerau, 116, 242
Hesychasm, 115
Hisa, Ota, 139
'holy theatre,' 19
Hosking, Geoffrey, 3
human spirit, Stanislavsky on, 31–2, 35, 40, 71, 85, 87–92, 97, 104–5, 116, 118, 122

'I am.' *See 'ya yesm'*
Ibsen, Henrik, 110, 147, 183–4
immediate action, 175–6
Imperial Theatres. *See also* state theatres
 Bolshoy Theatre, 2
 censors in, 4–5
 cultural influence of, 3–4
 Maly Theatre, 2
 monopoly of, abolishment of, 3
 star system in, 7
improvisation, 139–40
individuality, as distinct from individualism, 9–10
inert actors, 127–8
The Internationale (anthem), 62
Israfilov, Israfil, 237
Israfilov, Rifkat, 237
Ivanov, Vsevolod, 70, 72

James, William, 92
Jaques-Dalcroze, Émile, 116, 151–2

K. S. Stanislavsky's Teachings on the Word on the Stage (Galendeyev), 90
Kachalov, Vasily, 53, 72, 79–80
Kamerny Theatre, 65–6
Kandinsky, Vasily, 41
Kantor, Tadeusz, 19

Index

283

kapustnik (cabbage party), 59
Karbauskis, Mindaugas, 231
Kedrov, Mikhaïl, 155, 173, 226, 232
Kerzhentsev, Platon, 71, 80–1, 148–9
Khalutina, Svetlana, 151–2
Khlebnikov, Velimir, 41
Khmelyov, Nikolay, 155
The King of the Dark Chamber (Tagore),
    119–20
Knebel, Maria, xi, 84, 130, 155, 158
    at Opera-Dramatic Studio, 169, 172, 174–9
Knipper-Chekhova, Olga, 5, 53, 79–80
Kogan, Sam, 252
Komisarjevsky, Theodore, 3, 180–1, 246
Komissarzhevskaya, Vera, 40–1
Komissarzhevsky, Fyodor, 3
kommunalka (small communal apartment), 52–3
Komsomol (Communist Youth) theatre groups,
    73–4
Korovin, Konstantin, 26
Korsunovas, Oskaras, 263–4
Krasner, David, 240
Krechetova, Rima, 53, 84
Kristi, Grigory, 117, 167, 171–2, 174–5, 214
Kruchenykh, Aleksey, 41

laboratory (laboratory-studio), 10–11, 129, 136–7,
    143, 146, 153–4, 157–9, 162, 189, 255–6
Lady Macbeth of the Mtensk District
    (Shostakovich), 83
Lake Lyul (Fayko), 62
The Lamentations of Jeremiah (The Bible),
    259–61
Leblanc, Georgette, 134
LeCompte, Elizabeth, 19
Lecoq, Jacques, 242–3
LEF journal, 60
Lenin, Vladimir. *See also* Russia, post-
    Revolutionary period
    nationalization of theatres under, 5–6
    NEP period under, 56
Leonidov, Leonid, 71, 75–6, 79–80, 150
Leskov, Nikolay, 150
Levitan, Isaac, 23, 26, 204
Lieutenant Yegunov's Story (Turgenev), 150
Lieven, Dominic, 45
The Life of Man (Andreyev, Leonid), 111, 133,
    151
Lilina, Maria, 26, 70
Limanowski, Mieczyslaw, 255–6
Literature and Revolution (Trotsky), 64
Litovtseva, Nina, 70, 150
Littlewood, Joan, 247–8
The Lower Depths (Gorky), 13–14, 24, 45,
    184–5, 202–4

Lugné-Poe, Aurélien-Marie, 243
Lunacharsky, Anatoly, 6, 45–7, 68–9
    Commisariat of Enlightenment, 6, 46
    nationalization of theatres and, 5–6
Luzhsky, Vasily, 150, 158–61. *See also*
    Fourth Studio
Lyddiard, Alan, 251
Lynch, James, 196
Lyubimov, Yury, 155

MAAT2. *See* Second Moscow Art Theatre
A Mad Day or The Marriage of Figaro
    (Beaumarchais), 211–18
    throughaction in, 213
Maeterlinck, Maurice, 37, 133–4, 156
    'magic realism.' *See* 'fantastic realism'
The Magnanimous Cuckold (Crommelynck),
    55, 61
The Maid from Pskov (Rimsky-Korsakov), 173–4
Malaev-Babel, Andrei, 160
Malaya Bronnaya Theatre, 229
Malevich, Kasimir, 41, 43, 54–5, 57, 83
Malochevskaya, Irina, 266
Maly Drama Theatre (MDT, St. Petersburg),
    89–90, 140–1
Maly Theatre (Moscow), 2
Mamontov, Savva, x, 22–4. *See also* Private
    Opera Theatre
    Stanislavsky mentored by, 32–3
The Mandate (Erdman), 62
Mardzhanov, Konstantin, 185–6
Markov, Pavel, 133
Massalitinov, Nikolay, 149–50
Massenet, Jules, 166
MAT. *See* Moscow Art Theatre
Matyushin, Mikhaïl, 41
Maudsley, Henry, 119
A May Night (Rimsky-Korsakov), 169
Mayakovsky, Vladimir, 46, 57, 60, 64
Mchedelov, Vakhtang, 149–56. *See also* Second
    Studio
MDT. *See* Maly Drama Theatre
Medea-material (Müller), 261
Meisner, Sanford, 239
The Merchants of Glory (Pagnol and Nivoix),
    211–12
Merlin, Bella, 108
The Merry Wives of Windsor (opera) (Nicolai),
    174–5
metaphysics, of Silver Age, 37–42
    anthroposophists, 37–40
        First Studio and, 37–8
        yoga and, 38
    literary genres during, 7–39
    Rasputinites, 37

metaphysics, of Silver Age (cont.)
  Symbolists, 37, 40–1
  theosophists, 37
method of physical action, immediate action,
  175–6
Meyerhold, Vsevolod, 19, 57–67
  biomechanics, 48, 55, 61–2, 230, 257
  Blue Blouse groups and, 64–5
  Communist Party criticism of, 63–4
  Constructivism and, 61–2
  as director, 61–3
  gymnastic theatre of, 64–5
  during October Revolution, 57
  Proletkult and, 46
  public influence of, 64–5
  Stanislavsky's friendship with, xi, 65, 84–5
  theatrical theatre of, 57–9
The Miracle of St. Anthony (Maeterlinck), 156
The Mistress of the Inn (Goldoni), 159
Mitchell, Katie, 252–3
Mnouchkine, Ariane, 19, 201
  Théâtre du Soleil, 19, 233, 243
Molière, 159
Molière (A Cabal of Hypocrites) (Bulgakov), 79–82
A Month in the Country (Turgenev), 111–12,
  136–7, 206–7
monumentalism, 143
Morozov, Savva, 29, 185
Moscow Art Theatre (MAT), x–xi
  accessibility of, 4–5
  actors in, 9–10
  Agitprop as opponent of, xi
  as apolitical, 56
  artistic crisis within, 5
  artistic mission of, 4–5
  audience relationship with, 12
    dissatisfied audiences, 60–1
  'Bloody Sunday' and, 5
  Blue Blouse groups as opponents of, xi
  Communist Party and, 56
  directors at, 184–97
  as ensemble theatre, 7–21. *See also* ensemble
    theatre
  European tour of, 12–15
  individuality as distinct from individualism in,
    9–10
  MAAT2, 38–9
  nationalization of, 5–6
    as Academic Theatre, 6
  during October Revolution, 13–14
  in Prague, 53
  Proletkult as opponent of, xi
  promotion of, 56
  rejection of politics, xi
  restructuring of, 67

Second Studio merger with, 155–6
as socially inclusive, 4–5
stage structure of, 29
under Stalin, from 1926-1938, 67–86
  political attacks against, 73–4
  socio-political plays, 72–3
  studio affiliations with, xi–xii
    Opera-Dramatic Studio, xi–xii, 18–19
    Povarskaya Studio, xi–xii, 36, 62, 110, 129,
      228
  Tolstoy, Lev, and, 35–6
  TRAM as opponent of, xi
Moskvin, Ivan, 45
Müller, Heiner, 261
Munk, Erika, 239–40
Muratova, Yelena, 150
My Life in Art (Stanislavsky), 2–4, 8–9, 26, 32–3
  English translation of, 104–9
Mystery-Bouffe (Mayakovsky), 57, 60

narodniki ('advocates of the people'), 4, 52–3
Nekrasov, Nikolay, 159
Nekrosius, Eimuntas, 201
Nemirovich-Danchenko, Vladimir, x–xi, 1,
  79–80. *See also* Moscow Art Theatre
  as director, 182–97
    with Stanislavsky, 187–90
  on ensemble theatre, 8. *See also* ensemble
    theatre
Nepmen, 56–7
New Economic Policy (NEP), 56
  eradication of, 57
Nicholas II (Tsar), 44
Nicolai, Otto, 174–5
Nivoix, Paul, 211–12
No Way Out (Leskov), 150
Novitskaya, Lidiya, 172, 223–4
Nunn, Trevor, 249

October Revolution, x
  Bolshoy Theatre after, 6
  Imperial Theatres after, 2
  Maly Theatre after, 6
  MAT during, 13–14
  The Storming of the Winter Palace, 58–9, 62
Old Believer Orthodoxy, xi, 124
Old Believers, 30–1, 132
Opera-Dramatic Studio, xi–xii, 169–79
  active analysis in, 171–9
    restrictions on, 177
  Bolshoy Opera Theatre transition to, 169
  creative process in, for musical composition,
    171
  growth years for, 173–4
  Knebel at, 175, 177–9

Index

method of physical action in, 171–9
  immediate action, 175–6
  throughaction, 177
  word action, 176–7
System of acting and, 18–19
timeline for, 131
works performed at, 169–71, 174–5
Ormerod, Nick, 250
Orthodoxy, of Stanislavsky, 90, 93–5, 97, 113–14
Ostermeier, Thomas, 183–4, 201–2, 253–5
Osterwa, Juliusz, 255–6
Ostrovsky, Aleksandr, 20, 25, 62
Othello (Shakespeare), 218–19

Pagnol, Marcel, 211–12
passive actors, 127–8
Perceval, Luk, 262–3
Peter the Great, 2–3
The Petty Bourgeois (Gorky), 202
The Phantom Lady (Calderon de la Barca), 155
Philosophy of the Unconscious (von Hartmann), 118
The Pillars of Society (Ibsen), 110
Piscator, Erwin, 255
Pletnev, Valerian, 47
Podgorny, Nikolay, 149–52
Poem of Ecstasy (Scriabin), 41
Polenov, Vasily, 22–3
Polenova, Yelena, 22–3
Popov, Aleksey, 237
Popova, Lyubov, 54–5
Povarskaya Studio, xi–xii, 36, 62, 110, 129, 228
The Powers of Darkness (Tolstoy, Lev), 33
Princess Turandot (Gozzi), 59–60
Private Opera Theatre, x, 24–7
  Abramtsevo Circle and, 26–7
project-based theatre, 7
Proletkult (Proletarian Culture), xi, 46–7
  class definitions and, 47
  founding of, 46–7
  Meyerhold and, 46
  peak of, 55
  Smyshlyayev and, 45–6, 54–5
propaganda
  agitational, 57
  through newspapers, 84
  through state theatres, 6–7
Pryazhko, Pavel, 267–8
psychological gesture, 39
Pushkino, 22, 36

The Queen of Spades (Tchaikovsky), 28

Rabelais and His World (Bakhtin), 217–18
Rachmaninov, Sergey, 14

Radishcheva, Olga, 13–14, 75
Radlov, Sergey, 65–6
Rasputinites, 37
raznochintsy, 3
realism. *See also* 'fantastic realism';
   'socialist realism'
  for Stanislavsky, 201–5
Reinhardt, Max, 20, 209
Réjane, 134
repertory companies, ensemble theatre as, 11
Repin, Ilya, 22–3, 204
representation. *See* theatre of representation
result director, 233
Ribot, Théodule, 92
Richards, Thomas, 258
Rimsky-Korsakov, Nikolay, 24–5, 35, 169, 173–4
The Rite of Spring, 27
Rodchenko, Aleksandr, 54–5
Rodin, Auguste, 29
Roerich, Nikolay, 120
Roerich, Yelena, 120
Roksanova, Maria, 184
Romeo and Juliet (Shakespeare), 222–6
root directors, 233
Rosmersholm (Ibsen), 147
Rossi, Ernesto, 122
Rossini, Gioachino, 173–4, 216
Rudnitsky, Konstantin, 57, 203–4
Rumyantsev, Pavel, 165, 171
Russia. *See also* Union of Soviet Socialist
    Republics
  Civil War in, 45, 53–4
  proletarian insurrections in, 44–6
  tsarist era
    demise of, 44
    Duma established after, 44
Russia, post-Revolutionary period. *See also* Union
   of Soviet Socialist Republics
  Bolsheviks in, 44–6
  bourgeois culture during, 56
  NEP period, 56
  Nepmen, 56–7
  October Revolution
    Bolshoy Theatre after, 6
    Imperial Theatres after, 2
    Maly Theatre after, 6
    MAT during, 13–14
    The Storming of the Winter Palace, 58–9, 62
    promotion of MAT during, 56
Russian State Institute of Scenic Arts, 230
The Russian Theatre under the Revolution (Sayler), 14

Saint-Denis, Michel, 242–3
Sakhnovsky, Vasily, 71, 76–7

286   *Index*

Salvini, Tomaso, 122
Sats, Ilya, 36, 149
Sats, Natalya, 149
Saxe-Meiningen Court Theatre, 20
Sayler, Oliver, 14
Scriabin, Aleksandr, 41, 245
The Seagull (Chekhov, Anton), 12–14, 186–7
   Stanislavsky direction of, 187–90
Sechenov, Ivan, 92
Second Moscow Art Theatre (MAAT2), 38–9
Second Studio, 130, 149–56
   criticism of works at, 152–3, 155
   MAT merger with, 155–6
   Society of Art and Literature and, 180
   'studists' at, 150–1
   as theatre-studio, 153–4
   theatrical focus of, 153–4
   works performed at, 150–2, 154–5
Sellars, Peter, 264–5
Senelick, Laurence, 134
Serov, Valentin, 22–3
Shakespeare, William, 148, 218–19, 222–6
Shakhalov, Aleksandr, 209
Shchepkin, Mikhaïl, 1
Shchukin, Sergey, 30
Shekhtel, Fyodor, 29
Shostakovich, Dmitry, 84
   friendship with Meyerhold, 83–5
Silver Age. *See* metaphysics
Simov, Viktor, 8, 23
Sinitsyn, Vladimir, 220
Slowacki, Juliusz, 143
small communal apartment. *See kommunalka*
Smeliansky, Anatoly, 89–90
Smolin, Dmitri, 155
Smyshlyayev, Valentin, 39, 48–9, 135
   as Bolshevik, 44–6
   Proletkult and, 45–6, 54–5
The Snow Maiden (Rimsky-Korsakov),
   25, 35
Sobolevskaya, Olga, 170
Sobolyov, Yury, 155
sobornost, 22, 218
socialism, 48
'socialist realism,' 81–3
Society of Art and Literature, 2–4, 180–4. *See*
   also Moscow Art Theatre
   intelligentsia and, 3–4
   raznochintsy and, 3
Sokolova, Zinaïda, 52–3, 173
Sologub, Fyodr, 152
Solovyova, Inna, 186
Solovyova, Vera, 113–14
Soviet Writers' Union, 81
'spirit wrestlers.' *See* Dukhobors
'spirit-soul,' 106–7

spiritual communion, 100
stage creativity, of actors, 96
stage design, Stanislavsky on, 29, 66–7
Stalin, Josef
   Five-Year Plan, 57, 73
   MAT under, from 1926-1938, 67–86
   socio-political plays, 72–3
Stanislavski in America (Munk), 239–40
Stanislavsky, Konstantin, 2–3. *See also* Moscow
   Art Theatre; Society of Art and
   Literature; *specific studios*
   at Abramtsevo commune, 23
   on agitprop theatre, 65–6
   on American audiences, 16–17
   arrest of, 45
   on art, 33–4
   artistic legacy of, 235–40
      in England, 244–9
      in France, 241–4
      generational transmission of, 238
      international context for, 236–7
      temporal factors for, 238–9
      in US, 239–40
   Chekhov, Anton, works of
      directed by Stanislavsky, 187–201
      musicality and, 190–201
      production scores for, 190–201
   in Communist Party newspapers, 84
   Diaghilev and, 28
   as director. *See* directors
   as director-pedagogue, 177–8, 180
   Duncan as influence on, xi
   early years for, 1–2
   Gorky and, works directed by
      musicality of, 190–201
      production scores for, 190–201
   individuality as distinct from individualism
      for, 9–10
   inspiration for, 109–20
   line of physical action, 221
   Mamontov as mentor to, 32–3
   method of physical action, 171–9
      immediate action, 175–6
      throughaction, 177, 209–10, 213, 222, 232–3
      word action, 176–7
   Meyerhold friendship with, xi
   Old Believer Orthodoxy as influence on, xi
   Orthodoxy of, 90, 93–5, 97, 113–14
   spiritual practices, 40, 89–90
   as stage actor, 1–2
   on stage creativity, 96
   on stage design, 29, 66–7
   on the subconscious, 101–4, 117–19
   on the superconscious, 117–18
   Tchaikovsky and, 28
   Tolstoy as influence on, xi

Index

287

Tortsov (teacher/creator) and, 89, 96, 98, 102–3
on the unconscious, 117–19
on visualization, 109
'*ya yesm*' for, 101–4
yoga for, 97
Stanislavsky, Konstantin, works of
An Actor's Work on a Role, 8–9
An Actor's Work on Himself, Part One, 8–9, 78, 88, 99
English translation of, 89, 104–9
An Actor's Work on Himself, Part Two, 8–9, 88, 99, 125
English translation of, 89, 104–9
My Life in Art, 2–4, 8–9, 26, 32–3
Stanislavsky in Focus (Carnicke), 240
star system, in Imperial Theatres, 7
State Jewish Theatre, 65–6
state theatres
nationalization of, 5–6
propaganda through, 6–7
Stein, Peter, 254
Steiner, Rudolf, 37
The Storming of the Winter Palace, 58–9, 62
Strasberg, Lee, 239
Method acting theory and, 239
Stravinsky, Igor, 120
Strehler, Giorgio, ix–x, 197
Strindberg, August, 39
Student Studio, 156. *See also* Third Studio
'studists'
at Second Studio, 150–1
at Third Studio, 157–8
the subconscious, Stanislavsky on, 101–4, 117–19
Sudakov, Ilya, 68, 70
Sudbinin, Serafim, 195
The Suicide (Erdman), 77–8
Sulerzhitsky, Leopold, xi, 35–6, 38, 111–13, 115, 129–30, 132–51, 153, 222, 235, 255–6. *See also* First Studio
on affective memory, 138–9
on improvisation, 139–40
Orthodoxy of, 136
The Sunken Bell (Hauptmann), 182–3
the superconscious, 117–18
Sushkevich, Boris, 113–14, 142–3, 236
Symbolists, 37, 40–1
'synthetic' theatre, 65–6
System of acting, for Stanislavsky, 100–1, 109–10
discipline in, 124–5
in ensemble theatre, 13–14
ethics in, 124–5, 162
etudes in, 10–11, 49, 137, 139, 150, 174, 176, 223, 225, 262, 268

'fantastic realism' and, 19
in First Studio, 113–14
foundational points of, 112–13
four elements of, 114–15
method of physical action and, 6–7, 83–4, 171–2
'nature' and, 100–1
for opera, 164
Opera-Dramatic Studio and, 18–19
organic creative nature and, 123
practical purpose of, xi
theatre of emotional experiencing and, 123–4
yoga and, 114

Tagore, Rabindranath, 119–20
Taïrov, Aleksandr, 65–6
Fourth Studio and, 131
Talashkino community, 27
The Tale of Ivan the Fool and his Brothers (Tolstoy, Lev), 154
Tarasova, Alla, 152
Tatarinov, Vladimir, 39
Taylor, Frederick Winslow, 48
Taylorism, 48
Tchaikovsky, Pyotr, 28, 166–7
Tcherkasski, Sergei, 113–14, 116–17
The Teacher Bubus (Fayko), 62
teachers, at Bolshoy Opera Studio, 164–5
Telesheva, Yelena, 150
Telyakovsky, V. A., 193
Telyatinki community, 36–7
Tenisheva (Princess), 27
Théâtre du Soleil, 19, 233
Théâtre du Vieux Colombier, 200
Theatre for Young People, 230
Théâtre Libre, 21
Théâtre National Populaire, 243–4
'theatre of death,' 19
theatre of emotional experiencing, 121–4
actors in, 121–2
spectators in, 122
System of acting and, 123–4
theatre of representation, 121
Theatre of Worker Youth (TRAM), 73–4
MAT opposed by, xi
'theatre-church,' ensemble theatre as, 10–11
theatre-studio, 153–4
theatrical theatre, 57–9
'theatricality,' 19
Theory of the Development of a Stage Show (Smyshlyayev), 48–9
theosophists, 37
Third Studio, 130, 156–8
development of, 156
'studists' in, 157–8
The Three Sisters (Chekhov, Anton), 12–13, 186–7, 193–201

288   *Index*

throughaction, 177, 209–10, 213, 232–3
Tolstoy, Aleksey, 24, 27–8
Tolstoy, Lev, xi, 33, 154, 159, 181
    on art, 33–4
    MAT and, 35–6
Tolstoy, Sofya, 37
Toporkov, Vasily, 231–2
Tortsov (teacher/creator), 89, 96, 98, 102–3
Tovstonogov, Georgy, 237
TRAM. *See* Theatre of Worker Youth
Tree, Herbert Beerbohm, 244–5
Trench, Herbert, 244–5
Tretyakov, Pavel, 30
Tretyakov, Sergey, 47, 62
Trotsky, Lev, 62–4
Tsar Fyodor Ionnovich (Tolstoy, Aleksey), 24, 27–8
Turgenev, Ivan, 111–12, 136–7, 150, 206–7
Two Orphans (d'Ennery and Cormon), 211–12

Udaltsova, Zinaïda, 38–9, 149
Uncle Vanya (Chekhov, Anton), 12–14, 186–7,
    190–3
the unconscious, 117–19
Union of Soviet Socialist Republics (USSR), 6
    ensemble theatre in, 17–18
    First Five Year Plan in, 57
    socialism in, 48
    Taylorism in, 48
United States (US)
    Stanislavsky legacy in, 239–40
    theatre audiences in, Stanislavsky on, 16–18
Untilovsk (Leonov), 71
Uriel Costa (Gutskow), 181–2
US. *See* United States
Uspenskaya, Maria, 139, 238
USSR. *See* Union of Soviet Socialist Republics
Utopian communities
    Abramtsevo commune
        collective goals of, 23
        cross-arts explorations in, x
        Mamontov and, 22–4
        Stanislavsky at, 23
    ensemble theatre as, 21–37
    First Studio as, 136–7
    Pushkino, 22, 36
    sobornost and, 22
    Talashkino community, 27
    Telyatinki community, 36–7
    Yasnaya Polyana community, 36–7
    Yevpatoria community, 35–6, 38

Vakhtangov, Yevgeny, xi, 19, 59–60, 142–3,
    147, 156–8. *See also* Third Studio
    'fantastic realism' of, 60

Vasilyev, Anatoly, x, 90–1, 154–5, 259–61
Vasnetsov, Apollinary, 22–3, 26
Vasnetsov, Viktor, 22–3, 25–6
Verhaeren, Emile, 67
Vershilov, Boris, 170
Victory Over the Sun (Kruchenykh), 41
Le Vieux Colombier, 241–2
Vilar, Jean, 243–4
The Village of Stepanchikovo (Dostoyevsky), 26,
    119
Vinogradskaya, Irina, 112, 154
visualization, 109, 172, 179
Volkenstein, Vladimir, 142–3
Volkostrelov, Dmitry, 267
von Hartmann, Edouard, 118
Vrubel, Mikhaïl, 22–3, 26–7, 41
Vyakhireva, V. A., 222

The Wayfarers (Volkenstein), 142–3
Weigel, Helene, 248–9
Wells, H. G., 244–5
Werther (Massenet), 166
What is Art? (Tolstoy, Lev), 33
The White Guard (Bulgakov), 68
White Nights (Dostoyevsky), 150
Whyman, Rose, 92–3
Wilde, Oscar, 58
Wilson, Robert, ix–x
The Wooster Group, 19
word action, 176–7
World of Art, x
The World of Art (Diaghilev, journal), 26–7
The Wreck of the 'Hope' (Hejermans), 142–3

'ya yesm' ('I am'), 98, 101–4, 118
Yagoda, Genrikh, 77
Yasnaya Polyana community, 36–7
Yefremov, Oleg, 155
Yelizaveta Petrovna (Smolin), 155
Yermilov, Vladimir, 64
Yevgeny Onegin (Tchaikovsky), 166–7
Yevpatoria community, 35–6, 38
yoga, 38
    First Studio and, 113–14
    for Stanislavsky, 97
    System of acting and, 114

Zagorsky, Mikhaïl, 60
Zatvornik, Feofan, 91–5
Zavadsky, Yury, 214–17, 257
Zhenovach, Sergey, 229–30
Zola, Émile, 203
Zon, Boris, 140–1, 172–4, 228–9
Zuyeva, Anastasiya, 151–2

Printed in the United States
by Baker & Taylor Publisher Services